STUDY GUIDE

to accompany

FINANCIAL ACCOUNTING

DOUGLAS W. KIESO, PH.D., J.D., C.P.A.
Associate Professor of Accounting and Criminology
Aurora University
Aurora, Illinois

PAUL D. KIMMEL Ph.D., C.P.A.
Associate Professor of Accounting
University of Wisconsin—Milwaukee
Milwaukee, Wisconsin

JERRY J. WEYGANDT Ph.D., C.P.A.
Arthur Andersen Alumni Professor of Accounting
University of Wisconsin—Madison
Madison, Wisconsin

DONALD E. KIESO Ph.D., C.P.A.
KPMG Peat Marwick Emeritus Professor of Accountancy
Northern Illinois University
DeKalb, Illinois

John Wiley & Sons, Inc.

Cover Photo: ©David Madison/Stone/Getty Images

To order books or for customer service call 1-800-CALL-WILEY (225-5945).

ISBN 0-471-68410-4

Printed in the United States of America

10 9 8 7 6 5 4 3 2 1

Printed and bound by Malloy

To The Student

This study guide is provided as a significant aid in your study of ***Financial Accounting, 5th Edition*** by Jerry J. Weygandt and Donald E. Kieso and Paul D. Kimmel. The material in the study guide is designed to reinforce your understanding of the principles and procedures presented in the textbook. **It is important to recognize that the study guide is a supplement to and not a substitute for the textbook.**

This study guide contains the following materials for each chapter in the textbook: (a) study objectives, (b) a preview of the chapter, (c) a chapter review consisting of 20-30 key points, (d) a demonstration problem, (e) 20 true—false statements, (f) 20 multiple choice questions, (g) a matching question pertaining to key terms, and (h) 2-3 exercises. At the end of each chapter, answers to questions and exercises are provided in order to enable you to assess your comprehension of the material. Included are solutions explaining why the answer is what it is, so you get immediate feedback as to what, how, or why.

You will realize the maximum benefit from this study guide by following the approach suggested below.

1. Carefully read and study the chapter material in the textbook.
2. Read the chapter preview and review material in the study guide.
3. Answer the questions and exercises for the chapter in the study guide and compare your answers with those provided in the study guide. For any incorrect answers, refer back to the textbook for a discussion of the point you have missed.
4. Solve the end-of-chapter materials in the textbook assigned by your instructor.

The study guide should be helpful in preparing for examinations. The chapter review points, class notes, and other materials may be used to determine your recall of the information presented in specific chapters. When you have identified topics in need of further study, you can return to the textbook for a complete discussion of the subject matter.

I wish to acknowledge the valuable assistance of the proofers and checkers of this study guide, James Emig of Villanova University and Barbara J. Muller, Arizona State University West, and our compositor, Mary Ann Benson.

Douglas W. Kieso

MAKING YOUR STUDIES PAY

Suggestions for Effective Studying

WANT TO GET BETTER GRADES? READ ON!

Good students have a system to their studying. In the next few pages, we'll give you some guidelines that we think can help improve the way you study—not only for this course, but for any course.

How to Use a Textbook
How to Read a Chapter
How to Take Notes
How to Use a Study Guide (In General)
How to Take Tests

If you need more specific help, we suggest that you go to your teacher or your school's career counseling center.

And Good Luck in your College Career!

HOW TO USE A TEXTBOOK

Textbooks often include material designed to help you study. It's worth your while to flip through a textbook to look for:

- **The Preface.** If an author has a point of view, you can find it here, along with notes on how the book is meant to be used.

- **The Table of Contents.** Reading the table of contents will tell you how the book will be developed.

- **Glossary.** The most important terms and ideas for you to know will be in a glossary, either at the end of each chapter or at the end of the book.

- **Appendixes.** Found either after certain chapters or at the end of the book, appendixes contain such things as:
    * More difficult material.
    * Statistics or data, such as the present value of money. You may be able to use such data for most of the book.
    * Answers to selected problems.

HOW TO READ A CHAPTER

Before Class: Skim

Unless you're told to know a chapter completely by class time, it's a good idea just to skim an assigned chapter before class.

- Become familiar with the main ideas so that the lecture will make more sense to you.
- As you skim, ask yourself if you know something about the material.
- Keep any questions you have in mind for the lecture, so that you can listen for the answers.

In particular, look for:

- **Study Objectives.** These are what your teacher will expect you to know—and be able to do or explain—by the end of the chapter.
- **Chapter-Opening Vignettes.** This section is linked to the chapter topic, and gives a general idea of how accounting relates to your day-to-day life.
- **Boldface or *Italic* Terms.** These usually indicate important terms, people, or concepts.
- **Headings.** Read the major headings to see how the material fits together. How are the ideas related to each other? Do they make sense to you?
- **Summary.** A good summary will repeat the general ideas and conclusions of the chapter, but it won't explain them. It usually matches up well with the study objectives and chapter introduction.

After Class: Read

After skimming the chapter and attending class, you are ready to read a chapter in detail.

- **Check for Meaning.** Ask yourself as you read if you understand what the material means.
- **Don't Skip the Tables, Figures, and Illustrations.** These items usually contain important material and may all be on the test.
- **Read the "Sidebars."** These are features that are set off, usually in boxes or by color backgrounds. They can include real-world examples, amusing anecdotes, or additional material. The amusing anecdotes may not come up on the test, but the other kinds of sidebars probably will!
- **Review.** Read the chapter again, especially the parts you had trouble with. Review the study objectives, chapter introduction, summary, and key terms to make sure you understand them.
- **End-of-Chapter Questions.** Do all the end-of-chapter questions, exercises, or problems. For the exercises and problems, make sure you have memorized what equations or rules apply, and why. (Do any practice problems that your teacher gives you, too. These will not

only help you but show you what kind of questions might be on the test.) If you have trouble with any:

* Review the part of the chapter that applies.
* Look for similar questions.
* Ask yourself what concept or equation should be applied.

- **Use the Study Guide.** After you've read and studied the chapter, use the study guide to find out what areas you need to review in the text.

HOW TO TAKE NOTES

The ability to take notes is a skill, and one you can learn. First, a few practical tips:

- Arrive in class on time, and don't leave early. You might miss important notes or assignments.
- If you don't have assigned seating, sit close enough to your teachers so that you can hear them and read any overhead transparencies.
- If you don't understand, ask questions.
- Do not read the text during the class—you'll just miss what your teacher is saying. Listen, take notes, and ask questions.

Now, for the note-taking itself:

- **Listen for Ideas.** Don't try to write everything the instructor says. Instead, listen and take notes on the main ideas and any supporting ideas and examples. Make sure you include names, dates, and any new terms. In accounting classes, take down all rules, equations, and theories, as well as every step in a demonstration problem.
- **Use Outlines.** Organize these ideas into outlines. You don't have to use a numbered outline if you don't want to—just indent supporting ideas under the main ones.
- **Abbreviate.** Use any abbreviations you can, whether they're standard or ones you make up. (Leaving out vowels can sometimes help: Lvg out vwls can ...).
- **Leave Space.** Leave enough space in your notes so that you can add material if the instructor goes back to the topic or expands a problem later.

HOW TO USE A STUDY GUIDE (IN GENERAL)

A study guide is devoted to the particular text you're using. It can't replace the text; it can only point out places where you need more work. To make a study guide most effective:

- Use it only after you've read the chapter and reviewed your class notes.
- Ask yourself whether you really understand the chapter's main points and how they relate to one another.
- Go back and reread the sections of your text that deal with any questions you missed. Chances are that a text will not ask the same questions the study guide does, but the text can help you understand the material better. If that doesn't work, ask your instructor for help.
- Remember that a study guide can't cover any extra material that your teacher may have lectured on.

HOW TO TAKE TESTS

Studying for a Test

Studying for tests is a process that starts with the first class and ends only with the last test. All through the semester, it helps to:

- Follow the advice we gave about reading a chapter and taking notes.
- Review your notes:
  - immediately after class. Clear up anything you can't read and circle important items while the lecture is still fresh in your mind.
  - periodically during the semester.
  - before the test.
- Use any videotapes that may be made of lectures.

Now you're ready to do your final studying for this test. Leave as much time as you need, and study under the conditions that are right for you—alone or with a study group, in the library or another quiet place. It helps to schedule several short study sessions rather than to study all at one time.

- **Reread the chapter(s).** Follow this system:
  - Most importantly, look for things you don't remember or don't understand.
  - Reinforce your understanding of the main ideas by rereading the introduction, study objectives, and summary.
  - Read the chapter from beginning to end.
- **Redo the Problems.** Make sure you know what equation to apply or procedure to follow in different situations, and why.

- **Test Yourself.** Cover up something you've just read and try to explain it to yourself—or to a friend—out loud.

- **Use Memory Tricks.** If you're having trouble remembering something—such as a formula or items in a list—try associating it with something you know or by making a sentence up out of the first letters.

- **Study with a Group.** Group study is helpful after you've done all your own studying. You can help each other with problems and by quizzing each other, but you'll probably just distract each other if you try to review a chapter together.

(A Note About Cramming), DON'T! If you cram, you will probably only remember what you've read for a short time, and you'll have trouble knowing how to generalize from it. If you must cram, however, concentrate on the main ideas, the supporting ideas, main headings, boldface or italicized terms, and study objectives.)

Taking a Test

After the following general tips, we'll give you specifics on objective, problem, and essay tests.

- **Before the Test**
  * Make sure you eat well and get enough sleep before the exam.
  * If the instructor doesn't say in class what material will be covered or what kind of test—objective or essay—will be used, ask.
  * Arrive early enough to get settled.
  * Bring everything you need—bluebook, pens, pencils, eraser, calculator—even the book if it's an open-book test.

- **As You Begin the Test**
  * Read the instructions completely. Do you have to answer all of the questions? Do certain questions apply to others? Do some questions count more than others? Will incorrect answers be counted against you?
  * Schedule your time. How many questions are there? Try to estimate how much time to leave for each section. If sections are timed, so that you won't be able to go back to them, make sure you leave enough time to decide which questions to answer.

- **Taking the Test**
  * Read each question completely as you come to it.
  * Answer the easier questions first and go back to the harder ones.
  * Concentrate on questions that count more.
  * Jot notes or equations in the margin if you think it will help.
  * Review your answers, and don't change an answer unless you're sure you were wrong.

- **Dealing with Panic**
  * Relax. Do this by tightening and relaxing one muscle at a time.
  * Breathe deeply.
  * If you don't know an answer, go on to the next question.

Now for some notes on objective, problem, and essay tests.

- **Objective Tests.** (Multiple choice, true/false, matching, and completion or fill-in-the blank.)
    * Watch out for words like always/all/every/none/never. Very few things are always or never so. If a question or answer includes words like these, be careful.
    * If you are uncertain about a multiple choice answer, try to narrow the choices down to two and make an educated guess.
    * Match up the easy ones first on a matching test. This will leave less possibilities for the harder ones.
    * Make educated guesses for other objective questions. (If you really have no idea and wrong answers count against you, leave it blank.)

- **Problem Test**
    * If a formula or equation is quite long, jot it down before you work on the problem.
    * Remember that math builds one equation on another. If you can't remember a particular equation, try to remember how it was derived.
    * Don't despair if you can't figure out what a question is calling for. Try to figure out part of it first. If that doesn't work, go on; sometimes a later question will jog your memory.
    * If your teacher grants some credit for partially correct problems, make sure you include the way you worked out a problem.
    * Make sure you know how your calculator works before the test. And make sure you know how to do the problems without it. Sometimes you can hit the wrong button, so it helps to have a rough idea of what your calculator should be giving you.

- **Essay Test**
    * Write a rough outline before you begin. If that takes too much time, just jot down all the things you want to say and then number them. Organize what you're going to say into groups of related ideas.
    * Make a point in each paragraph. The easiest way is to make the point in the paragraph's first sentence and then to back it up.
    * Use examples, facts, and dates to back up what you are saying.
    * Do what the question asks for. If it asks you to compare two things, for example, go back and forth between them; don't spend all your time on one of them.
    * If you have no idea what to write, try to remember ideas that the teacher stressed in class and see if you can relate the question to those ideas.
    * Check your time. If you're running out, write your last points down without explaining them; your teacher will at least know what you are going to explain.

CONTENTS

CHAPTER 1

The Navigator ✓

- Scan Study Objectives ☐
- Read Preview ☐
- Read Chapter Review ☐
- Work Demonstration Problem ☐
- Answer True-False Statements ☐
- Answer Multiple-Choice Questions ☐
- Match Terms and Definitions ☐
- Solve Exercises ☐

ACCOUNTING MATTERS!

CHAPTER STUDY OBJECTIVES

After studying this chapter, you should be able to:

1. Explain what accounting is.
2. Identify the users and uses of accounting.
3. Understand why ethics is a fundamental business concept.
4. Explain the meaning of generally accepted accounting principles and the cost principle.
5. Explain the meaning of the monetary unit assumption and the economic entity assumption.
6. State the basic accounting equation and explain the meaning of assets, liabilities, and stockholders' equity.
7. Analyze the effects of business transactions on the basic accounting equation.
8. Understand what the four financial statements are and how they are prepared.

*9. Identify the three major fields of the accounting profession and potential accounting careers.

***Note:** All asterisked (*) items relate to material contained in the Appendix to the chapter.

The Navigator

PREVIEW OF CHAPTER 1

The purpose of this chapter is to show you that accounting is the system used to provide useful financial information. The content and organization of the chapter are as follows:

ACCOUNTING MATTERS!

- **Why Study Accounting?**
- **What is Accounting?**
  - Who uses accounting data
  - Brief history of accounting
  - Bookkeeping and accounting
  - Accounting and you
  - The accounting profession
- **The Building Blocks of Accounting**
  - Ethics—a fundamental business concept
  - Generally accepted accounting principles
  - Assumptions
  - Basic accounting equation
- **Using the Building Blocks**
  - Transaction analysis
  - Summary of transactions
- **Financial Statements**
  - Income Statement
  - Retained earnings statement
  - Balance sheet
  - Statement of cash flows

The Navigator

CHAPTER REVIEW

Accounting Defined

1. (S.O. 1) **Accounting** is an information system that identifies, records, and communicates the economic events of an organization to interested users.
   a. The first part of the process, **identifying,** involves selecting those events that are considered evidence of economic activity relevant to a particular business organization.
   b. **Recording** is the keeping of a systematic, chronological diary of events, measured in dollars and cents.
   c. **Communication** occurs through the preparation and distribution of accounting reports.

2. The accounting process consists of:

   Identification → Recording → Communication.

3. (S.O. 2) **Internal users** of accounting information are managers who plan, organize, and run a business. These include marketing managers, production supervisors, finance directors, and company officers.

4. **External users** include investors, creditors, taxing authorities, regulatory agencies, labor unions, customers, and economic planners outside the business.

5. **Bookkeeping** is not the same as accounting. Bookkeeping involves only the recording of economic events, while accounting includes identification, recording, and communication. Bookkeeping is therefore only a part of accounting.

6. Accounting is divided into financial versus managerial accounting. **Financial accounting** is the field of accounting that provides economic and financial information for investors, creditors, and other external users. **Managerial accounting** provides economic and financial information for managers and other internal users.

Ethics

7. (S.O. 3) The standards of conduct by which one's actions are judged as right or wrong, honest or dishonest, fair or not fair, are **ethics.** The process of analyzing ethical issues is to recognize that an ethical issue is involved, identify and analyze the principle elements in the situation (especially those harmed or benefited), identify the alternatives and weigh the impact of each alternative on the various stakeholders, then select the most ethical alternative.

GAAP and the Cost Principle

8. (S.O. 4) **Generally accepted accounting principles** (GAAP) are a common set of guidelines (standards) used by accountants in reporting economic events.

9. The **Securities and Exchange Commission** (SEC) is an independent regulatory agency of the United States government. The SEC has the legal power to enforce the form and content of financial statements of corporations that wish to sell securities to the public.

10. The **Financial Accounting Standards Board** (FASB) has been granted the power from the SEC to establish GAAP.

11. Under the **cost principle** assets should be recorded at their cost. Cost is the value exchanged at the time something is acquired.

The Monetary Unit and Economic Entity Assumptions

12. (S.O. 5) The accounting profession has developed certain assumptions that serve as guidelines for the accounting process.
    a. The **monetary unit assumption** requires that only transaction data that can be expressed in terms of money be included in the accounting records.
    b. The **economic entity assumption** requires that the activities of the entity be kept separate and distinct from (1) the activities of its owners and (2) all other economic entities.

Business Enterprises

13. Three types of business enterprises are proprietorships, partnerships, and corporations.
    a. A **proprietorship** is a business owned by one person.
    b. A **partnership** is a business owned by two or more persons associated as partners.
    c. A **corporation** is a business organized as a separate legal entity under state corporation law with ownership divided into transferable shares of stock.

The Accounting Equation

14. (S.O. 6) The **basic accounting equation** is:

    Assets = Liabilities + Stockholders' Equity.

    The accounting equation applies to all economic entities regardless of size, nature of business, or form of business organization.

15. The key components of the basic accounting equation are:
    a. **Assets** are resources owned by a business
    b. **Liabilities** are claims against assets.
    c. **Stockholders' equity** are the claims of the stockholders.

16. In corporations, there are five subdivisions of stockholders' equity:
    a. **Paid-in capital** is the stockholders' investment in the business.
    b. **Revenues** are the gross increases in stockholders' equity resulting from business activities entered into for the purpose of earning income.
    c. **Expenses** are the cost of assets consumed or services used in the process of earning revenue.
    d. **Dividends** are distributions of cash or other assets to stockholders.
    e. **Retained earnings** is determined by revenues, expenses, and dividends.

17. Revenues and expenses determine if a **net income** or **net loss** occurs as follows:
    a. Revenues > Expenses = Net Income.
    b. Revenues < Expenses = Net Loss.

Transactions

18. (S.O. 7) **Transactions** are the recorded economic events of the enterprise. Transactions may be identified as either external or internal transactions.

19. Each transaction must be analyzed in terms of its effect on the components of the basic accounting equation. The analysis must also identify the specific items affected and the amount of the change in each item.

20. Each transaction has a dual effect on the equation. For example, if an individual asset is increased, there must be a corresponding:
    a. decrease in another asset, or
    b. increase in a specific liability, or
    c. increase in stockholders' equity.

21. A tabular summary may be prepared to show the cumulative effect of transactions on the basic accounting equation. The summary demonstrates that:
    a. Each transaction must be analyzed in terms of its effect on (1) the three components of the equation and (2) specific types of items within each component.
    b. The two sides of the equation must always be equal.
    c. The causes of each change in the stockholders' claim on assets must be indicated in the stockholders' equity column.

The Financial Statements

22. (S.O. 8) Four financial statements are prepared from the summarized accounting data:
    a. An **income statement** presents the revenues and expenses and resulting net income (or net loss) of a company for a specific period of time.
    b. A **retained earnings statement** summarizes the changes in retained earnings for a specific period of time.
    c. A **balance sheet** reports the assets, liabilities, and stockholders' equity of a business enterprise at a specific date.
    d. A **statement of cash flows** summarizes information concerning the cash inflows (receipts) and outflows (payments) for a specific period of time.

23. The financial statements are **interrelated** because:
    a. Net income (or net loss) shown on the income statement is added (subtracted) to (from) the beginning balance of retained earnings in the retained earnings statement.
    b. Retained earnings at the end of the reporting period shown in the retained earnings statement is reported in the balance sheet.
    c. The amount of cash shown on the balance sheet is reported on the statement of cash flows.

24. In the income statement, revenues are listed first, followed by expenses. Then below expenses is the resulting amount of net income (or net loss).

25. The retained earnings statement shows the retained earnings at the beginning of the period, net income (or net loss) for the period, dividends, and the retained earnings at the end of the period.

26. In the balance sheet, assets are listed at the top, followed by liabilities and stockholders' equity.

27. The statement of cash flows reports the sources, uses, and net increase or decrease in cash. Chapter 14 will examine in detail how the statement is prepared.

*28. (S.O. 9) **Public accounting** provides the services of auditing, taxation, and management consulting.
   a. **Auditing** involves examining financial statements of companies and expressing an opinion as to the fairness of their presentation.
   b. **Taxation** includes providing tax advice and planning, preparing tax returns, and representing clients before governmental agencies.
   c. **Management consulting** involves providing advice for managers on such matters as financial planning and control and the development of computer systems.

*29. **Private accounting** involves the employment of accountants within individual companies. The private accountant performs a wide variety of duties such as cost accounting, budgeting, general accounting, accounting information systems, tax accounting, and internal auditing.

*30. **Not-for-profit accounting** pertains to not-for-profit organizations such as governmental units, foundations, hospitals, colleges, universities, and charities.

DEMONSTRATION PROBLEM (S.O. 8)

Prepare a balance sheet for the Morse Soybean Company on December 31, 2006, using the following list of accounts.

Accounts Payable	$4,000
Accounts Receivable	3,500
Cash	6,000
Equipment	7,000
Notes Payable	6,500
Retained Earnings	?
Salaries Payable	2,000
Supplies	2,500
Automobile	4,500
Common Stock	4,000

The Navigator

SOLUTION TO DEMONSTRATION PROBLEM

MORSE SOYBEAN COMPANY
Balance Sheet
December 31, 2006

Assets

Cash	$ 6,000
Accounts Receivable	3,500
Supplies	2,500
Equipment	7,000
Automobile	4,500
Total assets	$23,500

Liabilities and Stockholders' Equity

Liabilities	
Accounts Payable	$ 4,000
Salaries Payable	2,000
Notes Payable	6,500
Total liabilities	12,500
Stockholders' Equity	
Common Stock	4,000
Retained Earnings	7,000
Total liabilities and stockholders' equity	$23,500

REVIEW QUESTIONS AND EXERCISES

TRUE—FALSE

Indicate whether each of the following is true (T) or false (F) in the space provided.

_____ 1. (S.O. 1) Accounting provides the principal medium for communicating financial information of a business to all interested parties.

_____ 2. (S.O. 1) Identifying is the process of keeping a chronological diary of measured events in an orderly and systematic manner.

_____ 3. (S.O. 2) Customers and regulatory agencies are external users of accounting data.

_____ 4. (S.O. 2) Bookkeeping and accounting mean the same thing.

_____ 5. (S.O. 3) Accountants do not have to worry about issues of ethics.

_____ 6. (S.O. 4) GAAP is an acronym for "governmentally approved accounting principles."

_____ 7. (S.O. 4) At the time an asset is acquired, cost and value should be the same.

_____ 8. (S.O. 5) Under the economic entity assumption, it is assumed that the activity of a company is separate and distinct from activities of the owner(s).

_____ 9. (S.O. 5) The monetary unit assumption requires that all dollar amounts be rounded to the nearest dollar.

_____ 10. (S.O. 5) Proprietors are liable only for the amount they have invested in the business.

_____ 11. (S.O. 6) An asset may be intangible and represent nonphysical rights.

_____ 12. (S.O. 6) Stockholders' equity is the stockholders' claim on total assets.

_____ 13. (S.O. 6) Expenses are the decreases in stockholders' equity that result from operating the business.

_____ 14. (S.O. 6) If a liability increases, there would either have to be an equal decrease in another liability, a decrease in an asset, or an increase in stockholders' equity for the basic accounting equation to remain equal.

_____ 15. (S.O. 6) The basic accounting equation is in balance when the creditor(s) and ownership claims against the business equal the total assets.

_____ 16. (S.O. 7) External transactions involve economic events between the company and some other enterprise or party.

_____ 17. (S.O. 8) In the retained earnings statement, revenues are listed first, followed by expenses, and net income (or net loss).

_____ 18. (S.O. 8) The balance sheet is often referred to as the operating statement.

_____ *19. (S.O. 2) Management consulting includes examining the financial statements of companies and expressing an opinion as to the fairness of their presentation.

_____ *20. (S.O. 2) Cost accounting is part of private accounting.

The Navigator

MULTIPLE CHOICE

Circle the letter that best answers each of the following statements.

1. (S.O. 1) Which of the following is not part of the accounting process?
   a. Recording.
   b. Identifying.
   c. Financial decision making.
   d. Communicating.

2. (S.O. 2) Internal users of accounting data include:
   a. economic planners.
   b. investors.
   c. customers.
   d. company officers.

3. (S.O. 4) The organization(s) primarily responsible for establishing generally accepted accounting principles is(are) the:

	FASB	SEC
a.	no	no
b.	yes	no
c.	no	yes
d.	yes	yes

4. (S.O. 5) The monetary unit assumption:
   a. provides that the unit of measure fluctuates over time.
   b. is unimportant in applying the cost principle.
   c. is only used for financial statements of banks.
   d. requires that only transaction data capable of being expressed in terms of money be included in the accounting records of the economic entity.

5. (S.O. 5) A proprietorship is a business:
   a. owned by one person.
   b. owned by two or more persons.
   c. organized as a separate legal entity under state corporation law.
   d. owned by a governmental agency.

6. (S.O. 6) A net loss will result during a time period when:
   a. assets exceed liabilities.
   b. assets exceed stockholders' equity.
   c. expenses exceed revenues.
   d. revenues exceed expenses.

7. (S.O. 7) A company might carry on many activities that do not represent business transactions such as:
   a. borrowing money from the bank.
   b. placing an order for merchandise with a supplier.
   c. using office supplies.
   d. paying wages.

8. (S.O. 7) An example of an internal transaction is the:
   a. payment of monthly rent.
   b. hiring of employees.
   c. sale of pizza puffs to customers.
   d. use of paper, pens, and other office supplies.

9. (S.O. 7) The Relias Uptown Grill receives a bill of $400 from the Erml Advertising Agency. The owner, John Relias, is postponing payment of the bill until a later date. The effect on specific items in the basic accounting equation is:
   a. a decrease in Cash and an increase in Accounts Payable.
   b. a decrease in Cash and an increase in Retained Earnings.
   c. an increase in Accounts Payable and a decrease in Retained Earnings.
   d. a decrease in Accounts Payable and an increase in Retained Earnings.

10. (S.O. 7) Jim James, the inventory clerk of Nagy Co., indicates that $975 of supplies were used during the period. The effect on specific items in the basic accounting equation is:
    a. a decrease in Supplies and a decrease in Retained Earnings.
    b. a decrease in Cash and an increase in Supplies.
    c. an increase in Accounts Payable and a decrease in Supplies.
    d. an increase in Supplies Payable and a decrease in Retained Earnings.

11. (S.O. 7) Poindexter Co. pays a $500 dividend in cash. The effect on the specific items in the basic accounting equation is:
    a. an increase in Accounts Receivable and a decrease in Retained Earnings.
    b. an increase in Salary Expense and a decrease in Cash.
    c. an increase in Retained Earnings and a decrease in Cash.
    d. a decrease in Retained Earnings and a decrease in Cash.

12. (S.O. 7) Jeanie Company purchases $600 of equipment from Mundelein Inc. for cash. The effect on the components of the basic accounting equation of Jeanie Company is:
    a. an increase in assets and liabilities.
    b. a decrease in assets and liabilities.
    c. no change in total assets.
    d. an increase in assets and a decrease in liabilities.

13. (S.O. 7) The Vessely Company has the following at September 17: assets $13,000; liabilities $8,000; and stockholders' equity $5,000. On September 18, Vessely Company receives $500 of cash revenue and earns $200 of revenue on credit. Mike McEllen, the only worker that day, works 8 hours and receives a wage rate of $10 per hour. Mike will not get paid until September 21. No other transactions occur during the day. At the end of September 18 the new totals are:

	Assets	Liabilities	Stockholders' Equity
a.	$13,500	$7,880	$5,620
b.	$12,500	$8,000	$4,500
c.	$13,500	$8,120	$5,380
d.	$13,700	$8,080	$5,620

14. (S.O. 7) As of December 31, 2006, Morley Company has liabilities of $5,000 and stockholders' equity of $7,000. It received revenues of $23,000 during the year ended December 31, 2006. What are the assets for Morley Company as of December 31, 2006?
    a. $2,000.
    b. $12,000.
    c. $25,000.
    d. $35,000.

15. (S.O. 8) The statement that reports revenues and expenses is the:
    a. income statement.
    b. balance sheet.
    c. retained earnings statement.
    d. statement of cash flows.

16. (S.O. 8) Morreale Beaver Company buys a $12,000 van on credit. This transaction will affect the:
    a. income statement only.
    b. balance sheet only.
    c. income statement and retained earnings statement only.
    d. income statement, retained earnings statement, and balance sheet.

17. (S.O. 8) The financial statement that summarizes the financial position of a company is the:
    a. income statement.
    b. balance sheet.
    c. operating statement.
    d. retained earnings statement.

18. (S.O. 8) Which of the following would not appear on the DeFlippo Company's balance sheet?
    a. Accounts receivable.
    b. Retained earnings.
    c. Utilities expense.
    d. Wages payable.

*19. (S.O. 2) Auditing is:

a. the examination of financial statements by a CPA in order to express an opinion on their fairness.
b. a part of accounting that involves only recording of economic events.
c. an area of accounting that involves such activities as cost accounting, budgeting, and accounting information systems.
d. conducted by the Securities and Exchange Commission to ensure that registered financial statements are presented fairly.

*20. (S.O. 2) The private accountant might be involved in:

a. internal auditing.
b. tax accounting.
c. designing accounting and total information systems.
d. all of the above.

MATCHING

Match each term with its definition by writing the appropriate letter in the space provided.

Terms

____ 1. Revenues.

____ 2. Retained earnings statement.

____ 3. Stockholders' equity.

____ 4. Balance sheet.

____ 5. Monetary unit assumption.

____ 6. Income statement.

____ 7. Economic entity assumption.

____ 8. Assets.

____ 9. Accounting.

____ 10. Transactions.

____ 11. Expenses.

____ 12. Liabilities.

____ 13. Generally accepted accounting principles.

____ 14. Cost principle.

Definitions

a. Economic events of the enterprise recorded by accountants.

b. The process of identifying, recording, and communicating the economic information of an organization to interested users.

c. The gross increases in retained earnings resulting from business activities entered into for the purpose of earning income.

d. Resources owned by the business.

e. Reports the assets, liabilities, and stockholders' equity of a business enterprise at a specific date.

f. Presents the revenues and expenses and resulting net income of a company for a specific period of time.

g. Cost of assets consumed or services used in the process of earning revenue.

h. Creditorship claims on total assets.

i. Ownership claim on total assets.

j. Summarizes the changes in retained earnings for a specific period of time.

k. Requires that only transaction data capable of being expressed in terms of money be included in the accounting records of the economic entity.

l. States that economic events can be identified with a particular unit of accountability.

m. States that assets should be recorded at their cost.

n. A common set of rules, procedures, and guidelines (standards) used by accountants in reporting economic events.

The Navigator

EXERCISES

EX. 1-1 (S.O. 8) Some amounts are omitted in each of the following financial statements.

INCOME STATEMENT
For the Year Ended December 31, 2006

	Tang Company	June Company	Bruin Company
Revenues	$48,000	$ (D)	$82,000
Expenses	(A)	52,000	64,000

RETAINED EARNINGS STATEMENT
For the Year Ended December 31, 2006

	Tang Company	June Company	Bruin Company
Retained earnings, Jan. 1	$ (B)	$42,000	$43,000
Net income	15,000	24,000	(G)
Dividends	12,000	(E)	17,000
Retained earnings, Dec. 31	27,000	51,000	(H)

BALANCE SHEET
December 31, 2003

	Tang Company	June Company	Bruin Company
Total assets	$75,000	$ (F)	$91,000
Total liabilities	(C)	56,000	40,000
Common stock	5,000	3,000	7,000
Retained earnings	27,000	51,000	(I)

Instructions
Determine the missing amounts and indicate your answers in the spaces provided below.

(A)____________ (D)____________ (G)____________

(B)____________ (E)____________ (H)____________

(C)____________ (F)____________ (I)____________

EX. 1-2 (S.O. 7) On March 1, Laurie Fiala opened the Wahoo Beauty Salon. During the first month, the following selected transactions occurred.

1. Invested $5,000 cash in the business in exchange for $5,000 of common stock.
2. Paid $800 cash for beauty supplies.
3. Purchased equipment at a cost of $12,000, paying $2,000 in cash and the balance on account.
4. Received $1,200 cash for services rendered.
5. Paid $500 cash as a salary to a beautician.
6. Received $400 cash dividend.

Instructions

Prepare a tabular summary of the transactions, using the following column headings: Cash, Supplies, Equipment, Accounts Payable, Common Stock, and Retained Earnings.

Trans-action	Cash	+	Supplies	+	Equipment	=	Accounts Payable	+	Common Stock	+	Retained Earnings
1.	+5,000								+5000		
2.	-800		+800								
3.	-2,000				12,000		10,000				
4.	1200										1200
5.	-500										500
6.	400										

EX. 1-3 (S.O. 8) Selected financial statement items for the Geimer Company are presented below.

a. Accounts payable
b. Service revenue
c. Retained earnings, 1/1/06
d. Rent expense
e. Supplies
f. Advertising expense
g. Retained earnings, 12/31/06
h. Land
i. Utilities expense
j. Dividends
k. Net income
l. Salaries payable

Instructions

Indicate the financial statement(s) in which each item should be reported using the following code number(s): (1) Income statement for the year ended December 31, 2006, (2) Retained earnings statement for the year ended December 31, 2006, and (3) Balance sheet, December 31, 2006. (**Note:** More than one code number may be required for an item.)

Item	Financial Statement	Item	Financial Statement	Item	Financial Statement
a.		e.		i.	
b.		f.		j.	
c.		g.		k.	
d.		h.		l.	

The Navigator

SOLUTIONS TO REVIEW QUESTIONS AND EXERCISES

TRUE-FALSE

1. (T)
2. (F) **Identifying** is selecting those events that are considered evidence of economic activity relevant to a particular business organization. The process of keeping a chronological diary of measured events in an orderly and systematic manner is **recording.**
3. (T)
4. (F) **Bookkeeping** involves only the recording of economic events, while **accounting** encompasses the process of identification and communication along with recording.
5. (F) Accountants have to worry about ethical issues just like everybody else.
6. (F) GAAP is an acronym for "generally accepted accounting principles."
7. (T)
8. (T)
9. (F) The monetary unit assumption requires that only transaction data capable of being expressed in terms of money be included in the accounting records of the economic entity.
10. (F) A proprietor has unlimited liability for the debts incurred by the business. The stockholders of a corporation have limited liability.
11. (T)
12. (T)
13. (T)
14. (F) If a liability increases, there would have to be an equal decrease in another liability, an increase in an asset, or a decrease in stockholders' equity for the basic accounting equation to remain equal.
15. (T)
16. (T)
17. (F) It is the income statement which has revenues listed first, followed by expenses, and then net income (or net loss).
18. (F) The income statement is often referred to as the operating statement.

*19. (F) **Management consulting** provides advice to managers of companies concerning various aspects of a company's operations. Examining the financial statements of companies and expressing an opinion as to fairness of their presentation is the field of auditing.

*20. (T)

MULTIPLE CHOICE

1. (c) **Accounting** is defined as the process of identifying, recording, and communicating economic events of an organization to interested users. The interested users then make the financial decisions based on the information provided.

2. (d) Economic planners, customers, and investors are **external** users of accounting data. Company officers, managers, and employees are **internal** users of accounting data.

3. (d) Both the FASB and the SEC are the organizations primarily responsible for establishing generally accepted accounting principles.

4. (d) The **monetary unit assumption** requires that only transaction data capable of being expressed in terms of money be included in the accounting records of the economic entity. Choice (a) is false because this assumption assumes that the unit of measure remains sufficiently constant over time. Choice (b) is incorrect because the monetary unit assumption is vital in applying the cost principle. Choice (c) is incorrect because this assumption is used for all types of entities.

5. (a) A proprietorship is a business owned by only one person.

6. (c) A net loss will result when expenses exceed revenues. Net income results when revenues exceed expenses.

7. (b) Borrowing from the bank, using office supplies, and paying wages are all recognized as business transactions, thus causing (a), (c), and (d) to be incorrect. Placing an order for merchandise with a supplier is not recognized as a business transaction even though it may lead to a business transaction when the merchandise is delivered by the supplier.

8. (d) The use of office supplies is an internal transaction because an outside party is not involved when the office supplies are used. Answers (a) and (c) involve outside parties and are, therefore, external transactions. Choice (b) is not a transaction.

9. (c) The transaction is an advertising expense that has been incurred on account. Thus, the transaction decreases stockholders' equity Retained Earnings and increases the liability Accounts Payable.

10. (a) The using up of supplies is an expense. Thus, the transaction decreases the asset Supplies and decreases stockholders' equity Retained Earnings.

11. (d) The payment of a dividend reduces retained earnings. Dividends do not result in either an expense or a receivable.

12. (c) The transaction results in an increase in the asset Equipment and an equal decrease in the asset Cash. Therefore, there is no change in total assets.

13. (d) The effects of the transactions are summarized below.

	Assets	=	Liabilities	+	Stockholders' Equity
September 17	$13,000		$8,000		$5,000
Cash revenue	+ 500				+ 500
Credit revenue	+ 200				+ 200
Wage expense			+ 80		- 80
September 18	$13,700	=	$8,080	+	$5,620

14. (b) The balance sheet equation states: Assets = Liabilities + Stockholders' Equity. Thus, if liabilities are $5,000 and stockholders' equity is $7,000, assets must equal $12,000. The revenue is already in the December 31, 2006 totals and therefore is not relevant to the answer.

15. (a) The income statement reports revenues and expenses as well as net income. The balance sheet reports assets, liabilities, and stockholders' equity. The retained earnings statement explains the changes in retained earnings. The statement of cash flows shows cash flows.

16. (b) The transaction represents an increase in assets of $12,000 and an increase in liabilities of an equal amount. The transaction causes a change in balance sheet items only.

17. (b) The balance sheet reports the financial position of a company. The income statement (or operating statement) presents revenues and expenses. The retained earnings statement explains the changes in retained earnings that have occurred during a given period of time.

18. (c) Accounts Receivable, Retained Earnings and Wages Payable are all balance sheet items causing (a), (b), and (d) to be incorrect. Utilities Expense is an item that is reported on the income statement.

*19. (a) Auditing is the examination of financial statements by a CPA in order to express an opinion on their fairness. Choice (b) is incorrect because a part of accounting that involves only recording of economic events is bookkeeping. Choice (c) is incorrect because an area of accounting that involves such activities as cost accounting, budgeting, and accounting information systems is private (or managerial) accounting. Choice (d) is incorrect because CPAs perform the actual auditing function, not the SEC.

*20. (d) The private accountant might be involved in internal auditing, tax accounting, and designing accounting and information systems, as well as cost accounting, budgeting, and general accounting.

MATCHING

1. c.
2. j.
3. i.
4. e.
5. k.
6. f.
7. l.
8. d.
9. b.
10. a.
11. g.
12. h.
13. n.
14. m.

EXERCISES

EX. 1-1

(A)	$33,000	(Revenues $48,000 - net income $15,000).
(B)	$24,000	(Retained earnings, 12/31 $27,000 + dividends $12,000 - net income $15,000).
(C)	$43,000	[Assets $75,000 - (common stock $5,000 + retained earnings $27,000)].
(D)	$76,000	(Expenses $52,000 + net income $24,000)
(E)	$15,000	(Retained earnings, 1/1/ $42,000 + net income $24,000 - retained earnings 12/31 $51,000)
(F)	$110,000	(Liabilities $56,000 + common stock $3,000 + retained earnings $51,000).
(G)	$18,000	(Revenues $82,000 - expenses $64,000)
(H)	$44,000	(Retained earnings 1/1/ $43,000 + net income $18,000 - dividends $17,000)
(I)	$44,000	(Assets $91,000 - liabilities $40,000 - common stock $7,000).

EX. 1-2

Trans-action	Cash	+	Supplies	+	Equipment	=	Accounts Payable	+	Common Stock	+	Retained Earnings	
1.	+$5,000								+$5,000			Investment
2.	- 800		+$800									
	4,200	+	800			=			5,000			
3.	- 2,000				+$12,000		+$10,000					
	2,200	+	800	+	12,000	=	10,000	+	5,000			
4.	+ 1,200										+$1,200	Service Revenue
	3,400	+	800	+	12,000	=	10,000	+	5,000	+	1,200	
5.	- 500										- 500	Salary Expense
	2,900	+	800	+	12,000	=	10,000	+	5,000	+	700	
6.	- 400										- 400	Dividends
	$2,500	+	$800	+	$12,000	=	$10,000	+	$5,000	+	$300	

EX. 1-3

Item	Financial Statement	Item	Financial Statement	Item	Financial Statement
a.	3	e.	3	i.	1
b.	1	f.	1	j.	2
c.	2	g.	2, 3	k.	1, 2
d.	1	h.	3	l.	3

CHAPTER 2

THE RECORDING PROCESS

The Navigator ✓

- Scan Study Objectives ☐
- Read Preview ☐
- Read Chapter Review ☐
- Work Demonstration Problem ☐
- Answer True-False Statements ☐
- Answer Multiple-Choice Questions ☐
- Match Terms and Definitions ☐
- Solve Exercises ☐

CHAPTER STUDY OBJECTIVES

After studying this chapter, you should be able to:

1. Explain what an account is and how it helps in the recording process.
2. Define debits and credits and explain how they are used to record business transactions.
3. Identify the basic steps in the recording process.
4. Explain what a journal is and how it helps in the recording process.
5. Explain what a ledger is and how it helps in the recording process.
6. Explain what posting is and how it helps in the recording process.
7. Prepare a trial balance and explain its purposes.

PREVIEW OF CHAPTER 2

In Chapter 1, we analyzed business transactions in terms of the accounting equation and presented the cumulative effects of these transactions in tabular form. In this chapter, we will introduce and illustrate the basic procedures and records that are used. The organization and content of the chapter are as follows:

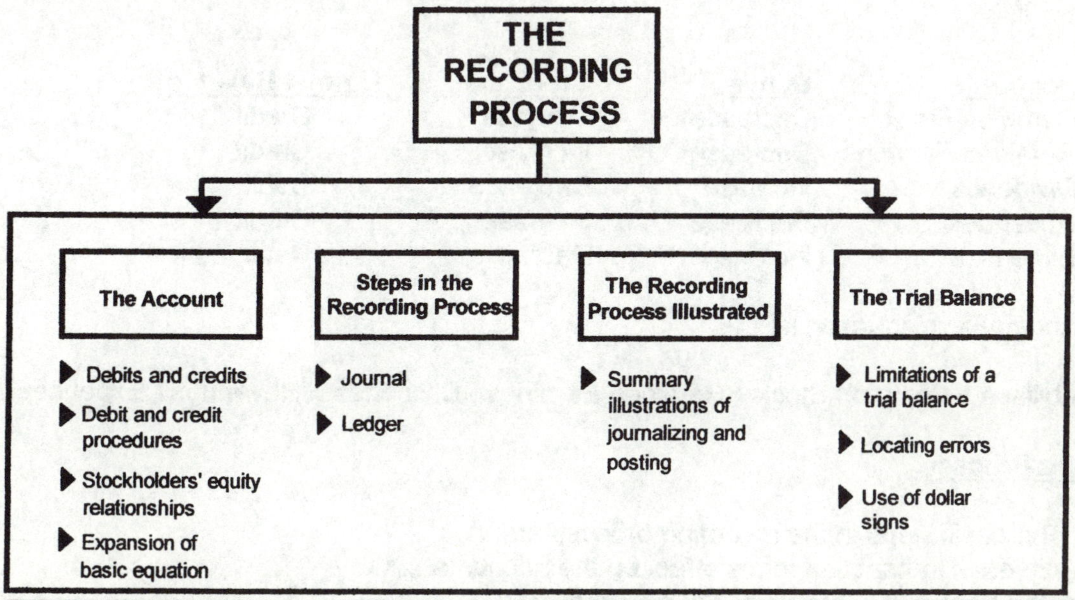

CHAPTER REVIEW

The Account

1. (S.O. 1) An **account** is an individual accounting record of increases and decreases in a specific asset, liability, or stockholders' equity item.

2. In its simplest form, an account consists of (a) the title of the account, (b) a left or debit side, and (c) a right or credit side. The alignment of these parts resembles the letter T, and therefore the account form is called a **T-account.**

Debits and Credits

3. (S.O. 2) The terms **debit** and **credit** mean left and right, respectively.
   a. The act of entering an amount on the left side of an account is called **debiting** the account and making an entry on the right side is **crediting** the account.
   b. When the debit amounts exceed the credits, an account has a **debit balance;** when the reverse is true, the account has a **credit balance.**

4. In a **double-entry** system, equal debits and credits are made in the accounts for each transaction. Thus, the total debits will always equal the total credits.

5. The effects of debits and credits on **assets** and **liabilities** and the normal balances are:

Accounts	Debits	Credits	Normal Balance
Assets	Increase	Decrease	Debit
Liabilities	Decrease	Increase	Credit

6. Accounts are kept for each of the five subdivisions of stockholders' equity: Common Stock, Retained Earnings, Dividends, Revenues, and Expenses.

7. The effects of debits and credits on the stockholders' equity accounts and the normal balances are:

Accounts	Debits	Credits	Normal Balance
Common Stock	Decrease	Increase	Credit
Retained Earnings	Decrease	Increase	Credit
Dividends	Increase	Decrease	Debit
Revenues	Decrease	Increase	Credit
Expenses	Increase	Decrease	Debit

8. The expanded basic equation is:

Assets = Liabilities + Common Stock + Retained Earnings - Dividends + Revenues - Expenses

The Recording Process

9. (S.O. 3) The basic steps in the recording process are:
   a. Analyze each transaction for its effect on the accounts.
   b. Enter the transaction information in a journal.
   c. Transfer the journal information to the appropriate accounts in the ledger.

The Journal

10. (S.O. 4) Transactions are initially recorded in a journal.
    a. A journal is referred to as a book of original entry.
    b. A **general journal** is the most basic form of journal.

11. The journal makes several significant contributions to the recording process:
    a. It discloses in one place the complete effect of a transaction.
    b. It provides a chronological record of transactions.
    c. It helps to prevent or locate errors because the debit and credit amounts for each entry can be readily compared.

12. Entering transaction data in the journal is known as **journalizing.** When three or more accounts are required in one journal entry, the entry is known as a **compound entry.**

The Ledger

13. (S.O. 5) The ledger is the entire group of accounts maintained by a company. It keeps in one place all the information about changes in account balances and it is a source of useful data for management.

14. The **standard form of a ledger account** has three money columns and the balance in the account is determined after each transaction.

15. (S.O. 6) **Posting** is the procedure of transferring journal entries to the ledger accounts. The following steps are used in posting:
    a. In the ledger, enter in the appropriate columns of the account(s) debited the date, journal page, and debit amount.
    b. In the reference column of the journal, write the account number to which the debit amount was posted.
    c. Perform the same steps in a. and b. for the credit amount.

The Chart of Accounts

16. A **chart of accounts** is a listing of the accounts and the account numbers which identify their location in the ledger. The numbering system usually starts with the balance sheet accounts and follows with the income statement accounts.

The Basic Steps

17. The basic steps in the recording process are illustrated as follows:

Transaction On September 4, Fesmire Inc. pays $3,000 cash to a creditor in full payment of the balance due.

Basic analysis The liability Accounts Payable is decreased $3,000, and the asset Cash is decreased $3,000.

Debit-credit analysis Debits decrease liabilities: debit Accounts Payable $3,000.
Credits decrease assets: credit Cash $3,000.

Journal entry

Date	Account Titles and Explanation	Ref.	Debit	Credit
Sept. 4	Accounts Payable	26	3,000	
	Cash	1		3,000
	(Paid creditor in full)			

Posting

Cash		1
	Sept. 4	3,000

Accounts Payable		26
Sept. 4	3,000	

The Trial Balance

18. (S.O. 7) A **trial balance** is a list of accounts and their balances at a given time. The primary purpose of the trial balance is to prove the mathematical equality of the debits and credits after posting.

19. A trial balance does not prove that all transactions have been recorded or that the ledger is correct because the trial balance may still balance when
    a. a transaction is not journalized.
    b. a correct journal entry is not posted.
    c. an entry is posted twice.
    d. incorrect accounts are used in journalizing or posting.
    e. offsetting errors are made in recording the amount of a transaction.

The Navigator

DEMONSTRATION PROBLEM (S.O. 4)

Accounting Consultants, Inc. had the following transactions occur during the month of January 2006:

Jan. 2 Stockholders invest $222,000 cash in business for common stock.

6 Buys an office building for $120,000.

10 Hires Pat Delaney as an assistant accountant, at a salary of $36,000 per year.

14 Performs consulting services for Simon, Inc. worth $10,000 but is not paid by J. Simon at this time.

17 Purchases supplies for $500 on credit.

20 Receives a $10,000 check from Simon, Inc.

28 Pays Pat Delaney $2,000 in wages for January.

30 Pays a $3,000 cash dividend.

Instructions

Prepare the general journal entries for each of these transactions.

SOLUTION TO DEMONSTRATION PROBLEM

General Journal			J1
Date	Account Title	Debit	Credit
2006			
Jan. 2	Cash	222,000	
	Common Stock		222,000
	(Investment in business)		
6	Office Building	120,000	
	Cash		120,000
	(Purchase of office building)		
10	(No journal entry required)		
14	Accounts Receivable	10,000	
	Consulting Revenue		10,000
	(Services performed for Simon, Inc.)		
17	Supplies	500	
	Accounts Payable		500
	(Purchase of supplies)		
20	Cash	10,000	
	Accounts Receivable		10,000
	(Received cash payment from Simon, Inc.)		
28	Wages Expense	2,000	
	Cash		2,000
	(Paid Delaney for his wages earned)		
30	Dividends	3,000	
	Cash		3,000
	(Pays cash dividends)		

REVIEW QUESTIONS AND EXERCISES

TRUE—FALSE

Indicate whether each of the following is true (T) or false (F) in the space provided.

_____ 1. (S.O. 2) In accounting the terms debit and credit mean left and right respectively.

_____ 2. (S.O. 2) The double-entry system is a logical method for recording transactions and results in equal debits and credits for each transaction.

_____ 3. (S.O. 2) Revenue accounts normally have debit balances.

_____ 4. (S.O. 2) The normal balance of an expense is a credit.

_____ 5. (S.O. 2) The expanded basic equation is: Assets = Liabilities + Common Stock + Retained Earnings + Dividends + Revenues - Expenses.

_____ 6. (S.O. 4) The journal discloses in one place the complete effect of a transaction.

_____ 7. (S.O. 4) The journal provides a chronological record of transactions.

_____ 8. (S.O. 4) Separate journal entries are made for each transaction.

_____ 9. (S.O. 4) The general journal is the most basic form of journal.

_____ 10. (S.O. 5) A ledger is a list of accounts and their balances at a given time.

_____ 11. (S.O. 5) The ledger is merely a bookkeeping device and therefore does not provide much useful data for management.

_____ 12. (S.O. 5) The standard form of ledger account has three money columns for debit, credit, and balance.

_____ 13. (S.O. 6) Posting is the procedure of entering transaction data in the general journal.

_____ 14. (S.O. 6) The chart of accounts is a listing of the accounts and the account numbers which identify their location in the ledger.

_____ 15. (S.O. 6) The purpose of transaction analysis is to first identify the type of account involved and then identify whether a debit or a credit to the account is required.

_____ 16. (S.O. 7) A trial balance lists the accounts and their location in the ledger.

_____ 17. (S.O. 7) The primary purpose of a trial balance is to prove the mathematical equality of the debits and credits after posting.

_____ 18. (S.O. 7) A trial balance is usually prepared daily.

_____ 19. (S.O. 7) A trial balance does not prove that all transactions have been recorded or that the ledger is correct.

_____ 20. (S.O. 7) The trial balance will not balance when incorrect account titles are used in journalizing or posting.

The Navigator

MULTIPLE CHOICE

Circle the letter that best answers each of the following statements.

1. (S.O. 1) An account is an individual accounting record of increases and decreases in specific:
   a. liabilities.
   b. assets.
   c. expenses.
   d. assets, liabilities, and stockholders' equity items.

2. (S.O. 2) Credits:
   a. increase both assets and liabilities.
   b. decrease both assets and liabilities.
   c. increase assets and decrease liabilities.
   d. decrease assets and increase liabilities.

3. (S.O. 2) An account which is increased by a credit is:
   a. an asset account.
   b. a liability account.
   c. a dividends account.
   d. an expense account.

4. (S.O. 2) Which of the following rules is **incorrect?**
   a. Credits decrease the dividends account.
   b. Debits increase the retained earnings account.
   c. Credits increase revenue accounts.
   d. Debits decrease liability accounts.

5. (S.O. 2) An account which is increased by a debit is a:
   a. liability account.
   b. dividends account.
   c. retained earnings account.
   d. revenue account.

6. (S.O. 2) An account which is increased by a credit is a(n):
   a. dividends account.
   b. revenue account.
   c. expense account.
   d. asset account.

7. (S.O. 3) Which of the following is the correct sequence of steps in the recording process?
   a. Posting, journalizing, analyzing.
   b. Journalizing, analyzing, posting.
   c. Analyzing, posting, journalizing.
   d. Analyzing, journalizing, posting.

8. (S.O. 4) The column in the general journal which is **not** used during journalizing is the:
   a. date column.
   b. account title column.
   c. reference column.
   d. debit amount column.

9. (S.O. 4) Which of the following is a **false** statement?
   a. The account Revenue from Fees is increased with a credit.
   b. A compound entry is when two or more accounts are required in one journal entry.
   c. Retained Earnings is increased by a credit entry.
   d. All transactions are initially recorded in a journal.

10. (S.O. 4) Which of the following is not considered a significant contribution of the journal to the recording process?
    a. The journal provides a chronological record of all transactions.
    b. The journal provides a means of accumulating in one place all the information about changes in account balances.
    c. The journal discloses in one place the complete effect of a transaction.
    d. The journal helps prevent or locate errors since the debit and credit amounts for each entry can be readily compared.

11. (S.O. 4) McClory Company purchases equipment for $900 and supplies for $300 from Rudnicky Co. for $1,200 cash. The entry for this transaction will include a:
    a. debit to Equipment $900 and a debit to Supplies Expense $300 for Rudnicky.
    b. credit to Cash for Rudnicky.
    c. credit to Accounts Payable for McClory.
    d. debit to Equipment $900 and a debit to Supplies $300 for McClory.

12. (S.O. 4) Reiner Company purchases $300 of equipment from Laventhal Company on credit. Reiner will enter the transaction in the journal with a:
    a. debit to Accounts Receivable and a credit to Sales.
    b. debit to Accounts Receivable and a credit to Equipment.
    c. credit to Accounts Payable and a debit to Equipment.
    d. credit to Cash and a debit to Equipment.

13. (S.O. 4) Szykowny Co. buys a machine from Scott Company paying half in cash and putting the balance on account. The journal entry for this transaction by Szykowny will include a:
    a. credit to Accounts Payable and a credit to Cash.
    b. credit to Notes Payable and a credit to Cash.
    c. debit to Supplies and a credit to Cash.
    d. debit to Machinery and a credit to Notes Payable.

14. (S.O. 4) Hrubec Company pays $900 cash for a one-year insurance policy on July 1, 2005. The policy will expire on June 30, 2006. The entry on July 1, 2005 is:
    a. Debit Insurance Expense $900; credit Cash $900.
    b. Debit Prepaid Insurance $900; credit Cash $900.
    c. Debit Insurance Expense $900; credit Accounts Payable $900.
    d. Debit Prepaid Insurance $900; credit Accounts Payable $900.

15. (S.O. 4) Kevin Walsh, Inc. pays a $300 cash dividend. The entry for this transaction will include a debit of $300 to:
    a. Dividends.
    b. Dividend Income.
    c. Dividends Expense.
    d. Salaries Expense.

16. (S.O. 4) Vicki Wagner Dance Studio bills a client for dancing lessons earned during the past week. The journal entry will include a credit to:
    a. Retained Earnings.
    b. Unearned Dance Fees.
    c. Dance Fees Earned.
    d. Accounts Receivable.

17. (S.O. 4) Golden Pork Company receives $400 from a customer on October 15 in payment of balance due for services billed on October 1. The entry by Golden Pork Company will include a credit of $400 to:
    a. Notes Receivable.
    b. Service Revenue.
    c. Accounts Receivable.
    d. Unearned Service Revenue.

18. (S.O. 4) On October 3, Mike Baker, Co. received a cash payment for services previously billed to a client. The company paid its telephone bill, and it also bought equipment on credit. For the three transactions, at least one of the entries will include a:
    a. credit to Retained Earnings.
    b. credit to Notes Payable.
    c. debit to Accounts Receivable.
    d. credit to Accounts Payable.

19. (S.O. 6) The chart of accounts is a:
    a. list of accounts and their balances at a given time.
    b. device used to prove the mathematical accuracy of the ledger.
    c. listing of the accounts and the account numbers which identify their location in the ledger.
    d. required step in the recording process.

20. (S.O. 7) A trial balance will not balance if:
    a. a journal entry is posted twice.
    b. a wrong amount is used in journalizing.
    c. incorrect account titles are used in journalizing.
    d. a journal entry is only partially posted.

The Navigator

MATCHING

Match each term with its definition by writing the appropriate letter in the space provided.

Terms

_____ 1. Account.

_____ 2. T-account.

_____ 3. Posting.

_____ 4. Trial balance.

_____ 5. Debit.

_____ 6. Credit.

_____ 7. Chart of accounts.

_____ 8. Ledger.

_____ 9. Journalizing.

_____ 10. Journal.

_____ 11. Double-entry system.

Definitions

a. The entire group of accounts maintained by a company.
b. A list of accounts and the account numbers which identify their location in the ledger.
c. An individual accounting record of increases and decreases in a specific asset, liability, or stockholders' equity item.
d. The right side of an account.
e. The left side of an account.
f. The procedure of transferring journal entries to the ledger accounts.
g. A list of accounts and their balances at a given time.
h. A system that records the dual effect of each transaction in appropriate accounts.
i. The form of an account with a title and a left or debit side and a right or credit side.
j. An accounting record in which transactions are initially recorded in chronological order.
k. The procedure of entering transaction data in the journal.

EXERCISES

EX. 2-1 (S.O. 3) The ledger of the Gilbert Company includes the following accounts:

a. Equipment
b. Wages Payable
c. Telephone Expense
d. Notes Receivable
e. Commissions Earned
f. Retained Earnings
g. Rent Expense
h. Supplies
i. Dividends
j. Fees Earned
k. Common Stock

Instructions

For each account indicate (a) whether it is an asset, liability, or stockholders' equity item, and (b) its normal balance. Use the following format for your answer. The account, Cash, is given as an example.

Account	(a) Type of Account	(b) Normal Balance
Cash	Asset	Debit
Equipment	asset	debit
Wages Payable	liabilty	credit
Telephone Expense	S.E.	credit
Notes Receivable	asset	~~credit~~
Commissions Earned	~~asset~~ SE	debit
Retained Earnings		
Rent Expense		
Supplies		
Dividends		
Fees Earned		
Common Stock		

EX. 2-2 (S.O. 4) Onassis Ship Lines, Inc., had the following transactions occur during the month of February 2006:

Feb. 3 Paid $1,000 to Jean Paul Getty, the ship's bursar, for wages earned in January. These wages were expensed in January.

7 Received $35,000 cash from J.P. Morgan for a cruise taken by J.P. and his family last month. This revenue was properly recorded last month.

11 Purchased equipment from J.D. Rockefeller for $50,000 on credit.

20 Received $25,000 cash from Andrew Carnegie upon completion of a cruise taken by Andrew and his friends this month. (Credit Cruise Revenues)

26 Received $31,000 cash from H.L. Hunt for a cruise to be taken next month.

28 Paid $20,000 cash to Vanderbilt Insurance Company for a 6-month insurance policy to expire August 31.

Instructions

Journalize the transactions in the journal provided below.

General Journal

J1

Date	Account Title	Debit	Credit
2006	wages payable	1,000	
	Cash salary expense		1,000
	Cash	35,000	
	accounts receivable		35,000
	equipment	50,000	
	accounts payable		50,000
	Cash	25,000	
	Service Rev		25,000
	cash	31,000	

unearned Rev 31,000

28 Insurance exp. 20,000

cash 20,000

General Journal

J1

Date	Account Title	Debit	Credit

EX. 2-3 (S.O. 7) The ledger for the Thorson Advertising Agency at October 31, 2006 shows the following data. Assume that all accounts have normal balances.

Accounts Receivable	$ 9,500
Accounts Payable	7,500
Common Stock	9,000
Dividends	500
Cash	?
Commissions Earned	7,000
Supplies	600
Rent Expense	900
Retained Earnings	1,500
Salaries Expense	4,060
Unearned Fees	1,200

Instructions

Prepare a trial balance at October 31, 2006.

THORSON ADVERTISING AGENCY
Trial Balance
October 31, 2006

	Debit	Credit
Assets:		
Cash	16,640	
Supplies	600	
accounts receivable	9,500	
Liabilities:		
acc. Payable		7,500
Unearned fees		1,2000
Common stock		9,000
Retained earnings		1,500
Dividends	500	
Commissioned earned		7,000
Rent Expense	900	
Salaries Expense	4060	
	26200	26200

As

The Navigator

SOLUTIONS TO REVIEW QUESTIONS AND EXERCISES

TRUE-FALSE

1. (T)
2. (T)
3. (F) The normal balance of a revenue account is a credit.
4. (F) The normal balance of an expense account is a debit.
5. (F) The expanded basic equation is:
   Assets = Liabilities + Common Stock + Retained Earnings - Dividends + Revenues - Expenses.
6. (T)
7. (T)
8. (T)
9. (T)
10. (F) The ledger is the entire group of accounts maintained by a company. It keeps in one place all the information about changes in account balances. The trial balance is a list of accounts and their balances at a given time.
11. (F) The ledger gives management useful information about account balances; e.g., Accounts Receivable can be inspected to ascertain the amounts due from customers.
12. (T)
13. (F) Posting is the procedure of transferring journal entries to the ledger accounts. Journalizing is the procedure of entering transaction data in a journal.
14. (T)
15. (T)
16. (F) The trial balance is a list of accounts and their balances at a given time. The chart of accounts is a listing of accounts and their location in the ledger.
17. (T)
18. (F) A trial balance can be prepared at any point in time, but is customarily prepared at the end of an accounting period.
19. (T)
20. (F) One of the limitations of the trial balance is that it will still balance when incorrect account titles are used in journalizing or posting.

MULTIPLE CHOICE

1. (d) An account is an individual accounting record of increases and decreases in specific asset, liability, and stockholders' equity items.

2. (d) Credits decrease assets and increase liabilities.

3. (b) An asset account (a), a dividends account (c), and an expense account (d) are all accounts that have normal debit balances; thus, they are increased by debits.

4. (b) Debits decrease the retained earnings account because the retained earnings account has a credit balance as its normal balance. Choices (a), (c), and (d) are all correct rules concerning increasing or decreasing accounts.

5. (b) A liability account (a), a retained earnings account (c), and a revenue account (d) are all accounts that have a normal balance as a credit; therefore, they are increased by a credit. The dividends account has a normal balance as a debit and will increase with a debit.

6. (b) A dividends account (a), an expense account (c), and an asset account (d) are all accounts that have a normal debit balance. A revenue account has a normal credit balance and will increase with a credit entry.

7. (d) The basic steps in the recording process are:
   1. Analyze each transaction.
   2. Enter the transaction information in a journal (journalizing).
   3. Post the journal information to the ledger.

8. (c) The date column (a), the account title column (b), and the debit amount column (d) are all used during the journalizing procedure. The reference column is used later when the journal entries are posted to the ledger.

9. (b) A compound entry is when three or more accounts are required in one journal entry. Choices (a), (c), and (d) are all true statements.

10. (b) The ledger—not the journal—provides a means of accumulating in one place all the information about changes in account balances. Answers (a), (c), and (d) are all considered significant contributions by the journal to the recording process.

11. (d) McClory Company will make the following entry:

Equipment	900	
Supplies	300	
Cash		1,200

12. (c) Reiner Co. will make the following entry:

Equipment	300	
Accounts Payable		300

13. (a) The journal entry for this transaction is as follows:

Equipment	XXXX	
Accounts Payable		XXXX
Cash		XXXX

14. (b) The one-year policy will benefit more than one accounting period. Therefore, the entry is:

Prepaid Insurance	900	
Cash		900

15. (a) The payment of dividends is not an expense. The entry is:

Dividends	300	
Cash		300

16. (c) The transaction is recorded in the journal as follows:

Accounts Receivable	XXXX	
Dance Fees Earned		XXXX

17. (c) The entry by Golden Pork Company is:

Cash	400	
Accounts Receivable		400

18. (d) The three transactions are recorded in the journal as follows:

Cash	XXXX	
Accounts Receivable		XXXX
Telephone Expense	XXXX	
Cash		XXXX
Equipment	XXXX	
Accounts Payable		XXXX

19. (c) The chart of accounts is a listing of the accounts and the account numbers which identify their location in the ledger. Both answers (a) and (b) are characteristics of a trial balance. Answer (d) is incorrect because a chart of accounts is not required.

20. (d) The trial balance may still balance even when a journal entry is posted twice (a), a wrong amount is used in journalizing (b), and incorrect account titles are used (c). A journal entry that is only partially posted means that a debit or credit posting is omitted; thus, the trial balance will not balance.

MATCHING

1. c	5. e	9. k
2. i	6. d	10. j
3. f	7. b	11. h
4. g	8. a	

EXERCISES

EX. 2-1

Account	(a) Type of Account	(b) Normal Balance
Equipment	Asset	Debit
Wages Payable	Liability	Credit
Telephone Expense	Stockholders' equity	Debit
Notes Receivable	Asset	Debit
Commissions Earned	Stockholders' equity	Credit
Retained Earnings	Stockholders' equity	Credit
Rent Expense	Stockholders' equity	Debit
Supplies	Asset	Debit
Dividends	Stockholders' equity	Debit
Fees Earned	Stockholders' equity	Credit
Common Stock	Stockholders' equity	Credit

EX. 2-2

General Journal

J1

Date	Account Title	Debit	Credit
2006			
Feb. 3	Wages Payable	1,000	
	Cash		1,000
	(Paid wages earned in January)		
7	Cash	35,000	
	Accounts Receivable		35,000
	(Received payment from J.P. Morgan)		
11	Equipment	50,000	
	Accounts Payable		50,000
	(Purchased equipment from J.D.		
	Rockefeller on account)		
20	Cash	25,000	
	Cruise Revenues		25,000
	(Received cash for revenue earned)		
26	Cash	31,000	
	Unearned Cruise Revenue		31,000
	(Received advance from H.L. Hunt		
	for future cruise)		
28	Prepaid Insurance	20,000	
	Cash		20,000
	(Paid 6-month policy; effective		
	date March 1)		

EX. 2-3

THORSON ADVERTISING AGENCY
Trial Balance
October 31, 2006

	Debit	Credit
Cash	$10,640	
Accounts Receivable	9,500	
Supplies	600	
Accounts Payable		$ 7,500
Unearned Fees		1,200
Common Stock		9,000
Retained Earnings		1,500
Dividends	500	
Commissions Earned		7,000
Rent Expense	900	
Salaries Expense	4,060	
	$26,200	$26,200

CHAPTER 3

ADJUSTING THE ACCOUNTS

The Navigator ✓

- *Scan Study Objectives* ☐
- *Read Preview* ☐
- *Read Chapter Review* ☐
- *Work Demonstration Problem* ☐
- *Answer True-False Statements* ☐
- *Answer Multiple-Choice Questions* ☐
- *Match Terms and Definitions* ☐
- *Solve Exercises* ☐

CHAPTER STUDY OBJECTIVES

After studying this chapter, you should be able to:

1. Explain the time period assumption.
2. Explain the accrual basis of accounting.
3. Explain why adjusting entries are needed.
4. Identify the major types of adjusting entries.
5. Prepare adjusting entries for prepayments.
6. Prepare adjusting entries for accruals.
7. Describe the nature and purpose of an adjusted trial balance.

*8. Prepare adjusting entries for the alternative treatment of prepayments.

***Note:** All **asterisked** (*) items relate to material contained in the Appendix to the chapter.

PREVIEW OF CHAPTER 3

In Chapter 2 we examined the recording process through the preparation of the trial balance. Before we will be ready to prepare financial statements from the trial balance, additional steps need to be taken. Before financial statements can be prepared, questions relating to the recognition of revenues and expenses must be answered. With the answers in hand, the relevant account balances can then be adjusted. The organization and content of the chapter are as follows:

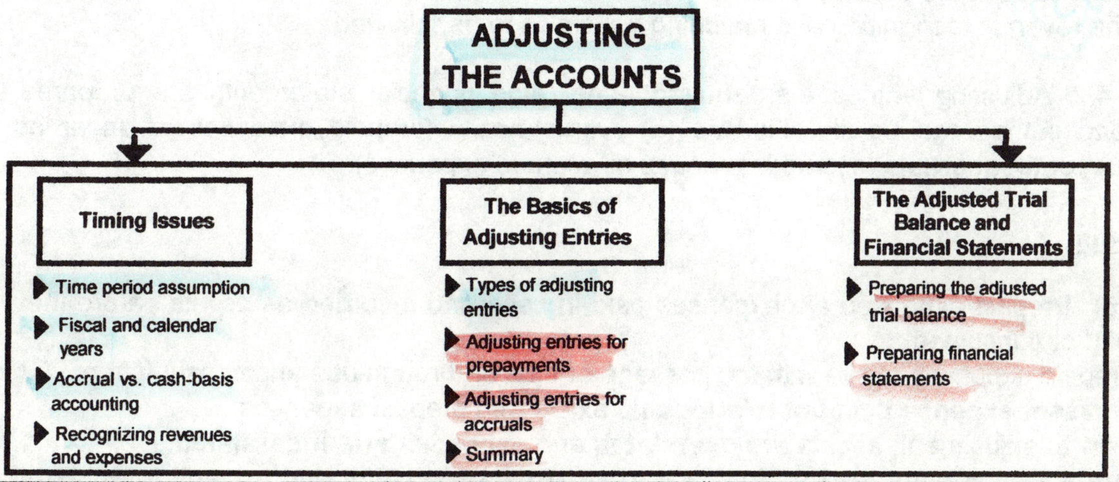

CHAPTER REVIEW

Time-Period Assumption

1. (S.O. 1) The **time period (or periodicity) assumption** assumes that the economic life of a business can be divided into artificial time periods.

2. Accounting time periods are generally a month, a quarter, or a year. The accounting time period of one year in length is usually known as a **fiscal year.**

Accrual Basis of Accounting

3. (S.O. 2) The revenue recognition and matching principles are used under the **accrual basis of accounting.** Under **cash basis accounting,** revenue is recorded only when cash is received and expenses are recorded only when paid.

4. Generally accepted accounting principles require accrual basis accounting rather than cash basis accounting because the cash basis of accounting often leads to misleading financial statements.

Revenue Recognition Principle

5. The **revenue recognition principle** states that revenue should be recognized in the accounting period in which it is earned.

The Matching Principle

6. The **matching principle** dictates that efforts (expenses) be matched with accomplishments (revenues).

Adjusting Entries

7. (S.O. 3) Adjusting entries are made in order for:
   a. Revenues to be recorded in the period in which they are earned, and for expenses to be recognized in the period in which they are incurred.
   b. The revenue recognition and matching principles to be followed.

8. (S.O. 4) Adjusting entries are required every time financial statements are prepared. Adjusting entries can be classified as (a) **prepayments** (prepaid expenses or unearned revenue) or (b) **accruals** (accrued revenues or accrued expenses).

Prepayments

9. (S.O. 5) Prepaid expenses are expenses paid in cash and recorded as assets before they are used or consumed.
   a. Prepaid expenses expire with the passage of time or through use and consumption.
   b. An **asset-expense account relationship** exists with prepaid expenses.
   c. Prior to adjustment, **assets are overstated** and **expenses are understated.**
   d. The adjusting entry results in a debit to an expense account and a credit to an asset account.
   e. Examples of prepaid expenses include supplies, insurance, and depreciation.

f. To illustrate a prepaid adjusting entry, assume on October 1, Kubitz Company pays $2,400 cash to Sandy Insurance Co. for a one-year insurance policy effective October 1. The adjusting entry at October 31 is:

Insurance Expense ($2,400 X 1/12)	200	
Prepaid Insurance		200

10. **Depreciation** is the process of allocating the cost of an asset to expense over its useful life in a rational and systematic manner.

a. The purchase of equipment or a building is viewed as a long-term prepayment of services and, therefore, is allocated in the same manner as other prepaid expenses.

b. Depreciation is an estimate rather than a factual measurement of the cost that has expired.

c. In recording depreciation, Depreciation Expense is debited and a contra asset account, Accumulated Depreciation, is credited.

d. In the balance sheet, Accumulated Depreciation is offset against the asset account. The difference between the cost of the asset and its related accumulated depreciation is referred to as the **book value** of the asset.

e. To illustrate an adjusting entry for depreciation, assume Resch Co. purchases a machine for $6,000 cash on January 1, 2005. Assuming that annual depreciation is $1,200, the adjusting entry at December 31, 2005 is:

Depreciation Expense	1,200	
Accumulated Depreciation—Machinery............		1,200

11. **Unearned revenues** are revenues received and recorded as liabilities before they are earned.

a. Unearned revenues are subsequently earned by rendering service to a customer.

b. A **liability-revenue account relationship** exists with unearned revenues.

c. Prior to adjustment, **liabilities are overstated** and **revenues are understated.**

d. The adjusting entry results in a debit to a liability account and a credit to a revenue account.

e. Examples of unearned revenues include rent, magazine subscriptions, and customer deposits for future service.

f. To illustrate an unearned revenue adjusting entry, assume on October 1, Schoen Co. receives $3,000 cash from a renter in payment of monthly rent for the period October through December. At October 31, the adjusting entry to record the rent earned in October is:

Unearned Rent Revenue	1,000	
Rent Revenue ($3,000 X 1/3)..........................		1,000

Accruals

12. (S.O. 6) **Accrued revenues** are revenues earned but not yet received in cash.

a. Accrued revenues may accumulate with the passing of time as in the case of interest and rent, or through services performed but not billed or collected.

b. An **asset-revenue account relationship** exists with accrued revenues.

c. Prior to adjustment, **both assets and revenues are understated.**

d. The adjusting entry results in a debit to an asset account and a credit to a revenue account.

e. To illustrate an accrued revenue adjusting entry, assume in October, Mayer, a dentist, performs $800 of services for patients who will not pay until November. The adjusting entry at October 31 is:

Accounts Receivable	800	
Dental Fees Earned		800

13. **Accrued expenses** are expenses incurred but not yet paid or recorded.
    a. Accrued expenses result from the same causes as accrued revenues and include interest, rent, taxes, and salaries.
    b. A **liability-expense account relationship** exists with accrued expenses.
    c. Prior to adjustment, both **liabilities and expenses are understated.**
    d. The adjusting entry results in a debit to an expense account and a credit to a liability account.
    e. To illustrate an accrued expense adjusting entry, assume Schwenk Company incurs salaries of $4,000 during the last week of October that will be paid in November. The adjusting entry on October 31 is:

Salaries Expense..	4,000	
Salaries Payable		4,000

14. Each adjusting entry affects one balance sheet account and one income statement account.

Adjusted Trial Balance

15. (S.O. 7) After all adjusting entries have been journalized and posted an **adjusted trial balance** is prepared. This trial balance shows the balances of all accounts, including those that have been adjusted, at the end of the accounting period.

16. The **purpose** of an adjusted trial balance is to prove the equality of the total debit balances and the total credit balances in the ledger after all adjustments have been made.

17. The accounts in the adjusted trial balance contain all data that are needed for the preparation of financial statements.

Alternative Treatment

*18. (S.O. 8) Under the alternative treatment, at the time an expense is prepaid, an expense account is debited, and when unearned revenues are received a revenue account is credited.

*19. The alternative treatment of prepaid expenses and unearned revenues has the same effect on the financial statements as the procedures described in the chapter.

*20. When a prepaid expense is initially debited to an expense account,
    a. No adjusting entry will be required if the prepayment is fully expired or consumed before the next financial statement date.
    b. If the prepayment is not fully expired or consumed, an adjusting entry is required.
    c. Prior to adjustment an **expense account is overstated** and an **asset account is understated.**
    d. The adjusting entry results in a debit (increase) to an asset account and a credit (decrease) to an expense account.

e. To illustrate the adjusting entry, assume Gonzalez Company purchases $1,200 of supplies and debits Office Supplies Expense. At the next financial statement date, $300 of supplies are on hand. The adjusting entry is:

	Debit	Credit
Office Supplies	300	
Office Supplies Expense		300

*21. When an unearned revenue is initially credited to a revenue account, the procedures are similar to those described above for prepaid expenses. In this case, however,

a. Prior to adjustment, a **revenue account is overstated** and a **liability account is understated.**

b. The adjusting entry results in a debit to a revenue account and a credit to a liability account.

DEMONSTRATION PROBLEM (S.O. 5 and 6)

At December 31, 2006, the unadjusted trial balance of Kari Thresher Company shows the following balances for selected accounts:

Supplies	$ 8,500
Prepaid Insurance	12,000
Equipment	40,000
Accumulated Depreciation	16,000
Unearned Fees	15,000
Notes Payable	50,000
Fees Earned	40,000

Analysis reveals the following additional data pertaining to these accounts:

1. Supplies on hand at December 31, 2006, $3,000.
2. Insurance began on July 1, 2006 for a one-year policy.
3. The equipment was purchased January 1, 2004. Annual depreciation is $8,000.
4. $12,000 of the unearned fees have been earned.
5. The note is dated July 1, 2006, payable in 2008 and bears interest at 10% per year.
6. Services rendered other customers but for which payment has not been collected at December 31, 2006 totaled $3,500.
7. Salaries of $2,500 were unpaid at December 31, 2006.

Instructions

Prepare the adjusting entries for the year ending December 31, 2006.

The Navigator

	General Journal	Debit	Credit
Dec 31	Supplies expense	5,500	
	Supplies		5,500
Dec.	Insurance expense	6,000	
	Prepaid Insurance		6000
Dec 31			

SOLUTION TO DEMONSTRATION PROBLEM

General Journal J1

Date	Account Title	Debit	Credit
2006 Dec. 31	Supplies Expense	5,500	
	Supplies		5,500
	($8,500 - $3,000)		
31	Insurance Expense	6,000	
	Prepaid Insurance		6,000
	($12,000 X 6/12)		
31	Depreciation Expense	8,000	
	Accumulated Depreciation		8,000
31	Unearned Fees	12,000	
	Fees Earned		12,000
31	Interest Expense	2,500	
	Interest Payable		2,500
	($50,000 X 10% X 6/12)		
31	Accounts Receivable	3,500	
	Fees Earned		3,500
31	Salaries Expense	2,500	
	Salaries Payable		2,500

REVIEW QUESTIONS AND EXERCISES

TRUE—FALSE

Indicate whether each of the following is true (T) or false (F) in the space provided.

_____ 1. (S.O. 1) The time-period assumption assumes that the economic life of a business can be divided into artificial time periods.

_____ 2. (S.O. 1) A calendar year and a fiscal year must be the same.

_____ 3. (S.O. 2) The revenue recognition principle states that revenue should be recognized in the accounting period cash is received.

_____ 4. (S.O. 2) The matching principle requires that expenses be matched with revenues.

_____ 5. (S.O. 3) Adjusting entries are journalized throughout the accounting period.

_____ 6. (S.O. 3) In general, adjusting entries are required each time financial statements are prepared.

_____ 7. (S.O. 3) In general, adjusting entries are necessary even if the records are free of errors.

_____ 8. (S.O. 3) Every adjusting entry affects one balance sheet account and one income statement account.

_____ 9. (S.O. 3) Adjusting entries are journalized but need not be posted.

_____ 10. (S.O. 5) Prepaid expenses are expenses paid in cash and recorded in an asset account before they are used or consumed.

_____ 11. (S.O. 5) Depreciation is a process of valuation.

_____ 12. (S.O. 5) The Accumulated Depreciation account is a contra asset account that is reported on the balance sheet.

_____ 13. (S.O. 5) The difference between the cost of an asset and its related accumulated depreciation is referred to as the asset's book value.

_____ 14. (S.O. 5) Revenues received in advance of the accounting period in which they are earned are liabilities.

_____ 15. (S.O. 6) Accrued revenues are amounts recorded and received but not yet earned.

_____ 16. (S.O. 6) Prior to an adjustment for accrued revenues, assets and revenues are both understated.

_____ 17. (S.O. 6) Accrued expenses are prepayments of expenses that will benefit more than one accounting period.

_____ 18. (S.O. 6) An adjusting entry for accrued expenses results in a debit to an expense account and a credit to a liability account.

_____ 19. (S.O. 7) An adjusted trial balance should be prepared before the adjusting entries are made.

_____ 20. (S.O. 7) The accounts in the adjusted trial balance contain all data that are needed for the preparation of financial statements.

_____ *21. (S.O. 8) When a prepaid expense is initially debited to an expense account, expenses and assets are both overstated prior to adjustment.

_____ *22. (S.O. 8) When an unearned revenue is initially credited to a revenue account, the adjusting entry will result in a debit to a revenue account and a credit to a liability account.

MULTIPLE CHOICE

Circle the letter that best answers each of the following statements.

1. (S.O. 2) Which of the following statements concerning the accrual basis of accounting is **incorrect?**
   a. The accrual basis of accounting follows the revenue recognition principle.
   b. The accrual basis of accounting is the method required by generally accepted accounting principles.
   c. The accrual basis of accounting recognizes expenses when they are paid.
   d. The accrual basis of accounting follows the matching principle.

2. (S.O. 2) The revenue recognition principle recognizes that:
   a. revenue should be recognized in the accounting period in which it is earned.
   b. the economic life of a business can be divided into artificial time periods.
   c. expenses should be matched with revenues.
   d. the fiscal year should correspond with the calendar year.

3. (S.O. 2) The matching principle dictates that:
   a. each debit be matched with an equal credit.
   b. revenue should be recognized in the accounting period in which it is earned.
   c. expenses should be matched with revenues.
   d. the fiscal year should match the calendar year.

4. (S.O. 5) For prepaid expense adjusting entries:
   a. an expense-liability account relationship exists.
   b. prior to adjustment, expenses are overstated and assets are understated.
   c. the adjusting entry results in a debit to an expense account and a credit to an asset account.
   d. none of the above.

5. (S.O. 5) The beginning balance of Supplies for Lu Inc. was $900. During the year additional supplies were purchased for $450. At the end of the year an inventory count indicates $700 of supplies on hand. The adjusting entry at December 31, is:

	Account	Debit	Credit
a.	Supplies	650	
	Supplies Expense		650
b.	Supplies	450	
	Supplies Expense		450
c.	Supplies Expense	250	
	Supplies		250
d.	Supplies Expense	650	
	Supplies		650

6. (S.O. 5) Demaet Cruise Lines purchased a five-year insurance policy for its ships on April 1, 2006 for $100,000. Assuming that April 1 is the effective date of the policy, the adjusting entry on December 31, 2006 is:

	Account	Debit	Credit
a.	Prepaid Insurance	15,000	
	Insurance Expense		15,000
b.	Insurance Expense	15,000	
	Prepaid Insurance		15,000
c.	Insurance Expense	20,000	
	Prepaid Insurance		20,000
d.	Insurance Expense	5,000	
	Prepaid Insurance		5,000

7. (S.O. 5) Cost less accumulated depreciation for a plant asset is often called:
   a. book value.
   b. market value.
   c. original value.
   d. none of the above.

8. (S.O. 5) Accumulated depreciation plus book value will equal the asset's:
   a. cost.
   b. market value.
   c. depreciable cost.
   d. none of the above.

9. (S.O. 5) Tamara Company purchased a machine on January 1, 2006. Annual depreciation is $800. At December 31, 2008, the balance in the accumulated depreciation account, after adjustment, should be:
   a. $800.
   b. $1,600.
   c. $2,400.
   d. $3,200.

10. (S.O. 5) For unearned revenue adjusting entries, the **incorrect** statement is:
   a. a liability-revenue account relationship exists.
   b. prior to adjustment, revenues are overstated and liabilities are understated.
   c. the adjusting entry results in a debit to a liability account and a credit to a revenue account.
   d. if the adjustment is not made, revenues will be understated.

11. (S.O. 5) On May 1, 2006, Maricel Advertising Company received $3,000 from Kathy Siska for advertising services to be completed April 30, 2007. At December 31, 2006, $2,000 of the fees have been earned. The adjusting entry on December 31, 2006 by Maricel will include a:
    a. $1,000 credit to Unearned Fees.
    b. $1,000 debit to Fees Earned.
    c. $2,000 credit to Unearned Fees.
    d. $2,000 debit to Unearned Fees.

12. (S.O. 5) The account Unearned Revenues is a(n):
    a. revenue account.
    b. contra revenue account.
    c. liability account.
    d. asset account.

13. (S.O. 6) For accrued revenue adjusting entries,
    a. an asset-revenue account relationship exists.
    b. prior to adjustment, assets and revenues are both overstated.
    c. the adjusting entry results in a debit to a revenue account and a credit to an asset account.
    d. none of the above.

14. (S.O. 6) On June 30, Wian Marketing Services is preparing its financial statements. $600 of fees were earned in June that were not billed to clients prior to June 30. The adjusting entry at June 30 is:

		Debit	Credit
a.	Unearned Fees	600	
	Fees Earned		600
b.	Accounts Receivable	600	
	Fees Earned		600
c.	Fees Earned	600	
	Accounts Receivable		600
d.	Fees Earned	600	
	Unearned Fees		600

15. (S.O. 6) For accrued expense adjusting entries, the **incorrect** statement is:
    a. a liability-expense account relationship exists.
    b. prior to adjustment, both expenses and liabilities are understated.
    c. if the adjusting entry is not made, expenses will be overstated in the income statement.
    d. the adjusting entry results in a debit to an expense account and a credit to a liability account.

16. (S.O. 6) Gardner Company purchased a truck from Kutner Co. by issuing a 6-month 10% note payable for $30,000 on November 1. On December 31, the accrued expense adjusting entry is:

		Debit	Credit
a.	No entry is required.		
b.	Interest Expense	3,000	
	Interest Payable		3,000
c.	Interest Expense	6,000	
	Interest Payable		6,000
d.	Interest Expense	500	
	Interest Payable		500

17. (S.O. 6) Cathy Cline, an employee of the Wheeler Company, will not receive her paycheck until April 2. Based on services performed from March 15 to March 30 her salary was $800. The adjusting entry for Wheeler Company on March 31 is:

		Debit	Credit
a.	Salaries Expense	800	
	Salaries Payable		800
b.	No entry is required.		
c.	Salaries Expense	800	
	Cash		800
d.	Salaries Payable	800	
	Cash		800

18. (S.O. 7) Financial statements are prepared directly from the:
    a. general journal.
    b. ledger.
    c. trial balance.
    d. adjusted trial balance.

*19. (S.O. 8) On January 2, Van Alstyne Food Services pays $3,000 cash for office supplies. Office Supplies Expense is debited because the supplies are expected to be used before financial statements are prepared on June 30. At June 30, there are $300 of office supplies on hand. The adjusting entry is:

		Debit	Credit
a.	Office Supplies	300	
	Office Supplies Expense		300
b.	Office Supplies	2,700	
	Office Supplies Expense		2,700
c.	Office Supplies Expense	2,700	
	Office Supplies		2,700
d.	Office Supplies Expense	300	
	Office Supplies		300

*20. (S.O. 8) On May 1, Walsh Inc. credited Fees Earned when $4,000 cash was received for future services. On June 30, the next date financial statements are prepared, $600 of the services have not been rendered. The June 30 adjusting entry will include a:
    a. credit to Fees Earned of $600.
    b. debit to Fees Earned of $600.
    c. debit to Unearned Fees of $3,400.
    d. credit to Unearned Fees of $3,400.

The Navigator

MATCHING

Match each term with its definition by writing the appropriate letter in the space provided.

Terms

_____ 1. Depreciation.

_____ 2. Time-period assumption.

_____ 3. Matching principle.

_____ 4. Revenue recognition principle.

_____ 5. Fiscal years.

_____ 6. Contra asset account.

_____ 7. Adjusted trial balance.

_____ 8. Prepaid expenses.

_____ 9. Unearned revenues.

_____ 10. Adjusting entries.

_____ 11. Accrued revenues.

_____ 12. Accrued expenses.

_____ 13. Accrual basis of accounting.

_____ 14. Cash basis of accounting.

Definitions

a. An account that is offset against an asset account in the balance sheet.

b. Expenses paid in cash and recorded in an asset account before they are used or consumed.

c. Revenues earned but not yet received or recorded at the statement date.

d. Accounting periods that are one year in length.

e. The principle that efforts (expenses) be matched with accomplishments (revenues).

f. An accounting basis in which events that change a company's financial statements are recorded in the periods in which the events occur.

g. Expenses incurred but not yet paid or recorded at the statement date.

h. A list of accounts and their balances after all adjustments have been made.

i. The assumption that the economic life of a business can be divided into artificial time periods.

j. Revenue is recorded only when cash is received and expense is recorded only when cash is paid.

k. The process of allocating the cost of an asset to expense over its useful life in a rational and systematic manner.

l. Revenues received and recorded as liabilities before they are earned.

m. Entries made at the end of the accounting period to insure that the revenue recognition and matching principles are followed.

n. The principle that revenue be recognized in the accounting period in which it is earned.

The Navigator

EXERCISES

EX. 3-1 (S.O. 5 and 6) McDaniels Painting Company is at the end of its fiscal year December 31, 2006 and needs to record its adjusting entries. Adjustment data are as follows:

a. Four months ago, Judy Bernstein made a $8,000 prepayment for the painting of her house. McDaniels recorded the original entry as Unearned Revenue. At December 31, one-fourth of the painting of the house remains to be done.

b. McDaniels purchased a truck from Donnelly Vehicles on January 1, 2005 at a cost of $20,000. Annual depreciation is $4,000. Depreciation was correctly recorded for 2005.

c. An employee, Pam Travis had earned wages of $500 for the last week in December. She will not be paid until January 5.

d. McDaniels purchased a $24,000, four-year insurance policy from Heinsen Insurance four months ago. The effective date of the policy was September 1, 2006.

e. McDaniels began painting Peggy Thompson's clubhouse in November at a price of $32,000. McDaniels determines that $20,000 of the revenue has been earned at December 31. Thompson has not made any payment to McDaniels, and McDaniels has not billed Thompson for services rendered.

Instructions
Prepare the adjusting entries at December 31, 2006.

General Journal J1

Date	Account Title	Debit	Credit
2006	(a) unearned revenue	6,000	
31	service revenue		6,000
31	depreciation expense	4,000	
	accumulated depreciation		4,000
	salaries expense	500	
	salaries payable		500
	insurance expense	2,000	
	prepaid insurance		2,000

General Journal J

Date	Account Title	Debit	Credit
	accounts receivable	20,000	
	Service Revenue		20,000

EX. 3-2 (S.O. 7) The adjusted trial balance of the Lauren Kutner Company at November 30, 2006, is as follows:

LAUREN KUTNER COMPANY
Adjusted Trial Balance
November 30, 2006

	Debit	Credit
Cash	$ 7,250	
Accounts Receivable	17,000	
Supplies	500	
Prepaid Insurance	2,500	
Land	12,000	
Equipment	40,000	
Accumulated Depreciation		$ 16,000
Notes Payable		7,500
Accounts Payable		5,950
Interest Payable		350
Unearned Fees		7,500
Salaries Payable		5,000
Common Stock		8,000
Retained Earnings, 12/1/05		32,000
Dividends	2,000	
Fees Earned		19,700
Salaries Expense	11,500	
Supplies Expense	400	
Rent Expense	2,000	
Insurance Expense	2,500	
Depreciation Expense	4,000	
Interest Expense	350	
	$102,000	$102,000

Instructions

(a) Prepare an income statement and a retained earnings statement for the year ended November 30, 2006.

(b) Prepare a balance sheet at November 30, 2006.

(a)

LAUREN KUTNER COMPANY
Income Statement
For the Year Ended November 30, 2006

LAUREN KUTNER COMPANY
Retained Earnings Statement
For the Year Ended November 30, 2006

(b)

LAUREN KUTNER
Balance Sheet
November 30, 2006

The Navigator

SOLUTIONS TO REVIEW QUESTIONS AND EXERCISES

TRUE-FALSE

1. (T)
2. (F) The calendar year begins January 1 and ends December 31. Fiscal years usually begin with the first day of any month and end on the last day of a month, twelve months later. Of course, the fiscal year could coincide with the calendar year.
3. (F) The revenue recognition principle states that revenue should be recognized in the accounting period in which it is earned. Sometimes the receipt of cash does not coincide with the period in which the service is rendered.
4. (T)
5. (F) Adjusting entries are only prepared at the end of an accounting period.
6. (T)
7. (T)
8. (T)
9. (F) Adjusting entries must be both journalized and posted.
10. (T)
11. (F) Depreciation is the process of allocating the cost of an asset to expense over its useful life in a rational and systematic manner.
12. (T)
13. (T)
14. (T)
15. (F) Accrued revenues are revenues earned but not yet received in cash.
16. (T)
17. (F) Accrued expenses are expenses incurred but not yet paid or recorded.
18. (T)
19. (F) The adjusted trial balance can only be prepared after the adjusting entries are made.
20. (T)

*21. (F) Prior to adjustment, expenses are overstated and assets are understated.

*22. (T)

MULTIPLE CHOICE

1. (c) The accrual basis of accounting recognizes expenses when they are incurred. Choices (a), (b), and (d) are all correct statements concerning the accrual basis of accounting.

2. (a) Choice (b) is the time-period assumption. Choice (c) is the matching principle. Answer (d) pertains to the time-period assumption. Also, the fiscal year does not have to correspond with the calendar year.

3. (c) Choice (a) is the dual effect of the double-entry system discussed in Chapter 2. Choice (b) is the revenue recognition principle. Choice (d) is an incorrect statement because the fiscal year does not necessarily have to be the calendar year.

4. (c) Answer (a) is incorrect because an asset-expense account relationship exists. Answer (b) is incorrect because prior to adjustment, assets are overstated and expenses are understated.

5. (d) The total cost of supplies is $1,350 ($900 + $450). Since the ending inventory is $700, the supplies expense for the period is $650 ($1,350 - $700).

6. (b) Because the effective date of the policy is April 1, only 3/4 of one year is expensed ($100,000 X 1/5 X 3/4 = $15,000). Insurance Expense is debited and Prepaid Insurance is credited because the $100,000 payment was debited to Prepaid Insurance.

7. (a) The market value (b) is the current exchange value of the asset. The original value (c) would refer to the cost.

8. (a) Cost less the related accumulated depreciation is equal to book value; therefore, changing the equation, accumulated depreciation plus book value equals the cost of the asset.

9. (c) The balance should be the accumulated depreciation for three years ($2,400 ($800 X 3).

10. (b) Prior to adjustment liabilities are overstated and revenues are understated. The other answer choices are correct.

11. (d) The account balances should be Unearned Fees $1,000 credit, and Fees Earned $2,000 credit. Thus, the adjusting entry is:

Unearned Fees..	2,000	
Fees Earned		2,000

12. (c) Unearned Revenue is the receipt of cash before the service has been performed. The obligation to perform this service is indicated in the records by crediting a liability account.

13. (a) Answer (b) is incorrect because prior to adjustment both assets and revenues are understated. Answer (c) is incorrect because an asset account is debited and a revenue account is credited.

14. (b) The amount owed by the clients is a receivable that is debited to an asset account. The services concerning this receivable have been performed and thus, earned; therefore, a revenue account is credited.

15. (c) In an accrued expense adjusting entry, expenses are understated prior to adjustment (b). Therefore, if the adjusting entry is not made, expenses will be understated.

16. (d) The accrued interest is $500 ($30,000 X 10% X 2/12).

17. (a) The accrued expense is recognized by debiting Salaries Expense and crediting Salaries Payable.

18. (d) The adjusted trial balance is prepared after all adjusting entries have been posted. Accordingly, the financial statements can be prepared directly from it.

*19. (a) At June 30, $300 of office supplies is on hand, which is the balance that should be in the asset account, Office Supplies. Since the unadjusted balance in this account is zero, Office Supplies must be debited for $300. Given the inventory on hand, office supplies expense for the period is $2,700 ($3,000 - $300). The unadjusted balance in Office Supplies Expense is $3,000. Therefore, this account must be credited for $300.

*20. (b) At June 30, $600 of the $4,000 of future services have not been rendered and $3,400 has been earned ($4,000 - $600). Prior to adjustment, the balances are Unearned Fees $0 and Fees Earned $4,000. Thus, the adjusting entry is a debit to Fees Earned $600 and a credit to Unearned Fees $600.

MATCHING

1. k	5. d	9. l	13. f
2. i	6. a	10. m	14. j
3. e	7. h	11. c	
4. n	8. b	12. g	

EX. 3-1

General Journal J1

Date	Account Title	Debit	Credit
2006			
	Adjusting Entries		
	a.		
Dec. 31	Unearned Revenue	6,000	
	Painting Revenue		6,000
	(To record revenue earned, $8,000 X		
	3/4)		
	b.		
31	Depreciation Expense	4,000	
	Accumulated Depreciation		4,000
	(To record annual depreciation)		
	c.		
31	Wages Expense	500	
	Wages Payable		500
	(To record accrued wages)		
	d.		
31	Insurance Expense	2,000	
	Prepaid Insurance		2,000
	(To record insurance expired;		
	$24,000 X 4/48)		
	e.		
31	Accounts Receivable	20,000	
	Painting Revenue		20,000
	(To accrued revenue earned)		

EX. 3-2

(a)

LAUREN KUTNER COMPANY
Income Statement
For the Year Ended November 30, 2006

Revenues		
Fees earned		$19,700
Expenses		
Salaries expense	$11,500	
Depreciation expense	4,000	
Insurance expense	2,500	
Rent expense	2,000	
Supplies expense	400	
Interest expense	350	
Total expense		20,750
Net loss		$ (1,050)

LAUREN KUTNER COMPANY
Retained Earnings Statement
For the Year Ended November 30, 2006

Retained earnings, December 1, 2005	$32,000
Less: Net loss	(1,050)
	30,950
Less: Dividends	2,000
Retained earnings, November 30, 2006	$28,950

(b)

LAUREN KUTNER COMPANY
Balance Sheet
November 30, 2006

Assets		
Cash		$ 7,250
Accounts receivable		17,000
Supplies		500
Prepaid insurance		2,500
Land		12,000
Equipment	$40,000	
Less: Accumulated depreciation	16,000	24,000
Total assets		$63,250
Liabilities and Stockholders' Equity		
Liabilities		
Notes payable		$ 7,500
Accounts payable		5,950
Interest payable		350
Unearned fees		7,500
Salaries payable		5,000
Total liabilities		26,300
Stockholders' Equity		
Common stock		8,000
Retained earnings		28,950
Total liabilities and stockholders' equity		$63,250

The Navigator ✓

- *Scan Study Objectives* ☐
- *Read Preview* ☐
- *Read Chapter Review* ☐
- *Work Demonstration Problem* ☐
- *Answer True-False Statements* ☐
- *Answer Multiple-Choice Questions* ☐
- *Match Terms and Definitions* ☐
- *Solve Exercises* ☐

CHAPTER 4

COMPLETION OF THE ACCOUNTING CYCLE

CHAPTER STUDY OBJECTIVES

After studying this chapter, you should be able to:

1. Prepare a work sheet.
2. Explain the process of closing the books.
3. Describe the content and purpose of a post-closing trial balance.
4. State the required steps in the accounting cycle.
5. Explain the approaches to preparing correcting entries.
6. Identify the sections of a classified balance sheet.

*7. Prepare reversing entries.

***Note:** All **asterisked** (*) items relate to material contained in the Appendix to the chapter.

PREVIEW OF CHAPTER 4

In this chapter we will explain the role of the work sheet in accounting as well as the remaining steps in the accounting cycle, most especially, the closing process. Then we will consider (1) correcting entries and (2) classified balance sheets. The organization and content of the chapter are as follows:

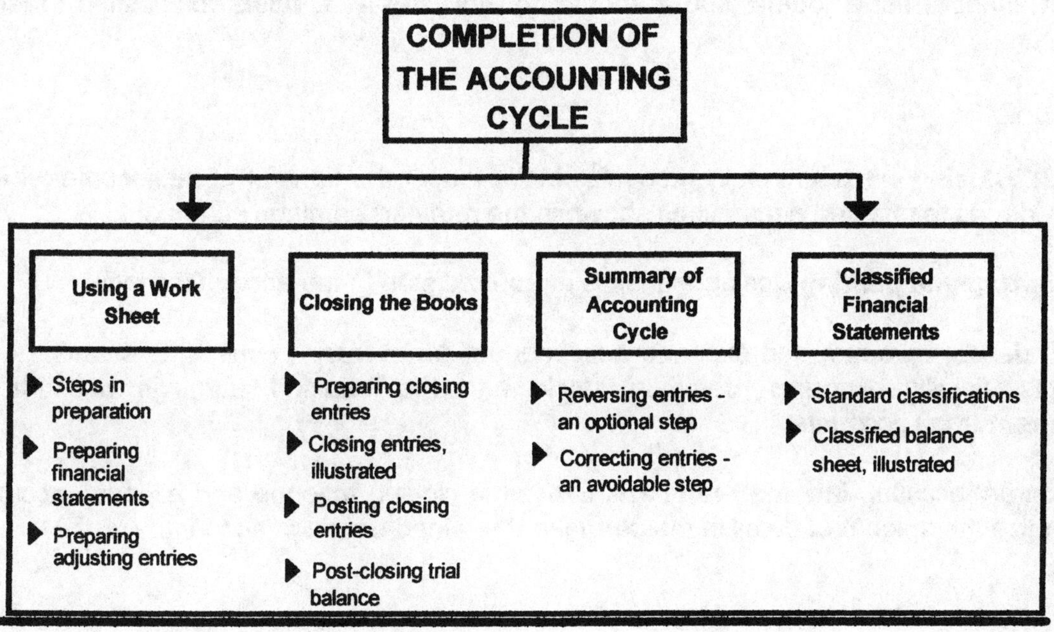

CHAPTER REVIEW

Preparing a Worksheet

1. (S.O. 1) The **steps** in preparing a work sheet are:
   a. Prepare a trial balance on the work sheet.
   b. Enter the adjustments in the adjustments columns.
   c. Enter adjusted balances in the adjusted trial balance columns.
   d. Extend adjusted trial balance amounts to appropriate financial statement columns.
   e. Total the statement columns, compute the net income (or loss), and complete the work sheet.

2. A **work sheet** is a multiple-column form that may be used in the adjustment process and in preparing financial statements. The **basic form** of a work sheet consists of the following columns:

Account Titles	Trial Balance		Adjustments		Adjusted Trial Balance		Income Statement		Balance Sheet	
	Dr.	Cr.	Dr.	Cr.	Dr.	Cr.	Dr.	Cr.	Dr.	Cr.

3. For each account in the work sheet, the amount in the **adjusted trial balance columns** is equal to the account balance that will appear in the ledger after the adjusting entries have been journalized and posted.

4. After the work sheet has been completed the **statement columns** contain all data that are required for the preparation of financial statements. The income statement is prepared from the income statement columns, and the retained earnings statement and balance sheet are prepared from the balance sheet columns.

5. Using a work sheet accountants can prepare financial statements **before** adjusting entries are journalized and posted.

6. A work sheet is not a journal and it should not be used as a **basis** for posting to ledger accounts.

Closing Entries

7. (S.O. 2) **Closing entries** formally recognize in the ledger the transfer of net income (or loss) and dividends to retained earnings as shown in the retained earnings statement.

8. **Journalizing and posting** closing entries is a required step in the accounting cycle.

9. The dividends, revenue, and expense accounts are **temporary** (nominal) accounts. Asset accounts, liability accounts, common stock, and the retained earnings account are **permanent** (real) accounts.

10. A temporary account, **Income Summary,** is used in closing revenue and expense accounts to minimize the amount of detail in the permanent retained earnings account.

11. In closing the books of a corporation:
    a. Debit each revenue account for its balance, and credit Income Summary for total revenues.
    b. Debit Income Summary for total expenses, and credit each expense account for its balance.
    c. Debit Income Summary, and credit Retained Earnings for the amount of net income; conversely, credit Income Summary and debit Retained Earnings if a net loss exists.
    d. Debit Retained Earnings for the balance in the Dividends account and credit Dividends for the same amount.

Post-Closing Trial Balance

12. (S.O. 3) After all closing entries have been journalized and posted, a **post-closing trial balance** is prepared. The purpose of this trial balance is to prove the equality of the **permanent account balances** that are carried forward into the next accounting period.

Steps in the Accounting Cycle

13. (S.O. 4) The required steps in the accounting cycle are:
    a. Analyze business transactions.
    b. Journalize the transactions.
    c. Post to ledger accounts.
    d. Prepare a trial balance.
    e. Journalize and post adjusting entries: Prepayments/Accruals.
    f. Prepare an adjusted trial balance.
    g. Prepare financial statements: Income statement, Retained earnings statement, Balance sheet.
    h. Journalize and post closing entries.
    i. Prepare a post-closing trial balance.

14. A **reversing entry** is the exact opposite of an adjusting entry. The preparation of reversing entries is an optional bookkeeping procedure that is not a required step in the accounting cycle.

Correcting Entries

15. (S.O. 5) Errors that occur in recording transactions should be corrected as soon as they are discovered by preparing **correcting entries.** Correcting entries:
    a. are unnecessary if the records are free of errors.
    b. are journalized and posted whenever an error is discovered.
    c. may involve any combination of balance sheet and income statement accounts.

16. To determine the correcting entry, it is useful to compare the incorrect entry with the correct entry, and then make a correcting entry. Another approach is to reverse the incorrect entry and then prepare the correct entry.

Classified Balance Sheet

17. (S.O. 6) Financial statements become more useful when the elements are classified into significant subgroups. A **classified balance sheet** generally has the following standard classifications:

Assets	Liabilities and Stockholders' Equity
Current assets	Current liabilities
Long-term investments	Long-term liabilities
Property, plant, and equipment	Stockholders' equity
Intangible assets	

Assets

18. **Current assets** are cash and other resources that are reasonably expected to be realized in cash or sold or consumed in the business within one year of the balance sheet date or the company's operating cycle, whichever is longer. Current assets are listed in the order of their liquidity.

19. The **operating cycle** of a company is the average time that is required to go from cash to cash in producing revenues.

20. **Long-term investments** are resources that can be realized in cash but the conversion into cash is not expected within one year or the operating cycle, whichever is longer.

21. Tangible resources of a relatively permanent nature that are used in the business and not intended for sale are classified as **property, plant, and equipment.**

22. **Intangible assets** are noncurrent resources that do not have physical substance, such as patents and copyrights.

Liabilities

23. **Current liabilities** are obligations that are reasonably expected to be paid from existing current assets or through the creation of other current liabilities within one year or the operating cycle, whichever is longer.

24. Obligations expected to be paid after one year are classified as **long-term liabilities (or long-term debt).**

Stockholders' Equity

25. The content of the stockholders' (owners') section varies with the form of business organization. In a proprietorship, there is a single owner's equity account, called (Owner's Name), Capital. In a partnership, there are separate capital accounts for each partner. For a corporation, owners' equity is called stockholders' equity and it consists of two accounts: Capital Stock and Retained Earnings.

Form of Balance Sheet

26. A balance sheet is most often presented in **report form** with the assets shown above the liabilities and stockholders' equity. It may also be presented in **account form** with the assets section placed on the left and the liabilities and owner's equity section on the right.

Reversing Entries

*27. (S.O. 7) A reversing entry is made at the beginning of the next accounting period. The **purpose** of reversing entries is to simplify the recording of a subsequent transaction related to an adjusting entry.

*28. Reversing entries are most often used to reverse two types of adjusting entries: **accrued revenues** and **accrued expenses.**

The Navigator

DEMONSTRATION PROBLEM (S.O. 1, 2, and 6)

Gardin Company's December 31, 2006 trial balance is as follows:

GARDIN COMPANY
December 31, 2006
Trial Balance

	Debit	Credit
Cash	$16,000	
Accounts Receivable	4,500	
Prepaid Insurance	2,500	
Supplies	3,000	
Equipment	41,500	
Accounts Payable		$ 5,500
Unearned Revenue		1,500
Notes Payable		28,000
Common Stock		6,000
Retained Earnings, 1/1/06		18,000
Dividends	2,500	
Revenue		16,000
Salaries Expense	3,700	
Utilities Expense	400	
Marketing Expense	900	
Totals	$75,000	$75,000

Gardin Company needs to make the year-end adjusting entries concerning the following data:

a. Insurance expires at the rate of $100 per month.
b. There are $2,400 of supplies on hand at December 31.
c. Monthly depreciation is $200 on the equipment.
d. Interest of $2,800 has accrued on the Notes Payable.
e. Unearned revenue amounted to $700 on December 31.
f. Accrued salaries are $3,200.

Instructions

(a) Prepare a work sheet.
(b) Prepare a classified balance sheet assuming $20,000 of the notes payable are long-term.
(c) Journalize the closing entries.

SOLUTION TO DEMONSTRATION PROBLEM

(a)

GARDIN COMPANY
Work Sheet
For the Year Ended Dec. 31, 2006

Account Titles	Trial Balance		Adjustments		Adjusted Trial Balance		Income Statement		Balance Sheet	
	Dr.	Cr.	Dr.	Cr.	Dr.	Cr.	Dr.	Cr.	Dr.	Cr.
Cash	16,000				16,000				16,000	
Accounts Receivable	4,500				4,500				4,500	
Prepaid Insurance	2,500			(a) 1,200	1,300				1,300	
Supplies	3,000			(b) 600	2,400				2,400	
Equipment	41,500				41,500				41,500	
Accounts Payable		5,500				5,500				5,500
Unearned Revenue		1,500	(e) 800			700				700
Notes Payable		28,000				28,000				28,000
Common Stock		6,000				6,000				6,000
Retained Earnings		18,000				18,000				18,000
Dividends	2,500				2,500				2,500	
Revenue		16,000		(e) 800		16,800		16,800		
Salaries Expense	3,700		(f) 3,200		6,900		6,900			
Utilities Expense	400				400		400			
Marketing Expense	900				900		900			
Totals	75,000	75,000								
Insurance Expense			(a) 1,200		1,200		1,200			
Supplies Expense			(b) 600		600		600			
Depreciation Expense			(c) 2,400		2,400		2,400			
Accum. Depr.—Equip.				(c) 2,400		2,400				2,400
Interest Expense			(d) 2,800		2,800		2,800			
Interest Payable				(d) 2,800		2,800				2,800
Salaries Payable				(f) 3,200		3,200				3,200
Totals			11,000	11,000	83,400	83,400	15,200	16,800	68,200	66,600
Net Income							1,600			1,600
Totals							16,800	16,800	68,200	68,200

(b)

GARDIN COMPANY
Balance Sheet
December 31, 2006

Assets

Current assets		
Cash		$16,000
Accounts Receivable		4,500
Prepaid Insurance		1,300
Supplies		2,400
Total current assets		24,200
Property, plant, and equipment		
Equipment	$41,500	
Less: Accumulated depreciation—equipment	2,400	39,100
Total assets		$63,300

Liabilities and Stockholders' Equity

Current liabilities	
Notes Payable	$ 8,000
Accounts Payable	5,500
Unearned Revenue	700
Salaries Payable	3,200
Interest Payable	2,800
Total current liabilities	20,200
Long-term liabilities	
Notes Payable	20,000
Total liabilities	40,200
Stockholders' equity	
Common Stock	6,000
Retained Earnings	17,100*
Total liabilities and stockholders' equity	$63,300

*Retained Earnings, $18,000 less dividends $2,500 and plus net income $1,600.

(c)

Date	Account	Debit	Credit
Dec. 31	Revenue	16,800	
	Income Summary		16,800
	(To close revenue account)		
31	Income Summary	15,200	
	Salaries Expense		6,900
	Utilities Expense		400
	Marketing Expense		900
	Insurance Expense		1,200
	Supplies Expense		600
	Depreciation Expense		2,400
	Interest Expense		2,800
	(To close expense account)		

Dec. 31	Income Summary	1,600	
	Retained Earnings		1,600
	(To close net income to retained earnings)		
31	Retained Earnings	2,500	
	Dividends		2,500
	(To close dividends to retained earnings)		

REVIEW QUESTIONS AND EXERCISES

TRUE—FALSE

Indicate whether each of the following is true (T) or false (F) in the space provided.

_____ 1. (S.O. 1) A work sheet is not a permanent accounting record.

_____ 2. (S.O. 1) If total debits exceed total credits in the income statement columns on a work sheet, net income has resulted.

_____ 3. (S.O. 1) After a work sheet has been completed, the statement columns contain all data that are required for the preparation of financial statements.

_____ 4. (S.O. 1) A work sheet is not a journal, but it can be used as a basis for posting to ledger accounts.

_____ 5. (S.O. 2) All balance sheet accounts are considered to be permanent or real accounts.

_____ 6. (S.O. 2) After the closing entries are posted, all nominal accounts will have zero balances.

_____ 7. (S.O. 2) The journalizing and posting of closing entries is a required step in the accounting cycle.

_____ 8. (S.O. 2) To close net income to retained earnings, Income Summary is debited and Retained Earnings is credited.

_____ 9. (S.O. 2) Revenue accounts are closed by debiting the individual revenue accounts and crediting Income Summary for total revenues.

_____ 10. (S.O. 2) In closing, Dividends is credited and Income Summary is debited.

_____ 11. (S.O. 2) Income Summary is used in preparing both adjusting and closing entries.

_____ 12. (S.O. 3) The post-closing trial balance will contain only retained earnings statement accounts and balance sheet accounts.

_____ 13. (S.O. 3) The preparation of reversing entries is an optional step in the accounting cycle.

_____ 14. (S.O. 5) Correcting entries are only made at the end of an accounting period.

_____ 15. (S.O. 6) The operating cycle of a company is the average time required to collect the receivables resulting from producing revenues.

_____ 16. (S.O. 6) Current assets are listed in the order of liquidity.

_____ 17. (S.O. 6) Long-term investments are resources that are not expected to be converted into cash within one year or the operating cycle, whichever is longer.

_____ 18. (S.O. 6) Property, plant, and equipment are tangible assets that are reported at market value in the balance sheet.

_____ 19. (S.O. 6) Current liabilities must be expected to be payable out of existing current assets or through the creation of other current liabilities.

_____ 20. (S.O. 6) The relationship of current assets and current liabilities is important in evaluating a company's liquidity.

MULTIPLE CHOICE

Circle the letter that best answers each of the following statements.

1. (S.O. 1) The following is **not** a column heading in a work sheet:
   a. Trial Balance.
   b. Income Statement.
   c. Post-Closing Trial Balance.
   d. Adjusted Trial Balance.

2. (S.O. 1) The steps in the preparation of a work sheet do **not** include:
   a. analyzing documentary evidence.
   b. preparing a trial balance on the work sheet.
   c. entering the adjustments in the adjustment columns.
   d. entering adjusted balances in the adjusted trial balance columns.

3. (S.O. 1) Which of the following account balances is extended to the income statement columns on a work sheet?
   a. Prepaid Insurance.
   b. Unearned Revenue.
   c. Depreciation Expense.
   d. Accumulated Depreciation.

4. (S.O. 1) The work sheet is:
   a. used as a basis for posting to the ledger accounts.
   b. never computerized.
   c. part of the ledger.
   d. essentially a working tool of the accountant.

5. (S.O. 2) Balance sheet accounts are considered to be:
   a. temporary stockholders' equity accounts.
   b. permanent accounts.
   c. retained earnings accounts.
   d. nominal accounts.

6. (S.O. 2) The dividends account is a(n):
   a. expense account.
   b. revenue account.
   c. permanent account.
   d. temporary account.

7. (S.O. 2) Income Summary has a credit balance of $12,000 in J. Spencer, Co. after closing revenues and expenses. The entry to close Income Summary is:
   a. credit Income Summary $12,000, debit Retained Earnings $12,000.
   b. credit Income Summary $12,000, debit Dividends $12,000.
   c. debit Income Summary $12,000, credit Dividends $12,000.
   d. debit Income Summary $12,000, credit Retained Earnings $12,000.

8. (S.O. 3) The account that will appear on the post-closing trial balance is:
   a. Fees Earned.
   b. Accumulated Depreciation.
   c. Depreciation Expense.
   d. Dividends.

9. (S.O. 3) The number of accounts appearing in the trial balance will normally be:
   a. less than the number of accounts in the post-closing trial balance.
   b. equal to the number of accounts in the adjusted trial balance.
   c. more than the number of accounts in the post-closing trial balance.
   d. more than the number of accounts in the adjusted trial balance.

10. (S.O. 3) The post-closing trial balance contains only:
    a. income statement accounts.
    b. balance sheet accounts.
    c. balance sheet and income statement accounts.
    d. income statement, balance sheet, and stockholders' equity statement accounts.

11. (S.O. 4) One of the following statements concerning the accounting cycle is **incorrect.** The incorrect statement is:
    a. The accounting cycle includes journalizing transactions and posting to ledger accounts.
    b. The accounting cycle includes only one optional step.
    c. The steps in the accounting cycle are performed in sequence.
    d. The steps in the accounting cycle are repeated in each accounting period.

12. (S.O. 5) On September 23, the Polar Company received a $350 check from Mike Moluf for services to be performed in the future. The bookkeeper for Polar Company incorrectly debited Cash for $350 and credited Accounts Receivable for $350. The amounts have been posted to the ledger. To correct this entry, the bookkeeper should:
    a. debit Cash $350 and credit Unearned Fees $350.
    b. debit Accounts Receivable $350 and credit Unearned Fees $350.
    c. debit Accounts Receivable $350 and credit Cash $350.
    d. debit Accounts Receivable $350 and credit Fees Earned $350.

13. (S.O. 5) On June 19, the Pinkowski Company bought office supplies on account from the Ewell Company for $550. Pinkowski Company incorrectly debited Office Equipment for $500 and credited Accounts Payable for $500. The entries have been posted to the ledger. The correcting entry should be:

		Debit	Credit
a.	Office Supplies	550	
	Accounts Payable		550
b.	Office Supplies	550	
	Accounts Payable		500
	Office Equipment		50
c.	Office Supplies	550	
	Office Equipment		550
d.	Office Supplies	550	
	Office Equipment		500
	Accounts Payable		50

14. (S.O. 6) Which of the following accounts is not classified under the current asset section of the balance sheet?
    a. Prepaid Expenses.
    b. Supplies.
    c. Equipment.
    d. Cash.

15. (S.O. 6) One of the following statements about current assets is correct. The correct statement is:
    a. The time period for current assets is within one year after the balance sheet date or the company's operating cycle, whichever is longer.
    b. The time period for current assets is within one year after the balance sheet date or the company's operating cycle, whichever is shorter.
    c. The operating cycle is the average time to collect accounts receivable in the process of earning revenue.
    d. Current assets are listed in the balance sheet in the order of magnitude.

16. (S.O. 6) Long-term investments are:
    a. reported in the balance sheet after property, plant, and equipment.
    b. resources that are not expected to be realized in cash within one year or operating cycle, whichever is longer.
    c. resources that are intended for use or consumption.
    d. resources that may include rights and privileges granted by governmental authority.

17. (S.O. 6) Which of the following statements is **incorrect?** Property, plant and equipment:
   a. includes tangible resources that are held for use and not for sale.
   b. is reported in the balance sheet at cost less accumulated depreciation.
   c. includes long-lived, non-physical resources such as patents and copyrights.
   d. includes land, buildings, equipment, and machinery.

18. (S.O. 6) Current liabilities:
   a. must reasonably be expected to be paid from existing current assets or through the creation of other current liabilities.
   b. are listed in the balance sheet in order of their expected maturity.
   c. must reasonably be expected to be paid within one year or the operating cycle, whichever is shorter.
   d. should not include long-term debt that is expected to be paid within the next year.

*19. (S.O. 7) Malikowski Company had accrued salaries between September 15 and September 30 of $6,000 that will be paid on October 5. The appropriate adjusting entry was made at the year end, September 30. If a reversing entry is made on October 1, the entry would be:
   a. debit Salaries Payable $6,000 and credit Salaries Expense $6,000.
   b. credit Salaries Payable $6,000 and debit Salaries Expense $6,000.
   c. debit Salaries Payable $6,000 and credit Income Summary $6,000.
   d. credit Salaries Payable $6,000 and debit Income Summary $6,000.

*20. (S.O. 7) On November 1, 2005, Nilsson Company issued a $12,000, 10% three-month note payable to Barshinger Bank. At the year end, Nilsson made the appropriate adjusting and reversing entries. On February 1, 2006, Nilsson paid Barshinger Bank the amount of the note payable plus the appropriate interest. The entry on February 1, 2006 is:

a.	Notes Payable	12,000	
	Cash		12,000
b.	Notes Payable	12,000	
	Interest Expense	300	
	Cash		12,300
c.	Notes Payable	12,000	
	Interest Payable	200	
	Interest Expense	100	
	Cash		12,300
d.	Notes Payable	12,000	
	Interest Payable	300	
	Cash		12,300

MATCHING

Match each term with its definition by writing the appropriate letter in the space provided.

Terms

_____ 1. Reversing entry.

_____ 2. Operating cycle.

_____ 3. Income summary.

_____ 4. Work sheet.

_____ 5. Property, plant, and equipment.

_____ 6. Current liabilities.

_____ 7. Intangible assets.

_____ 8. Classified balance sheet.

_____ 9. Long-term liabilities.

_____ 10. Current assets.

_____ 11. Liquidity.

_____ 12. Closing entries.

_____ 13. Long-term investments.

_____ 14. Post-closing trial balance.

_____ 15. Correcting entries.

Definitions

a. A listing of the accounts and their balances after closing entries have been journalized and posted.

b. Cash and other assets that are reasonably expected to be realized in cash or sold or consumed in the business within one year of the balance sheet date or the company's operating cycle, whichever is longer.

c. The ability of a company to meet obligations expected to come due in the next year or operating cycle.

d. Noncurrent resources that do not have physical substance.

e. Entries made when errors are discovered.

f. Entries at the end of the accounting period that transfer each nominal account to the permanent retained earnings account.

g. Resources that can be realized in cash but conversion is not expected within one year or the operating cycle, whichever is longer.

h. The exact reverse of an adjusting entry.

i. The average time that is required to go from cash to cash in producing revenues.

j. A multiple-column form that may be used in the adjustment process and in preparing financial statements.

k. A balance sheet that contains significant subgroups.

l. An account that is used when making closing entries so excessive detail does not occur in the permanent Retained Earnings account.

m. Obligations expected to be paid after one year.

n. Obligations that are reasonably expected to be paid from existing current assets or through the creation of other current liabilities within one year or the operating cycle, whichever is longer.

o. Tangible resources of a relatively permanent nature that are being used in the business and not intended for sale.

EXERCISES

EX. 4-1 (S.O. 1, 2, and 3) King Oliver began Jazz Company on January 1, 2006. At December 31, 2006, the company had the following adjustment data.

a. Inventory clerk, Count Basie, determined that $4,000 of supplies were on hand.
b. The insurance was obtained through the Dizzy Gillespie Insurance Agency; during the year $3,000 of the insurance had expired.
c. The equipment was purchased from Miles Davis on January 1, 2006 and it is depreciated at a rate of $1,000 per year.
d. Unearned fees of $450 were earned as a result of the Duke Ellington concert on December 4.
e. Fees earned from the Ella Fitzgerald performance on December 31 totaling $2,250 have not been billed.
f. The note payable was a loan from Louis Armstrong; interest of $300 has accrued at December 31.
g. A salary of $850 earned by Jimmy Dorsey in December has not been recorded or paid.

Instructions

(a) Enter the adjustments in the adjustment columns of the work sheet that follows and complete the work sheet (use 10-column paper).
(b) Prepare the closing entries at December 31.
(c) Prepare a post-closing trial balance at December 31.

(a)

JAZZ COMPANY
Work Sheet
For the Year Ended Dec. 31, 2006

Account Titles	Trial Balance Dr.	Trial Balance Cr.	Adjustments Dr.	Adjustments Cr.	Adjusted Trial Balance Dr.	Adjusted Trial Balance Cr.	Income Statement Dr.	Income Statement Cr.	Balance Sheet Dr.	Balance Sheet Cr.
Cash	6,000									
Accounts Receivable	7,850									
Supplies	6,000									
Prepaid Insurance	9,000									
Equipment	10,000									
Note Payable		9,750								
Unearned Fees		3,100								
Common Stock		4,000								
Retained Earnings		8,000								
Fees Earned		22,000								
Salaries Expense	8,000									
Totals	46,850	46,850								
Supplies Expense										
Insurance Expense										
Accumulated Depr.										
Depreciation Expense										
Interest Expense										
Interest Payable										
Salaries Payable										
Totals										
Net Income										
Totals										

(b)

General Journal

J1

Date	Account Title	Debit	Credit
2006			

(c)

JAZZ COMPANY
Post-Closing Trial Balance
December 31, 2006

	Debit	Credit

SOLUTIONS TO REVIEW QUESTIONS AND EXERCISES

TRUE-FALSE

1. (T)
2. (F) If total debits exceed total credits, a net loss has occurred.
3. (T)
4. (F) Since a work sheet is not a journal, it should not be used as a basis for posting to ledger accounts.
5. (T)
6. (T)
7. (T)
8. (T)
9. (T)
10. (F) Dividends is credited and Retained Earnings is debited.
11. (F) Income Summary is only used in preparing closing entries.
12. (F) The post-closing trial balance will contain only balance sheet accounts.
13. (T)
14. (F) Correcting entries are made whenever an error is discovered.
15. (F) The operating cycle is the average time required to go from cash to cash in producing revenues.
16. (T)
17. (T)
18. (F) Property, plant, and equipment are reported at cost less accumulated depreciation.
19. (T)
20. (T)

MULTIPLE CHOICE

1. (c) The trial balance (a), income statement (b), and adjusted trial balance (d), are all columns on the work sheet. A post-closing trial balance is not presented on the work sheet.

2. (a) The preparation of a work sheet involves the following steps:
   1. Prepare a trial balance on the work sheet.
   2. Enter the adjustments in the adjustment columns.
   3. Enter adjusted balances in the adjusted trial balance columns.
   4. Extend adjusted trial balance amounts to appropriate financial statement columns.
   5. Total the statement columns, compute the net income (or loss), and complete the work sheet.

3. (c) Prepaid Insurance (a), Unearned Revenue (b), and Accumulated Depreciation (d) are all account balances that are extended to the balance sheet columns. Depreciation Expense is transferred to the income statement columns.

4. (d) The work sheet is not used as a basis for posting to the ledger, however, it is frequently used as a substitute for posting to the ledger. The work sheet is frequently computerized using a spreadsheet software program (like Lotus 1-2-3). The work sheet is not part of the ledger.

5. (b) The dividends, revenue, and expense accounts are considered to be temporary stockholders' equity accounts (a) or nominal accounts (d). At the end of an accounting period, these accounts are transferred to the retained earnings account. Not all balance sheet accounts are retained earnings accounts (c), but all are permanent accounts.

6. (d) The dividends account is not an expense account (a) or a revenue account (b). It is also not a permanent account (c) because it is transferred to the retained earnings account.

7. (d) A credit balance in Income Summary indicates the company has earned net income. The closing entry results in a debit to Income Summary and a credit to the Retained Earnings account.

8. (b) Fees Earned, Depreciation Expense, and Dividends are temporary accounts that are closed annually.

9. (c) The post-closing trial balance would have the least number of accounts because it would only have the real accounts. The trial balance would have both the real and nominal accounts. The adjusted trial balance would probably have more accounts than the trial balance, because it would have the same real and nominal accounts plus any new accounts resulting from any adjustments.

10. (b) The post-closing trial balance contains only balance sheet accounts because income statement accounts are nominal accounts and are closed out.

11. (b) The accounting cycle contains two optional steps: (1) use of a work sheet and (2) preparing reversing entries. Each of the other statements about the accounting cycle is true.

12. (b) The correct entry in this case was Cash (Dr) $350 and Unearned Fees (Cr) $350. A comparison with the incorrect entry shows that both Accounts Receivable and Unearned Fees are understated by $350. The correcting entry, therefore, is (b).

13. (d) The error has caused three accounts to be incorrect. Office Equipment is overstated by $500. Office Supplies is understated by $550, and Accounts Payable is understated by $50. The correcting entry is therefore (d).

14. (c) Prepaid Expenses, Supplies, and Cash are current assets. Equipment would be classified as Property, Plant, and Equipment

15. (a) The time period for current assets is within one year or the operating cycle, whichever is longer, not shorter as in (b). Choice (c) is incorrect because the operating cycle is the average time to go from cash to cash in producing revenues. Choice (d) is incorrect because current assets are listed in order of liquidity.

16. (b) Long-term investments are not expected to be realized in cash within the next year or operating cycle, whichever is longer. Choice (a) is incorrect because long-term investments are reported between current assets and property, plant, and equipment. Choice (c) is incorrect because long-term investments are not expected to be used or consumed. Choice (d) is a correct statement for intangible assets.

17. (c) Long-lived, non-physical resources are intangible assets. Each of the other statements is true.

18. (a) This answer choice correctly states the expected source of payment. Choice (b) is incorrect because current liabilities are not listed in order of maturity. Choice (c) is incorrect because the time period is one year or the operating cycle, whichever is longer. Choice (d) is incorrect because current maturities of long-term debt should be reported under current liabilities.

*19. (a) First, the adjusting entry should be determined. For this transaction the following adjusting entry would be made:

Salaries Expense	6,000	
Salaries Payable		6,000

Then, to make the reversing entry, the above adjusting entry is reversed, both amount and account titles.

Salaries Payable	6,000	
Salaries Expense		6,000

*20. (b) On December, 31, 2005 an adjusting entry was made to accrue $200 ($12,000 X 10% X 2/12) of interest by debiting Interest Expense for $200 and crediting Interest Payable for $200. By reversing the entry after the closing entries are made, the balance in the Interest Payable account will be zero, and Interest Expense will have a credit balance of $200. Therefore, by making the entry in (b), which includes a debit to Interest Expense of $300, the correct amount of interest, $100 ($300 - $200) for January willl be shown in Interest Expense.

MATCHING

1. h	5. o	9. m	13. g
2. i	6. n	10. b	14. a
3. l	7. d	11. c	15. e
4. j	8. k	12. f	

EXERCISES

EX. 4-1
(a)

JAZZ COMPANY
Work Sheet
For the Year Ended Dec. 31, 2006

Account Titles	Trial Balance Dr.	Trial Balance Cr.	Adjustments Dr.	Adjustments Cr.	Adjusted Trial Balance Dr.	Adjusted Trial Balance Cr.	Income Statement Dr.	Income Statement Cr.	Balance Sheet Dr.	Balance Sheet Cr.
Cash	6,000				6,000				6,000	
Accounts Receivable	7,850		(e) 2,250		10,100				10,100	
Supplies	6,000			(a) 2,000	4,000				4,000	
Prepaid Insurance	9,000			(b) 3,000	6,000				6,000	
Equipment	10,000				10,000				10,000	
Note Payable		9,750				9,750				9,750
Unearned Fees		3,100	(d) 450			2,650				2,650
Common Stock		4,000				4,000				4,000
Retained Earnings		8,000				8,000				8,000
Fees Earned		22,000		(d) 450 (e) 2,250		24,700		24,700		
Salaries Expense	8,000		(g) 850		8,850		8,850			
Totals	46,850	46,850								
Supplies Expense			(a) 2,000		2,000		2,000			
Insurance Expense			(b) 3,000		3,000		3,000			
Accumulated Depr.				(c) 1,000		1,000				1,000
Depreciation Expense			(c) 1,000		1,000		1,000			
Interest Expense			(f) 300		300		300			
Interest Payable				(f) 300		300				300
Salaries Payable				(g) 850		850				850
Totals			9,850	9,850	51,250	51,250	15,150	24,700	36,100	26,550
Net Income							9,550			9,550
Totals							24,700	24,700	36,100	36,100

(b)

General Journal

J1

Date	Account Title	Debit	Credit
2006			
	Closing entries		
	(1)		
Dec. 31	Fees Earned	24,700	
	Income Summary		24,700
	(To close revenue account)		
	(2)		
31	Income Summary	15,150	
	Salaries Expense		8,850
	Supplies Expense		2,000
	Insurance Expense		3,000
	Depreciation Expense		1,000
	Interest Expense		300
	(To close expense accounts)		
	(3)		
31	Income Summary	9,550	
	Retained Earnings		9,550
	(To close net income to capital)		

(c)

JAZZ COMPANY
Post-Closing Trial Balance
December 31, 2006

	Debit	Credit
Cash	$ 6,000	
Accounts Receivable	10,100	
Supplies	4,000	
Prepaid Insurance	6,000	
Equipment	10,000	
Accumulated Depreciation		$ 1,000
Note Payable		9,750
Unearned Fees		2,650
Salaries Payable		850
Interest Payable		300
Common Stock		4,000
Retained Earnings ($8,000 + $9,550)		17,550
	$36,100	$36,100

The Navigator ✓

- Scan Study Objectives
- Read Preview
- Read Chapter Review
- Work Demonstration Problem
- Answer True-False Statements
- Answer Multiple-Choice Questions
- Match Terms and Definitions
- Solve Exercises

Chapter 5

ACCOUNTING FOR MERCHANDISING OPERATIONS

CHAPTER STUDY OBJECTIVES

After studying this chapter, you should be able to:

1. Identify the differences between a service enterprise and a merchandiser.
2. Explain the entries for purchases under a perpetual inventory system.
3. Explain the entries for sales revenues under a perpetual inventory system.
4. Explain the steps in the accounting cycle for a merchandiser.
5. Distinguish between a multiple-step and a single-step income statement.
6. Explain the computation and importance of gross profit.
7. Determine cost of goods sold under a periodic inventory system.

*8. Prepare the entries for purchases and sales of inventory under a periodic inventory system.
*9. Prepare a work sheet for a merchandiser.

***Note:** All **asterisked** (*) items relate to material contained in the Appendices to the chapter.

PREVIEW OF CHAPTER 5

The steps in the accounting cycle for a merchandising company are the same as the steps for a service enterprise. However, merchandising companies use additional accounts and entries which are required in recording merchandising transactions. The content and organization of this chapter are as follows:

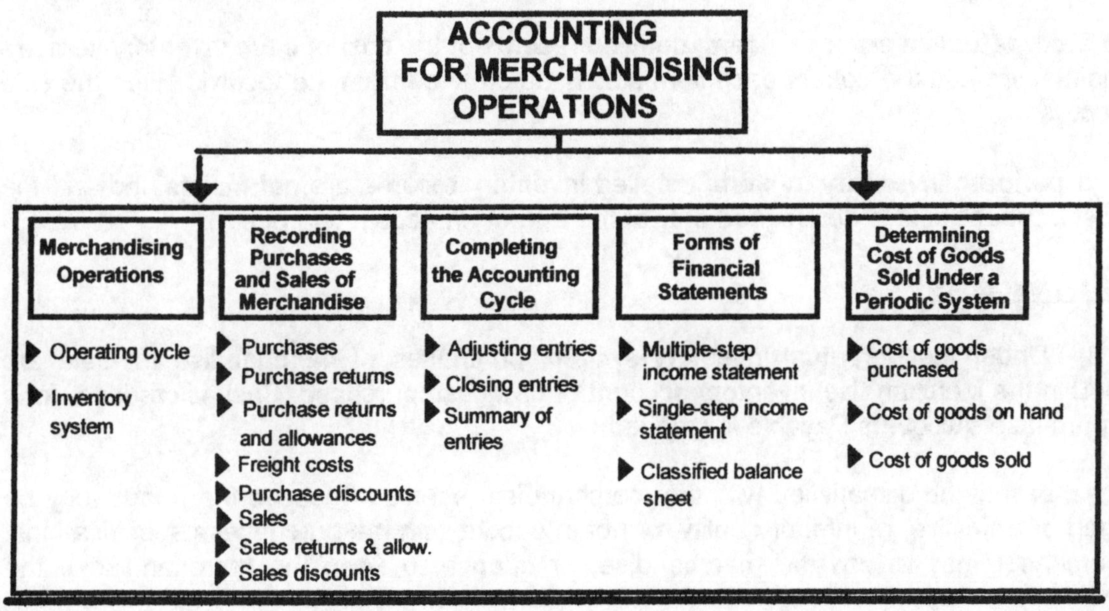

CHAPTER REVIEW

Measuring Net Income

1. (S.O. 1) A merchandiser is an enterprise that buys and sells goods to earn a profit. Merchandisers that purchase and sell directly to consumers are **retailers,** and those that sell to retailers are known as **wholesalers.**

2. The primary source of revenue for a merchandiser is **sales revenue.** Expenses are divided into two categories: (1) cost of goods sold and (2) operating expenses.

3. Sales less cost of goods sold is called the gross profit (or gross margin) on sales. For example, if sales are $5,000 and cost of goods sold is $3,000, gross profit is $2,000.

4. After gross profit is calculated, operating expenses are deducted to determine net income (or loss).

5. **Operating expenses** are expenses incurred in the process of earning sales revenue.

Operating Cycles

6. The operating cycle of a merchandiser is as follows:

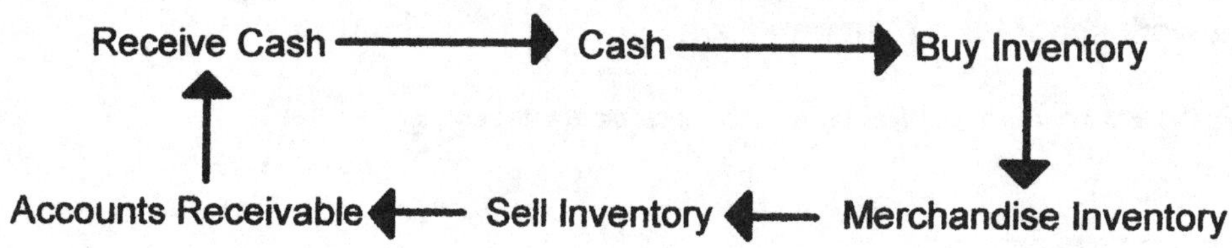

Inventory Systems

7. A merchandiser may use either a perpetual or a periodic inventory system in determining cost of goods sold.

   a. In a **perpetual inventory system,** detailed records of the cost of each inventory item are maintained and the cost of each item sold is determined from the records when the sale occurs.

   b. In a **periodic inventory system,** detailed inventory records are not maintained and the cost of goods sold is determined only at the end of an accounting period.

Purchase Transactions

8. (S.O. 2) Under the perpetual inventory system, purchases of merchandise for sale are recorded in the Merchandise Inventory account. For a cash purchase, Cash is credited; for a credit purchase, Accounts Payable is credited.

9. A purchaser may be dissatisfied with the merchandise received because the goods may be damaged or defective, of inferior quality, or not in accord with the purchaser's specifications. The purchaser may **return** the merchandise, or choose to keep the merchandise if the

supplier is willing to grant an **allowance** (deduction) from the purchase price. When merchandise is returned, Merchandise Inventory is credited.

10. When the credit terms of a purchase on account permits the purchaser to claim a cash discount for the prompt payment of a balance due, this is called a **purchase discount.** If a purchase discount has terms 3/10, n/30, then a 3% discount is taken on the invoice price (less any returns or allowances) if payment is made within 10 days. If payment is not made within 10 days, then there is no purchase discount, and the net amount of the bill is due within 30 days.

11. When an invoice is paid within the discount period, the amount of the discount is credited to Merchandise Inventory. When an invoice is not paid within the discount period, then the usual entry is made with a debit to Accounts Payable and a credit to Cash.

12. **FOB shipping point** means that goods are placed free on board the carrier by the seller, and the buyer must pay the freight costs. **FOB destination** means that goods are placed free on board at the buyer's place of business, and the seller pays the freight.

13. When the purchaser pays the freight, Merchandise Inventory is debited and Cash is credited. When the seller pays the freight, Delivery Expense or Freight-out is debited and cash is credited. This account is classified as an operating expense by the seller.

Sales Transactions

14. (S.O. 3) In accordance with the **revenue recognition principle,** sales revenues are recorded when earned. Typically sales revenues are earned when the goods are transferred from the seller to the buyer.

15. All sales transactions should be supported by a **business document**. Cash register tapes provide evidence of cash sales; sales invoices provide support for credit sales.

16. A sale on credit is recorded as follows:

	Debit	Credit
Accounts Receivable	XXXX	
Sales		XXXX
Cost of Goods Sold	XXXX	
Merchandise Inventory		XXXX

After the cash payment is received by the seller, the following entry is recorded:

	Debit	Credit
Cash	XXXX	
Accounts Receivable		XXXX

A cash sale is recorded by a debit to Cash and a credit to Sales, and a debit to Cost of Goods Sold and a credit to Merchandise Inventory.

Sales Returns and Allowances

17. A **sales return** results when a customer is dissatisfied with merchandise and is allowed to return the goods to the seller for credit or for a cash refund. A **sales allowance** results when a customer is dissatisfied with merchandise and the seller is willing to grant an allowance (deduction) from the selling price.

18. To give the customer a sales return or allowance, the seller normally prepares a business document known as a **credit memorandum** to inform the customer that a credit has been made to the customer's account receivable. The seller makes the following entry if the sale had been a credit sale (the second entry is made only if the goods are returned):

Sales Returns and Allowances	XXXX	
Accounts Receivable		XXXX
Merchandise Inventory	XXXX	
Cost of Goods Sold		XXXX

For a sales return or allowance on a cash sale, a cash refund is made and Cash is credited instead of Accounts Receivable. The second entry is the same as above.

19. Sales Returns and Allowances is a **contra revenue account** and the normal balance of the account is a debit.

Sales Discounts

20. A **sales discount** is the offer of a cash discount to a customer for the prompt payment of a balance due. If a credit sale has terms 2/10, n/30, then a 2% discount is taken on the invoice price (less any returns or allowances) if payment is made within 10 days. If payment is not made within 10 days, then there is no sales discount, and the net amount of the bill, without discount, is due within 30 days. Sales Discounts is a **contra revenue account** and the normal balance of this account is a debit.

21. Both Sales Returns and Allowances and Sales Discounts are subtracted from Sales in the income statement to arrive at **net sales.**

The Accounting Cycle

22. (S.O. 4) Each of the required steps in the accounting cycle applies to a merchandiser.

Adjusting Entries and Closing Entries

23. A merchandiser generally has the same types of adjusting entries as a service company but a merchandiser using a perpetual inventory system will require an additional adjustment to reflect the difference between a physical count of the inventory and the accounting records. In addition, like a service company, a merchandiser makes closing entries to and from Income Summary.

Multiple-Step vs. Single-Step Income Statement

24. (S.O. 5) A **multiple-step income statement** shows numerous steps in determining net income. It shows two steps: (1) cost of goods sold is subtracted from net sales for determining gross profit and (2) operating expenses are deducted from gross profit to determine net income. In addition, there may be nonoperating sections for:

    a. Revenues and expenses that result from secondary or auxiliary operations, and

    b. Gains and losses that are unrelated to the company's operations.

Gross Profit and Operating Expenses

25. (S.O. 6) **Gross profit** is net sales less cost of goods sold. The gross profit rate is expressed as a percentage by dividing the amount of gross profit by net sales. Operating expenses are the third component in measuring net income for a merchandising company.

26. Nonoperating sections are reported in the income statement after income from operations and are classified as (a) Other revenues and gains and (b) Other expenses and losses.

27. A multiple-step income statement may also subdivide operating expenses into two functional groupings: (a) selling expenses, and (b) administrative expenses.

28. The income statement is referred to as a **single-step income statement** when all data are classified under two categories: (a) Revenues and (b) Expenses, and only one step is required in determining net income or net loss.

Classified Balance Sheet

29. A merchandiser generally has the same type of balance sheet as a service company except merchandise inventory is reported as a current asset.

Determining Cost of Goods Sold Under a Periodic System

30. (S.O. 7) Under a **periodic system** separate accounts are used to record freight costs, returns, and discounts. In addition, a running account of changes in inventory is not maintained. Instead, the balance in ending inventory, as well as cost of goods sold for the period, is calculated at the end of the period. The determination of cost of goods sold for Tsutsui Co. using a periodic inventory system, is as follows:

Tsutsui Company
Cost of Goods Sold
For the Year Ended December 31, 2006

Cost of goods sold				
Inventory, January 1			$28,000	
Purchases		$234,000		
Less: Purchases returns and allowances	$8,200			
Purchase discounts	4,600	12,800		
Net Purchases		221,200		
Add: Freight-in		10,800		
Cost of goods purchased			232,000	
Cost of goods available for sale			260,000	
Inventory, December 31			30,000	
Cost of goods sold				230,000

Periodic Inventory System

*31. (S.O. 8) In a **periodic inventory system** revenues from the sale of merchandise are recorded when sales are made in the same way as in a perpetual system. But, no attempt is made on the date of sale to record the cost of the merchandise sold. Instead, a physical inventory count is taken at the end of the period to determine (1) the cost of the merchandise then on hand and (2) the cost of the goods sold during the period.

*32. Under the periodic inventory system, purchases of merchandise for sale are recorded in a Purchases account. For a cash purchase, Cash is credited; for a credit purchase, Accounts Payable is credited.

*33. A purchase return and allowance is recorded by debiting Accounts Payable or Cash and crediting the account Purchase Returns and Allowances. Purchase Returns and Allowances is a temporary account whose normal balance is a credit.

*34. If payment is made within a discount period, the amount of the discount is credited to the account Purchases Discounts. When an invoice is not paid within the discount period, then the usual entry is made with a debit to Accounts Payable and a credit to Cash.

Cost of Goods Sold

*35. To determine the **cost of goods sold** under a periodic inventory system, three steps are required: (1) Record purchases of merchandise; (2) Determine the cost of goods purchased; and (3) Determine the cost of goods on hand at the beginning and end of the accounting period.

Cost of Goods Purchased

*36. In determining cost of goods purchased, (a) contra purchase accounts are subtracted from purchases to produce **net purchases,** and (b) freight-in is then added to net purchases.

Cost of Inventory

*37. **Cost of inventory on hand** under the periodic inventory method is obtained from a physical inventory. Taking a physical inventory involves:
   a. Counting the units on hand for each item of inventory.
   b. Applying unit costs to the total units on hand for each item.
   c. Totaling the costs for each item of inventory, to determine the total cost of goods on hand.

Cost of Goods Sold

*38. **Cost of goods sold** is determined by two steps:
   a. The cost of goods purchased is added to the cost of goods on hand at the beginning of the period to obtain the cost of goods available for sale.
   b. The cost of goods on hand at the end of the period is subtracted from **the cost of goods available for sale.**

*39. The income statement for retailers and wholesalers under a periodic inventory system will generally contain more detail listing the above calculations.

Using a Work Sheet

*40. (S.O. 9) As indicated in Chapter 4, a work sheet enables financial statements to be prepared before the adjusting entries are journalized and posted. The steps in preparing a work sheet for a merchandiser are the same as they are for a service enterprise except the additional merchandising accounts are included.

The Navigator

DEMONSTRATION PROBLEM No. 1 (S.O. 2)

Presented below is the following information for JoAnne Company for 2006:

1. On November 4, purchased merchandise from A. Mobley Company for $20,000 terms 2/10, net/30, FOB shipping point.
2. On November 5, paid freight cost of $800 on merchandise purchased from A. Mobley.
3. On November 6, purchased equipment on account for $15,000.
4. On November 7, returned damaged merchandise to A. Mobley Company and was granted a $4,000 allowance.
5. On November 13, paid the amount due to A. Mobley Company in full.

Instructions

(a) Prepare the journal entries to record these transactions on the books of JoAnne Company under a perpetual inventory system.

(b) Assume that JoAnne Company paid the balance due to A. Mobley Company on November 23 instead of November 13. Prepare the journal entry to record this payment.

The Navigator

SOLUTION TO DEMONSTRATION PROBLEM No. 1

(a)

Date	Account	Debit	Credit
Nov. 4	Merchandise Inventory	20,000	
	Accounts Payable		20,000
Nov. 5	Merchandise Inventory	800	
	Cash		800
Nov. 6	Equipment	15,000	
	Accounts Payable		15,000
Nov. 7	Accounts Payable	4,000	
	Merchandise Inventory		4,000
Nov. 13	Accounts Payable	16,000	
	Cash		15,680
	Merchandise Inventory		320

(b)

Date	Account	Debit	Credit
Nov. 23	Accounts Payable	16,000	
	Cash		16,000

DEMONSTRATION PROBLEM No. 2 (S.O. 7)

The following information is given for Jennifer Company for 2006:

Purchases	$28,500
Purchase Discounts	2,400
Merchandise Inventory, 1/1/06	7,500
Freight-in	700
Purchase Returns and Allowances	1,500
Merchandise Inventory, 12/31/06	10,600

Instructions
Prepare the cost of goods sold section of the income statement for Jennifer Company.

The Navigator

SOLUTION TO DEMONSTRATION PROBLEM No. 2

Cost of goods sold			
Merchandise Inventory, 1/1/06			$ 7,500
Purchases		$28,500	
Less: Purchase returns and allowances	$1,500		
Purchase discounts	2,400	3,900	
Net Purchases		24,600	
Add: Freight-in		700	
Cost of goods purchased			25,300
Cost of goods available for sale			32,800
Merchandise Inventory, 12/31/06			10,600
Cost of goods sold			$22,200

REVIEW QUESTIONS AND EXERCISES

TRUE—FALSE

Indicate whether each of the following is true (T) or false (F) in the space provided.

_____ 1. (S.O. 1) Merchandisers that sell to wholesalers are known as retailers.

_____ 2. (S.O. 1) Merchandise inventory is reported as a long-term asset on the balance sheet.

_____ 3. (S.O. 1) In a perpetual inventory system no attempt is made to keep detailed inventory records of the goods on hand throughout the period.

_____ 4. (S.O. 1) Under a perpetual inventory system, inventory shrinkage and lost or stolen goods are more readily determined.

_____ 5. (S.O. 2) Under the perpetual inventory system, purchases of merchandise for sale are recorded by a credit to the Merchandise Inventory account.

_____ 6. (S.O. 2) A purchase return is where the purchaser chooses to keep the merchandise if the supplier is willing to grant an allowance (deduction) from the purchase price.

_____ 7. (S.O. 2) The terms 2/10, n/30 state that a 2% discount is available if the invoice is paid within the first 10 days of the next month.

_____ 8. (S.O. 2) When the terms are FOB shipping point, the seller pays the freight costs from the seller's location.

_____ 9. (S.O. 3) Gross profit is computed by subtracting cost of goods sold from net sales.

_____ 10. (S.O. 3) Sales should be recorded in accordance with the matching principle.

_____ 11. (S.O. 3) To record a sale, an asset account is debited and the revenue account Sales is credited.

_____ 12. (S.O. 3) Upon approval of the customer's request for a sales return or allowance, the seller normally prepares a business document known as a credit memorandum.

_____ 13. (S.O. 3) Sales Returns and Allowances is a contra expense account.

_____ 14. (S.O. 3) A sales discount is the offer of a cash discount to a customer for the prompt payment of a balance due.

_____ 15. (S.O. 3) Sales returns and allowances and sales discounts are subtracted from sales in reporting net sales in the income statement.

_____ 16. (S.O. 4) A merchandiser using a perpetual inventory system will usually need to make an adjusting entry to ensure that the recorded inventory agrees with physical inventory count.

_____ 17. (S.O. 5) When a company has other revenues and gains, sales revenue less cost of goods sold and operating expenses equals net income (or loss).

_____ 18. (S.O. 5) If a merchandising company sells land at more than its cost, the gain should be reported in the sales revenue section of the income statement.

_____ 19. (S.O. 5) The single-step statement is so named because only one step, subtracting total expenses from total revenues, is required in determining net income or net loss.

_____ 20. (S.O. 6) The major difference between the balance sheets of a service company and a merchandising company is inventory.

_____ 21. (S.O. 7) Net purchases is determined by subtracting purchase returns and allowances and purchase discounts from purchases.

_____ 22. (S.O. 7) In determining the cost of goods purchased, Freight-out is added to purchases.

_____ 23. (S.O. 7) Ending merchandise inventory is subtracted from the cost of goods available for sale in determining the cost of goods sold.

_____ 24. (S.O. 7) The cost of ending inventory is added to the cost of goods available for sale to determine cost of goods sold.

_____ *25. (S.O. 8) Under a periodic inventory system, when the purchaser directly incurs freight cost, the account Freight-in is credited.

The Navigator

MULTIPLE CHOICE

Circle the letter that best answers each of the following statements.

1. (S.O. 1) A merchandising company sells goods to:

	Retailers	Consumers
a.	yes	yes
b.	yes	no
c.	no	yes
d.	no	no

2. (S.O. 1) Brent Company has sales revenue of $13,000, cost of goods sold of $8,000 and operating expenses of $3,000 for the year ended December 31. Brent's gross profit is:
   a. $10,000.
   b. $ 5,000.
   c. $ 2,000.
   d. $ 0.

3. (S.O. 1) For the year ended 2000, Degas Co. has the following amounts: Sales Revenue $350,000; Gross Profit $120,000; and Operating Expenses $90,000. What are the amounts of Cost of Goods Sold and Net Income (Loss)?
   a. $260,000 and $140,000.
   b. $230,000 and $30,000.
   c. $230,000 and $140,000.
   d. $130,000 and $90,000.

4. (S.O. 1) Which of the following is **not** associated with a perpetual inventory system?
   a. Detailed records of the cost of each inventory purchase and sale are maintained.
   b. The system is usually more expensive.
   c. Shrinkage and lost or stolen goods are more readily determined.
   d. The cost of goods sold is determined only at the end of the accounting period.

5. (S.O. 2) Monet Company made a purchase of merchandise on credit from Claude Corporation on August 3, for $3,000, terms 2/10, n/45. On August 10, Monet makes the appropriate payment to Claude. The entry (perpetual inventory) on August 10 for Monet Company is:

		Debit	Credit
a.	Accounts Payable	3,000	
	Cash		3,000
b.	Accounts Payable	2,940	
	Cash		2,940
c.	Accounts Payable	3,000	
	Purchase Returns and Allowances		60
	Cash		2,940
d.	Accounts Payable	3,000	
	Merchandise Inventory		60
	Cash		2,940

6. (S.O. 2) On August 28, Renoir Company purchased merchandise from Sisley Company for $2,375 on credit. Under the perpetual system, the entry by Renoir Company is:

		Debit	Credit
a.	Merchandise Inventory	2,375	
	Accounts Payable		2,375
b.	Accounts Payable	2,375	
	Merchandise Inventory		2,375
c.	Cash	2,375	
	Accounts Payable		2,375
d.	Sales	2,375	
	Accounts Payable		2,375

7. (S.O. 2) Cezanne Co. returned defective goods costing $5,000 to the Bazille Company on March 19, for credit. The goods were purchased March 10, on credit, terms 3/10, n/30. The entry by Cezanne Co. on March 19, in receiving full credit is:

		Debit	Credit
a.	Accounts Payable	5,000	
	Merchandise Inventory		150
	Cash		4,850
b.	Accounts Payable	5,000	
	Merchandise Inventory	150	
	Cash		5,150
c.	Accounts Payable	5,000	
	Purchase Discounts		150
	Merchandise Inventory		4,850
d.	Accounts Payable	5,000	
	Merchandise Inventory		5,000

8. (S.O. 2) Seurat Company made a purchase of merchandise on credit from Van Gogh Company on August 3, for $6,000, terms 3/10, n/30. On August 17, Seurat makes the appropriate payment to Van Gogh. The entry on August 17 for Seurat Company is:

		Debit	Credit
a.	Accounts Payable	6,000	
	Cash		6,000
b.	Accounts Payable	5,820	
	Cash		5,820
c.	Accounts Payable	6,000	
	Purchase Returns and Allowances		180
	Cash		5,820
d.	Accounts Payable	6,000	
	Merchandise Inventory		180
	Cash		5,820

9. (S.O. 2) Caillebotte Company purchased inventory from Pissaro Company. The shipping costs were $400 and the terms of the shipment were FOB shipping point. Caillebotte would have the following entry regarding the shipping charges:

a. There is no entry on Caillebotte's books for this transaction.

		Debit	Credit
b.	Freight Expense	400	
	Cash		400
c.	Freight-out	400	
	Cash		400
d.	Merchandise Inventory	400	
	Cash		400

10. (S.O. 3) Every credit sale should be supported by a:

	Cash Register Tape	Sales Invoice
a.	yes	yes
b.	yes	no
c.	no	yes
d.	no	no

11. (S.O. 3) El Greco Co. made a credit sale to Rubens Company when terms were n/30. Upon payment by Rubens, El Greco Co. should debit Cash and credit:
    a. Sales.
    b. Accounts Receivable and Sales Discounts.
    c. Accounts Receivable.
    d. None of the above.

12. (S.O. 3) On October 2, 2006, DaVinchi Company has cash sales of $3,200 from merchandise having a cost of $2,500. The entries to record the day's cash sales will include:
    a. a $2,500 debit to Cost of Goods Sold.
    b. a $3,200 credit to Cash.
    c. a $2,500 debit to Merchandise Inventory.
    d. a $2,500 debit to Accounts Receivable.

13. (S.O. 3) On October 4, 2006, Terry Corporation had credit sales transactions of $2,500 from merchandising having cost $1,900. The entries to record the day's credit transactions include:
    a. a debit of $2,500 to Merchandise Inventory.
    b. a credit of $2,500 to Sales.
    c. a debit of $1,900 to Merchandise Inventory.
    d. a credit of $1,900 to Cost of Goods Sold.

14. (S.O. 3) A customer, Zurbaran, is dissatisfied with merchandise purchased for $2,000 cash from the Rembrandt Company. Rembrandt Company gives Zurbaran a cash refund of $2,000. The journal entry by Rembrandt Company for the refund will include a:
    a. debit to Sales Returns and Allowances.
    b. credit to Accounts Receivable.
    c. debit to Accounts Receivable.
    d. credit to Sales Returns and Allowances.

15. (S.O. 3) On July 9, Goya Company sells goods on credit to Ed Manet for $3,500, terms 1/10, n/60. Goya receives payment on July 18. The entry by Goya on July 18 is:

	Account	Debit	Credit
a.	Cash	3,500	
	Accounts Receivable		3,500
b.	Cash	3,500	
	Sales Discounts		35
	Accounts Receivable		3,465
c.	Cash	3,465	
	Sales Discounts	35	
	Accounts Receivable		3,500
d.	Cash	3,535	
	Sales Discounts		35
	Accounts Receivable		3,500

16. (S.O. 3) Which of the following are contra revenue accounts?

	Sales Returns and Allowances	Sales Discounts	Freight-out
a.	yes	yes	no
b.	yes	no	yes
c.	no	yes	yes
d.	yes	no	no

17. (S.O. 4) In the Clark Company, sales were $320,000, sales returns and allowances were $20,000 and cost of goods sold was $180,000. The gross profit rate was:
   a. 60%.
   b. 40%.
   c. 37.5%.
   d. 56.3%.

18. (S.O. 4) When the physical count of BIM company inventory had a cost of $2,700 at year end and the unadjusted balance in Merchandise Inventory was $2,500, BIM will have to make the following entry:

		Debit	Credit
a.	Cost of Goods Sold	200	
	Merchandise Inventory		200
b.	Merchandise Inventory	200	
	Cost of Goods Sold		200
c.	Income Summary	200	
	Merchandise Inventory		200
d.	Cost of Goods Sold	2,500	
	Merchandise Inventory		2,500

19. (S.O. 6) The nonoperating sections of the income statement will include a section entitled other:
   a. revenues and losses.
   b. revenues and gains.
   c. expenses and gains.
   d. expenses and casualty losses.

20. (S.O. 6) In the balance sheet, ending merchandise inventory is reported:
   a. in current assets immediately following accounts receivable.
   b. in current assets immediately following prepaid expenses.
   c. in current assets immediately following cash.
   d. under property, plant, and equipment.

21. (S.O. 7) Which of the following is true concerning Freight-in?
   a. Freight-in is subtracted from net purchases in determining cost of goods purchased.
   b. Freight-in is added to net purchases in determining cost of goods purchased.
   c. Freight-in is a selling expense.
   d. Freight-in is an administrative expense.

22. (S.O. 7) On December 31, Degas Co. has the following account balances: Purchases $307,000; Purchase Returns and Allowances $34,000; Purchase Discounts $26,000; and Freight-in $18,000. The cost of goods purchased for Degas Co. is:
    a. $265,000.
    b. $281,000.
    c. $349,000.
    d. $229,000.

23. (S.O. 7) On December 31, Seurat Company has the following amounts in the determination of cost of goods purchased; Purchases $60,000; Freight-in $10,000; Net purchases $48,000; Purchase returns and allowances $7,000; and Cost of goods purchased $58,000. What is the amount of purchase discounts?
    a. $2,000.
    b. $3,000.
    c. $5,000.
    d. $15,000.

24. (S.O. 7) On December 31, Van Gogh Company has the following data: Cost of goods purchased $184,500; Beginning Inventory $19,000, Ending inventory $25,000, and Sales $300,000. The cost of goods sold for Van Gogh Corporation is:
    a. $121,500.
    b. $190,500.
    c. $178,500.
    d. $109,500.

25. (S.O. 7) Caillebotte Company has the following amounts in the determination of cost of goods sold: Cost of Goods Purchased $76,000; Ending Inventory $34,000; Cost of Goods Sold $82,000. The dollar amount of beginning inventory is:
    a. $28,000.
    b. $40,000.
    c. $42,000.
    d. $48,000.

The Navigator

MATCHING

Match each term with its definition by writing the appropriate letter in the space provided.

Terms

_____ 1. Net sales.

_____ 2. Periodic inventory system.

_____ 3. Perpetual inventory system.

_____ 4. Multiple-step income statement.

_____ 5. Gross profit.

_____ 6. Income from operations.

_____ 7. Other revenues and gains.

_____ 8. Single-step income statement.

_____ 9. FOB shipping point.

_____ 10. Contra revenue account.

_____ 11. Sales discount.

_____ 12. Other expenses and losses.

_____ 13. FOB destination.

_____ 14. Cost of goods sold.

Definitions

a. A system in which detailed inventory records are not maintained and the cost of goods sold is determined only at the end of an accounting period through the taking of physical inventory.

b. Goods are placed free on board at the buyer's place of business, and the seller must pay the freight costs.

c. A detailed inventory system in which the cost of each inventory item is maintained and the records continuously show the inventory that should be on hand.

d. Net sales less cost of goods sold.

e. A nonoperating section of the income statement that shows expenses pertaining to auxiliary operations and losses unrelated to the company's operations.

f. A nonoperating section of the income statement that shows revenues from auxiliary operations and gains unrelated to the company's operations.

g. Sales less sales returns and allowances and sales discounts.

h. Cost of goods available for sale less ending merchandise inventory.

i. An income statement in which numerous steps are involved before net income or net loss is reported.

j. An income statement that shows only one step in determining net income or net loss.

k. An account that is offset against a revenue account on the income statement.

l. Net sales less cost of goods sold and operating expenses.

m. A reduction given by a seller from prompt payment of a credit sale.

n. Goods are placed free on board the carrier by the seller, and the buyer must pay the freight costs.

The Navigator

EXERCISES

EX. 5-1 (S.O. 2 and 3) During the month of October, 2006, the American Fiction Merchandising Company had the following transactions:

Oct.	2	Sold $5,000 of goods that originally cost $4,200 to Jim Michener for cash.
	10	Sold goods to Irving Stone for $2,500 on credit, terms 2/10, n/30. The goods originally cost $1,700.
	12	Gave a cash refund of $2,500 to Jim Michener because half of the goods purchased on October 2 were defective. The goods were not returned.
	15	Purchased $8,000 of merchandise from L'Amour Company on credit, terms 2/10, n/30.
	17	Received cash from Irving Stone in full payment of the sale on October 10, less the sales discount.
	21	Received an allowance from L'Amour Company of $1,000 because the goods purchased on October 15 did not meet specifications.
	24	Paid L'Amour Company the amount due less the purchase discount.

Instructions
Journalize the transactions using a perpetual inventory system. (Omit explanations.)

GENERAL JOURNAL J1

Date	Account Title	Debit	Credit

General Journal			J1
Date	Account Title	Debit	Credit

EX. 5-2 (S.O. 7) On December 31, 2006, the adjusted trial balance of the Mailer Company was as follows:

	Debits		Credits
Cash	$ 3,500	Accumulated Depreciation	$ 12,000
Accounts Receivable	13,000	Accounts Payable	16,250
Merchandise Inventory	40,500	Common Stock	10,000
Equipment	70,000	Retained Earnings	56,500
Dividends	15,000	Sales	505,000
Sales Returns and Allowances	13,850	Interest Revenue	10,900
Sales Discounts	7,750		
Cost of Goods Sold	277,850		
Freight-out	6,000		
Advertising Expense	9,500		
Sales Commissions Expense	35,000		
Office Salaries	83,000		
Utilities Expense	23,000		
Interest Expense	8,700		
Depreciation Expense	4,000		

Other data:
Utilities expense and depreciation expense are both 40% selling and 60% administrative.

Instructions
Prepare a multiple-step income statement for the year ended December 31, 2006.

MAILER COMPANY
Income Statement
For the Year Ended December 31, 2006

MAILER COMPANY
Income Statement
For the Year Ended December 31, 2006
(continued)

EX. 5-3 (S.O. 7) Westphal Company uses a periodic inventory system. On December 31, 2006, the adjusted trial balance of the Westphal Company was as follows:

	Debits		Credits
Cash	$ 3,500	Accumulated Depreciation	$ 12,000
Accounts Receivable	13,000	Accounts Payable	16,250
Merchandise Inventory	42,000	Common Stock	50,000
Equipment	70,000	Retained Earnings	16,500
Dividends	15,000	Sales	505,000
Sales Returns and Allowances	13,850	Purchase Returns and Allowances	14,350
Sales Discounts	7,750		
Purchases	300,000	Purchase Discounts	22,000
Freight-in	12,700	Interest Revenue	10,900
Freight-out	6,000		
Advertising Expense	9,500		
Sales Commissions Expense	35,000		
Office Salaries	83,000		
Utilities Expense	23,000		
Interest Expense	8,700		
Depreciation Expense	4,000		

Other data:

1. Merchandise inventory December 31, 2006 is $40,500.
2. Utilities expense and depreciation expense are both 40% selling and 60% administrative.

Instructions

Prepare a multiple-step income statement for the year ended December 31, 2006.

WESTPHAL COMPANY
Income Statement
For the Year Ended December 31, 2006

WESTPHAL COMPANY
Income Statement
For the Year Ended December 31, 2006
(continued)

*** EX. 5-4** (S.O. 8) Aurora Company uses a periodic inventory system. The following transactions occur in July.

1. On July 2, Aurora Company purchased $90,000 of merchandise from Sparta Company, terms 2/10, n/30.
2. On July 6, Aurora Company returned $13,000 of the merchandise purchased on July 2 because it was defective.
3. On July 12, Aurora Company paid the balance due to Sparta Company.

Instructions
Prepare the journal entries to record these transactions.

GENERAL JOURNAL J1

Date	Account Title	Debit	Credit

SOLUTIONS TO REVIEW QUESTIONS AND EXERCISES

TRUE-FALSE

1. (F) Merchandisers that sell to retailers are known as wholesalers; retailers are merchandising companies that purchase and sell directly to consumers.
2. (F) Merchandise inventory is reported as a current asset on the balance sheet.
3. (F) In a perpetual inventory system detailed records of the cost of each inventory purchase and sale are maintained and continuously (perpetually) show the inventory that should be on hand for every item.
4. (T)
5. (F) Under a perpetual inventory system, purchases of merchandise for sale are recorded by a debit to the Merchandise Inventory account.
6. (F) A purchase return is where the purchaser returns the goods to the supplier for credit if the sale was made on credit, or for a cash refund if the purchase was originally for cash.
7. (F) The terms 2/10, n/30 state that a 2% discount is available if the invoice is paid within 10 days of the invoice date otherwise the net balance, without cash discount, is due 30 days from the invoice date.
8. (F) When the terms are FOB shipping point, the buyer pays the freight costs; when the terms are FOB destination, the seller pays the freight costs.
9. (T)
10. (F) Sales should be recorded in accordance with the revenue recognition principle.
11. (T)
12. (T)
13. (F) Sales Returns and Allowances is a contra revenue account. It is subtracted from Sales in the computation of Net Sales.
14. (T)
15. (T)
16. (T)
17. (F) The difference between the amounts is income (loss) from operations, not net income (or loss).
18. (F) If a merchandiser sells land at more than its cost, the gain should be reported in the other revenues and gains section.
19. (T)
20. (T)
21. (T)
22. (F) Freight-in is added to net purchases; Freight-out is a selling expense.
23. (T)
24. (F) The cost of ending inventory is subtracted from the cost of goods available for sale to determine the cost of goods sold.

*25. (F) Under a periodic inventory system, when the purchaser directly incurs freight costs, the account Freight-in is debited.

MULTIPLE CHOICE

1. (a) A merchandising company sells goods to both retailers and consumers.

2. (b) The gross profit is equal to sales revenue minus cost of goods sold ($13,000 - $8,000 = $5,000).

3. (b) Cost of Goods Sold equals Sales Revenue less Gross Profit ($350,000 - $120,000 = $230,000) and Net Income equals Gross Profit less Operating Expenses ($120,000 - $90,000 = $30,000).

4. (d) Under a periodic inventory system, the cost of goods sold is determined only at the end of the accounting period. In a perpetual inventory system, the cost of goods sold is determined and recorded each time a sale occurs. Answers (a), (b), and (c) are all associated with perpetual inventory systems.

5. (d) Because the payment was within 10 days, Monet was allowed a purchase discount of $60 ($3,000 X 2%). Thus, credits are needed to Cash $2,940 and Merchandise Inventory $60.

6. (a) The purchase of inventory on credit results in a debit to Merchandise Inventory and a credit to Accounts Payable.

7. (d) A purchase discount is not involved because a payment was never made. The credit of $5,000 is recorded by debiting Accounts Payable, $5,000 and crediting Merchandise Inventory $5,000.

8. (a) Because Seurat failed to make the payment with the time period of 10 days, the full payment must be made on August 17. Therefore, Accounts Payable is debited for $6,000 and Cash is credited for $6,000.

9. (d) The terms FOB shipping point mean that goods are placed free on board the carrier by the seller, and the buyer pays the freight costs. When the purchaser directly incurs the freight costs, the account Merchandise Inventory is debited.

10. (c) Cash register tapes support cash sales, and sales invoices support credit sales.

11. (c) The entry for a receipt of a balance due from a credit sale when terms were n/30 is debit Cash and credit Accounts Receivable.

12. (a) The entries to record the day's cash sales are as follows:

Cash	3,200	
Sales		3,200
Cost of Goods Sold	2,500	
Merchandise Inventory		2,500

13. (b) The credit transactions by Terry Corporation would be as follows:

Accounts Receivable	2,500	
Sales		2,500
Cost of Goods Sold	1,900	
Merchandise Inventory		1,900

14. (a) The entry for the cash refund is debit Sales Returns and Allowances $2,000 and credit Cash $2,000.

15. (c) The payment was made within the discount period. Therefore, Cash is debited for $3,465, Sales Discount is debited for $35 ($3,500 X 1%), and the Accounts Receivable account is credited for $3,500.

16. (a) Both Sales Returns and Allowances and Sales Discounts are contra revenue accounts. Freight-out is a selling expense.

17. (b) The gross profit rate is computed by dividing gross profit by net sales. Gross profit is $120,000 [($320,000 - $20,000) - $180,000], and net sales are $300,000; $120,000 ÷ $300,000 = 40%.

18. (b) The account Merchandise Inventory for BIM should be adjusted to reflect the physical count and therefore Merchandise Inventory is increased by $200 ($2,700 - 2,500) with a debit, and Cost of Goods Sold is credited for $200.

19. (b) The nonoperating sections are either entitled (1) Other revenues and gains or (2) Other expenses and losses. Answer (d) is incorrect because other types of losses besides casualty losses can be recorded in this section.

20. (a) Ending inventory is reported in current assets immediately following accounts receivable.

21. (b) Freight-in is a temporary account whose normal balance is a debit; therefore, it is added to purchases in determining the cost of goods purchased.

22. (a) The cost of goods purchased is computed as follows:

Purchases		$307,000
Less: Purchase returns and allowances	$34,000	
Purchase discounts	26,000	60,000
Net purchases		247,000
Add: Freight-in		18,000
Cost of goods purchases		$265,000

23. (c) Purchase discounts is determined as follows:

Purchases	$60,000
Less: Purchase returns and allowances	7,000
	53,000
Less: Net purchases	48,000
Purchase discounts	$ 5,000

24. (c) The cost of goods sold is computed as follows:

Beginning inventory	$ 19,000
Cost of goods purchased	184,500
Cost of goods available for sale	203,500
Ending inventory	25,000
Cost of goods sold	$178,500

25. (b) Beginning inventory is determined as follows:

Cost of goods sold	$ 82,000
Add: Ending inventory	34,000
Cost of good available for sale	116,000
Less: Cost of goods purchased	76,000
Beginning inventory	$ 40,000

MATCHING

1.	g	6.	l	11.	m
2.	a	7.	f	12.	e
3.	c	8.	j	13.	b
4.	i	9.	n	14.	h
5.	d	10.	k		

EXERCISES

EX. 5-1

General Journal J1

Date	Account Title	Debit	Credit
2006 Oct. 2	Cash	5,000	
	Sales		5,000
	Cost of Goods Sold	4,200	
	Merchandise Inventory		4,200
10	Accounts Receivable	2,500	
	Sales		2,500
	Cost of Goods Sold	1,700	
	Merchandise Inventory		1,700
12	Sales Returns and Allowances	2,500	
	Cash		2,500
15	Merchandise Inventory	8,000	
	Accounts Payable		8,000
17	Cash	2,450	
	Sales Discounts ($2,500 x 2%)	50	
	Accounts Receivable		2,500
21	Accounts Payable	1,000	
	Merchandise Inventory		1,000
24	Accounts Payable	7,000	
	Merchandise Inventory [($8,000 - $1,000) X 2%]		140
	Cash		6,860

EX. 5-2

MAILER COMPANY
Income Statement
For the Year Ended December 31, 2006

Sales revenues			
Sales			$505,000
Less: Sales returns and allowances		$ 13,850	
Sales discounts		7,750	21,600
Net sales			483,400
Cost of goods sold			277,850
Gross profit			205,550
Operating expenses			
Selling expenses			
Sales commissions expense	35,000		
Advertising expense	9,500		
Utilities expense ($23,000 X 40%)	9,200		
Freight-out	6,000		
Depreciation expense ($4,000 X 40%)	1,600		
Total selling expenses		61,300	
Administrative expenses			
Office salaries	83,000		
Utilities expense ($23,000 X 60%)	13,800		
Depreciation (4,000 X 60%)	2,400		
Total administrative expenses		99,200	
Total operating expenses			160,500
Income from operations			45,050
Other revenues and gains			
Interest revenue		10,900	
Other expenses and losses			
Interest expense		8,700	2,200
Net income			$ 47,250

EX. 5-3

WESTPHAL COMPANY
Income Statement
For the Year Ended December 31, 2006

Sales revenues				
Sales				$505,000
Less: Sales returns and allowances			$ 13,850	
Sales discounts			7,750	21,600
Net sales				483,400
Cost of goods sold				
Inventory, January 1			42,000	
Purchases		$300,000		
Less: Purchase returns and allowances	$14,350			
Purchase discounts	22,000	36,350		
Net purchases		263,650		
Add: Freight-in		12,700		
Cost of goods purchased			276,350	
Cost of goods available for sale			318,350	
Inventory, December 31			40,500	
Cost of goods sold				277,850
Gross profit				205,550
Operating expenses				
Selling expenses				
Sales commissions expense		35,000		
Advertising expense		9,500		
Utilities expense ($23,000 X 40%)		9,200		
Freight-out		6,000		
Depreciation expense ($4,000 X 40%)		1,600		
Total selling expenses			61,300	
Administrative expenses				
Office salaries		83,000		
Utilities expense ($23,000 X 60%)		13,800		
Depreciation (4,000 X 60%)		2,400		
Total administrative expenses			99,200	
Total operating expenses				160,500
Income from operations				45,050
Other revenues and gains				
Interest revenue			10,900	
Other expenses and losses				
Interest expense			8,700	2,200
Net income				$ 47,250

***EX. 5-4**

General Journal			J1
Date	**Account Title**	**Debit**	**Credit**
July 2	Purchases	90,000	
	Accounts Payable		90,000
6	Accounts Payable	13,000	
	Purchase Returns and Allowances		13,000
12	Accounts Payable ($90,000 - $13,000)	77,000	
	Purchase Discounts ($77,000 X 2%)		1,540
	Cash ($77,000 - $1,540)		75,460

Chapter **6**

The Navigator	✓
■ *Scan Study Objectives*	☐
■ *Read Preview*	☐
■ *Read Chapter Review*	☐
■ *Work Demonstration Problem*	☐
■ *Answer True-False Statements*	☐
■ *Answer Multiple-Choice Questions*	☐
■ *Match Terms and Definitions*	☐
■ *Solve Exercises*	☐

INVENTORIES

CHAPTER STUDY OBJECTIVES

After studying this chapter, you should be able to:

1. Describe the steps in determining inventory quantities.
2. Explain the basis of accounting for inventories and describe the inventory cost flow methods.
3. Explain the financial statement and tax effects of each of the inventory cost flow methods.
4. Explain the lower of cost or market basis of accounting for inventories.
5. Indicate the effects of inventory errors on the financial statements.
6. Compute and interpret inventory turnover.

*7. Apply the inventory cost flow methods to perpetual inventory records.
*8. Describe the two methods of estimating inventories

The Navigator

***Note:** All **asterisked** (*) items relate to material contained in the Appendix to the chapter.

PREVIEW OF CHAPTER 6

In this chapter we will explain the procedures for determining the cost of inventory on hand at the balance sheet date. In addition, we will discuss the effects of inventory errors on a company's financial statements. The content and organization of this chapter are as follows:

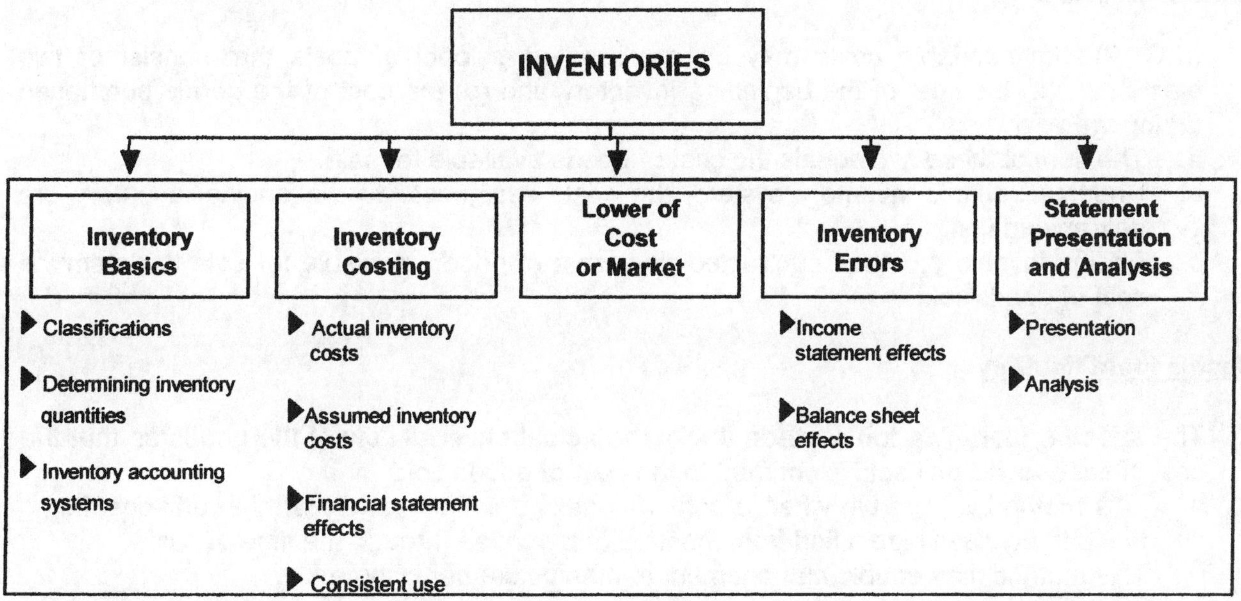

CHAPTER REVIEW

Classifying Inventory

1. (S.O. 1) **Merchandise inventory** has two common characteristics: (a) it is owned by the company and (b) it is in a form ready for sale in the ordinary course of business.

2. A manufacturer's inventory is usually classified into three categories:
   a. **Finished goods** that are completed and ready for sale.
   b. **Work in process** that is in various stages of production but not yet completed.
   c. **Raw materials** that are on hand waiting to be used in production.

Determination of Inventory Quantities

3. The determination of inventory quantities involves (a) taking a physical inventory of goods on hand and (b) determining the ownership of goods.

4. Taking a physical inventory involves counting, weighing or measuring each kind of inventory on hand. Internal control procedures should be followed in taking the inventory in order to minimize errors.

5. For goods in transit, **legal title** is determined by the terms of sale. When the terms are:
   a. **FOB (free on board) shipping point,** ownership of the goods passes to the buyer when the public carrier accepts the goods from the seller.
   b. **FOB destination,** legal title to the goods remains with the seller until the goods reach the buyer.

6. Under a consignment arrangement, the holder of the goods (called the consignee) does not own the goods. Ownership remains with the shipper of the goods (consignor) until the goods are actually sold to a customer. Consigned goods should be included in the consignor's inventory—not the consignee's inventory.

Inventory Costing

7. (S.O. 2) Inventoriable costs may be regarded as a pool of costs that consist of two elements: (a) the cost of the beginning inventory and (b) the cost of the goods purchased during the year.
   a. The sum of these two equals the cost of goods available for sale.
   b. Under a periodic inventory system, the costs assignable to the ending inventory are determined first.
   c. Ending inventory is then subtracted from cost of goods available for sale to determine cost of goods sold.

Specific Identification

8. The **specific identification method** tracks the actual physical flow of the goods so that the cost of the specific unit sold is charged to the cost of goods sold.
   a. This method is possible when a company sells a limited variety of high unit-cost items that can be clearly identified from the time of purchase through the time of sale.
   b. This method may enable management to manipulate net income.

9. The allocation of inventoriable costs may be made under any of the following assumptions as to the **flow of costs** (a) first-in, first-out (FIFO), (b) last-in, first-out (LIFO), or (c) average cost.

FIFO

10. The **FIFO method** assumes that the costs of the earliest goods purchased are the first to be sold.
    a. This method often parallels the actual physical flow of the merchandise.
    b. Under this method, the ending inventory is based on the latest units purchased.

LIFO

11. The **LIFO (periodic) method** assumes that the costs of the latest units purchased are the first to be sold.
    a. This method seldom coincides with the actual physical flow of inventory.
    b. Under this method, all goods purchased during the period are assumed to be available for the first sale, regardless of the date of purchase.
    c. The ending inventory is found by taking the unit cost of the oldest goods and working forward until all units of inventory are costed.

Average Cost

12. The **average cost method** assumes that the goods available for sale are identical.
    a. Under this method, the cost of goods available for sale is allocated on the basis of **weighted-average unit** cost.
    b. The formula for determining the weighted average unit cost is: Cost of goods available for sale divided by total units available for sale.

Financial Statement Effects

13. (S.O. 3) In periods of rising prices, FIFO produces a higher net income, LIFO the lowest, and average cost falls in the middle. The reverse is true when prices are falling.

14. Companies adopt different inventory costing methods because of:
    a. Balance sheet effects: the inventory costs are closer to current costs under FIFO than under LIFO.
    b. Income statement effects: in addition to the effects on net income in (13) above, LIFO enables the company to avoid reporting paper or phantom profit as economic gain.
    c. Tax effects: in a period of inflation LIFO results in the lowest income taxes.

Lower of Cost of Market

15. (S.O. 4) When the value of inventory is lower than its cost, the inventory is written down to its market value. This is known as the **lower of cost or market (LCM) method.**

16. Market is measured by the **current replacement cost** of the goods, not selling price.

Effects of Inventory Errors

17. (S.O. 5) The effects of **inventory errors** on the current year's income statement are:

Inventory Error	Cost of Goods Sold	Net Income
Beginning inventory understated	Understated	Overstated
Beginning inventory overstated	Overstated	Understated
Ending inventory understated	Overstated	Understated
Ending inventory overstated	Understated	Overstated

18. The effects of ending inventory errors on the balance sheet are:

Ending Inventory	Assets	Liabilities	Owner's Equity
Overstated	Overstated	None	Overstated
Understated	Understated	None	Understated

19. In the financial statements:
    a. Inventory is usually classified as a current asset after receivables in the balance sheet, and cost of goods sold is subtracted from sales in the income statement.
    b. There should be disclosure of (1) the major inventory classifications, (2) the basis of accounting, and (3) the costing method.

Inventory Turnover Ratio

20. (S.O. 6) The **inventory turnover ratio** measures the number of times on average the inventory is sold during the period.

Cost of Goods Sold ÷ Average Inventory = Inventory Turnover

*Applying Perpetual Inventory

*21. (S.O. 7) Each of the inventory cost flow methods may be used in a perpetual inventory system.
    a. Under FIFO, the cost of the earliest goods on hand prior to each sale is charged to cost of goods sold.
    b. When the **moving average method** is used, a new average is computed after each purchase by dividing the cost of goods available for sale by the units on hand.
    c. Under the LIFO method, the most recent purchase prior to sale is allocated to the units sold.

Estimating Inventories

*22. (S.O. 8) Inventories may have to be estimated when (a) management wants monthly or quarterly financial statements or (b) a fire or other type of casualty makes it impossible to take a physical inventory.

Gross Profit Method

*23. The **gross profit method** is widely used to estimate the ending inventory. Two steps are involved in using this method.

a. The estimated cost of goods sold is determined by subtracting the estimated gross profit from net sales.

b. The estimated cost of goods sold is subtracted from cost of goods available for sale to determine the estimated cost of the ending inventory.

Retail Inventory Method

*24. The **retail inventory method** is used by retail companies to estimate the cost of the inventory. The steps in using this method are:

a. Goods Available for Sale at Retail − Net Sales = Ending Inventory at Retail

b. Goods Available for Sale at Cost ÷ Goods Available for Sale at Retail = Cost to Retail Ratio

c. Ending Inventory at Retail X Cost to Retail Ratio = Estimated Cost of Ending Inventory

DEMONSTRATION PROBLEM No. 1 (S.O. 2)

Paul Company sells a stereo amplifying system. Below is information relating to Paul's purchases of the stereo systems during October. During the same month, 150 stereo systems were sold. Paul uses a periodic inventory system:

Date	Explanation	Units	Unit Cost	Total Cost
Oct. 1	Inventory	44	$125	$ 5,500
Oct. 4	Purchases	75	$128	$ 9,600
Oct. 15	Purchases	80	$122	$ 9,760
Oct. 28	Purchases	70	$126	$ 8,820
		269		$33,680

Instructions
Complete the ending inventory and cost of goods sold at October 31, using the FIFO and LIFO methods.

The Navigator

SOLUTION TO DEMONSTRATION PROBLEM No. 1

Ending Inventory = 269 – 150 = 119
FIFO Method:

Ending Inventory

Date	Units	Unit Cost	Total Cost
Oct. 28	70	$126	$ 8,820
Oct. 15	49	$122	5,978
Total	119		$14,798

Cost of Goods Sold

Cost of Goods available for sale	$33,680
Less: Ending Inventory	14,798
Cost of Goods Sold	$18,882

LIFO Method:

Ending Inventory

Date	Units	Unit Cost	Total Cost
Oct. 1	44	$125	$ 5,500
Oct. 4	75	$128	9,600
Total			$15,100

Cost of Goods Sold

Cost of Goods available for sale	$33,680
Less: Ending Inventory	15,100
Cost of Goods Sold	$18,580

*DEMONSTRATION PROBLEM No. 2 (S.O. 8)

The inventory of Edison Company was destroyed by fire on October 1, 2006. From an examination of the accounting records, the following data for the prior months of the year 2006 were obtained: Sales $462,000, Sales Returns and Allowances $8,500, Purchases $73,000, Freight-in $5,600, and Purchase Returns and Allowances $7,200.

Instructions
Determine the merchandise lost by fire, assuming a beginning inventory of $252,000 and a gross profit rate of 35% on net sales.

SOLUTION TO DEMONSTRATION PROBLEM No. 2

Sales	$462,000	
Sales Returns and Allowances	8,500	
Net sales		$453,500
Less: Estimated gross profit (35% X $453,500)		158,725
Estimated cost of goods sold		$294,775
Beginning inventory		$252,000
Purchases	$73,000	
Add: Freight-in	5,600	
Less: Purchases returns and allowances	(7,200)	
Cost of goods purchased		71,400
Cost of goods available for sale		323,400
Less: Estimated cost of goods sold		294,775
Estimated cost of ending inventory		$ 28,625

REVIEW QUESTIONS AND EXERCISES

TRUE—FALSE

Indicate whether each of the following is true (T) or false (F) in the space provided.

_____ 1. (S.O. 1) Merchandise inventory has two common characteristics: (a) it is owned by the company and (b) it is on hand waiting to be used in production.

_____ 2. (S.O. 1) Finished goods are a classification of inventory in a manufacturing enterprise that are completed and ready for sale.

_____ 3. (S.O. 1) The determination of inventory quantities involves taking a physical inventory and determining the ownership of goods.

_____ 4. (S.O. 1) Under the terms FOB destination, ownership of the goods passes to the buyer when the public carrier accepts the goods from the seller.

_____ 5. (S.O. 2) The primary basis of accounting for inventories is market value.

_____ 6. (S.O. 2) The pool of inventory costs consists of the beginning inventory plus the cost of goods purchased.

_____ 7. (S.O. 2) The inventory method of specific identification is appropriate for costly, easily distinguishable items such as pianos, automobiles, fur coats, and antiques.

_____ 8. (S.O. 2) Under the FIFO method, the costs of the earliest units purchased are the first charged to cost of goods sold.

_____ 9. (S.O. 3) In a period of falling prices, the LIFO method results in a lower cost of goods sold than the FIFO method.

_____ 10. (S.O. 3) In a period of rising prices, the FIFO method reports the highest net income, LIFO the lowest, and average cost falls in the middle.

_____ 11. (S.O. 4) Under the lower of cost or market basis, market is defined as selling price.

_____ 12. (S.O. 4) The lower of cost or market basis is an example of the accounting concept of conservatism.

_____ 13. (S.O. 4) The lower of cost or market basis must be applied to each individual item of inventory.

_____ 14. (S.O. 5) If beginning inventory is overstated, net income will be overstated in the same year.

_____ 15. (S.O. 5) Inventories are reported in the current asset section of the balance sheet immediately below receivables.

_____ *16. (S.O. 7) In a perpetual inventory system, the cost of goods sold under the FIFO method is based on the cost of the latest goods on hand during the period.

_____ *17. (S.O. 7) Under the LIFO method, the cost of the most recent purchase prior to sale is allocated to the units sold in a perpetual inventory system.

_____ *18. (S.O. 8) The gross profit method is based on the assumption that the rate of gross profit remains constant from one year to the next.

_____ *19. (S.O. 8) In the retail method, the cost to retail ratio is applied to the goods available for sale at retail to determine the estimated cost of the inventory.

_____ *20. (S.O. 8) It is not necessary to take a physical inventory under the retail method to determine the estimated cost of goods on hand at any given time.

The Navigator

MULTIPLE CHOICE

Circle the letter that best answers each of the following statements.

1. (S.O. 1) Inventory items on an assembly line in various stages of production are classified as:
   a. Finished goods.
   b. Work in process.
   c. Raw materials.
   d. Merchandise inventory.

2. (S.O. 1) L. Pasteur Company's inventory at December 31, 2006, was $300,000 based on a physical count of goods made on December 31. The following items were in transit:

   * Goods costing $5,000 were shipped FOB shipping point on December 29, 2006 to a customer and received by the customer on January 3, 2007.

   * Goods costing $10,000 were shipped FOB destination on December 30, 2006 to a customer and received by the customer on January 4, 2007.

   What amount should L. Pasteur report as inventory on its December 31, 2006 balance sheet?
   a. $290,000.
   b. $305,000.
   c. $310,000.
   d. $315,000.

3. (S.O. 2) Rudolf Diesel Company's inventory records show the following data:

		Units	Unit Cost
Inventory, January 1		10,000	$9.00
Purchases:	June 18	9,000	8.00
	November 8	6,000	7.00

A physical inventory on December 31 shows 8,000 units on hand. Under the FIFO method, the December 31 inventory is:
a. $56,000.
b. $58,000.
c. $64,000.
d. $72,000.

4. (S.O. 2) Fermat Company had 300 units of inventory on hand at January 1 costing $32 each. Purchases during the month of January were as follows:

	Units	Unit Cost
Jan. 15	400	$33
23	550	34
29	100	35

A physical count on January 31 shows 450 units on hand. The cost of the inventory at January 31 under the LIFO method is:
a. $15,400.
b. $14,900.
c. $14,550.
d. $14,400.

Items 5 and 6 are based on the following data:

Sig Freud Bookstore had 200 electric pencil sharpeners on hand at January 1, costing $18 each. Purchases and sales of electric pencil sharpeners during the month of January were as follows:

Date		Purchases	Sales
Jan.	14		150@ $28
	17	100 @ $20	
	25	100 @ $22	
	29		100 @ $32

Sig Freud does not maintain perpetual inventory records. According to a physical count, 150 electric pencil sharpeners were on hand at January 31.

5. (S.O. 2) The cost of the inventory at January 31, under the FIFO method is:
a. $400.
b. $2,700.
c. $3,100.
d. $3,200.

6. (S.O. 2) The cost of the inventory at January 31, under the LIFO method is:
   a. $400.
   b. $2,700.
   c. $3,100.
   d. $3,200.

7. (S.O. 2) Ampere Company recorded the following data:

	Units			Unit
Date	Received	Sold	On Hand	Cost
1/1 Inventory			400	$1.00
1/8 Purchased	600		1,000	1.10
1/12 Sold		800	200	

   The weighted average unit cost of the inventory at January 31 is:
   a. $1.00.
   b. $1.05.
   c. $1.06.
   d. $1.10.

8. (S.O. 3) In a period of rising prices, FIFO will have a
   a. lower net income than LIFO.
   b. lower cost of goods sold than LIFO.
   c. lower income tax expense than LIFO.
   d. lower net purchases than LIFO.

9. (S.O. 3) In a period of inflation, the use of the LIFO method will result in:
   a. a more realistic inventory value than FIFO.
   b. a better matching of costs and revenues than FIFO.
   c. higher income taxes than FIFO.
   d. higher net income than FIFO.

Items 10 and 11 are based on the following data:

Langmuir, Inc. has 5 personal computers which have been part of the inventory for over two years. Each personal computer cost $800 and originally retailed for $1,100. At the statement date, each personal computer has a current replacement cost of $450.

10. (S.O. 4) What value should Langmuir, Inc., have for the personal computers at the end of the year balance sheet?
    a. $1,750.
    b. $2,250.
    c. $4,000.
    d. $5,500.

11. (S.O. 4) How much loss should Langmuir, Inc., record the for year ended?
    a. $1,500.
    b. $1,750.
    c. $1,800.
    d. $2,250.

12. (S.O. 5) On December 31, 2006, Cavendish, Inc. overstated its ending inventory by $4,000. Assuming no correcting entry was made, the effects on the following **2007** income statement items are :

	Net Income	Sales	Cost of Goods Sold
a.	overstated	no effect	understated
b.	understated	no effect	overstated
c.	overstated	overstated	understated
d.	understated	no effect	understated

13. (S.O. 5) Euler Company made an inventory count on December 31, 2006. During the count, one of the clerks made the error of counting an inventory item twice. For the balance sheet at December 31, 2006, the effects of this error are:

	Assets	Liabilities	Owner's Equity
a.	overstated	understated	overstated
b.	understated	no effect	understated
c.	overstated	no effect	overstated
d.	overstated	overstated	understated

Items *14-*16 relate to the perpetual inventory system of the Zollmer Company. During May, the following purchases and sales were made for Product X298. There was no beginning inventory.

	Purchases		Sales
May 3	20 units @ $20	May 15	25 units
14	20 units @ $22	24	10 units
21	10 units @ $25		

*14. (S.O. 7) Under the FIFO method, the cost of goods sold for each sale is:

	May 15	May 24
a.	$500	$200
b.	550	220
c.	510	220
d.	625	250

*15. (S.O. 7) Under the LIFO method, the cost of goods sold for each sale is:

	May 15	May 24
a.	$540	$250
b.	625	220
c.	500	200
d.	550	250

*16. (S.O. 7) Under the average cost method, the cost of goods sold for each sale is:

	May 15	May 24
a.	$575	$235
b.	525	226
c.	550	240
d.	525	218

*17. (S.O. 8) Doppler Company wishes to prepare an income statement for the month of March when its records show Net Sales, $300,000; Beginning Inventory, $59,000; and Cost of Goods Purchased, $155,000. The company realizes a 30% gross profit rate. The estimated cost of the ending inventory at March 31 under the gross profit method is:

a. $4,000.
b. $55,000.
c. $63,000.
d. $72,000.

*18. (S.O. 8) Oppenheimer Company's records indicate the following information for the year:

Merchandise inventory, 1/1	$ 550,000
Purchases	2,250,000
Net Sales	3,000,000

On December 31, a physical inventory determined that ending inventory of $600,000 was in the warehouse. Oppenheimer's gross profit on sales has remained constant at 30%. Oppenheimer suspects some of the inventory may have been taken by some new employees. At December 31, what is the estimated cost of missing inventory?

a. $100,000.
b. $200,000.
c. $300,000.
d. $700,000.

Items *19 and *20 are based on the following data: On December 31, Gottlieb Retailers has the following information under the retail inventory method.

	Cost	Retail
Beginning inventory	$40,500	$ 57,000
Cost of goods purchased	57,000	73,000
Goods available for sale	$97,500	130,000
Sales (net)		72,000
Ending inventory at retail		$ 58,000

*19. (S.O. 8) The cost to retail ratio is:

a. 71%.
b. 78%.
c. 75%.
d. 80%.

*20. (S.O. 8) The estimated cost of the ending inventory is:

a. $41,210.
b. $45,286.
c. $43,500.
d. $22,500.

MATCHING

Match each term with its definition by writing the appropriate letter in the space provided.

Terms

_____ 1. Inventoriable costs.

_____ 2. Perpetual inventory system.

_____ 3. Specific identification method.

_____ 4. First-in, first-out method (FIFO).

_____ 5. Last-in, first-out method (LIFO).

_____ 6. Average cost method.

_____ 7. Retail inventory method.

_____ 8. Gross profit method.

_____ 9. Lower of cost or market basis.

_____ 10. Cost of goods available for sale.

Definitions

a. An inventory system in which the accounting records continuously show the inventory that should be on hand at any point in time.

b. The inventory costing method that tracks the actual physical flow of the goods available for sale.

c. The inventory costing method which assumes that the latest units purchased are the first to be allocated to cost of goods sold.

d. The inventory costing method which assumes that the earliest goods acquired are the first to be recognized as cost of goods sold.

e. The inventory costing method which assumes that the goods available for sale are homogeneous.

f. A method used to estimate the cost of the ending inventory in which the estimated cost of goods sold is subtracted from the cost of goods available for sale.

g. A pool of costs that consists of the cost of the beginning inventory and the cost of goods purchased during the period.

h. The sum of the beginning merchandise inventory plus the cost of goods purchased.

i. A method used to estimate the cost of the ending inventory by using a cost to retail ratio.

j. A method of valuing inventory that recognizes the decline in the value when the current purchase price (market) is less than cost.

EXERCISES

EX. 6-1 (S.O. 2) On January 1, Fermi Company had a beginning inventory of 200 units that cost $30 each. The following purchases were made during the year.

May	5	240 units at $28
Aug.	8	350 units at $31
Nov.	29	300 units at $33

Fermi Company uses a periodic inventory system. The count of the ending inventory was 500 units at December 31.

Instructions
Compute the cost of the ending inventory and the cost of goods sold for Fermi Company for the year ended December 31 for each of the following methods: (a) FIFO, (b) LIFO, and (c) average cost (round to two decimals)

Pool of Costs
Cost of Goods Available for Sale

Date	Units	Unit Cost	Total Cost

FIFO Method

Ending Inventory:

Date	Units	Unit Cost	Total Cost

FIFO Method (continued)

Cost of goods sold:

Date	Units	Unit Cost	Total Cost

LIFO Method

Ending Inventory:

Date	Units	Unit Cost	Total Cost

Cost of goods sold:

Average Cost Method

Weighted average unit cost:

Ending Inventory:

Cost of goods sold:

***EX. 6-2** (S.O. 8) The records of A.G. Bell Company show the following data for the month of October:

Net sales	$230,000
Inventory at cost, October 1	122,500
Inventory at retail, October 1	175,000
Goods purchased at cost	149,600
Goods purchased at retail	220,000

Instructions

(a) Using the retail inventory method, compute the estimated cost of the inventory at October 31. (Round to two decimals.)

(b) Assuming a gross profit rate of 30%, compute the estimated cost of the inventory at October 31 using the gross profit method.

(a)

(b)

The Navigator

SOLUTIONS TO REVIEW QUESTIONS AND EXERCISES

TRUE-FALSE

1. (F) Merchandise inventory has two common characteristics: (1) it is owned by the company and (2) it is in a form ready for sale to customers in the ordinary course of business.
2. (T)
3. (T)
4. (F) Under the terms, FOB destination, legal title to the goods remains with the seller until the goods are delivered to the buyer by the transportation company.
5. (F) The primary basis of accounting for inventories is cost.
6. (T)
7. (T)
8. (T)
9. (T)
10. (T)
11. (F) Under the lower of cost or market basis, market is defined as current replacement cost, not selling price.
12. (T)
13. (F) This basis may also be applied to major categories of inventory or to total inventory.
14. (F) If beginning inventory is overstated, net income will be understated in the same year.
15. (T)

*16. (F) The cost of goods sold is based on the earliest goods on hand prior to the sale.
*17. (T)
*18. (T)
*19. (F) The cost to retail ratio is applied to the ending inventory at retail.
*20. (T)

MULTIPLE CHOICE

1. (b) Finished Goods (a) are inventory that is completed and ready for sale. Raw Materials (c) are inventory that is on hand waiting to be used in production. Merchandise inventory (d) does not apply to a manufacturing company.

2. (c) The company should add the cost of the goods ($10,000) that are in transit with the terms FOB destination. The goods were not included in the physical count because they were in transit on December 31. They should be included in inventory because legal title to these goods remains with the seller until these goods are delivered to the buyer by the transportation company.

3. (b) Under the FIFO method, the costs of the most recent purchases are assigned to the goods on hand as follows:

Date	Units		Unit Cost		Total Cost
Nov. 8	6,000	X	$7.00	=	$42,000
June 18	2,000	X	8.00	=	16,000
	8,000				$58,000

4. (c) Under the LIFO method, the costs of the earliest units purchased remain in inventory as follows:

Date	Units		Unit Cost		Total Cost
Jan. 1	300	X	$32.00	=	$ 9,600
Jan. 15	150	X	33.00	=	4,950
	450				$14,550

5. (d) Under the FIFO method, the costs of the most recent purchases are assigned to the goods on hand as follows:

Date	Units		Unit Cost		Total Cost
Jan. 25	100	X	$22.00	=	$2,200
Jan. 17	50	X	20.00	=	1,000
	150				$3,200

6. (b) Under the LIFO method, the cost of the earliest units purchased remains in inventory as follows:

Date	Units		Unit Cost		Total Cost
Jan. 1	150	X	$18.00	=	$2,700

7. (c) Average cost must be computed at the end of the accounting period based on the weighted average unit cost of goods available for sale during the period. The computation is as follows:

Date	Units		Unit Cost		Total Cost
Jan. 1	400	X	$1.00	=	$ 400
Jan. 8	600	X	1.10	=	660
	1,000				$1,060

$1,060 ÷ 1,000 = $1.06

8. (b) In a period of rising prices, FIFO will have a lower cost of goods sold than LIFO. This is because under FIFO, the earliest costs are assigned to cost of goods sold whereas under LIFO, the latest costs are assigned to cost of goods sold. Net purchases will be the same under either method.

9. (b) The use of LIFO method will result in a better matching of costs and revenues. The use of FIFO method will result in a more realistic inventory value (a). The use of the LIFO method will result in lower income taxes and lower net income not higher as answer (c) and (d) indicate.

10. (b) Under lower of cost or market (LCM), the personal computers cost $4,000 ($800 x 5) and a replacement cost of $2,250 ($450 x 5), therefore the personal computers should be valued at $2,250.

11. (b) The amount of loss is calculated by subtracting the market value of $2,250 from the cost of $4,000. Therefore, the loss for the personal computers is $1,750.

12. (b) The ending inventory on December 31, 2006, is the beginning inventory on January 1, 2007. When beginning inventory is overstated, then cost of goods sold will be overstated and net income will be understated. The Sales account will not be affected.

13. (c) By counting an inventory item twice, the ending inventory will be overstated. When ending inventory is overstated, net income is overstated and, therefore, owner's equity is overstated. The overstatement will have no effect on liabilities.

*14. (c) The cost of the 25 units sold on May 15: (20 X $20) + (5 X $22) = $510. The cost of the 10 units sold on May 24 is 10 X $22 = $220.

* 15. (a) The cost of the 25 units sold on May 15: (20 X $22) + (5 X $20) = $540. The cost of the 10 units sold on May 24 is 10 X $25 = $250.

* 16. (b) A moving average cost is computed after each purchase. The average unit cost is $21 after the May 14 purchase [($400 + $440) ÷ 40]. Thus, the cost of the May 15 sale is 25 X $21 = $525. After the May 21 purchase, average cost is $22.60 [($315 + $250) ÷ 25]. Thus, the cost of the May 24 sale is 10 X $22.60 = $226.

*17. (a) The estimated cost of ending inventory at March 31 under the gross profit method is as follows:

Net sales	$300,000
Less: Estimated gross profit ($30% X $300,000)	90,000
Estimated cost of goods sold	$210,000

Beginning inventory	$ 59,000
Cost of goods purchased	155,000
Cost of goods available for sale	214,000
Less: Estimated cost of goods sold	210,000
Estimated cost of ending inventory	$ 4,000

*18. (a) The estimated cost of ending inventory at December 31 under the gross profit method is as follows:

Net sales	$3,000,000
Less: Estimated gross profit (30% X $3,000,000)	900,000
Estimated cost of goods sold	$2,100,000

Beginning inventory	$ 550,000
Cost of goods purchased	2,250,000
Cost of goods available for sale	2,800,000
Less: Estimated cost of goods sold	2,100,000
Estimated cost of ending inventory	$ 700,000

Therefore the estimated cost of missing inventory is $100,000 ($700,000 - $600,000).

*19. (c) The cost to retail ratio is based on the cost of goods available for sale. The ratio is 75% ($97,500 ÷ $130,000).

*20. (c) The cost to retail ratio (75%) times the ending inventory at retail ($58,000) equals the ending inventory at cost ($43,500).

MATCHING

1. g
2. a
3. b
4. d
5. c
6. e
7. i
8. f
9. j
10. h

EXERCISES

EX. 6-1

For each of the inventory methods, the number of units available for sale and cost of goods available for sale should be computed as follows:

Pool of Costs
Cost of Goods Available for Sale

Date	Units		Unit Cost		Total Cost
1/1	200	X	$30	=	$ 6,000
5/5	240	X	28	=	6,720
8/8	350	X	31	=	10,850
11/29	300	X	33	=	9,900
	1,090				$33,470

Since 500 units are in ending inventory, 590 (1,090 - 500) units were sold.

FIFO Method

Ending inventory:

Date	Units		Unit Cost		Total Cost
11/29	300	X	$33	=	$ 9,900
8/8	200	X	31	=	6,200
	500				$16,100

Cost of goods sold: $33,470 - $16,100 = $17,370.

LIFO Method

Ending inventory:

Date	Units		Unit Cost		Total Cost
1/1	200	X	$30	=	$ 6,000
5/5	240	X	28	=	6,720
8/8	60	X	31	=	1,860
	500				$14,580

Cost of goods sold: $33,470 - $14,580 = $18,890.

Average Cost Method

Weighted average cost: = $33,470 ÷ 1,090 = $30.71 (rounded).

Ending inventory: = 500 X $30.71 = $15,355.

Cost of goods sold: = $33,470 - $15,355 = $18,115 or 590 units sold X $30.71 = $18,115 (rounded).

***EX. 6-2**

(a)

	Cost	Retail
Beginning inventory	$122,500	$175,000
Goods purchased	149,600	220,000
Goods available for sale	$272,100	395,000
Net sales		230,000
(1) Ending inventory at retail		$165,000

(2) Cost to retail ratio = ($272,100 ÷ $395,000) = 68.89%.

(3) Ending inventory at cost = ($165,000 X 68.89%) = $113,688.50.

(b)

Net sales	$230,000
Less: Estimated gross profit (30% X $230,000)	69,000
Estimated cost of goods sold	$161,000

Beginning inventory	$122,500
Cost of goods purchased	149,600
Cost of goods available for sale	272,100
Less: Estimated cost of goods sold	161,000
Estimated cost of ending inventory	$111,100

The Navigator ✓

- Scan Study Objectives ☐
- Read Preview ☐
- Read Chapter Review ☐
- Work Demonstration Problem ☐
- Answer True-False Statements ☐
- Answer Multiple-Choice Questions ☐
- Match Terms and Definitions ☐
- Solve Exercises ☐

CHAPTER 7

ACCOUNTING PRINCIPLES

CHAPTER STUDY OBJECTIVES

After studying this chapter, you should be able to:

1. Explain the meaning of generally accepted accounting principles and identify the key items of the conceptual framework.
2. Describe the basic objectives of financial reporting.
3. Discuss the qualitative characteristics of accounting information and elements of financial statements.
4. Identify the basic assumptions used by accountants.
5. Identify the basic principles of accounting.
6. Identify the two constraints in accounting.
7. Understand and analyze classified financial statements.
8. Explain the accounting principles used in international operations.

PREVIEW OF CHAPTER 7

This chapter explores the basic accounting principles followed in developing specific accounting guidelines. The content and organization of the chapter are as follows:

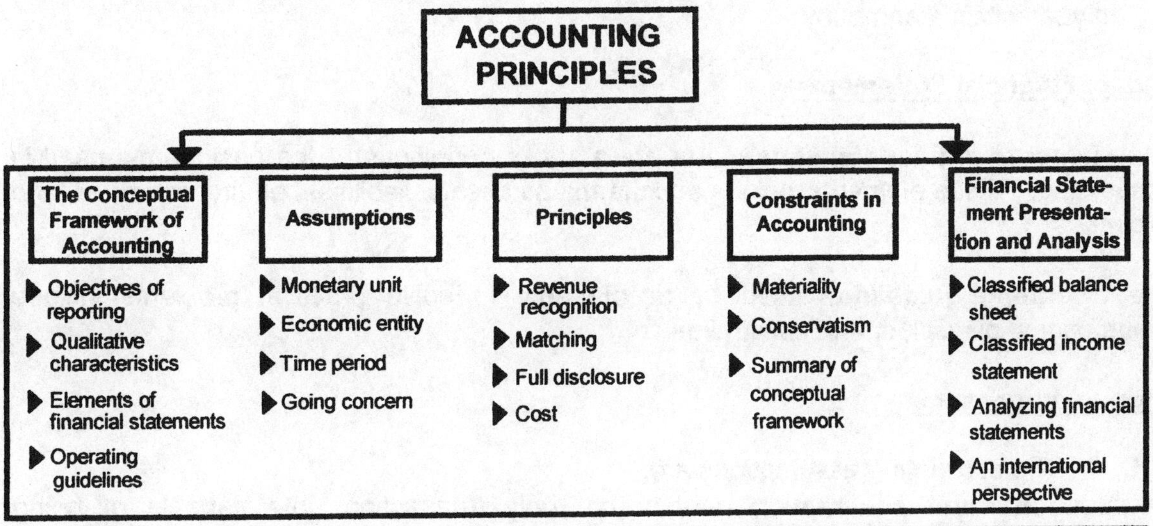

CHAPTER REVIEW

GAAP

1. (S.O. 1) **Generally accepted accounting principles (GAAP)** are a set of standards and rules that are recognized as a general guide for financial reporting purposes. These principles must have "substantial authoritative support."

2. The Financial Accounting Standards Board (FASB) has developed a **conceptual framework** to serve as a basis for resolving accounting and reporting problems. This framework consists of the following:
   a. Objectives of financial reporting.
   b. Qualitative characteristics of accounting information.
   c. Elements of financial statements.
   d. Operating guidelines (assumptions, principles, and constraints).

Objectives of Financial Reporting

3. (S.O. 2) The **objectives** of financial reporting are to provide information that is useful in (a) making investment and credit decisions; (b) assessing future cash flows; and (c) identifying the economic resources (assets), the claims to those resources (liabilities), and the changes in those resources and claims.

Qualitative Characteristics

4. (S.O. 3) The accounting alternative selected or policy adopted should be one that generates the most useful financial information for decision making. To be useful, information should possess the following **qualitative characteristics:**
   a. **Relevance.** The information must be capable of making a difference in a decision. Relevant information has either predictive or feedback value; and is also timely.
   b. **Reliability.** The information should be free of error and bias and be dependable.
   c. **Comparability.** The information should be comparable with accounting information about other enterprises.
   d. **Consistency**. The same accounting principles and methods should be used from year to year within a company.

Elements of Financial Statements

5. The **elements of financial statements** are a set of definitions of the basic terms used in accounting. These elements include such terms as assets, liabilities, equity, revenues, and expenses.

6. The **operating guidelines** used by accountants to solve practical problems include assumptions, principles, and constraints.

Accounting Assumptions

7. (S.O. 4) The accounting assumptions are:
   a. **Monetary unit assumption**—states that only transaction data capable of being expressed in terms of money should be included in the accounting records of the

economic entity. An important corollary is the added assumption that the unit of measure remains sufficiently constant over time.

b. **Economic entity assumption**—states that economic events can be identified with a particular unit of accountability.

c. **Time period assumption**—states that the economic life of a business can be divided into artificial time periods.

d. **Going concern assumption**—states that the enterprise will continue in operation long enough to carry out its existing objectives.

Principles

8. (S.O. 5) On the basis of these assumptions, the accounting profession has developed principles that dictate how transactions and other economic events should be recorded and reported.

9. The **revenue recognition principle** dictates that revenue should be recognized in the accounting period in which it is earned. When a sale is involved, revenue is recognized at the point of sale.

10. The **matching principle** requires that expenses be matched with revenues in the period in which efforts are expended to generate revenues. Expenses are not recognized when cash is paid, or the work performed; they are recognized when the labor (service) or product actually makes its contributions to revenue.
    a. Incurred costs that will only generate revenues in the current period are expended immediately. These costs are expired costs.
    b. Incurred costs that will generate revenues in current and future periods are recognized as **assets** when incurred, these costs are unexpired costs.
    c. Unexpired costs become expenses either as cost of goods sold or operating expenses.

11. The **full disclosure principle** requires that circumstances and events that make a difference to financial statement users be disclosed. Compliance with this principle occurs through the data contained in the financial statements and the information in the notes that accompany the statements. The first note in most cases is a **summary of significant accounting policies.**

12. The most basic principle of accounting is the **cost principle.**
    a. Cost is relevant because it represents the price paid, the assets sacrificed, or the commitment made at the date of acquisition.
    b. Cost is reliable because it is objectively measurable, factual and verifiable.

Price-Level Adjusted Data

13. While admitting that some changes in prices do occur, the accounting profession believes the unit of measure (e.g., the dollar) has remained sufficiently constant over time to produce meaningful financial information. If presented, the disclosure of price-level adjusted data is in the form of supplemental information presented with financial statements.

Constraints

14. (S.O. 6) There are **two constraints** in applying the operating guidelines.
    a. **Materiality** means that an item is likely to influence the decision of a reasonably prudent investor.
    b. **Conservatism** means that when in doubt choose the method that will be least likely to overstate assets and income.

Classified Statements

15. (S.O. 7) The **classified balance sheet** segregates assets into (1) current assets, (2) long-term investments, (3) property, plant and equipment, and (4) intangible assets. Liabilities are segregated into (1) current liabilities and (2) long-term liabilities.

16. If the form of organization is a proprietorship, the term "owner's equity" is used instead of "stockholders' equity." If the form of organization is a partnership, each partner has a separate capital account.

17. The **multiple-step income statement** includes the following:
    a. Sales revenue—presents sales, discounts, allowances and other related information.
    b. Cost of goods sold—indicates the cost of goods sold to produce sales.
    c. Operating expenses—provides information on both selling and administrative expenses.
    d. Other revenues and gains—indicates revenues earned or gains incurred from nonoperating transactions.
    e. Other expenses and losses—indicates expenses or losses incurred from nonoperating transactions.
    f. Income tax expense—indicates the taxes that must be paid.
    g. Earnings per share—indicates the net income earned by each share of outstanding common stock.

Earnings Per Share

18. Earnings per share is reported only for common stock. The formula for computing earnings per share when there has been no change in outstanding shares during the year is:

$$\frac{\text{Net income}}{\text{Number of common shares outstanding}} = \text{Earnings per share}$$

Analyzing Financial Statements

19. In analyzing and interpreting financial statement information, three major characteristics are generally evaluated: liquidity, profitability and solvency.

20. Liquidity is important in assessing the safety of a loan. Two methods of analyzing liquidity are (1) the current ratio and (2) working capital.
    a. The **current ratio** is calculated as follows: current assets ÷ current liabilities
    b. **Working capital** is calculated as follows: current assets - current liabilities

21. Profitability ratios measure the income or operating success of an enterprise for a given period of time. Three methods of analyzing profitability are (1) the profit margin percentage, (2) return on assets, and (3) return on common stockholders' equity.
    a. The profit margin percentage is calculated as follows: net income ÷ net sales
    b. The return on assets is calculated as follows: net income ÷ total assets
    c. The return on common stockholders' equity is calculated as follows: net income ÷ common stockholders' equity.

22. Solvency measures the ability of an enterprise to survive over a long period of time. One method of analyzing solvency is the debt to total assets ratio as follows:

total debt ÷ total assets

International Accounting Standards

23. (S.O. 8) World markets are becoming increasingly intertwined. Firms that conduct their operations in more than one country through subsidiaries, or branches in foreign countries are referred to as multinational corporations.

24. The International Accounting Standards Board (IASB) exists to obtain uniformity in international accounting practices. To date, numerous International Accounting Standards have been issued for IASB members to introduce to their respective countries.

The Navigator

DEMONSTRATION PROBLEM (S.O. 7)

The ledgers of Zullo's Inc. contain the following balances as of December 31, 2006 (its year end):

Advertising expense	$216,000
Depreciation expense	103,000
Gain on sale of land	16,200
Insurance expense	109,000
Interest expense	14,300
Interest revenue	26,900
Inventory, January 1	588,200
Inventory, December 31	608,300
Managerial salaries	262,800
Miscellaneous administrative expenses	43,500
Miscellaneous selling expenses	78,000
Net purchases	3,346,200
Net sales	5,347,100
Rent expense	168,000
Sales staff wages	318,000
Transportation in	55,800
Transportation out	13,200
Utilities expense	60,600

Income taxes are calculated at 30 percent of income; the company had 168,000 shares of common stock outstanding for the entire year.

Instructions

Prepare in good form a multi-step income statement for Zullo's Inc.

SOLUTION TO DEMONSTRATION PROBLEM

ZULLO'S INC.
Income Statement
For the Year Ended December 31, 2006

Net sales			$5,347,100
Cost of goods sold			
Inventory, January 1		$ 588,200	
Net purchases	$3,346,200		
Add: Transportation in	55,800		
Cost of goods purchased		3,402,000	
Cost of goods available		3,990,200	
Inventory, December 31		608,300	
Cost of goods sold			3,381,900
Gross profit			1,965,200
Operating expenses			
Selling expenses			
Advertising expense	216,000		
Sales staff wages	318,000		
Transportation out	13,200		
Miscellaneous selling expenses	78,000		
Total selling expenses		625,200	
Administrative expenses			
Managerial salaries	262,800		
Depreciation expense	103,000		
Insurance expense	109,000		
Rent expense	168,000		
Utilities expense	60,600		
Miscellaneous administrative expenses	43,500		
Total administrative expenses		746,900	
Total operating expenses			1,372,100
Income from operations			593,100
Other revenues and gains			
Interest revenue	26,900		
Gain on sale of land	16,200	43,100	
Other expenses and losses			
Interest expense		14,300	28,800
Income before income taxes			621,900
Income tax expense			186,570
Net income			$ 435,330
Earnings per share			$ 2.59

REVIEW QUESTIONS AND EXERCISES

TRUE—FALSE

Indicate whether each of the following is true (T) or false (F) in the space provided.

_____ 1. (S.O. 1) To be considered part of generally accepted accounting principles, a principle should have substantial authoritative support.

_____ 2. (S.O. 1) The conceptual framework consists of objectives, qualitative characteristics, elements, and operating guidelines.

_____ 3. (S.O. 2) The information provided by financial reporting cannot be used in assessing future cash flows.

_____ 4. (S.O. 3) If information is reliable, it has either predictive value or feedback value.

_____ 5. (S.O. 3) Comparability means using the same accounting principles and methods from year to year within a company.

_____ 6. (S.O. 3) It is not possible for a company to change to a new method of accounting because the information would not be consistent.

_____ 7. (S.O. 3) Elements of financial statements include a set of definitions for such terms as assets, liabilities, equity, revenues, and expenses.

_____ 8. (S.O. 4) The economic entity assumption states that the economic life of a business can be divided into artificial time periods.

_____ 9. (S.O. 4) The going concern assumption has been proven invalid due to numerous business failures.

_____ 10. (S.O. 4) The monetary unit assumption states that only transaction data capable of being expressed in terms of money should be included in the accounting records of the economic entity.

_____ 11. (S.O. 4) The time period assumption states that companies will pay their debts within specified time periods.

_____ 12. (S.O. 5) When the savings and loan industry recorded a large portion of its fees for granting a loan as revenue immediately, many thought this may have violated the revenue recognition principle.

_____ 13. (S.O. 5) Costs that will generate revenues only in the current accounting period are expensed immediately.

_____ 14. (S.O. 5) Costs carried as merchandise inventory are expensed in the period the goods are purchased by the merchandising company.

_____ 15. (S.O. 5) For most companies, the first note to the financial statements is the summary of significant accounting policies.

_____ 16. (S.O. 5) The cost principle is justified because it is considered both relevant and reliable.

_____ 17. (S.O. 7) In the classified income statement, "operating expenses" indicates the cost of goods sold to produce sales.

_____ 18. (S.O. 7) Because of the importance of earnings per share (EPS), most companies are required to report it on the face of the income statement.

_____ 19. (S.O. 7) The current ratio is often used to analyze a company's profitability.

_____ 20. (S.O. 7) The excess of current assets over current liabilities is called working capital.

_____ 21. (S.O. 7) Liquidity measures the ability of an enterprise to survive over a long period of time.

The Navigator

MULTIPLE CHOICE

Circle the letter that best answers each of the following statements.

1. (S.O. 2) According to the FASB's study, which of the following is **not** among the items concluded to be an objective of financial reporting?
   a. Provide information that is helpful in assessing future cash flows.
   b. Provide information that identifies the economic resources (assets), the claims to those resources (liabilities), and the changes in those resources and claims.
   c. Provide economic and financial information for managers and other internal users.
   d. Provide information that is useful to those making investment and credit decisions.

2. (S.O. 3) The characteristic of relevance does **not** include:
   a. predictive value.
   b. feedback value.
   c. faithful representation.
   d. timeliness.

3. (S.O. 3) "Last year's report is useless because it lost its capacity to influence decisions." Grumpy said to Dopey. What characteristic of relevancy is Grumpy trying to explain to Dopey?
   a. Predictive value.
   b. Feedback value.
   c. Timeliness.
   d. Verifiable value.

4. (S.O. 3) The characteristic of reliability does **not** include:
   a. verifiability.
   b. comparability.
   c. faithful representation.
   d. neutrality.

5. (S.O. 3) Consistency means that:
   a. accounting information is always relevant.
   b. accounting information is always reliable.
   c. different companies use the same accounting principles for similar transactions.
   d. the same accounting methods are used from year to year within a company.

6. (S.O. 3) Doc was looking at the financial statements of Sneezy Company and Bashful Company. Which qualitative characteristic is most important to Doc?
   a. Comparability.
   b. Consistency.
   c. Feedback value.
   d. Neutrality.

7. (S.O. 4) The time period assumption recognizes that:
   a. revenue should be recognized in the accounting period in which it is earned.
   b. the economic life of a business can be divided into artificial time periods.
   c. expenses should be recognized in the period of their association with earned revenue.
   d. economic events can be identified with a particular unit of accountability.

8. (S.O. 4) The going concern assumption recognizes that:
   a. economic events can be identified with a particular unit of accountability.
   b. when a sale is involved, revenue is recognized at the point of sale.
   c. because of numerous business failures, enterprises should be accounted for based on a finite life.
   d. the enterprise will continue in operation long enough to carry out its existing objectives and commitments.

9. (S.O. 5) The principle that expense recognition is traditionally tied to revenue recognition is the:
   a. matching principle.
   b. revenue recognition principle.
   c. comparability principle.
   d. consistency principle.

10. (S.O. 5) The principle that dictates that circumstances and events that make a difference to financial statement users be disclosed is the:
    a. reliability principle.
    b. relevance principle.
    c. full disclosure principle.
    d. monetary unit assumption.

11. (S.O. 5) Which of the following is considered an unexpired cost?
    a. Prepaid Insurance.
    b. Advertising.
    c. Sales Salaries.
    d. Repairs.

12. (S.O. 5) Cost is criticized as irrelevant because:
    a. it represents the price paid at the date of acquisition.
    b. it is the amount for which someone should be accountable.
    c. it is objectively measurable.
    d. subsequent to acquisition, cost is not equivalent to market value.

13. (S.O. 6) Zendejas Company purchased a ruler for $2.00. The ruler is expected to last for ten years. Leo, the accountant, expensed the cost of the ruler in the year of the purchase. Which constraint has Leo taken into account when making his accounting decision?
    a. Conservatism.
    b. Faithful Representation.
    c. Neutrality.
    d. Materiality.

14. (S.O. 6) Which of the following is an example of conservatism?
    a. Use of only the market method for inventories.
    b. Use of the FIFO method when prices are rising.
    c. Use of an accelerated depreciation method over a straight-line depreciation method.
    d. Use of the higher amount to record an asset than a lower amount.

15. (S.O. 7) Davies, Inc. had net income of $255,000 for the year ended December 31, 2006. On December 31, 2006 Davies had 200,000 shares of common stock authorized and 100,000 shares of common stock outstanding. On the same date, Davies had 20,000 shares of preferred stock authorized and 10,000 shares of preferred stock outstanding. What is Davies, Inc.'s earnings per share for December 31, 2006?
    a. $1.16.
    b. $1.28.
    c. $2.32.
    d. $2.55.

16. (S.O. 7) Callahan Company has total assets of $320,000, total liabilities of $220,000, current assets of $80,000 and current liabilities of $100,000. What is Callahan's current ratio?
    a. .69.
    b. .80.
    c. 1.25.
    d. 1.45.

17. (S.O. 7) Based on the information in question 16, what is Callahan's working capital?
    a. $100,000.
    b. ($100,000).
    c. $20,000.
    d. ($20,000).

18. (S.O. 7) Scacco Inc. has sales of $160,000, costs of goods sold of $80,000, net income of $10,000, total assets of $80,000, and total liabilities of $60,000. What is Scacco's return on assets?
    a. 12.50%.
    b. 16.67%.
    c. 20.00%.
    d. 75.00%

19. (S.O. 7) Which of the following is a ratio used to analyze profitability?
    a. The current ratio.
    b. Working capital.
    c. Return on assets.
    d. Debt to total assets.

20. (S.O. 8) Which of the following statements concerning international accounting is **incorrect?**
    a. There is little uniformity in accounting standards from country to country.
    b. There has been no effort to obtain uniformity in international accounting practices.
    c. Firms that conduct their operations in more than one country through subsidiaries, divisions, or branches in foreign countries are referred to as multinational corporations.
    d. World markets are becoming increasingly intertwined.

The Navigator

MATCHING

Match each term with its definition by writing the appropriate letter in the space provided.

Terms

_____ 1. Generally accepted accounting principles.

_____ 2. Conceptual framework.

_____ 3. Elements of financial statements.

_____ 4. Going concern assumption.

_____ 5. Comparability.

_____ 6. Materiality.

_____ 7. Full disclosure principle.

_____ 8. Monetary unit assumption.

_____ 9. Purchasing power.

_____ 10. Reliability.

_____ 11. Earnings per share.

_____ 12. Current ratio

Definitions

a. Definitions of basic terms used in accounting.

b. A set of rules and practices that are recognized as a general guide for financial reporting purposes.

c. The assumption that the enterprise will continue in operation long enough to carry out its existing objectives and commitments.

d. The quality of information that gives assurance that it is free of error and bias.

e. A coherent system of interrelated objectives and fundamentals that can lead to consistent standards.

f. The real value of the dollar determined by the goods and services for which it can be exchanged.

g. The constraint of determining if an item is important enough to likely influence the decision of a reasonably prudent investor or creditor.

h. Ability to compare accounting information of different companies because they use the same accounting principles.

i. Accounting assumption that only transaction data capable of being expressed in monetary terms should be included in accounting records.

j. Circumstances and events that make a difference to financial statement users that must be disclosed.

k. Current assets divided by current liabilities.

l. The net income earned by each share of outstanding common stock.

EX. 7-1 (S.O. 4, 5, and 6) Presented below are some business transactions that occurred during 2006 for Puck Company.

(a) The account receivable of $15,000 from Hermia Inc. was written off using the direct write-off method. The following entry was made:

Bad Debt Expense	15,000	
Accounts Receivable—Hermia		15,000

(b) A letter opener purchased from Helena, Co. costing $10 is being depreciated over 10 years. At year end the following entry was made:

Depreciation Expense—Letter Opener	1	
Accumulated Depreciation—Letter Opener		1

(c) The president of Puck Company, Demetrius, purchased a van for personal use and charged it to his expense account. The following entry was made:

Travel Expense	25,000	
Cash		25,000

Instructions

In each of the situations above, identify the assumption, principle, or constraint that has been violated, if any, and discuss the appropriateness of the journal entries. Give the correct journal entry, if necessary.

EX. 7-2 (S.O. 7) The adjusted trial balance of Mobile Fastners, Inc. as of December 31, 2006 (its year end) contains the following information:

Accounts payable	$235,000
Accounts receivable	210,000
Accumulated depreciation—Buildings	90,000
Accumulated depreciation—Equipment	287,200
Bonds payable	850,000
Buildings-Manufacturing plant	340,000
Cash	39,000
Common stock	250,000
Equipment	830,000
Income taxes payable	23,500
Interest payable	35,000
Interest receivable	11,000
Inventories	820,000
Investment in Wisnewski bonds (long-term)	300,000
Land	100,000
Mortgage payable (long-term)	155,500
Notes payable (short-term)	100,000
Prepaid advertising	4,800
Retained earnings (December 31, 2006)	645,600
Supplies	17,000

Instructions

Prepare in good form a classified balance sheet for Mobile Fastners, Inc.

SOLUTIONS TO REVIEW QUESTIONS AND EXERCISES

TRUE-FALSE

1. (T)
2. (T)
3. (F) One of the objectives of financial reporting is to provide information that is helpful in assessing future cash flows.
4. (F) If information is reliable, it is verifiable, a faithful representation, and neutral.
5. (F) Comparability means different companies use the same accounting principles to record similar transactions.
6. (F) It is possible for a company to change to a new method of accounting if management can justify that the new method results in more meaningful financial information.
7. (T)
8. (F) The economic entity assumption states that economic events can be identified with a particular unit of accountability.
9. (F) The going concern assumption is considered valid because experience indicates that, in spite of numerous business failures, companies have a fairly high continuance rate.
10. (T)
11. (F) The time period assumption states that the economic life of a business can be divided into artificial time periods.
12. (T)
13. (T)
14. (F) Costs carried as merchandise inventory are expensed as cost of goods sold in the period when the sale occurs.
15. (T)
16. (T)
17. (F) In the classified income statement, "operating expenses" provides information on both selling and administrative expenses.
18. (T)
19. (F) The current ratio is often used to analyze a company's liquidity.
20. (T)
21. (F) Solvency measures the ability of an enterprise to survive over a long period of time.

MULTIPLE CHOICE

1. (c) Providing economic and financial information for managers and other internal users is the primary objective of managerial accounting. Answers (a), (b), and (d) were all the items concluded as the objectives of financial reporting based on the FASB's study.

2. (c) Faithful representation pertains to the characteristic of reliability.

3. (c) For accounting information to be relevant it must be timely. That is, it must be available to decision makers before it loses its capacity to influence decisions.

4. (b) Comparability is one of the four qualitative characteristics.

5. (d) Choices (a) and (b) pertain to the characteristics of relevance and reliability, respectively. Choice (c) is a definition of comparability.

6. (a) Because Doc is looking at two different companies, he would like both companies to use the same accounting principles so he can compare one to the other.

7. (b) Choice (a) is the revenue recognition principle, choice (c) is the matching principle, and choice (d) is the economic entity assumption.

8. (d) Answer (a) is the economic entity assumption and answer (b) is the revenue recognition principle. Answer (c) is the opposite viewpoint from the going concern assumption.

9. (a) The principle that expense recognition is traditionally tied to revenue recognition is the matching principle.

10. (c) The principle that dictates that circumstances and events that make a difference to financial statement users be disclosed is the full disclosure principle.

11. (a) Examples of unexpired costs are Merchandise Inventory not sold yet, Supplies, Prepaid Insurance and Prepaid Rent. Answers (b), (c), and (d) are all examples of expired costs.

12. (d) Choices (a), (b), and (c) are all arguments in favor of the cost principle.

13. (d) Leo has taken "materiality" into account. Materiality relates to an item's impact on a firm's overall financial operations. Although the proper accounting would be to depreciate the ruler over a ten-year period, the cost and time to depreciate the item is far greater than the impact of $2.00 on the financial statements. Leo's ultimate decision to expense or capitalize would rest on whether the cost of the item would impact the decision of a reasonably prudent investor or creditor.

14. (c) Conservatism in accounting means that when in doubt the accountant should choose the method that will be least likely to overstate assets and income. Answer (a) is incorrect because the lower of cost of market would be conservative. Answer (b) is incorrect because using the LIFO method when prices are rising would be conservative. Answer (d) is incorrect because using a lower amount to record an asset would be conservative.

15. (d) Earnings per share is calculated by dividing net income of $255,000 by the number of shares outstanding

($2.55 = $255,000 ÷ 100,000).

16. (b) The current ratio is calculated by dividing current assets by current liabilities

(.80 = $80,000 ÷ $100,000).

17. (d) Working capital is the excess of current assets over current liabilities

(-$20,000 = $80,000 - $100,000).

18. (a) The return on assets is calculated by dividing net income by total assets

(12.5% = $10,000 ÷ $80,000).

19. (c) Profitability is analyzed by the return on assets.

20. (b) Some efforts have been made to obtain uniformity in international accounting practices. In 1973 the International Accounting Standards Board (IASB) was formed by agreement of accounting organizations from many countries.

MATCHING

1.	b	5.	h	9.	f
2.	e	6.	g	10.	d
3.	a	7.	j	11.	l
4.	c	8.	i	12.	k

EXERCISES

EX. 7-1

(a) The matching principle requires that expenses be matched with revenues in the period in which the efforts are expended to generate revenues. The direct write-off method is not acceptable according to GAAP. Instead, the bad debt expenses are better matched with revenue if an estimate is made during each period and an allowance for doubtful accounts is used. If Puck Company had been estimating a bad debt expense each year, the following entry would have been made at the time it was determined the Hermia account receivable was uncollectible.

Allowance for Doubtful Accounts	15,000	
Accounts Receivable		15,000

(b) Although the proper accounting would be to depreciate the letter opener over a ten-year period, the cost and time to depreciate the item is far greater than the impact of $10.00 on the financial statements. Therefore, taking materiality into account, it would probably be acceptable to expense the whole $10.00 in the year of the purchase. To decide whether an item is material or not, an accountant should take into account whether the item is likely to influence the decision of a reasonably prudent investor or creditor. At the time of the purchase, the letter opener could have been expensed as follows:

Supplies Expense	10	
Cash		10

(c) By including personal assets within the company, the economic entity assumption has been violated. The economic entity assumption states that economic events can be identified with a particular unit of accountability. At the time of purchasing the van, the company should not have paid for the van and therefore no entry would have been needed.

EX. 7-2

MOBILE FASTNERS, INC.
Balance Sheet
December 31, 2006

Assets

Current assets			
Cash		$ 39,000	
Accounts receivable		210,000	
Interest receivable		11,000	
Supplies		17,000	
Inventories		820,000	
Prepaid advertising		4,800	
Total current assets			$1,101,800
Long-term investments			
Investments in Wisnewski bonds			300,000
Property, plant, and equipment			
Equipment	$830,000		
Less: Accumulated depreciation	287,200	542,800	
Buildings—Manufacturing plant	340,000		
Less: Accumulated depreciation	90,000	250,000	
Land		100,000	
Total property, plant, and equipment			892,800
Total Assets			$2,294,600

Liabilities and Stockholders' Equity

Current liabilities			
Accounts payable		$235,000	
Notes payable		100,000	
Interest payable		35,000	
Income taxes payable		23,500	
Total current liabilities			$ 393,500
Long-term liabilities			
Mortgage payable		155,500	
Bonds payable		850,000	
Total long-term liabilities			1,005,500
Total liabilities			1,399,000
Stockholders' equity			
Common stock		250,000	
Retained earnings		645,600	
Total stockholders' equity			895,600
Total Liabilities and Stockholders' Equity			$2,294,600

The Navigator ✓

- Scan Study Objectives ☐
- Read Preview ☐
- Read Chapter Review ☐
- Work Demonstration Problem ☐
- Answer True-False Statements ☐
- Answer Multiple-Choice Questions ☐
- Match Terms and Definitions ☐
- Solve Exercises ☐

Chapter 8

INTERNAL CONTROL AND CASH

CHAPTER STUDY OBJECTIVES

After studying this chapter, you should be able to:

1. Define internal control.
2. Identify the principles of internal control.
3. Explain the applications of internal control principles to cash receipts.
4. Explain the applications of internal control principles to cash disbursements.
5. Describe the operation of a petty cash fund.
6. Indicate the control features of a bank account.
7. Prepare a bank reconciliation.
8. Explain the reporting of cash.

PREVIEW OF CHAPTER 8

The organization and content of Chapter 8 are as follows:

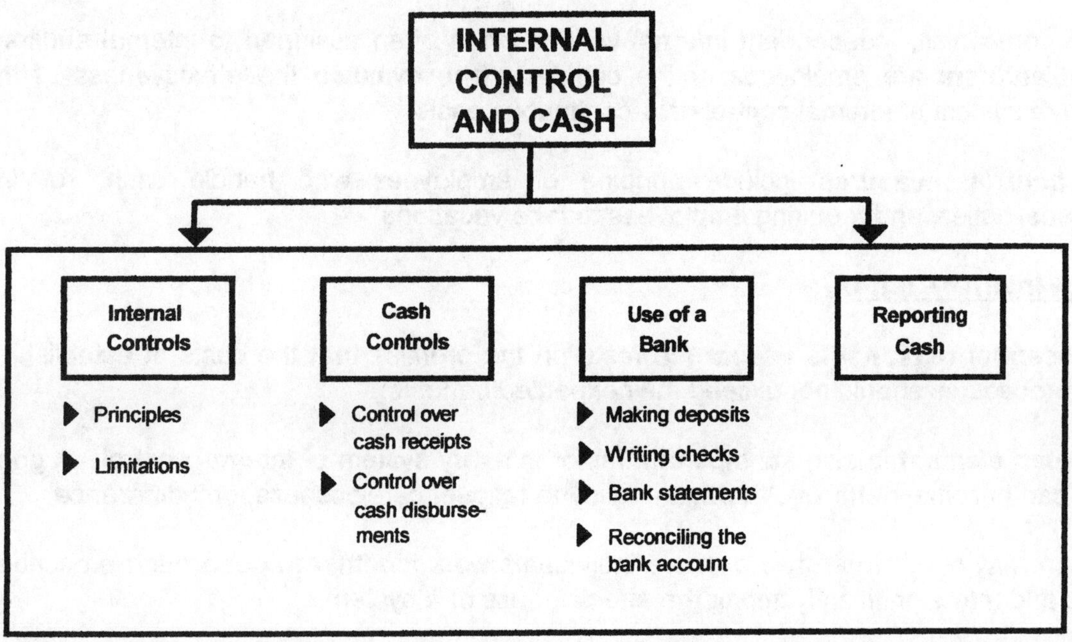

CHAPTER REVIEW

Internal Control

1. (S.O. 1) **Internal control** consists of the plan of organization and all the related methods and measures adopted within a business to (a) safeguard its assets and (b) enhance the accuracy and reliability of its accounting records.

2. (S.O. 2) An essential characteristic of internal control is the **establishment of responsibility** to specific employees. Control is most effective when only one person is responsible for a given task.

3. The rationale for segregation of duties is this: The work of one employee should, without a duplication of effort, provide a reliable basis for evaluating the work of another employee.

4. The responsibility for related transactions should be assigned to different individuals, and the responsibility for establishing the **accountability for an asset** should be separate from the physical custody of that asset.

5. **Documentation procedures** provide evidence that transactions and events have occurred.

6. **Physical, mechanical, and electronic controls** relate primarily to the safeguarding of assets and include such measures as safes for the storage of cash prior to deposit, bank vaults for the deposit of cash, safety deposit boxes for the storage of important business papers, fences around storage areas, and locked warehouses for inventories.

7. Mechanical and electronic controls include electronic burglar alarms, television monitors, sensors on garments, cash registers, time clocks and built-in hardware controls.

8. Most systems of internal control provide for **independent internal verification.** This principle involves the review, comparison, and reconciliation of data prepared by one or several employees.

9. In large companies, independent internal verification is often assigned to internal auditors. **Internal auditors** are employees of the company who evaluate the effectiveness of the company's system of internal control on a continuous basis.

10. **Other control measures** include bonding of employees who handle cash, rotating employees' duties, and requiring employees to take vacations.

Limitations of Internal Control

11. The concept of **reasonable assurance** rests on the premise that the costs of establishing control procedures should not exceed their expected benefits.

12. The **human element** is also an important factor in every system of internal control. A good system can become ineffective through employee fatigue, carelessness, or indifference.

13. **Collusion** may result when two or more individuals work together to get around prescribed controls and may significantly impair the effectiveness of a system.

Cash

14. Cash consists of coins, currency (paper money), checks, money orders, and money on hand or on deposit in a bank or similar depository. To safeguard cash and to assure the accuracy of the accounting records for cash, effective internal control over cash is imperative.

Internal Control Over Cash Receipts

15. (S.O. 3) The application of internal control principles to **cash receipts transactions** includes: (1) only designated personnel should be authorized to handle or have access to cash receipts; (2) different individuals should be assigned the duties of receiving cash, recording cash receipt transactions, and having custody of cash; (3) documents should include remittance advices, cash register tapes, and deposit slips; (4) cash should be stored in company safes and bank vaults, access to storage areas should be limited to authorized personnel, and cash registers should be used in executing over-the-counter receipts; (5) daily cash counts and daily comparisons of total receipts should be made; and (6) all personnel who handle cash receipts should be bonded and required to take vacations.

16. Control of over-the-counter receipts is centered on cash registers that are visible to customers.

Internal Control Over Cash Disbursements

17. (S.O. 4) Generally, internal control over cash disbursements is more effective when payments are made by check rather than by cash, except for incidental amounts that are paid out of petty cash.

18. The application of internal control principles to **cash disbursements transactions** includes: (1) only specified individuals should be authorized to sign checks; (2) different departments or individuals should be assigned the duties of approving an item for payment and paying it; (3) prenumbered checks should be used and each check should be supported by an approved invoice or other document; (4) blank checks should be stored in a safe and access should be restricted to authorized personnel, and a check writer machine should be used to imprint the amount on the check in indelible ink; (5) each check should be compared with the approved invoice before it is issued; and (6) following payment, the approved invoice (or form) should be stamped PAID.

Voucher System

19. A **voucher system** is often used to enhance the internal control over cash disbursements. A voucher system is an extensive network of approvals by authorized individuals acting independently to ensure that all disbursements by check are proper. A voucher system includes the use of authorization forms called **vouchers** which are recorded by the accounting department in the voucher register.

Electronic Funds Transfer

20. **Electronic Funds Transfer (EFT)** is a disbursement system that uses wire, telephone, telegraph or computer to send cash from one location to another.

Petty Cash Fund

21. (S.O. 5) A petty cash fund is a cash fund used to pay relatively small amounts.
    a. The operation of the fund, often called an imprest system, involves (1) establishing the fund, (2) making payments from the fund, and (3) replenishing the fund.
    b. Accounting entries are required when (1) the fund is established, (2) the fund is replenished, and (3) the amount of the fund is changed.

Use of a Bank

22. (S.O. 6) The use of a bank minimizes the amount of currency that must be kept on hand and therefore contributes significantly to good internal control over cash.

23. A check is a written order signed by the depositor directing the bank to pay a specified sum of money to a designated recipient. The three parties to a check are as follows:
    a. The maker (or drawer) who issues the check.
    b. The bank (or payer) on which the check is drawn.
    c. The payee to whom the check is payable.

24. A bank statement shows (a) checks paid and other debits charged against the account, (b) deposits and other credits made to the account, and (c) the account balance after each day's transactions.

25. A bank debit memoranda is usually included with the bank statement to indicate charges against the depositor's account such as a bank service charge, cost of printing checks, issuing traveler's checks, and when a previously deposited customer's check "bounces" because of insufficient funds (NSF check).

26. A bank credit memoranda shows such items as the collection of a note receivable for the depositor by the bank.

Reconciling the Bank Account

27. (S.O. 7) A **reconciliation** of a bank account is necessary because the balance per bank and balance per books are seldom in agreement. The lack of agreement may be the result of **time lags** and **errors.**

28. To obtain maximum benefit from a **bank reconciliation,** the reconciliation should be prepared by an employee who has no other responsibilities pertaining to cash.

29. In reconciling the bank statement, it is customary to reconcile the balance per books and balance per bank to their adjusted cash balances. The reconciliation schedule consists of two sections. The steps in preparing a bank reconciliation are:

a. Determine deposits in transit.
b. Determine outstanding checks.
c. Note any errors discovered.
d. Trace bank memoranda to the records.

30. Each reconciling item used in determining the adjusted cash balance per books should be recorded by the depositor.

Reporting Cash

31. (S.O. 8) Cash on hand, cash in banks, and petty cash are often combined and reported simply as **Cash.** Because it is the most liquid asset, cash is listed first in the current asset section of the balance sheet under the title "cash and cash equivalents." **Cash equivalents** are highly liquid investments, with maturities of 3 months or less when purchased, that can be converted into a specific amount of cash. They include money market funds, money market savings certificates, bank certificates of deposit, and U.S. Treasury bills and notes.

DEMONSTRATION PROBLEM (S.O. 7)

The information below relates to the Cash in Bank account in the ledger of Mozart Corporation for November, 2006:

Balance November 1—$27,100.	Cash deposited—$94,500.
Balance November 30—$28,200.	Checks written—$93,400.

The November bank statement shows:

Balance, November 30	$26,950
Credit memorandum:	
Collection of note by bank including $27 of interest	1,000
Debit memorandum:	
NSF check: G.F. Handel	425
Bank service charge	25

At November 30, deposits in transit amounted to $7,200 and outstanding checks totaled $5,400.

Instructions
Prepare the bank reconciliation at November 30, 2006.

The Navigator

SOLUTION TO DEMONSTRATION PROBLEM

MOZART CORPORATION
Bank Reconciliation
November 30, 2006

Cash balance per bank statement		$26,950
Add: Deposits in transit		7,200
		34,150
Less: Outstanding checks		5,400
Adjusted cash balance per bank		$28,750
Cash balance per books		$28,200
Add: Collection of note receivable		1,000
		29,200
Less: NSF check	$425	
Bank service charge	25	450
Adjusted cash balance per books		$28,750

REVIEW QUESTIONS AND EXERCISES

TRUE—FALSE

Indicate whether each of the following is true (T) or false (F) in the space provided.

_____ 1. (S.O. 1) Internal control consists of the plan of organization and all of the related methods and measures adopted within a business to (a) safeguard its assets, and (b) enhance the accuracy and reliability of its accounting records.

_____ 2. (S.O. 2) Internal control is most effective when only one person is responsible for a given task.

_____ 3. (S.O. 2) The responsibility for related transactions should be assigned to one person.

_____ 4. (S.O. 2) The responsibility for establishing the accountability for an asset should be separate from the physical custody of that asset.

_____ 5. (S.O. 2) In general, documents should be prenumbered and all documents should be accounted for.

_____ 6. (S.O. 2) Internal auditors are specialists hired from other companies to evaluate the effectiveness of the company's system of internal control.

_____ 7. (S.O. 2) The concept of reasonable assurance rests on the premise that the costs of establishing control procedures should not exceed their expected benefits.

_____ 8. (S.O. 2) The human element is an important factor in every system of internal control.

_____ 9. (S.O. 2) Collusion may result when one individual circumvents prescribed controls and may significantly impair the effectiveness of a system.

_____ 10. (S.O. 3) Only designated personnel should be authorized to handle or have access to cash receipts.

_____ 11. (S.O. 3) Personnel who handle cash receipts should have the option of taking a vacation or not.

_____ 12. (S.O. 3) Control of over-the-counter receipts is centered on cash registers that are visible to customers.

_____ 13. (S.O. 4) The duties of approving an item for payment and paying the item should be done by different departments or individuals.

_____ 14. (S.O. 4) Electronic Funds Transfer is a system that uses computers to send cash from one location to another.

_____ 15. (S.O. 5) The custodian of the petty cash fund has the responsibility of recording a journal entry every time cash is used from the fund.

_____ 16. (S.O. 6) The three parties to a check are the maker, the drawer, and the bank.

_____ 17. (S.O. 6) A debit memoranda could show the collection of a note receivable by the bank.

_____ 18. (S.O. 7) The lack of agreement between the balance of the bank and the balance of the books may be the result of time lags and errors.

_____ 19. (S.O. 7) To obtain maximum benefit from a bank reconciliation, the reconciliation should be prepared by an employee who has no other responsibilities pertaining to cash.

_____ 20. (S.O. 7) In a bank reconciliation, outstanding checks are added to the balance per books to obtain the adjusted balance per books.

The Navigator

MULTIPLE CHOICE

Circle the letter that best answers each of the following statements.

1. (S.O. 1) Which of the following is **not** considered a part of the definition of internal control?
   a. Safeguard its assets.
   b. Enhance the accuracy and reliability of its accounting records.
   c. Assignment of responsibility to specific individuals.
   d. The plan of organization.

2. (S.O. 2) An example of poor internal control is:
   a. The accountant should not have physical custody of the asset nor access to it.
   b. The custodian of an asset should not maintain or have access to the accounting records.
   c. One person should be responsible for handling related transactions.
   d. A salesperson should make the sale, and a different person ships the goods.

3. (S.O. 2) Independent internal verification is not involved when an independent person:
   a. reconciles the cash balance per books with the cash balance per the bank.
   b. reviews the accounts receivable subsidiary ledger.
   c. makes a surprise count of the petty cash fund.
   d. is responsible for making sales and recording the entries in the books.

4. (S.O. 2) Internal auditors

	are employees of the company	review activities of departments for compliance with prescribed internal controls
a.	yes	yes
b.	yes	no
c.	no	yes
d.	no	no

5. (S.O. 2) Which of the following is **not** a physical, mechanical, or electronic control?
   a. Bonding employees who handle cash.
   b. Employee identification badges.
   c. Safety deposit boxes.
   d. Fences around storage areas.

6. (S.O. 2) Which of the following is **not** an example of an effective internal control measure?
   a. Requiring employees to take vacations.
   b. Prenumbering sales invoices.
   c. Bonding employees who handle cash.
   d. Permitting collusion among employees.

7. (S.O. 2) Which of the following statements concerning the limitations of internal control is **correct?**
   a. The human factor is unimportant.
   b. The costs of establishing control procedures should not exceed their expected benefit.
   c. Collusion among employees may result in more effective control.
   d. A system of internal control should be infallible.

8. (S.O. 3) Which of the following is **not** cash?
   a. Money orders.
   b. Postdated checks.
   c. Bank deposits.
   d. Currency.

9. (S.O. 3) Effective control over cash receipts transactions does **not** result when:
   a. cash registers are used in executing cash receipts transactions.
   b. personnel who handle cash receipts are bonded.
   c. company safes and vaults are used for the storage of cash prior to deposit.
   d. one individual is responsible for the receiving, recording, and custody of cash receipts.

10. (S.O. 3) Independent internal verification over cash receipts transactions does **not** occur when:
    a. cashiers make daily cash counts of cash register totals.
    b. the treasurer's office makes daily comparisons of total receipts and receipts deposited in the bank.
    c. an internal auditor reconciles bank and book balances monthly.
    d. none of the above.

11. (S.O. 3) Storing cash in a company safe is an application of which internal control principle?
    a. Segregation of duties.
    b. Documentation procedures.
    c. Physical controls.
    d. Establishment of responsibility.

12. (S.O. 4) All but one of the following statements about internal control over cash disbursements are correct. The **incorrect** statement is:
    a. More effective internal control results when payments are made by check rather than in cash.
    b. The bank reconciliation should be prepared by the employee who writes the checks.
    c. The use of a bank contributes significantly to good internal control over cash disbursements.
    d. Prenumbered checks should be used and all checks in a series should be accounted for.

13. (S.O. 4) An application of good internal control over cash disbursements is:
    a. Following payment, the approved invoice should be stamped PAID.
    b. Blank checks should be stored in the treasurer's desk.
    c. Each check should be compared with the approved invoice after the check is issued.
    d. Check signers should record the cash disbursements.

14. (S.O. 5) When making a payment from the petty cash fund for postage stamps, the following journal entry is made.

		Debit	Credit
a.	Office Supplies	XXXX	
	Petty Cash		XXXX
b.	Postage Expense	XXXX	
	Petty Cash		XXXX
c.	Miscellaneous Expense.........	XXXX	
	Petty Cash		XXXX
d.	No entry is made.		

15. (S.O. 5) A $100 petty cash fund contains $92 in receipts and $7 in cash. The entry to record replenishments of the fund will include a debit to:
    a. Petty Cash for $100.
    b. Cash Over and Short for $1.
    c. Expenses for $93.
    d. Petty Cash for $8.

16. (S.O. 6) Which of the following statements is **false?**
    a. The use of a bank contributes significantly to good internal control over cash.
    b. Many companies have only one bank account.
    c. Use of a bank minimizes the amount of currency that must be kept on hand.
    d. A company can safeguard its cash by using a bank as a depository and clearing house for checks received and checks written.

17. (S.O. 6) The person who issues the check is known as the:
    a. maker.
    b. payer.
    c. payee.
    d. drawee.

18. (S.O. 6) A bank may issue a credit memoranda for:
    a. a bank service charge.
    b. an NSF (not sufficient funds) check from a customer.
    c. the collection of a note receivable for the depositor by the bank.
    d. the cost of printing checks.

19. (S.O. 7) Which of the following reconciling items would be added to the balance per bank statement to determine the adjusted balance per bank?

	Deposits in transit	Outstanding checks	NSF checks
a.	yes	yes	yes
b.	no	yes	no
c.	yes	no	no
d.	yes	yes	no

20. (S.O. 8) Cash equivalents are highly liquid investments that can be converted into a specific amount of cash with maturities of:
    a. 1 month or less when purchased.
    b. 3 months or less when purchased.
    c. 6 months or less when purchased.
    d. 1 year or less when purchased.

The Navigator

MATCHING

Match each term with its definition by writing the appropriate letter in the space provided.

Terms

_____ 1. Internal control.

_____ 2. Cash.

_____ 3. NSF check.

_____ 4. Internal auditors.

_____ 5. Outstanding checks.

_____ 6. Deposits in transit.

_____ 7. Bank statement.

_____ 8. Petty cash fund.

_____ 9. Electronic funds transfer.

Definitions

a. Resources that consist of coins, currency, checks, money orders, and money on hand or on deposit in a bank.

b. Company employees who evaluate the effectiveness of the company's system of internal control on a continuous basis.

c. A cash fund used to pay small amounts.

d. A check that is not paid by a bank because of insufficient funds in a customer's bank account.

e. The plan of organization and all of the related methods and measures adopted within a business to safeguard its assets and enhance the accuracy and reliability of its accounting records.

f. A statement received monthly from the bank that shows the depositor's bank transactions and balances.

g. A disbursement system that uses wire, telephone, telegraph or computer to transfer cash from one location to another.

h. Deposits recorded by the depositor that have not been recorded by the bank.

i. Checks issued and recorded by the company that have not been paid by the bank.

The Navigator

EXERCISES

EX. 8-1 Avison Company uses a petty cash fund for small cash disbursements. The following transactions occurred during July.

July 1 Established a petty cash fund of $200.

4 Paid freight costs on goods purchased $52. Issued receipt ticket No. 1.

8 Paid $37 postage expense. Issued receipt ticket No. 2.

15 Paid miscellaneous expenses $29. Issued receipt tickets Nos. 3 and 4.

20 Paid delivery costs on goods sold $44. Issued receipt ticket No. 5.

24 Paid $35 for office supplies expense. Issued receipt ticket No. 6.

25 Replenished petty cash fund by issuing a check for $197.

31 Increased petty cash fund to $300.

Instructions
Journalize the entries that affect the Petty Cash account by using the general journal on the next page.

General Journal			J1
Date	Account Title	Debit	Credit

EX. 8-2 (S.O. 6) As of January 31, 2006, the Beethoven Company had the following facts concerning cash in bank.

1. Balance per bank, $55,000.
2. Balance per books, $53,965.
3. Deposits in transit, $4,000.
4. Outstanding checks: No. 305, $1,000; No. 308, $2,500; and No. 310, $3,000.
5. Error: Check No. 301 for $3,416 was correctly paid by the bank but was recorded by the company for $3,461. This check was a payment on account to a creditor.
6. Two bank debit memoranda are unrecorded.
   a. NSF check from Franz Schubert for $3,000 on account.
   b. A bank service charge of $10.
7. One bank credit memorandum is unrecorded. A note receivable for $1,450 plus interest of $50 was collected by the bank. The interest has been accrued by Beethoven Company.

Instructions

(a) Prepare a bank reconciliation for the Beethoven Company for the month ended January 31, 2006.

(b) Journalize the adjusting entries for Beethoven Company on January 31, 2006.

(a)

BEETHOVEN COMPANY
Bank Reconciliation
January 31, 2006

(b)

General Journal			J1
Date	Account Title	Debit	Credit

The Navigator

SOLUTIONS TO REVIEW QUESTIONS AND EXERCISES

TRUE-FALSE

1. (T)
2. (T)
3. (F) The responsibility for related transactions should be assigned to different individuals.
4. (T)
5. (T)
6. (F) Internal auditors are employees of the company.
7. (T)
8. (T)
9. (F) Collusion results when two or more individuals circumvent prescribed controls and may significantly impair the effectiveness of the system.
10. (T)
11. (F) For good internal control, all persons who handle cash should be required to take vacations.
12. (T)
13. (T)
14. (T)
15. (F) An entry is not made every time petty cash is used.
16. (F) The maker and drawer are one and the same. The three parties to a check are the maker (or drawer), the bank (or payer), and the payee.
17. (F) A debit memoranda shows charges to the account such as a bank service charge, and the cost of printing checks. A credit memoranda will show the collection of a note receivable.
18. (T)
19. (T)
20. (F) Outstanding checks are subtracted from the balance per bank to obtain the adjusted balance per bank.

MULTIPLE CHOICE

1. (c) Internal control consists of the plan of organization and all of the related methods and measures adopted within a business to safeguard its assets and enhance the accuracy and reliability of its accounting data.

2. (c) Answers (a), (b), and (d) are all considered a part of good internal control. The responsibility for related transactions should be assigned to different individuals.

3. (d) Independent internal verification involves the review, comparison, and reconciliation of information from two different sources. Answers (a), (b), and (c) are all considered to be independent internal verification. Answer (d) has nothing to do with internal verification and actually is considered poor internal control.

4. (a) Internal auditors are employees of the company who evaluate the effectiveness of the company's system of internal control on a year-round basis. In addition, they review the activities of departments for compliance with prescribed internal controls.

5. (a) Physical, mechanical, and electronic controls relate primarily to the safeguarding of assets and include the measures identified in (b), (c), and (d). Another control measure, but not a physical control, is the bonding of employees who handle cash.

6. (d) Answers (a), (b), and (c) are effective internal control measures. Permitting collusion among employees is bad internal control, because collusion between two or more individuals to circumvent prescribed controls may significantly impair the effectiveness of a system.

7. (b) The human factor (a) is important because internal control may become ineffective through employee fatigue and indifference. Answer (c) may significantly impair the system of internal control because collusion circumvents prescribed controls. No internal control system is infallible.

8. (b) Cash consists of coins, currency (paper money), checks, money orders, and money on deposit in a bank or similar depository. Postdated checks are classified as accounts receivable.

9. (d) Answers (a), (b), and (c) are valid statements. Answer (d) is a violation of the principle of segregation of duties.

10. (a) A cashier department supervisor should make the daily cash count, not the cashiers, because the cashiers would be checking their own work. Answers (b) and (c) are applications of independent internal verification.

11. (c) Storing cash in a company safe is an application of physical controls.

12. (b) This answer choice is a violation of the principle of independent internal verification. An independent individual should prepare the bank reconciliation.

13. (a) Following payment, the approved invoice (or form) should be stamped PAID to prevent it from being resubmitted for payment at a later date. Answer (b) is incorrect because blank checks should be stored in a safe. Answer (c) is incorrect because the comparison should be made before the check is issued. Answer (d) is a violation of segregation of duties; check signers should not record the checks.

14. (d) No entry is made when a petty cash payment occurs. Each payment, though, must be documented on a prenumbered petty cash receipt.

15. (b) The entry is:

Expenses	92.00	
Cash Over and Short	1.00	
Cash		93.00

16. (b) Many companies have more than one bank account. They use regional bank accounts, payroll bank accounts and other accounts to obtain short-term loans.

17. (a) The three parties to a check are (1) the maker (or drawer) who issues the check, (2) the bank (or payer) on which the check is drawn, and (3) the payee to whom the check is payable.

18. (c) The collection of a note receivable results in a credit memoranda. The bank service charge (a), NSF checks (b), and the cost of printing checks (d) all result in debit memoranda.

19. (c) Deposits in transit are added to the balance per bank statement, outstanding checks are deducted from the balance per bank, and NSF checks are deducted from the balance per books.

20. (b) A cash equivalent is defined as a highly liquid investment with a maturity of 3 months or less when purchased, that can be converted into a specific amount of cash.

MATCHING

1. e.	4. b.	7. f.
2. a.	5. i.	8. c.
3. d.	6. h.	9. g.

EXERCISES

EX. 8-1

General Journal			J1
Date	Account Title	Debit	Credit
July 1	Petty Cash	200	
	Cash in Bank		200
	(To establish petty cash fund)		
25	Freight-in	52	
	Postage Expense	37	
	Miscellaneous Expense	29	
	Delivery Expense	44	
	Office Supplies Expense	35	
	Cash in Bank		197
	(To replenish petty cash fund)		
31	Petty Cash	100	
	Cash in Bank		100
	(To increase petty cash fund)		

EX. 8-2

(a)

BEETHOVEN COMPANY
Bank Reconciliation
January 31, 2006

Cash balance per bank statement			$55,000
Add:	Deposits in transit		4,000
			59,000
Less:	Outstanding checks		
	No. 305	$1,000	
	No. 308	2,500	
	No. 310	3,000	6,500
Adjusted cash balance per bank			$52,500
Cash balance per books			$53,965
Add:	Collection of $1,450 note receivable plus interest $50	$1,500	
	Error in recording check No. 301	45	1,545
			55,510
Less:	NSF check	3,000	
	Bank service charge	10	3,010
Adjusted cash balance per books			$52,500

(b)

General Journal			J1
Date	Account Title	Debit	Credit
2006 Jan. 31	Cash	1,500	
	Miscellaneous Expense	25	
	Notes Receivable		1,450
	Interest Receivable		75
	(To record collection of note		
	receivable by bank)		
31	Cash	45	
	Accounts Payable		45
	(To correct error in recording		
	check No. 301)		
31	Accounts Receivable—Franz Schubert	3,000	
	Cash		3,000
	(To replenish NSF check)		
31	Miscellaneous Expense	10	
	Cash		10
	(To record January bank service		
	charge)		

The Navigator ✓

- *Scan Study Objectives* ☐
- *Read Preview* ☐
- *Read Chapter Review* ☐
- *Work Demonstration Problem* ☐
- *Answer True-False Statements* ☐
- *Answer Multiple-Choice Questions* ☐
- *Match Terms and Definitions* ☐
- *Solve Exercises* ☐

Chapter 9

ACCOUNTING FOR RECEIVABLES

CHAPTER STUDY OBJECTIVES

After studying this chapter, you should be able to:

1. Identify the different types of receivables.
2. Explain how accounts receivable are recognized in the accounts.
3. Distinguish between the methods and bases used to value accounts receivable.
4. Describe the entries to record the disposition of accounts receivable.
5. Compute the maturity date of and interest on notes receivable.
6. Explain how notes receivable are recognized in the accounts.
7. Describe how notes receivable are valued.
8. Describe the entries to record the disposition of notes receivable.
9. Explain the statement presentation and analysis of receivables.

PREVIEW OF CHAPTER 9

The content and organization of this chapter is as follows:

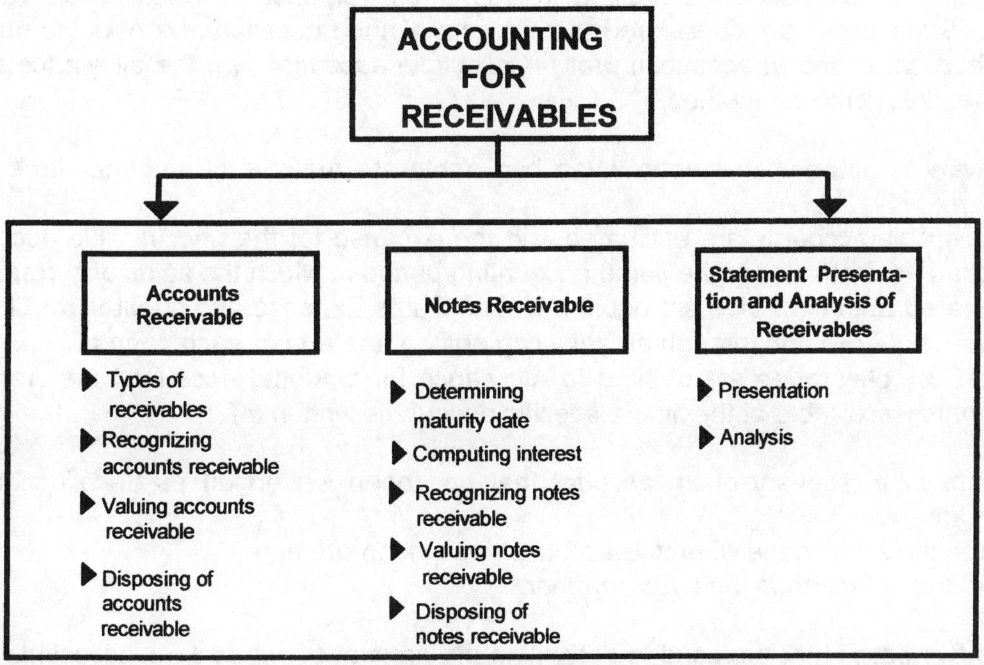

CHAPTER REVIEW

Types of Receivables

1. (S.O. 1) **Receivables** are claims that are expected to be collected in cash. The three major classes of receivables are usually classified as: (a) accounts, (b) notes, and (c) other.

2. **Accounts receivable** are amounts owed by customers on account. **Notes receivable** represent claims for which formal instruments of credit are issued as evidence of debt. And **other receivables** include nontrade receivables such as interest receivable, loans to company officers, advances to employees, and income taxes refundable.

Recognizing Accounts Receivable

3. (S.O. 2) When a business sells merchandise to a customer on credit, Accounts Receivable is debited and Sales is credited.

4. If a payment is received by a customer within the discount period, the following entry is made:

Cash	XXX	
Sales Discounts	XXX	
Accounts Receivable		XXX

Valuing Accounts Receivable

5. (S.O. 3) To ensure that receivables are not overstated on the balance sheet, they are stated at their cash (net) realizable value. Cash (net) realizable value is the net amount expected to be received in cash.

6. In accounting, credit losses are debited to Bad Debts Expense or Uncollectible Accounts Expense. Such losses are considered to be a normal and necessary risk of doing business. Two methods are used in accounting for uncollectible accounts: (a) the allowance method and (b) the direct write-off method.

7. The **allowance method** is required when bad debts are material in amount. Its essential features are:
   a. Uncollectible accounts are estimated and the expense for the uncollectible accounts is matched against sales in the same accounting period in which the sales occurred.
   b. **Estimated uncollectibles** are debited to Bad Debts Expense and credited to Allowance for Doubtful Accounts through an adjusting entry at the end of each period.
   c. **Actual uncollectibles** are debited to Allowance for Doubtful Accounts and credited to Accounts Receivable at the time a specific account is written off.

8. When there is a recovery of an account that has been written off as uncollectible, it is necessary to:
   a. reverse the entry made when the account was written off, and
   b. record the collection in the usual manner.

9. There are two bases that are used to determine the amount of expected uncollectibles. One is the percentage of sales basis, and the other is the percentage of receivables basis.

Percentage of Sales Basis

10. Under the **percentage of sales basis,**
    a. Management establishes a percentage relationship between the amount of credit sales and expected losses from uncollectible accounts.
    b. The expected bad debt losses are determined by applying the percentage to the sales base of the current period.
    c. This basis better matches expenses with revenues.

Percentage of Receivables Basis

11. Under the **percentage of receivables basis,**
    a. The balance in the allowance account is derived from an analysis of individual customer accounts. The analysis is often called **aging the accounts receivable.**
    b. The amount of the adjusting entry is the difference between the required balance and the existing balance in the allowance account.
    c. This basis produces the better estimate of **cash realizable value** of the accounts receivable.

Direct Write-off Method

12. Under the direct write-off method, bad debt losses are not anticipated and no allowance account is used.
    a. No entries are made for bad debts until an account is determined to be uncollectible at which time the loss is charged to Bad Debts Expense.
    b. This method makes no attempt to match bad debts expense to sales revenue in the income statement or to show the cash realizable value of the accounts receivable in the balance sheet.
    c. This method is not acceptable for financial reporting purposes, unless bad debt losses are insignificant.

Disposing of Accounts Receivable

13. (S.O. 4) In order to accelerate the receipt of cash from receivables, owners frequently (1) sell to a factor such as finance company or bank, or (2) make credit card sales.

14. A factor buys receivables from businesses for a fee and then collects the payments directly from the customers. The entry for a sale to a factor is:

Cash	XXX	
Service Charge Expense	XXX	
Accounts Receivable		XXX

15. Credit cards are frequently used by retailers because the retailer does not have to be concerned with the customer's credit history and the retailer can receive cash more quickly from the credit card issuer. However, the credit card issuer usually receives a fee of from 2-6% of the invoice price from the retailer.

Notes Receivable

16. (S.O. 5) A **promissory note** is a written promise to pay a specified amount of money on demand or at a definite time. The party making the promise is called the maker; the party to whom payment is made is called the payee.

17. When the life of a note is expressed in terms of months, the due date is found by counting the months from the date of issue. When the due date is stated in terms of days, it is necessary to count the days. In counting days, the date of issue is omitted but the due date is included.

18. The basic formula for computing interest on an interest bearing note is:

$$\text{Face Value of Note} \times \text{Annual Interest Rate} \times \text{Time in Terms of One Year} = \text{Interest}$$

Recognizing Notes Receivable

19. (S.O. 6) Entries for notes receivable are required when the note is received and at maturity. To illustrate, assume that on June 1, 2005, Raider Company receives a $2,000, 3-month, 12% note receivable from Paul Revere in settlement of an open account. The entry is:

June 1	Notes Receivable	2,000	
	Accounts Receivable		2,000

Valuing Notes Receivable

20. (S.O. 7) Like accounts receivable, short-term notes receivable are reported at their cash (net) realizable value and an Allowance for Doubtful Accounts is used.

Disposing Notes Receivable

21. (S.O. 8) On September 1, the maturity date, Paul Revere honors the note by paying the face amount, $2,000 plus interest of $60 ($2,000 X 12% X 3/12). Assuming that interest has not been accrued, the entry is:

Sept. 1	Cash	2,060	
	Notes Receivable		2,000
	Interest Revenue		60

22. (S.O. 9) In the balance sheet, short-term receivables are reported within the current assets section below temporary investments. Both the gross amount of receivables and the allowance for doubtful accounts should be reported. In a multiple-step income statement, Bad Debts Expense and Service Charge Expense are reported as selling expenses in the operating expenses section.

The Navigator

DEMONSTRATION PROBLEM (S.O. 3, 4, 5, 6, 7, and 8)

The December 31, 2005 balance sheet of Zunich Company reported the following amounts:

Accounts Receivable	$190,000
Allowance for Doubtful Accounts (credit balance)	4,200

During 2006, Zunich had the following transactions:

February	5	Wrote off as uncollectible an account receivable from Stoldt Co. for $750 and an account receivable from Scanlon for $1,200.
March	31	Credit sales for the first quarter were $125,000. Zunich records its bad debts expense at the end of each quarter based on 2% of credit sales.
May	25	Received $1,200 from Scanlon for the account receivable written off on February 5th.
June	30	Credit sales for the second quarter were $130,000.
July	17	Received a two-month, 11% note from Hammond to replace her account receivable balance of $5,000.
September	17	Hammond dishonored her note. It is expected that Hammond will still pay in the future.
September	30	Credit sales for the third quarter were $90,000.
December	15	Hammond declared bankruptcy. Her account is written off as uncollectible.
December	31	Credit sales for the fourth quarter were $120,000.

Instructions
Prepare the journal entries for Zunich's transactions.

The Navigator

SOLUTION TO DEMONSTRATION PROBLEM

Date		Account	Debit	Credit
February	5	Allowance for Doubtful Accounts	750	
		Accounts Receivable		750
		(Write-off account of Stoldt)		
		Allowance for Doubtful Accounts	1,200	
		Accounts Receivable		1,200
		(Write-off account of Scanlon)		
March	31	Bad Debts Expense ($125,000 X 2%)	2,500	
		Allowance for Doubtful Accounts		2,500
		(To record estimated bad debts)		
May	25	Accounts Receivable	1,200	
		Allowance for Doubtful Accounts		1,200
		(Reverse the write-off entry)		
		Cash	1,200	
		Accounts Receivable		1,200
		(Record collection from Scanlon)		
June	30	Bad Debts Expense ($130,000 X 2%)	2,600	
		Allowance for Doubtful Accounts		2,600
		(To record estimated bad debts)		
July	17	Notes Receivable	5,000	
		Accounts Receivable		5,000
September	17	Accounts Receivable	5,092	
		Interest Revenue ($5,000 X 11% X 2/12)		92
		Notes Receivable		5,000
		(Hammond dishonored note)		
September	30	Bad Debts Expense ($90,000 X 2%)	1,800	
		Allowance for Doubtful Accounts		1,800
		(To record estimated bad debts)		
December	15	Allowance for Doubtful Accounts	5,092	
		Accounts Receivable		5,092
		(Hammond account write-off)		
December	31	Bad Debts Expense ($120,000 X 2%)	2,400	
		Allowance for Doubtful Accounts		2,400
		(To record estimated bad debts)		

REVIEW QUESTIONS AND EXERCISES

TRUE—FALSE

Indicate whether each of the following is true (T) or false (F) in the space provided.

_____ 1. (S.O. 1) Accounts receivable generally are expected to be collected within 90-120 days.

_____ 2. (S.O. 1) Notes receivable represent claims for which formal instruments of credit are issued as evidence of debt.

_____ 3. (S.O. 3) The two methods of accounting for uncollectible accounts are (a) percentage of sales and (b) percentage of receivables.

_____ 4. (S.O. 3) Under the allowance method, estimated uncollectibles are debited to Bad Debts Expense and credited to Allowance for Doubtful Accounts through an adjusting entry at the end of each period.

_____ 5. (S.O. 3) Actual uncollectibles are debited to Accounts Receivable and credited to Allowance for Doubtful Accounts at the time the specific account is written off.

_____ 6. (S.O. 3) Allowance for Doubtful Accounts is a contra asset account that shows the portion of gross claims on customers that is expected to become uncollectible in the future.

_____ 7. (S.O. 3) The account Allowance for Doubtful Accounts is closed out at the end of the year.

_____ 8. (S.O. 3) To record the recovery of a bad debt, the only entry needed is the entry that reverses the customer's account.

_____ 9. (S.O. 3) Under both the percentage of sales basis and the percentage of receivables basis, it is necessary to determine the company's past experience with bad debt losses.

_____ 10. (S.O. 3) The percentage of sales basis for estimating uncollectibles emphasizes income statement relationships.

_____ 11. (S.O. 3) Under the percentage of receivables basis for estimating uncollectibles, the balance in the allowance account is derived from an analysis of individual customer accounts.

_____ 12. (S.O. 3) Under the direct write-off method, bad debt losses are not anticipated and an allowance account is not used.

_____ 13. (S.O. 3) The direct write-off method is not acceptable in accounting unless bad debt losses are insignificant.

_____ 14. (S.O. 4) In order to accelerate the receipt of cash from receivables, owners may sell the receivables to another company for cash.

_____ 15. (S.O. 4) National credit cards involve three parties: (a) the credit card issuer, (b) the customer, and (c) a bank.

_____ 16. (S.O. 5) A promissory note is a written promise to pay a specified amount of money at some unknown time in the future.

_____ 17. (S.O. 5) When counting the exact number of days to determine the maturity date of a note, the date of issue is included but the due date is omitted.

_____ 18. (S.O. 8) A note is dishonored when it is not fully paid at maturity.

_____ 19. (S.O. 9) Short-term receivables are reported in the current asset section before temporary investments.

_____ 20. (S.O. 9) Bad Debts Expense is reported in the income statement as a selling expense in the operating expenses section.

The Navigator

MULTIPLE CHOICE

Circle the letter that best answers each of the following statements.

1. (S.O. 1) Which of the following are also called trade receivables?
   a. Accounts receivable.
   b. Other receivables.
   c. Advances to employees.
   d. Income taxes refundable.

2. (S.O. 2) On February 1, 2006, Chudzick Company sells merchandise on account to Livingston Company for $5,000. The entry to record this transaction by Chudzick Company is:

		Debit	Credit
a.	Sales	5,000	
	Accounts Payable		5,000
b.	Cash	5,000	
	Sales		5,000
c.	Accounts Receivable	5,000	
	Sales		5,000
d.	Notes Receivable	5,000	
	Accounts Receivable		5,000

Questions 3 and 4 are based on the following information: On March 1, 2006, Etheredge, Inc. sells merchandise on account to Brooks Company for $7,000 terms 2/10, n/30. On March 3, Brooks returns $500 of the merchandise to Etheredge. On March 9, payment is received from Brooks for the balance due.

3. (S.O. 2) The entry on March 3 by Etheredge is:

		Debit	Credit
a.	Sales	500	
	Cash		500
b.	Sales	500	
	Accounts Receivable		500
c.	Sales Discount	500	
	Cash		500
d.	Sales Returns and Allowances	500	
	Accounts Receivable		500

4. (S.O. 2) The entry on March 9 by Etheredge is:

		Debit	Credit
a.	Cash	7,000	
	Accounts Receivable		7,000
b.	Cash	6,500	
	Accounts Receivable		6,500
c.	Cash	6,360	
	Sales Discount	140	
	Accounts Receivable		6,500
d.	Cash	6,370	
	Sales Discount	130	
	Accounts Receivable		6,500

5. (S.O. 3) When the allowance method of recognizing bad debts expense is used, the entry to recognize that expense:
   a. increases net income.
   b. decreases current assets.
   c. has no effect on current assets.
   d. has no effect on net income.

6. (S.O. 3) A basis of estimating uncollectible accounts that focuses on the income statement rather than the balance sheet is the:
   a. direct write-off of receivables.
   b. aging of the accounts receivable.
   c. percentage of sales.
   d. percentage of receivables.

7. (S.O. 3) Morgan Marie Company provides for bad debts expense at the rate of 2% of credit sales. The following data are available for 2006:

Allowance for doubtful accounts, 1/1/06 (Cr.)	$ 21,000
Accounts written off as uncollectible during 2006	13,000
Credit sales in 2006	3,000,000

The Allowance for Doubtful Accounts balance at December 31, 2006, should be:
a. $68,000.
b. $60,000.
c. $50,000.
d. $13,000.

8. (S. O. 3) In 2006, the Slowe Company had credit sales of $600,000 and granted sales discounts of $12,000. On January 1, 2006, Allowance for Doubtful Accounts had a credit balance of $15,000. During 2006, $25,000 of uncollectible accounts receivable were written off. Past experience indicates that 3% of net credit sales become uncollectible. What should be the adjusted balance of Allowance for Doubtful Accounts at December 31, 2006?
a. $7,640.
b. $8,000.
c. $17,640.
d. $33,000.

9. (S.O. 3) An analysis and aging of the accounts receivable of Shawn Green Company at December 31 revealed the following data:

Accounts Receivable	$600,000
Allowance for Doubtful Accounts per books before adjustment (Cr.)	75,000
Amounts expected to become uncollectible	82,000

The cash realizable value of the accounts receivable at December 31, after adjustment, is:
a. $593,000.
b. $525,000.
c. $518,000.
d. $443,000.

10. (S.O. 3) Erin Danielle Company's account balances at December 31 for Accounts Receivable and Allowance for Doubtful Accounts were $1,400,000 and $70,000 (Cr.), respectively. An aging of accounts receivable indicated that $108,000 are expected to become uncollectible. The amount of the adjusting entry for bad debts at December 31 is:
a. $108,000.
b. $38,000.
c. $178,000.
d. $70,000.

11. (S.O. 3) Debra Joan Company decides that the past-due account of Sheldon Stahl is uncollectible. Under the allowance method, the $865 balance owed by Sheldon Stahl is written off as follows:

		Debit	Credit
a.	Bad Debts Expense	865	
	Accounts Receivable—S. Stahl		865
b.	Allowance for Doubtful Accounts	865	
	Accounts Receivable—S. Stahl		865
c.	Accounts Receivable—S. Stahl	865	
	Allowance for Doubtful Accounts		865
d.	Allowance for Doubtful Accounts	865	
	Bad Debt Expense		865

12. (S.O. 3) Aurora Company has insignificant bad debt losses and therefore uses the direct write-off method. On October 19, the $300 balance of Becky Sherrick becomes uncollectible. The entry to record the write-off is:

		Debit	Credit
a.	Allowance for Doubtful Accounts	300	
	Accounts Receivable—Becky Sherrick		300
b.	Bad Debts Expense	300	
	Allowance for Doubtful Accounts		300
c.	Accounts Receivable—Becky Sherrick	300	
	Bad Debts Expense		300
d.	Bad Debts Expense	300	
	Accounts Receivable—Becky Sherrick		300

13. On March 1, 2006, Tom Zarle purchased a suit at Madden's Fine Apparel Store. The suit cost $350 and Tom used his Madden credit card. Madden charges 2% per month interest if payment on credit charges is not made within 30 days. On April 30, 2006, Tom had not yet made his payment. What entry should Madden make on April 30th?

		Debit	Credit
a.	Uncollectible Account	350	
	Accounts Receivable		350
b.	Bad Debts Expense	343	
	Interest Expense	7	
	Accounts Receivable		350
c.	Accounts Receivable	357	
	Interest Revenue		7
	Sales		350
d.	Accounts Receivable	7	
	Interest Revenue		7

14. (S.O. 4) Cole William Co., makes a credit card sale to a customer for $250. The credit card sale has a grace period of 30 days and then an interest charge of 18% per year or 1.5% per month is added to the balance. If the unpaid balance on the above sale is $150 at the end of the grace period, the interest charge is:
a. $3.75.
b. $3.00.
c. $1.50.
d. $2.25.

15. (S.O. 4) On October 1, 2006, Arteberry Company sells (factors) $300,000 of receivables to Church Factors, Inc. Church assesses a service charge of 3% of the amount of receivables sold. The journal entry to record the sale by Arteberry will include:
    a. a debit of $300,000 to Accounts Receivable.
    b. a credit of $309,000 to Cash.
    c. a debit of $309,000 to Cash.
    d. a debit of $9,000 to Service Charge Expense.

16. (S.O. 5) On April 3, 2006, Sublette, Inc. issued a promissory note to Biterman Company that was to mature in 90 days. The maturity date of the 90-day note is:
    a. July 1, 2004.
    b. July 2, 2004.
    c. July 3, 2004.
    d. July 4, 2004.

17. (S.O. 5) On February 1, Lowery Company received a $5,000, 10%, four-month note receivable. The cash to be received by Lowery Company when the note becomes due is:
    a. $167.
    b. $5,000.
    c. $5,167.
    d. $5,500.

Questions 18 and 19 are based on the following information: On February 15, 2006, Gilbert Company received a two-month, 10%, $2,000 note from Vincent Nathan for the settlement of his open account.

18. (S.O. 6) The entry by Gilbert Company on February 15, 2006 is:

		Debit	Credit
a.	Notes Receivable	2,000	
	Accounts Receivable—V. Nathan		2,000
b.	Accounts Receivable—V. Nathan	2,000	
	Notes Receivable		2,000
c.	Cash	2,000	
	Notes Receivable		2,000
d.	Cash	2,000	
	Accounts Receivable—V. Nathan		2,000

19. (S.O. 8) The entry by Gilbert Company on April 15, 2006 if Nathan dishonors the note and collection is expected is:

		Debit	Credit
a.	Accounts Receivable—V. Nathan	2,000	
	Notes Receivable		2,000
b.	Accounts Receivable—V. Nathan	2,033	
	Notes Receivable		2,000
	Interest Revenue		33
c.	Accounts Receivable—V. Nathan	1,067	
	Interest Lost	33	
	Notes Receivable		2,000
d.	Bad Debts Expense	2,033	
	Notes Receivable		2,033

20. (S.O. 9) Which of the following statements concerning receivables is **incorrect?**
    a. Notes receivable are often listed last under receivables.
    b. The contingent liability from selling notes receivable should be disclosed.
    c. Both the gross amount of receivables and the allowance for doubtful accounts should be reported.
    d. Interest revenue and gain on sale of notes receivable are shown under other revenues and gains.

The Navigator

MATCHING

Match each term with its definition by writing the appropriate letter in the space provided.

Terms

______ 1. Promissory note.

______ 2. Aging of accounts receivable.

______ 3. Percentage of sales basis.

______ 4. Allowance method.

______ 5. Percentage of receivables basis.

______ 6. Cash net realizable value.

______ 7. Dishonored note.

______ 8. Honored note.

______ 9. Maker.

______ 10. Payee.

______ 11. Direct write-off method.

Definitions

a. Management establishes a percentage relationship between the amount of credit sales and expected losses from uncollectible accounts.
b. The net amount expected to be received in cash.
c. A method of accounting for bad debts that is required when bad debts are material.
d. The party who promises to pay a promissory note.
e. A note that is not paid in full at maturity.
f. A written promise to pay a specified amount of money on demand or at a definite time.
g. Management establishes a percentage relationship between the amount of receivables and the expected losses from uncollectible accounts.
h. An analysis of individual customer accounts by the length of time they have been unpaid.
i. The party to whom a promissory note is to be paid.
j. A note that is paid in full at maturity.
k. A method of accounting for bad debts that is only acceptable when bad debts are insignificant.

The Navigator

EXERCISES

EX. 9-1 (S.O. 3) The N. Hawthorne Co. had a credit balance in Allowance for Doubtful Accounts of $10,000 at January 1, 2006. During 2006 credit sales totaled $300,000. A summary of the aging of accounts receivable at December 31, 2006 is as follows:

Classification by Month of Sale	Balance in Each Category	Estimated % Uncollectible
Nov.—Dec., 2006	$ 60,000	2%
Jul.—Oct., 2006	30,000	10
Jan.—June, 2006	10,000	25
Prior to 1/1/06	5,000	75
	$105,000	

On April 2, 2006, $750 was received from Hermann Hesse; his account for $750 had been written off as uncollectible in 2005. During 2006, accounts receivable totaling $8,400 were written off as uncollectible.

Instructions

(a) Prepare the journal entries on April 2 for the collection of the account previously written off and a summary entry on December 31 for the accounts written off in 2006.

(b) Assuming N. Hawthorne Co. estimates uncollectibles as 2% of credit sales, prepare the adjusting entry at December 31, 2006.

(c) Assuming the N. Hawthorne Co. estimates uncollectibles by using the percentage of accounts receivables, prepare the adjusting entry at December 31, 2006 (use an aging schedule).

General Journal **J1**

Date	Account Title	Debit	Credit
2006 (a)			

General Journal			J
Date	Account Title	Debit	Credit
(b)			
(c)			

EX. 9-2 (S.O. 5, 6, 7, and 8) Hemingway Company had the following transactions for the year ended December 31, 2006.

July 1 Received a $2,000, three-month 10% promissory note from Damon Runyon in settlement of an open account.

Aug. 1 Received a $1,000, three-month 12% note receivable from Carl Sandburg for cash borrowed by Sandburg.

Oct. 1 Received notice that the Damon Runyon note had been dishonored. It is expected that Runyon will eventually pay the amount owed.

Nov. 1 Sandburg honored the note receivable in full. (Assume that interest has not been accrued.)

Instructions
Prepare the entries for the transactions above.

General Journal J1

Date	Account Title	Debit	Credit

The Navigator

SOLUTIONS TO REVIEW QUESTIONS AND EXERCISES

TRUE-FALSE

1. (F) Accounts receivable generally are expected to be collected within 30 to 60 days.
2. (T)
3. (F) The two methods are (a) the allowance method and (b) the direct write-off method.
4. (T)
5. (F) Actual uncollectibles are debited to Allowance for Doubtful Accounts and credited to Accounts Receivable at the time the specific account is written off.
6. (T)
7. (F) The account Allowance for Doubtful Accounts is a contra asset account on the balance sheet and is therefore a permanent account that is not closed out.
8. (F) Two entries are required to record the recovery of a bad debt: (1) the entry made in writing off the account is reversed to reinstate the customer's account, and (2) the collection is journalized in the usual manner.
9. (T)
10. (T)
11. (T)
12. (T)
13. (T)
14. (T)
15. (F) The three parties are (a) the credit card issuer, (b) the retailer, and (c) the customer.
16. (F) A promissory note is a written promise to pay a specified amount of money on demand or at a definite time.
17. (F) When counting the exact number of days to determine the maturity date, the date of issue is omitted but the due date is included.
18. (T)
19. (F) Short-term receivables are reported in the current asset section immediately after temporary investments.
20. (T)

MULTIPLE CHOICE

1. (a) Accounts receivables, also called trade receivables, are amounts owed by customers on account. Answer (b), other receivables, include non-trade receivables. Advances to employees (c) and income taxes refundable (d) are included under the category of other receivables.

2. (c) When a business sells merchandise on credit they must recognize an asset by debiting Accounts Receivable and revenue earned by crediting Sales.

3. (d) When merchandise is returned, the seller must recognize the return by debiting Sales Returns and Allowance, which is a contra account to Sales. A decrease in assets must be recognized by crediting Accounts Receivable.

4. (d) The sales discount is $130 ($6,500 X 2%). The correct entry is Cash (Dr.) $6,370, Sales Discounts (Dr.) $130, and Accounts Receivable (Cr.) $6,500.

5. (b) Estimated uncollectibles are debited to Bad Debts Expense and credited to Allowance for Doubtful Accounts through an adjusting entry at the end of each period. Bad Debts Expense, being an expense decreases net income. The Allowance for Doubtful Accounts is a contra asset account to accounts receivable, thus decreasing current assets.

6. (c) The allowance method using the percentage of sales basis focuses on the income statement. The direct write-off of receivables (a) is not an allowance method. The aging of the accounts receivable (b) and a percentage of the accounts receivable (d) are the same; they focus on the balance sheet.

7. (a) The balance in the Allowance for Doubtful Accounts prior to adjustment is a credit of $8,000 ($21,000 - $13,000). The adjusting entry under the percentage of sales method is $60,000 ($3,000,000 X 2%). Thus, the adjusted balance is $68,000 ($8,000 + $60,000).

8. (a) The balance in Allowance for Doubtful Accounts prior to adjustment is a debit of $10,000 ($25,000 - $15,000). The adjusting entry is $17,640 [$600,000 - $12,000) X .03]. Thus the ending balance is $7,640 ($17,640 - $10,000).

9. (c) The cash realizable value of the accounts receivable at December 31 should be accounts receivable ($600,000) less the amounts deemed uncollectible ($82,000) or $518,000.

10. (b) Under the percentage of receivables basis, the allowance account is adjusted to the estimated uncollectibles. In this case, the required balance is $108,000 and the amount of the adjusting entry is $38,000 ($108,000 - $70,000).

11. (b) Under the allowance method, every bad debt write-off is made against the allowance account and not to Bad Debts Expense. A debit to Bad Debts Expense would be incorrect because the expense is recognized when the adjusting entry is made for estimated bad debts. The write-off of the account reduces both Accounts Receivable and the Allowance for Doubtful Accounts.

12. (d) Under the direct write-off method, bad debt loses are not anticipated and an allowance account is not used. No entries are made for bad debts until an account is determined to be uncollectible, at which time the loss is charged to Bad Debts Expense and credited to Accounts Receivable.

13. (d) Madden should recognize revenue earned of $7 ($350 X 2%). The amount is simply added to the accounts receivable balance.

14. (d) The interest charge is $150 X 1.5% or $2.25.

15. (d) The entry to record the sale (factor) of receivables by Arteberry is as follows:

Cash	291,000	
Service Charge Expense	9,000	
Accounts Receivable		300,000

16. (b) In calculating the maturity date, the date the note is issued is omitted but the due date is included.

Term on the note		90
April (30 - 3)	27	
May	31	
June	30	88
Maturity date, July		2

17. (c) The cash to be received by Lowery Company will be the face value, $5,000, plus the interest earned, $167 ($5,000 X 10% X 4/12).

18. (a) A transfer from one asset account, Accounts Receivable, to another asset account, Notes Receivable, is made by debiting Notes Receivable and crediting Accounts Receivable.

19. (b) By dishonoring the note, the Notes Receivable is reverted back to Accounts Receivable. The amount of interest that has been earned $33 - ($2,000 X .10 X 2/12) is recognized by crediting interest revenue and by increasing Accounts Receivable.

20. (a) Notes receivable are often listed first under receivables because they can be quickly realized in cash through sale. Answers (b), (c), and (d) are all correct statements.

MATCHING

1. f	5. g	9. d
2. h	6. b	10. i
3. a	7. e	11. k
4. c	8. j	

EXERCISES

EX. 9-1

General Journal J1

Date	Account Title	Debit	Credit
2006 (a)			
Apr. 2	Accounts Receivable – H. Hesse	750	
	Allowance for Doubtful Accounts		750
	(To reverse write-off of H. Hesse account)		
2	Cash	750	
	Accounts Receivable – H. Hesse		750
	(To record collection from H. Hesse)		
Dec. 31	Allowance for Doubtful Accounts	8,400	
	Accounts Receivable		8,400
	(Write-off of 2004 uncollectibles)		
(b)			
Dec. 31	Bad Debts Expense ($300,000 X 2%)	6,000	
	Allowance for Doubtful Accounts		6,000
	(To record estimated bad debts for year)		
(c)			
Dec. 31	Bad Debts Expense	8,100	
	Allowance for Doubtful Accounts		8,100
	(To adjust allowance account to total		
	estimated uncollectibles)		

Aging Schedule

Classification by Month of Sale	Balance in Each Category	Estimated % Uncollectible	Estimated Bad Debts
Nov.—Dec. 2006	$ 60,000	2%	$ 1,200
July—Oct. 2006	30,000	10	3,000
Jan.—June 2006	10,000	25	2,500
Prior to 1/1/06	5,000	75	3,750
	$105,000		$10,450

The balance in Allowance for Doubtful Accounts prior to adjustment is $2,350 (Cr.) ($10,000 + $750 - $8,400). Therefore, the adjusting entry is $8,100 ($10,450 - $2,350).

EX. 9-2

General Journal J1

Date	Account Title	Debit	Credit
2006			
July 1	Notes Receivable	2,000	
	Accounts Receivable – D. Runyon		2,000
	(To record acceptance of D. Runyon note)		
Aug. 1	Notes Receivable	1,000	
	Cash		1,000
	(To record acceptance of C. Sandburg note)		
Oct. 1	Accounts Receivable	2,050	
	Notes Receivable		2,000
	Interest Revenue ($2,000 X 10% X 3/12)		50
	(To record Runyon dishonored note)		
Nov. 1	Cash	1,030	
	Notes Receivable		1,000
	Interest Revenue ($1,000 X 12% X 3/12)		30
	(To record honoring of C. Sandburg note)		

The Navigator

- Scan Study Objectives
- Read Preview
- Read Chapter Review
- Work Demonstration Problem
- Answer True-False Statements
- Answer Multiple-Choice Questions
- Match Terms and Definitions
- Solve Exercises

Chapter 10

PLANT ASSETS, NATURAL RESOURCES, AND INTANGIBLE ASSETS

CHAPTER STUDY OBJECTIVES

After studying this chapter, you should be able to:

1. Describe how the cost principle applies to plant assets.
2. Explain the concept of depreciation.
3. Compute periodic depreciation using different methods.
4. Describe the procedure for revising periodic depreciation.
5. Distinguish between revenue and capital expenditures, and prepare the entries for these expenditures.
6. Explain how to account for the disposal of a plant asset.
7. Compute periodic depletion of natural resources.
8. Explain the basic issues related to accounting for intangible assets.
9. Indicate how plant assets, natural resources, and intangible assets are reported and analyzed.

*10. Explain how to account for the exchange of plant assets.

Note: All asterisked (*) items relate to material contained in the Appendix to the chapter.

The Navigator

PREVIEW OF CHAPTER 10

In this chapter, we explain the application of the cost principle of accounting to natural resources and intangible assets. We also describe the methods that may be used to allocate an asset's cost over its useful life. In addition, the accounting for expenditures incurred during the useful life of assets is discussed. The organization and content of this chapter are as follows:

PLANT ASSETS, NATURAL RESOURCES, AND INTANGIBLE ASSETS

Plant Assets
- Determining the cost of plant assets
- Depreciation
- Expenditures during useful life
- Plant asset disposals

Natural Resources

Intangible Assets
- Accounting for intangibles
- Research and development costs

Statement Presentation and Analysis
- Presentation
- Analysis

The Navigator

CHAPTER REVIEW

Plant Assets

1. (S.O. 1) **Plant assets** are resources that have a physical substance (a definite size and shape), are used in the operations of a business and are not intended for sale to customers. They are also called **property, plant, and equipment**; **plant and equipment**; or **fixed assets.**

Cost of Plant Assets

2. Plant assets are recorded at cost in accordance with the **cost principle** of accounting. Cost consists of all expenditures necessary to (1) acquire the asset and (2) make it ready for its intended use.

3. The cost of **land** includes the cash purchase price, closing costs such as title and attorney's fees, real estate brokers' commissions, and accrued property taxes and other liens on the land assumed by the purchaser. All necessary costs incurred in making land ready for its intended use are debited to the Land Account.

4. **Land improvements** are structural additions made to land, such as driveways, parking lots, fences, landscaping, and underground sprinklers. The cost of **land improvements** includes all expenditures needed to make the improvements ready for their intended use.

5. The cost of **buildings** includes **all** necessary costs related to the purchase or construction of a building:
   a. When a building is purchased, such costs include the purchase price, closing costs, and real estate broker's commission.
   b. Costs to make the building ready for its intended use include expenditures for remodeling and replacing or repairing the roof, floors, wiring, and plumbing.
   c. When a new building is constructed, cost consists of the contract price plus payments for architects' fees, building permits, interest payments during construction, and excavation costs.

6. The cost of **equipment** consists of the cash purchase price, sales taxes, freight charges, and insurance paid by the purchaser during transit. Cost includes all expenditures required in assembling, installing, and testing the unit. Recurring costs such as licenses and insurance are expensed as incurred.

Depreciation

7. (S.O. 2) **Depreciation** is the process of allocating to expense the cost of a plant asset over its useful (service) life in a rational and systematic manner.
   a. The cost allocation is designed to provide for the proper matching of expenses with revenues in accordance with the **matching principle.**
   b. During an asset's life, its usefulness may decline because of wear and tear or obsolescence.
   c. Recognition of depreciation does not result in the accumulation of cash for the replacement of the asset.

8. Three factors that affect the computation of depreciation are (1) cost, (2) useful life, and (3) salvage value.

9. Three methods of recognizing depreciation are (a) straight-line, (b) units of activity, and (c) declining-balance.
   a. Each method is acceptable under generally accepted accounting principles.
   b. Management selects the method that is appropriate in the circumstances.
   c. Once a method is chosen, it should be applied consistently.

Straight-Line Method

10. Under the **straight-line method** depreciation is the same for each year of the asset's useful life.
   a. The formula for computing annual depreciation expense is:

      Depreciable Cost ÷ Useful Life (in years) = Depreciation Expense

   b. To illustrate the computation, assume that the Benson Company purchased a delivery truck for $11,000 on January 1 with an estimated salvage value of $1,000 at the end of its four-year service life. Annual depreciation is $2,500 [($11,000 - $1,000 ÷ 4)].
   c. The straight-line method predominates in practice.
   d. This method is simple to apply and it matches expenses and revenues appropriately when the use of the asset is reasonably uniform throughout the service life.

Units-of-Activity Method

11. Under the **units-of-activity method,** service life is expressed in terms of the total units of production or expected use from the asset, rather than time.
   a. The formulas for computing depreciation expense are:

      (1) Depreciable Cost ÷ Total Units of Activity = Depreciation Cost per Unit

      (2) Depreciation Cost per Unit X Units of Activity During the Year = Depreciation Expense

   b. To illustrate the computation, assume that Benson Company expects to drive the truck purchased in (10b) above for 100,000 miles and that 30,000 miles are driven in the first year. Depreciation for the first year is $3,000.

      (1) $10,000 ÷ 100,000 = $.10 per mile.

      (2) $.10 X 30,000 = $3,000.

   c. In using this method, it is often difficult to make a reasonable estimate of total activity.
   d. When the productivity of an asset varies significantly from one period to another, this method results in the best matching of expenses with revenues.

Declining-Balance Method

12. The **declining-balance method** produces a decreasing annual depreciation expense over the useful life of the asset.

a. The formula for computing depreciation expense is:

Book Value at Beginning of Year X Declining Balance Rate = Depreciation Expense

b. To illustrate the computation, assume that Benson Company uses a declining-balance rate that is double the straight-line rate of 25%. Depreciation in the first year is $5,500 ($11,000 X 50%).

c. Under this method, the depreciation rate remains constant from year to year, but the book value to which the rate is applied declines each year.

d. This method is compatible with the matching principle because the higher depreciation in early years is matched with the higher benefits received in these years.

13. Taxpayers must use on their tax returns either the straight-line method or a special accelerated depreciation method called the Modified Accelerated Cost Recovery System (MACRS).

Revising Periodic Depreciation

14. (S.O. 4) If wear and tear or obsolescence indicate that annual depreciation is inadequate or excessive, a change in the periodic amount should be made.
    a. When a change is made, (1) there is no correction of previously recorded depreciation expense, and (2) depreciation expense for current and future years is revised.
    b. To determine the new annual depreciation expense, the depreciable cost at the time of the revision is divided by the remaining useful life.

Expenditures During Useful Life

15. (S.O. 5) **Ordinary repairs** are expenditures to maintain the operating efficiency and expected productive life of the plant asset. They are debited to Repairs Expense as incurred and are often referred to as **revenue expenditures.**

16. **Additions and improvements** are costs incurred to increase the operating efficiency, productive capacity, or expected useful life of the plant asset. These expenditures are usually material in amount and occur infrequently during the period of ownership.

17. **Capital expenditures** increase the company's investment in productive facilities. These expenditures include additions and improvements.

Plant Asset Disposals

18. (S.O. 6) Plant assets may be disposed of by (a) retirement, (b) sale, or (c) exchange.

19. At the time of disposal, it is necessary to determine the **book value** of the plant asset.
    a. If the disposal occurs during the year, depreciation for the fraction of the year to the date of disposal must be recorded.
    b. The book value is then eliminated by debiting the Accumulated Depreciation account for the total depreciation to the date of disposal and crediting the asset account for the cost of the asset.

Retirement of Plant Assets

20. In accounting for a disposal by **retirement,**
    a. if the asset is fully depreciated, the entry is a debit to Accumulated Depreciation and a credit to the plant asset account.
    b. if the asset is retired before it is fully depreciated and no scrap or salvage value is received, a loss on disposal occurs.
    c. the loss on disposal is reported in the Other Expenses and Losses section of the income statement.

Sale of Plant Assets

21. In a disposal by **sale,** the book value of the asset is compared with the **proceeds** received from the sale.
    a. If the proceeds of the sale exceed the book value, a **gain on disposal** occurs which is reported in the Other Revenues and Gains section of the income statement.
    b. If the proceeds of the sale are less than the book value of the asset, a **loss on disposal** occurs which is reported in the Other Expenses and Losses section of the income statement.

Natural Resources

22. (S.O. 7) **Natural resources** consist of standing timber and underground deposits of oil, gas, and minerals. These assets are frequently called wasting assets.

Acquisition Cost

23. The acquisition cost of a natural resource is the price needed to acquire the resource and prepare it for its intended use.

Depletion

24. **Depletion** is the systematic write-off of the cost of natural resources. The **units of activity method** is generally used to compute depletion because periodic depletion is generally a function of the units extracted during the year. The formulas for computing depletion expense are:
    a. Total Cost minus Salvage Value ÷ Total Estimated Units = Depletion Cost per Unit.
    b. Depletion Cost per Unit X Number of Units Extracted and Sold = Depletion Expense.

25. To record depletion expense, Depletion Expense is debited and a contra asset account, Accumulated Depletion, is credited.
    a. Depletion expense is reported as a cost of producing the product.
    b. Accumulated Depletion is deducted from the cost of the natural resource in the balance sheet.

Intangible Assets

26. (S.O. 8) **Intangible assets** are rights, privileges, and competitive advantages that result from the ownership of assets that do not possess physical substance. Intangibles may arise from government grants, acquisition of another business, and private monopolistic arrangements.

27. In general, **accounting for intangible assets** parallels the accounting for plant assets. Intangible assets are (a) recorded at cost, (b) cost is written off over useful life in a rational and systematic manner, assuming the useful life is limited, and (c) at disposal, book value is eliminated and gain or loss, if any, is recorded. If the life of the intangible is indefinite, the cost of the intangible should not be allocated.

28. Differences between the accounting for intangible assets and the accounting for plant assets include:
    a. The systematic write-off of an intangible asset is referred to as **amortization.**
    b. To record amortization, Amortization Expense is debited and the specific intangible asset is credited.
    c. Amortization is typically computed on a straight-line basis.

Patents

29. A **patent** is an exclusive right issued by the U.S. Patent Office that enables the recipient to manufacture, sell, or otherwise control his or her invention for a period of twenty years from the date of grant.
    a. The initial cost of a patent is the cash or cash equivalent price paid when the patent is acquired.
    b. When legal costs are incurred in successfully defending the patent, they are added to the Patent account and amortized over the remaining useful life of the patent.
    c. The cost of the patent should be amortized over its legal life (20 years) or useful life, whichever is shorter.

Copyrights

30. Copyrights are granted by the federal government, giving the owner the exclusive right to reproduce and sell an artistic or published work.

Trademark or Trade name

31. A **trademark** or **trade name** is a word, phrase, jingle, or symbol that distinguishes or identifies a particular enterprise or product.

Franchise

32. A **franchise** is a contractual arrangement under which the franchisor grants the franchisee the right to sell certain products, to render specific services, or to use certain trademarks or trade names, usually within a designated geographical area. Another type of franchise, commonly referred to as a **license** or **permit,** is entered into between a governmental body and a business enterprise and permits the enterprise to use public property in performing its services.

Goodwill

33. **Goodwill** is the value of all favorable attributes that relate to a business enterprise such as exceptional management, skilled employees, high-quality products, fair pricing policies, and harmonious relations with labor unions.
    a. Goodwill can be identified only with the business as a whole.

b. Goodwill is recorded only when there is an exchange transaction that involves the purchase of an entire business.
c. When an entire business is purchased, goodwill is the excess of cost over the fair market value of the net assets (assets less liabilities) acquired.

34. Goodwill is not amortized because it is considered to have an indefinite life, but it must be written down if its value is determined to have declined (been permanently impaired).

Research and Development

35. **Research and development** costs are costs that are spent on developing new products and processes. Such costs are usually recorded as an expense when incurred.

Financial Statement Presentation

36. (S.O. 9) In the balance sheet, plant assets and natural resources are usually combined under Property, Plant, and Equipment and intangibles are shown separately under Intangible Assets.
    a. There should be disclosure of the balances in the major classes of assets and accumulated depreciation of major classes of assets or in total.
    b. Depreciation and amortization methods used should be described and the amount of depreciation and amortization expense for the period disclosed.

Exchanges of Plant Assets

*37. (S.O. 10) An **exchange of similar assets** involves assets of the same type. In this type of exchange, the new asset performs the same function as the old asset. The accounting depends on whether there is a gain or loss on the old asset.
    a. When a gain occurs in the exchange of similar assets:
        (1) The acquisition cost of the new asset is equal to the fair market value of the old asset exchanged plus any cash or other consideration given up.
        (2) The gain or loss is the difference between the fair market value and the book value of the asset given up.
        (3) The gain is then offset against the cost of the new asset (instead of being credited to Gain on Disposal).
    b. When a loss occurs in the exchange of similar assets, the loss is recognized immediately—it is not deferred.

The Navigator

DEMONSTRATION PROBLEM (S.O. 2 and 3)

On January 1, 2006, Hume Company purchases a machine that includes a cash price of $7,000, freight charges of $250, insurance during transit of $50, assembly costs of $150, and a license of $35 per year. Hume depreciates the machine using the straight-line method based on a five-year useful life with an estimated salvage value of $700.

Instructions

(a) Make the entry for the purchase on January 1, 2006.
(b) Make the depreciation expense entries for December 31, 2006, 2007, and 2008.

SOLUTION TO DEMONSTRATION PROBLEM

			Debit	Credit
(a)		2006		
	Jan. 1	Equipment	7,450	
		License Expense	35	
		Cash		7,485
		($7,000 + $250 + $50 + $150)		
(b)		2006, 2007, 2008		
	Dec. 31	Depreciation Expense	1,350	
		Accumulated Depreciation—Equipment		1,350
		[($7,450 - $700) ÷ 5]		

REVIEW QUESTIONS AND EXERCISES

TRUE—FALSE

Indicate whether each of the following is true (T) or false (F) in the space provided.

_____ 1. (S.O. 1) To be classified as a plant asset, an asset must possess physical substance.

_____ 2. (S.O. 1) All plant assets should be depreciated over their useful life.

_____ 3. (S.O. 1) The cost of tearing down an old building on a newly purchased lot to make the site suitable for a new building should be debited to Buildings.

_____ 4. (S.O. 1) The cost of driveways and parking lots is debited to Land.

_____ 5. (S.O. 1) When constructing a building, a company is permitted to include the acquisition cost and certain interest costs incurred in financing the project.

_____ 6. (S.O. 1) The cost of equipment includes the cash price, freight charges, expenditures required in the assembling, motor vehicle licenses, and accident insurance.

_____ 7. (S.O. 2) Recognition of depreciation permits the accumulation of cash for the replacement of the asset.

_____ 8. (S.O. 3) Under the straight-line method, depreciation decreases for each year of service life of the asset.

_____ 9. (S.O. 3) Under the units of activity method, the decline in service potential is attributed to time rather than activity.

_____ 10. (S.O. 3) The declining-balance method is often called an accelerated depreciation method.

_____ 11. (S.O. 3) The declining-balance method is compatible with the matching principle.

_____ 12. (S.O. 3) When an asset is purchased during the year, it is not necessary to record depreciation expense in the first year under the declining-balance depreciation method.

_____ 13. (S.O. 3) Taxpayers must use either the straight-line method or a special accelerated depreciation method called Modified Accelerated Cost Recovery System on their tax returns.

_____ 14. (S.O. 3) The book value of a plant asset is the difference between the asset's fair market value and accumulated depreciation.

_____ 15. (S.O. 6) The retirement of a fully depreciated plant asset will usually result in a loss.

_____ 16. (S.O. 6) If the proceeds from the sale of a plant asset exceed the asset's book value, a gain should be recognized.

_____ 17. (S.O. 7) Wasting assets are natural resources which no longer have any value.

_____ 18. (S.O. 7) The acquisition cost of a natural resource is the cash or cash equivalent price necessary to acquire the resource and prepare it for its intended use.

_____ 19. (S.O. 7) The units of activity method is generally used to compute depletion.

_____ 20. (S.O. 7) Depletion expense is reported in the income statement as an operating expense.

_____ 21. (S.O. 8) In general, the accounting for intangible assets parallels the accounting for plant assets.

_____ 22. (S.O. 8) The straight-line method is generally used to compute amortization expense on intangible assets.

_____ 23. (S.O. 8) The cost of successfully defending a patent in an infringement suit should be expensed when incurred.

_____ 24. (S.O. 8) Goodwill is not recognized in accounting unless it is acquired from another business enterprise.

_____ 25. (S.O. 8) Research and development costs should be charged to expense when incurred.

_____ *26. (S.O. 6) A gain can be recognized on the exchange of similar assets.

_____ *27. (S.O. 6) A loss on the exchange of plant assets occurs when the fair market value of the old asset is less than its book value.

_____ *28. (S.O. 6) Gains resulting from the exchange of similar assets are deferred and reduce the cost basis of the new asset acquired.

The Navigator

MULTIPLE CHOICE

Circle the letter that best answers each of the following statements.

1. (S.O. 1) A term which is not synonymous with property, plant, and equipment is:
   a. plant assets.
   b. fixed assets.
   c. intangible assets.
   d. long-lived tangible assets.

2. (S.O. 1) Plant assets are often subdivided into four groups. Which of the following would not be classified as a plant asset?
   a. Land.
   b. Land improvements.
   c. Supplies.
   d. Buildings.

3. (S.O. 1) Plato Company acquired land with a purchase price of $150,000 plus attorney's fee $6,000, demolition and removal costs of an old building $4,000, and grading and filling the land $3,000. The land should be recorded at:
   a. $137,000.
   b. $150,000.
   c. $157,000.
   d. $163,000.

4. (S.O. 1) Land improvements do **not** include:
   a. building sites.
   b. driveways.
   c. parking lots.
   d. fencing.

5. (S.O. 1) Schopenhauer Company purchased a delivery truck and incurred the following costs:

Cash price	$15,000
Sales tax	750
Painting	600
Motor vehicle license	75
2-year accident insurance policy	700
Total costs	$17,125

What amount should be recorded as the cost of the delivery truck?
a. $15,750.
b. $16,350.
c. $16,425.
d. $17,125.

6. (S.O. 2) The factor that is not relevant in computing depreciation is:
a. Replacement value.
b. Cost.
c. Salvage value.
d. Useful life.

7. (S.O. 3) Using the straight-line method, depreciation expense is calculated with the formula:
a. (Cost ÷ Useful life) - Salvage value.
b. (Cost + Salvage value) ÷ Useful life.
c. (Cost - Salvage value) ÷ Useful life.
d. (Cost ÷ Useful life) + Salvage value.

8. (S.O. 3) Bruno Company purchased equipment on January 1, 2006 at a total invoice cost of $280,000; additional costs of $5,000 for freight and $25,000 for installation were incurred. The equipment has an estimated salvage value of $10,000 and an estimated useful life of five years. The amount of accumulated depreciation at December 31, 2007 if the straight-line method of depreciation is used is:
a. $108,000.
b. $110,000.
c. $120,000.
d. $124,000.

9. (S.O. 3) Spinoza Enterprises purchased a truck for $27,000 on January 1, 2006. The truck will have an estimated salvage value of $2,000 at the end of five years. Using the units of activity method, the accumulated depreciation at December 31, 2007 can be computed by the following formula:
a. ($27,000 ÷ Total estimated activity) X Units of activity for 2007.
b. ($25,000 ÷ Total estimated activity) X Units of activity for 2007.
c. ($27,000 ÷ Total estimated activity) X Units of activity for 2006 and 2007.
d. ($25,000 ÷ Total estimated activity) X Units of activity for 2006 and 2007.

10. (S.O. 3) Nietzsche Company purchased a machine on January 1, 2006, for $350,000. The machine has an estimated useful life of five years and a salvage value of $50,000. The machine is being depreciated using the double-declining balance method. The book value at December 31, 2007 is:
    a. $126,000.
    b. $158,000.
    c. $170,000.
    d. $224,000.

11. (S.O. 4) Santayana Company purchased a machine on January 1, 2004, for $8,000 with an estimated salvage value of $2,000 and an estimated useful life of 8 years. On January 1, 2006, Santayana decides the machine will last 12 years from the date of purchase. The salvage value is still estimated at $2,000. Using the straight-line method the new annual depreciation will be:
    a. $450.
    b. $500.
    c. $600.
    d. $667.

12. (S.O. 5) Which of the following would be considered an ordinary repair?
    a. Constructing a new wing on a building.
    b. A major motor overhaul of a new truck.
    c. Painting of buildings.
    d. Replacing a stairway with an escalator.

13. (S.O. 5) Improvements are:
    a. revenue expenditures.
    b. debited to an appropriate asset account when they increase useful life.
    c. debited to accumulated depreciation when they do not increase useful life.
    d. debited to an appropriate asset account when they do not increase useful life.

14. (S.O. 6) Which of the following is an example of a plant asset disposal?
    a. Retirement.
    b. Sale.
    c. Exchange.
    d. All of the above are examples.

15. (S.O. 6) A plant asset cost $27,000 when it was purchased on January 1, 1999. It was depreciated by the straight-line method based on a 9-year life with no salvage value. On June 30, 2006, the asset was discarded with no cash proceeds. What gain or loss should be recognized on the retirement?
    a. No gain or loss.
    b. $6,000 loss.
    c. $4,500 loss.
    d. $3,000 gain.

Use the following information for questions 16 and 17:

On May 1, 2006, Bentham Company sells office furniture for $60,000 cash. The office furniture originally cost $150,000 when purchased on January 1, 1999. Depreciation is recorded by the straight-line method over 10 years with a salvage value of $15,000.

16. (S.O. 3) What depreciation expense should be recorded on this asset in 2006?
    a. $4,500.
    b. $5,000.
    c. $6,750.
    d. $13,500.

17. (S.O. 6) What gain should be recognized on the sale?
    a. $4,500.
    b. $9,000.
    c. $9,500.
    d. $18,000.

18. (S.O. 6) On January 1, Averroes Company sold a machine that had a book value of $7,500 for $8,000 cash. The entry by Averroes Company on January 1, will include a:
    a. debit to Loss on Disposal.
    b. credit to Loss on Disposal.
    c. debit to Gain on Disposal.
    d. debit to Cash.

19. (S.O. 7) Natural resources include all of the following except:
    a. standing timber.
    b. land improvements.
    c. oil deposits.
    d. mineral deposits.

20. (S.O. 7) The entry to record depletion expense:
    a. decreases stockholders' equity and assets.
    b. decreases net income and increases liabilities.
    c. decreases assets and liabilities.
    d. decreases assets and increases liabilities.

21. (S.O. 7) Abelard Company expects to extract 15 million tons of coal from a mine that cost $25 million. If no salvage value is expected, and 3,000,000 tons are mined and sold in the first year, the entry to record depletion in the first year will include a:
    a. debit to Accumulated Depletion of $3,000,000.
    b. credit to Depletion Expense of $5,000,000.
    c. debit to Depletion Expense of $5,000,000.
    d. credit to Accumulated Depletion of $1,800,000.

22. (S.O. 8) All of the following are intangible assets except:
    a. franchises.
    b. copyrights.
    c. accounts receivable.
    d. goodwill.

23. (S.O. 8) A purchased patent has a legal life of 20 years. It should be:
    a. expensed in the year of acquisition.
    b. amortized over 20 years regardless of its useful life.
    c. amortized over its useful life if less than 20 years.
    d. not amortized.

24. (S.O. 8) Eloise Company incurred $350,000 of research and development costs in its laboratory to develop a patent granted on January 1, 2006. On July 31, 2006, Eloise paid $52,000 for legal fees in a successful defense of the patent. The total amount debited to Patents through July 31, 2006, should be:
    a. $350,000.
    b. $52,000.
    c. $402,000.
    d. $298,000.

25. (S.O. 8) Goodwill from the acquisition of a business enterprise:
    a. should be expensed in the year of acquisition.
    b. is an asset that is not subject to amortization, but must be written down if its value is determined to have declined.
    c. is not an intangible asset.
    d. is granted by the federal government.

*26. (S.O. 10) In exchanges of similar assets:
    a. neither gains nor losses are recognized immediately.
    b. gains, but not losses, are recognized immediately.
    c. losses, but not gains, are recognized immediately.
    d. both gains and losses are recognized immediately.

*27. (S.O. 10) Hobbes Company exchanges a used truck (original cost, $41,000) plus $20,000 cash for a new truck costing $45,000. At the time of exchange, accumulated depreciation on the used truck is $23,000. What gain or loss should Hobbs recognize on the exchange?
    a. $16,000 loss.
    b. $7,000 loss.
    c. $0 gain or loss.
    d. $7,000 gain.

*28. (S.O. 10) Voltaire Company exchanged an old machine, with a book value of $53,000 and a fair market value of $49,000, and paid $7,000 cash for a similar used machine. At what amount should the machine acquired in the exchange be recorded on the books of Voltaire?
    a. $49,000.
    b. $53,000.
    c. $56,000.
    d. $60,000.

MATCHING

Match each term with its definition by writing the appropriate letter in the space provided.

Terms

_____ 1. Revenue expenditures.

_____ 2. Declining-balance method.

_____ 3. Natural resources.

_____ 4. Cash equivalent price.

_____ 5. Additions and improvements.

_____ 6. Ordinary repairs.

_____ 7. Units of activity method.

_____ 8. Straight-line method.

_____ 9. Patent.

_____ 10. Intangible assets.

_____ 11. Copyright.

_____ 12. Full cost approach.

_____ 13. Successful efforts approach.

_____ 14. Depletion.

_____ 15. Amortization

_____ 16. Franchise.

_____ 17. Goodwill.

_____ 18. Trademark.

_____ 19. Research and development costs.

Definitions

a. A depreciation method where the computation of periodic depreciation is based on the book value of the asset which declines each year.

b. Expenditures that are immediately charged against revenues as an expense.

c. An exclusive right that enables the recipient to manufacture, sell, or otherwise control his or her invention for a period of 20 years from the date of grant.

d. A depreciation method in which the decline in service potential is attributable to activity rather than time.

e. The fair market value of the asset given up or the fair market value of the asset received, whichever is more clearly determinable.

f. Costs incurred to increase the operating efficiency, productive capacity, or expected productive life of the unit.

g. Expenditures to maintain the operating efficiency and expected productive life of the unit.

h. The value of all favorable attributes that relate to a business enterprise.

i. A depreciation method where periodic depreciation is the same throughout the service life of the asset.

j. Rights, privileges, and competitive advantages that result from the ownership of assets that do not possess physical substance.

k. Costs relating to the development of new products and processes that are usually recorded as expense when incurred.

l. The costs of both successful and unsuccessful explorations are capitalized.

m. Assets that consist of standing timber and underground deposits of oil, gas, and minerals.

n. Only the costs of successful explorations are capitalized.

o. A word, phrase, or symbol that distinguishes or identifies a particular enterprise or product.

Definitions (continued)

p. A right granted by the federal government giving the owner the exclusive right to reproduce and sell an artistic or published work.
q. A contractual agreement granting rights to sell certain products, or render specific services, or to use certain trademarks.
r. The systematic write-off of the cost of natural resources.
s. The rational and systematic write-off of the cost of an intangible asset.

The Navigator

EXERCISES

EX. 10-1 (S.O. 1 and 5) During 2006, Bergson Company had the following plant asset transactions.

Jan. 1 Purchased a bus for company tours. The bus had a purchase price of $23,000 plus costs of $500 for delivery charges, $250 for insurance during transit to the company, $700 for painting and lettering, $300 for sales tax, $30 for motor vehicle license, and $800 for accident insurance for two years.

July 1 Purchased a factory machine by making a $500 down payment and signing a $2,500 1-year, 10% note.

Instructions
Journalize the transactions. (Omit explanations.)

General Journal J1

Date	Account Title	Debit	Credit
	Dr. equipment	24750	
	Dr. insurance expense	800	
	Dr. license expense	30	
	Cr. cash		25580
	Dr. equipment	3000	
	Cr. cash	~~500~~	500
	Cr. Notes payable		2,500

EX. 10-2 (S.O. 3) On January 1, 2006, Dewey Company purchased a mainframe computer for $150,000. The computer is estimated to have a $30,000 salvage value after its four-year useful life.

Instructions

(a) Fill in the appropriate amounts concerning the depreciation on the computer for the depreciation methods identified below.

(b) Show the depreciation schedules for each method for the years 2006 and 2007.

	Straight-Line Method	Declining Balance Method
Depreciation Expense: 2006	$______	$______
Book Value: 12/31/06	$______	$______
Depreciation Expense: 2007	$______	$______
Book Value: 12/31/07	$______	$______

Schedules

Straight-Line Method

	Computation				End of Year	
Year	Depreciable Cost	X	Depreciation Rate	= Depreciation Expense	Accumulated Depreciation	Book Value

Declining-Balance Method

	Computation				End of Year	
Year	Book Value Beginning of Year	X	Depreciation Rate	= Depreciation Expense	Accumulated Depreciation	Book Value

EX. 10-3 (S.O. 6 and *10) During 2006, the Leibniz Company had the following plant asset transactions.

Jan. 1 Exchange a delivery truck and $3,000 of cash for another delivery truck from Goethe Company. The Leibniz truck had a book value of $5,000 (accumulated depreciation of $2,500) and a fair market value of $7,000. The Goethe truck had a book value of $4,000 (accumulated depreciation of $9,500).

July 1 Sold machinery costing $17,000 for $2,200 cash. The machinery had accumulated depreciation of $12,000 at December 31, 2005, based on annual depreciation of $2,000 per year.

Instructions

(a) Journalize the plant asset transactions.

(b) Assume the same facts in the January 1 exchange except that the fair market value of the Leibniz truck was $3,500. Journalize this exchange transaction.

General Journal			J1
Date 2006 (a)	**Account Title**	**Debit**	**Credit**
	Dr. Equipment (new)	8,000	
	Dr. Accum. Dep-old	2,500	
	Cr. Equip (old)		7500
	Cr. Cash		3,000
		10,500	10,500
	Dr. Cash	2,200	
	Dr. Loss on Sale of asset	1,800	
	Dr. accum. dep -	13,000	4,000
	Cr. Equipment		17,000
Dec			
	Dr. Depreciation exp	1,000	
	Cr. accumulated de		1,000
(b)	Dr. Equipment (new)	6,500	
	Dr. accumulation Dep	2,500	
	Dr. Loss on disposal	1,500	
	Cr. Office equipment		7,500
	Cr. cash		3,000

3,500
3,000
6500

3,500
5,000

5000
−3500
1500

EX 10-4 (S.O. 8) On December 31, 2005, the intangible asset section of Mill Company's balance sheet was:

Patents (net of $9,000 accumulated amortization)	$109,000
Trademarks (net of $10,000 accumulated amortization)	90,000
Copyrights (net of $48,000 accumulated amortization)	12,000
Total intangibles	$211,000

Mill owns two patents, one purchased for $50,000 on 1/1/05 with a total useful life of 10 years , and the other purchased for $68,000 on 1/1/05 with a total useful life of 17 years. The trademark was obtained on 1/1/02 for $100,000. The copyrights were also capitalized on 1/1/00 at a cost of $60,000. During 2006, Mill purchased a patent on July 1 at a cost of $72,000. This patent has a total useful life of 12 years from 7/1/06.

Instructions

Prepare the December 31, 2006 intangible asset section of Mill Company's balance sheet.

MILL COMPANY
Partial Balance Sheet
December 31, 2006

Patents (net of 21,000 accumul amortization) = 88000
9,000 + 5000 + 4000 + 3000 = 21,000
Trademarks net of 12,500 accu. amor) = 87500
10000 + 2,500 = 12,500

Copyrights net accum of 60,000)
48,000 + 12,000
60000

SOLUTIONS TO REVIEW QUESTIONS AND EXERCISES

TRUE-FALSE

1. (T)
2. (F) Land is a plant asset that is not depreciated over its useful life.
3. (F) The cost of tearing down the old building should be debited to Land.
4. (F) The cost of driveways and parking lots is debited to Land Improvements.
5. (T)
6. (F) The cost of equipment includes the cash price, freight charges, expenditures required in assembling, etc. Motor vehicle licenses and accident insurance are expensed as incurred because they represent annual recording expenditures.
7. (F) Recognition of depreciation permits a matching of expenses and revenues, but does not result in the accumulation of cash for the replacement of the asset.
8. (F) Under the straight-line method, depreciation is the same for each year of service life of the asset.
9. (F) Under the units of activity method the decline in service potential is attributed to activity rather than time.
10. (T)
11. (T)
12. (F) When an asset is purchased during the year, it is necessary to prorate the declining balance depreciation in the first year on a time basis.
13. (T)
14. (F) Book value is cost less accumulated depreciation.
15. (F) A fully depreciated plant asset has no book value, so a retirement at a loss is impossible. Generally, the entry would consist of a debit to accumulated depreciation and an equal credit to the asset account.
16. (T)
17. (F) Wasting assets have value but they are not replaceable.
18. (T)
19. (T)
20. (F) Depletion expense is reported as part of the cost of producing the product.
21. (T)
22. (T)
23. (F) The cost of defending the patent should be added to the Patent account and amortized over the remaining life of the patent.
24. (T)
25. (T)

*26. (F) A gain cannot be recognized on the exchange of similar assets.

*27. (T)

*28. (T)

MULTIPLE CHOICE

1. (c) Property, plant and equipment, plant assets (a), fixed assets (b), and long-lived tangible assets (d) are all terms which mean tangible long-lived resources that are used in the operations of the business and are not intended for sale to customers. Intangible assets are not considered to be plant assets.

2. (c) Plant assets are subdivided into the four classes of (a) Land, (b) Land improvements, (c) Buildings, and (d) Equipment. Supplies is classified as a current asset.

3. (d) The acquisition of land will consist of the purchase price ($150,000), attorney's fee ($6,000), demolition and removal costs of an old building ($4,000), and grading and filling ($3,000) for a total of $163,000.

4. (a) Land improvements include driveways (b), parking lots (c), fencing (d), underground sprinkler systems, and similar assets. Building sites (a) are recorded in the Land account.

5. (b) The cost of a plant asset consists of all expenditures necessary to acquire the asset and make it ready for its intended use ($15,000 + $750 + $600 = $16,350). The payment for the license is expensed as incurred because it is an annual recurring expenditure. The insurance premium is recorded as prepaid insurance and expensed over its two-year life.

6. (a) Replacement value is not relevant in computing depreciation.

7. (c) The formula for calculating depreciation expense under the straight-line method is (Cost - Salvage value) ÷ Useful life.

8. (c) The cost of the equipment includes the invoice cost of $280,000, freight costs of $5,000 and installation costs of $25,000. The annual depreciation is then calculated as follows:

   ($310,000 - $10,000) ÷ 5 = $60,000 X 2 = $120,000

9. (d) The salvage value is subtracted from the cost to compute the depreciable cost. The depreciable cost is divided by the total estimated activity (e.g., miles) to compute the depreciable cost per unit. Since the accumulated depreciation for the years 2006 and 2007 is needed, the depreciable cost per unit should be multiplied by the units of activity for both 2006 and 2007.

10. (a) Annual depreciation expense is computed by multiplying the book value at the beginning of the year times the declining balance rate. Salvage value is ignored. The depreciation rate is double the straight-line rate: 1/5 or 20% X 2 = 2/5 or 40%.

	Book Value at Beginning of Year		Depreciation Rate	Annual Depreciation	Book Value
2006	$350,000	X	40%	$140,000	$210,000
2007	210,000	X	40%	84,000	126,000

11. (a) To determine the new annual depreciation expense, the depreciable cost is divided by the revised remaining useful life as follows:

Book value, 1/1/06 ($8,000 - $1,500)	$6,500
Less: Salvage value	2,000
Depreciable cost	$4,500
Remaining useful life (12-2)	10 years
Revised annual depreciation ($4,500 ÷ 10)	$450

12. (c) Ordinary repairs include such expenses as motor tune-ups on delivery trucks, the painting of buildings and the replacing of worn-out tires on delivery trucks. Additions and improvements include costs for (a) constructing a new wing on a building, (b) a major motor overhaul of a new truck, and (d) replacing a stairway with an escalator.

13. (d) Improvements are capital expenditures, not revenue expenditures (a). When the expenditure does not increase useful life, it should be debited to an appropriate asset account.

14. (d) Plant assets may be disposed of by retirement, sale, or exchange.

15. (c) On June 30, 2006, the plant asset would have a book value of $4,500:

Cost	$27,000
Depreciation, 1999-05 (7 X $3,000)	(21,000)
Depreciation, 1/1/03-6/30/03 (6/12 X $3,000)	(1,500)
Book value, 6/30/05	$ 4,500

Since the asset was discarded with no cash proceeds, a loss of $4,500 should be recognized.

16. (a) In 2006, depreciation expense should be recorded for four months (1/1/06 to 5/1/06). This amount is computed below:

$$\text{Annual depreciation} = \frac{\$150{,}000 - \$15{,}000}{10} = \underline{\underline{\$13{,}500}}.$$

Four months' depreciation = $13,500 X 4/12 = $4,500.

17. (b) On May 1, 2006, the office furniture would have a book value of $51,000, as computed below:

Cost	$150,000
Depreciation, 1999-05 (7 X $13,500)	(94,500)
Depreciation, 1/1/06-5/1/06 (4/12 X $13,500)	(4,500)
Book value, 5/1/06	$ 51,000

The gain recognized is the excess of the proceeds ($60,000) over the book value ($51,000) or $9,000.

18. (d) The $8,000 cash is recorded with a debit to Cash and since the amount of cash received is more than the book value of the asset, a gain would be recorded with a credit to Gain on Disposal. Therefore, answers (a), (b), and (c) are all incorrect.

19. (b) Natural resources consist of standing timber and underground deposits of oil, gas, and minerals. Land improvements are reported as plant assets.

20. (a) The entry to record depletion expense results in a debit to Depletion Expense and a credit to Accumulated Depletion. The debit to Depletion Expense decreases net income and stockholders' equity.

21. (c) The computations for depletion are:

$$\frac{\$25{,}000{,}000}{15{,}000{,}000} = \$1.67 \text{ and } \$1.67 \text{ X } 3{,}000{,}000 = \$5{,}000{,}000.$$

The entry is as follows:

Depletion Expense	5,000,000	
Accumulated Depletion		5,000,000

22. (c) Intangible assets are rights, privileges and competitive advantages that result from the ownership of long-lived assets that do not possess physical substance. They include patents, copyrights, trademarks, trade names, franchises, licenses, and goodwill. Accounts receivable are included in current assets.

23. (c) The cost of a patent should be amortized over its legal life or useful life, whichever is shorter; therefore, if its useful life is less than 20 years, then it should be amortized over its useful life.

24. (b) The research and development costs of $350,000 should be expensed when incurred. The legal fees in a successful defense of the patent of $52,000 are debited to the Patent account.

25. (b) Goodwill is an intangible asset that is not recognized in accounting unless it is acquired from another business enterprise. Goodwill is not amortized, but it must be written down if its value is determined to have declined.

*26. (c) In exchanges of similar assets, any loss on the old asset is recognized immediately.

*27. (c) The book value of the used truck is $18,000 ($41,000 - $23,000), while its fair market value is $25,000 ($45,000 value of land obtained less $20,000 in cash paid). In an exchange of **similar** assets, any gain ($7,000 in this case) is deferred. Thus, zero gain or loss is recognized.

*28. (c) Because a loss occurs in this exchange, the acquisition cost is equal to the fair market value of the asset given up ($49,000) plus any cash paid by the purchaser ($7,000) or a total of $56,000. The entry is as follows:

Machine	56,000	
Loss on Disposal	4,000	
Machine		53,000
Cash		7,000

MATCHING

1. b
2. a
3. m
4. e
5. f
6. g
7. d
8. i
9. c
10. j
11. p
12. l
13. n
14. r
15. s
16. q
17. h
18. o
19. k

EXERCISES

EX. 10-1

General Journal			J1
Date	Account Title	Debit	Credit
2006			
Jan. 1	Bus	24,750	
	License Expense	30	
	Prepaid Insurance	800	
	Cash		25,580
July 1	Factory Machinery	3,000	
	Cash		500
	Notes Payable		2,500

EX. 10-2

	Straight-Line Method	**Declining Balance Method**
Depreciation Expense: 2006	$ 30,000	$ 75,000
Book Value: 12/31/06	$120,000	$ 75,000
Depreciation Expense: 2007	$ 30,000	$ 37,500
Book Value: 12/31/07	$ 90,000	$ 37,500

Schedules

Straight-Line Method

	Computation				End of Year	
Year	**Depreciable Cost**	X	**Depreciation Rate**	= **Depreciation Expense**	**Accumulated Depreciation**	**Book Value**
2006	$120,000		25%	$30,000	$30,000	$120,000
2007	120,000		25%	30,000	60,000	90,000

Declining-Balance Method

	Computation				End of Year	
Year	**Book Value Beginning of Year**	X	**Depreciation Rate**	= **Depreciation Expense**	**Accumulated Depreciation**	**Book Value**
2006	$150,000		50%	$75,000	$ 75,000	$75,000
2007	75,000		50%	37,500	112,500	37,500

EX. 10-3

General Journal J1

Date 2006	Account Title	Debit	Credit
(a) Jan. 1	Delivery Equipment	8,000	
	Accumulated Depreciation – Delivery Equipment	2,500	
	Delivery Equipment		7,500
	Cash		3,000
	(To record exchange of similar assets		
	The $2,000 gain reduces the cost of the		
	new truck from $10,000 to $8,000.)		
July 1	Depreciation Expense	1,000	
	Accumulated Depreciation – Machinery		1,000
	(To record six-months' depreciation:		
	$2,000 ÷ 2)		
1	Cash	2,200	
	Accumulated Depreciation – Machinery		
	($12,000 + $1,000)	13,000	
	Loss on Disposal ($4,000 - $2,200)	1,800	
	Machinery		17,000
	(To record sale of machinery)		
2006			
(b) Jan. 1	Delivery Equipment ($3,000 + $3,500)	6,500	
	Accumulated Depreciation – Delivery Equipment	2,500	
	Loss on Disposal ($5,000 - $3,500)	1,500	
	Delivery Equipment		7,500
	Cash		3,000
	(To record exchange of assets and		
	loss on disposal)		

EX. 10-4

MILL COMPANY
Partial Balance Sheet
December 31, 2006

Intangible assets:	
Patents: (net of $21,000 accumulated amortization)	$169,000
Trademarks: (net of $12,500 accumulated amortization)	87,500
Total intangibles	$256,500

Computations:	
Patents: $50,000 + $68,000 + $72,000 =	$190,000
Accumulated amortization: $9,000 + $5,000 + $4,000 + $3,000 =	(21,000)
Patents, net	$169,000
Trademarks:	$100,000
Accumulated Amortization: $10,000 + $2,500 =	(12,500)
Trademarks, net	$ 87,500
Copyrights:	$ 60,000
Accumulated amortization: $48,000 + $12,000 =	(60,000)
Copyrights, net	$ -0-

CHAPTER 11

LIABILITIES

The Navigator ✓

- Scan Study Objectives ☐
- Read Preview ☐
- Read Chapter Review ☐
- Work Demonstration Problem ☐
- Answer True-False Statements ☐
- Answer Multiple-Choice Questions ☐
- Match Terms and Definitions ☐
- Solve Exercises ☐

CHAPTER STUDY OBJECTIVES

After studying this chapter, you should be able to:

1. Explain a current liability and identify the major types of current liabilities.
2. Describe the accounting for notes payable.
3. Explain the accounting for other current liabilities.
4. Explain why bonds are issued and identify the types of bonds.
5. Prepare the entries for the issuance of bonds and interest expense.
6. Describe the entries when bonds are redeemed or converted prior to maturity.
7. Describe the accounting for long-term notes payable.
8. Identify the methods for the financial statement presentation and analysis of long-term liabilities.

*9. Compute the market price of a bond.
*10. Apply the effective-interest method of amortizing bond discount and bond premium.
*11. Apply the straight-line method of amortizing bond discount and bond premium.

The Navigator

***Note:** All **asterisked** (*) items relate to material contained in the Appendix to the chapter.

PREVIEW OF CHAPTER 11

In Chapter 4, we defined liabilities as "creditors" claims on total assets" and as "existing debts and obligations." These claims, debts, and obligations must be settled or paid at some time in the future by the transfer of assets or services. The future date on which they are due or payable (maturity date) is a significant feature of liabilities. This "future date" feature gives rise to two basic classifications of liabilities: (1) current liabilities and (2) long-term liabilities. Thus, our discussion of liabilities in this chapter is divided into these two classifications. The content and organization of the chapter are as follows:

LIABILITIES

Current Liabilities	Long-Term Liabilities
▶ Notes payable	▶ Bond basics
▶ Sales taxes payable	▶ Accounting for bond issues
▶ Payroll and payroll taxes	▶ Accounting for bond retirements
▶ Unearned revenues	▶ Accounting for other long-term notes payable
▶ Current maturities of long-term debt	▶ Statement presentation and analysis
▶ Statement presentation and analysis	

The Navigator

CHAPTER REVIEW

Current Liabilities

1. (S.O. 1) A **current liability** is a debt that can reasonably be expected to be paid (1) from existing current assets or in the creation of other current liabilities, and (2) within one year or the operating cycle whichever is longer. Current liabilities include notes payable, accounts payable, unearned revenues, and accrued liabilities.

Notes Payable

2. (S.O. 2) **Notes payable** are obligations in the form of written promissory notes that usually require the borrower to pay interest. Notes due for payment within one year of the balance sheet date are usually classified as current liabilities.

3. When an **interest-bearing note** is issued, the assets received generally equal the face value of the note:
   a. During the term of the note, it is necessary to accrue interest expense.
   b. At maturity, Notes Payable is debited for the face value of the note and Interest Payable is debited for accrued interest.

Sales Taxes Payable

4. (S.O. 3) A **sales tax** is expressed as a stated percentage of the sales price on goods sold to customers by a retailer. The entry by the retailer to record sales taxes is as follows:

Cash	XXXX	
Sales		XXXX
Sales Taxes Payable		XXXX

When sales taxes are not rung up separately on the cash register, receipts are divided by 100% plus the sales tax percentage to determine the sales.

Wages and Salaries Payable

5. The amount of unpaid pay owed to employees is **wages and salaries payable.** Mandatory payroll deductions remitted to government authorities are withholding taxes, such as personal, state, and federal income taxes, social security taxes, and medicare taxes. Also, with every payroll, the employer incurs liabilities to pay various **payroll taxes,** such as social security taxes and the state and federal unemployment taxes.

6. The payroll and payroll tax liability accounts are classified as current liabilities.

Unearned Revenues

7. **Unearned Revenues** (advances from customers) are recorded by a debit to Cash and a credit to a current liability account identifying the source of the unearned revenue. When the revenue is earned, the unearned revenue account is debited and an earned revenue account is credited.

Current Maturities of Long-Term Debt

8. Another item classified as a current liability is **current maturities of long-term debt.** Current maturities of long-term debt are often identified on the balance sheet as long-term debt due within one year.

Financial Statement Presentation of Current Liabilities

9. Current liabilities is the first category under liabilities on the balance sheet.
   a. Each of the principal types of current liabilities is listed separately.
   b. Current liabilities are usually in order of magnitude with the largest obligations being listed first. However, many companies, as a matter of custom, show notes payable and accounts payable first regardless of amount.

10. The excess of current assets over current liabilities is **working capital.** The **current ratio** is current assets divided by current liabilities.

Bonds

11. (S.O. 4) **Long-term liabilities** are obligations that are expected to be paid after one year. Long-term liabilities include bonds, long-term notes, and lease liabilities.

12. Bonds offer the following **advantages** over common stock:
    a. Stockholder control is not affected.
    b. Tax savings result.
    c. Earnings per share of common stock may be higher.

13. The **major disadvantages** in the use of bonds are that interest must be paid on a periodic basis, and the principal (face value) of the bonds must be paid at maturity.

Types of Bonds

14. **Secured bonds** have specific assets of the issuer pledged as collateral for the bonds. A **mortgage bond** is secured by real estate. **Unsecured bonds** are issued against the general credit of the borrower; they are called **debenture bonds.**

15. Bonds that mature at a single specified future date are called **term bonds.** In contrast, bonds that mature in installments are called **serial bonds.**

16. **Registered bonds** are issued in the name of the owner and have interest payments made by check to bondholders of record. **Bearer or coupon bonds** are not registered; thus bondholders must send in coupons to receive interest payments.

17. **Convertible bonds** permit bondholders to convert the bonds into common stock at their option. **Callable bonds** are subject to call and retirement at a stated dollar amount prior to maturity at the option of the issuer.

18. State laws grant corporations the power to issue bonds.
    a. Within the corporation, formal approval by both the board of directors and stockholders is usually required before bonds can be issued.
    b. In authorizing a bond issue, the board of directors must stipulate the total number of bonds to be authorized and the contractual interest rate.

c. The terms of the bond issue are set forth in a formal legal document called a **bond indenture.**

Market Value of Bonds

19. The **market value** (present value of a bond) is a function of three factors: (a) the dollar amounts to be received, (b) the length of time until the amount is received, and (c) the market rate of interest. The process of finding the present value is referred to as discounting the future amounts.

Bond Issues

20. (S.O. 5) The issuance of bonds at **face value** results in a debit to Cash and a credit to Bonds Payable.
    a. Over the term of the bonds, entries are required for bond interest.
    b. At the maturity date, it is necessary to record the final payment of interest and payment of the face value of the bonds.

21. Bonds may be issued below or above face value.
    a. If the market (effective) rate of interest is higher than the contractual (stated) rate, the bonds will sell at less than face value, or at a discount.
    b. If the market rate of interest is less than the contractual rate on the bonds, the bonds will sell above face value, or at a premium.

Bond Issues at Discount

22. When bonds are issued at a **discount,**
    a. The discount is debited to a contra account, Discount on Bonds Payable, that is deducted from Bonds Payable on the balance sheet to show the carrying (or book) value of the bonds.
    b. Bond discount is an additional cost of borrowing that should be recorded as bond interest expense over the life of the bonds.

Bond Issues at Premium

23. When bonds are issued at a **premium,**
    a. The premium is credited to the account, Premium on Bonds Payable, that is added to Bonds Payable on the balance sheet.
    b. Bond premium is a reduction in the cost of borrowing that should be credited to Bond Interest Expense over the life of the bonds.

Bond Retirements

24. (S.O. 6) When bonds are **retired before maturity** it is necessary to (a) eliminate the carrying value of the bonds at the redemption date, (b) record the cash paid, and (c) recognize the gain or loss on redemption. A gain (loss) is reported as an **extraordinary item** on the income statement.

25. In recording the **conversion of bonds** into common stock the current market prices of the bonds and the stock are ignored. Instead, the carrying value of the bonds is transferred to paid-in capital accounts and no gain or loss is recognized.

Long-term Notes Payable

26. (S.O. 7) A **long-term note payable** may be secured by a document called a mortgage that pledges title to specific assets as security for the loan.
    a. Typically, the terms require the borrower to make installment payments consisting of (1) interest on the unpaid balance of the loan and (2) a reduction of loan principal.
    b. Mortgage notes payable are recorded initially at face value; each installment payment results in a debit to Interest Expense and a debit to Mortgage Notes Payable.

Presentation and Analysis of Long-Term Notes Payable

27. (S.O. 8) Long-term liabilities are reported in a separate section of the balance sheet immediately following current liabilities.

28. The **debt to total assets ratio** measures the percentage of the total assets provided by creditors. It is computed by dividing total debt by total assets.

29. The **times interest earned ratio** provides an indication of the company's ability to meet interest payments as they become due. It is computed by dividing income before interest expense and income taxes by interest expense.

Present Value Variables

*30. (S.O. 9) The present value is based on three variables: (1) the dollar amount to be received (future amount), (2) the length of time until the amount is received (number of periods), and (3) the interest rate (the discount rate).

PV = FV/(1 + 1)

PV = present value
FV = future value
I = interest rate

*31. The present value of 1 may also be determined through tables that show the present value of 1 for n periods.

Present Value of an Annuity

*32. In computing the present value of an annuity, it is necessary to know (1) the discount rate, (2) the number of discount periods, and (3) the amount of the periodic receipts or payments. When the future receipts are the same in each period, there are two other ways to compute the present value. First, the annual cash flow can be multiplied by the sum of the three present value factors. Second, annuity tables may be used.

Time Periods and Discounting

*33. Discounting may also be done over shorter periods of time such as monthly, quarterly, or semiannually. When the time frame is less than one year, it is necessary, to convert the annual interest rate to the applicable time frame.

Computing the Present Value of a Long-Term Note or Bond

*34. The present value (or market price) of a long-term note or bond is a function of three variables: (1) the payment amounts, (2) the length of time until the amounts are paid, and (3) the discount rate. When the investor's discount rate is equal to the bond's contractual interest rate, the present value of the bonds will equal the face value of the bonds.

Effective-Interest Method

*35. (S.O. 10) The **effective interest method** of amortization is an alternative to the straight-line method. Under this method,

a. Bond Interest Expense is computed first by multiplying the carrying value of the bonds at the beginning of the period by the effective interest rate.

b. The credit to Cash (or Bond Interest Payable) is computed by multiplying the face value of the bonds by the contractual interest rate.

c. The bond discount or premium amortization amount is then determined by comparing bond interest expense with the interest paid or accrued.

*36. The effective interest method produces a periodic interest expense equal to a constant percentage of the carrying value of the bonds. When the amounts of bond interest expense are materially different under the two methods, the effective interest method is required under generally accepted accounting principles.

Straight-Line Method

*37. (S.O. 11) The straight-line method of amortization allocates the same amount of bond discount each interest period. The formula is:

Bond Discount ÷ Number of Interest Periods = Bond Discount Amortization

Bond discount amortization is recorded by debiting Bond Interest Expense and crediting Discount on Bonds Payable.

DEMONSTRATION PROBLEM 1 (S.O. 1, 2, and 3)

On January 1, 2006, the ledger of Reichenbacher Company contains the following liability accounts:

Note Payable	$52,000
Accounts Payable	61,500
Interest Payable	520
Sales Taxes Payable	7,700
Advances from Customers	4,000

The note payable was issued on November 30, 2005. It bears 12% interest and matures on May 31, 2006. During 2006, the following selected transactions occurred:

Feb.	5	Sold merchandise for cash totaling $13,650 which includes 5% sales tax.
Mar.	13	Provided services for customers who had made advance payments of $2,000.
Apr.	22	Paid $32,000 of accounts payable.
May	31	Accrued interest on note payable for five months.
May	31	Paid the note due.
June	15	Borrowed $22,000 in cash from Sandwich Bank on a 10% interesting-bearing, three-month note having face value of $22,000.
Aug.	7	Sold merchandise on credit totaling $28,350 which includes 5% sales tax.
Sept.	15	Recognized interest expense on Sandwich Bank note.
Sept.	15	Paid the note due.
Nov.	30	Borrowed $30,000 in cash from Somonauk Bank on a six-month, 12%, $30,000 note.

Instructions

(a) Journalize the 2006 transactions.

(b) Journalize the adjusting entry at December 31, 2006 for the outstanding notes payable.

The Navigator

SOLUTION TO DEMONSTRATION PROBLEM 1

Date		Account	Debit	Credit
Feb.	5	Cash	13,650	
		Sales ($13,650 ÷ 105%)		13,000
		Sales Taxes Payable		650
		(To record sales and sales taxes)		
Mar.	13	Advances From Customers	2,000	
		Sales		2,000
		(To record services performed)		
Apr.	22	Accounts Payable	32,000	
		Cash		32,000
		(To record payment of Accounts Payable)		
May	31	Interest Expense	2,600	
		Interest Payable		2,600
		(To record accrued interest: $52,000 X 12% X 5/12)		
May	31	Notes Payable	52,000	
		Interest Payable ($520 + $2,600)	3,120	
		Cash		55,120
		(To record payment of interest-bearing note)		
June	15	Cash	22,000	
		Notes Payable		22,000
		(To record receipt of cash and issuance of 3-month, 10% interesting-bearing note)		
Aug.	7	Accounts Receivable	28,350	
		Sales		27,000
		Sales Taxes Payable		1,350
		(To record sales and sales taxes)		
Sept.	15	Interest Expense	550	
		Interest Payable		550
		(To recognize interest expense for 3 months $22,000 X 10% X 3/12)		
Sept.	15	Notes Payable	22,000	
		Interest Payable	550	
		Cash		22,550
		(To recognize payment of 10% interest-bearing note)		
Nov.	30	Cash	30,000	
		Notes Payable		30,000
		(To record receipt of cash and issuance of 12%, 6-month note)		

(continued)

(b)

Dec. 31	Interest Expense ($30,000 X 12% X 1/12)	300	
	Interest Payable		300
	(To record interest expense for one month on $30,000 interest-bearing note)		

DEMONSTRATION PROBLEM 2 (S.O. 4, 5, and 6)

The following is taken from the Brent Company balance sheet at December 31, 2006:

Current liabilities		
Bond interest payable		$ 225,000
Long-term liabilities		
Bond payable, 10%, due December 31, 2016	$4,500,000	
Add: Premium on Bonds Payable	300,000	4,800,000

The bonds originally sold for $5,100,000 when they were issued on January 1, 1997. Bond interest is payable semiannually on January 1 and July 1. The bonds are callable on any semiannual interest date. Brent uses straight-line amortization for any bond premium or discount.

Instructions

(a) Prepare the necessary journal entries to record the semiannual interest payments, the premium amortization, and accrued interest in 1997. (Note that as of December 31, 2006, the bonds will be outstanding for 10 additional years.)

(b) Prepare the journal entry to record the redemption of $2,000,000 face value bonds on January 1, 2008, after accrued interest was paid. The bonds were called at 103.

(c) Prepare the journal entry to record the payment of bond interest on July 1, 2008 on the remaining bonds. Include the amortization of the remaining bond premium.

SOLUTION TO DEMONSTRATION PROBLEM 2

(a)

Date		Account	Debit	Credit
Jan.	1	Bond Interest Payable	225,000	
		Cash		225,000
July	1	Bond Interest Expense	210,000	
		Premium on Bonds Payable ($300,000 X 6/120)	15,000	
		Cash		225,000
Dec.	31	Bond Interest Expense	210,000	
		Premium on Bonds Payable	15,000	
		Bond Interest Payable		225,000

(b)

Date		Account	Debit	Credit
Jan.	1	Bonds Payable	2,000,000	
		Premium on Bonds Payable	120,000	
		Gain on Bond Redemption		60,000
		Cash ($2,000,000 X 1.03)		2,060,000

Premium on Bonds Payable:	
Balance, Dec. 31, 2006	$300,000
July 1, 2007 amortization	(15,000)
Dec. 31, 2007	(15,000)
Balance, January 1	270,000
Pro rata	X 20/45
Amount redeemed	$120,000

(c)

Date		Account	Debit	Credit
July	1	Bond Interest Expense	116,667	
		Premium on Bonds Payable ($15,000 X 25/45)	8,333	
		Cash ($2,500,000 X 5%)		125,000

Alternatively:

Premium on Bonds Payable:	
Amount before redemption	$270,000
Amount redeemed	120,000
Total	150,000
Months outstanding at Jan. 1	÷ 108
Amortized per month	1,389
Six months of 2008	X 6
Total amortization	$ 8,334

DEMONSTRATION PROBLEM 3 (S.O. 3)

Gardner Co. is about to issue $1,000,000 of 10-year bonds paying a 10% interest rate, with interest payable semiannually. The discount rate for such securities is 8%. How much can Gardner expect to receive for the sale of these bonds?

SOLUTION TO DEMONSTRATION PROBLEM 3

Present value of principal to be received at maturity	
$1,000,000 X PV of 1 due in 20 periods at 4%	
$1,000,000 X .45639 (Table 1)	$ 456,390
Present value of interest to be received periodically over the terms of the bonds	
$50,000 X PV of 1 due periodically for 20 periods at 4%	
$50,000 X 13.5903 (Table 2)	679,515
Present value of bonds	$1,135,905

REVIEW QUESTIONS AND EXERCISES

TRUE—FALSE

Indicate whether each of the following is true (T) or false (F) in the space provided.

_____ 1. (S.O. 1) A debt that is expected to be paid within one year through the creation of long-term debt is a current liability.

_____ 2. (S.O. 2) Obligations in the form of written promissory notes are recorded as accounts payable.

_____ 3. (S.O. 2) Notes payable usually are issued to meet long-term financing needs.

_____ 4. (S.O. 3) A company does not report sales taxes as an expense but merely forwards the amount paid by the customer to the government.

_____ 5. (S.O. 3) Unearned Revenues are classified as a current asset.

_____ 6. (S.O. 3) Current maturities of long-term debt are often identified as long-term debt due within one year on the balance sheet.

_____ 7. (S.O. 3) Current liabilities are usually listed in the order of maturity.

_____ 8. (S.O. 4) A disadvantage of issuing bonds over common stock is that bondholders do not have voter rights.

_____ 9. (S.O. 4) Unsecured bonds, also known as debenture bonds, are issued against the general credit of the borrower.

_____ 10. (S.O. 4) Bonds that mature at a single specified future date are called term bonds.

_____ 11. (S.O. 4) Bonds that permit bondholders to convert them into common stock at their option are known as callable bonds.

_____ 12. (S.O. 4) The terms of the bond issue are set forth in a formal legal document called a bond indenture.

_____ 13. (S.O. 5) Bond Interest Payable on long-term bonds is classified as a long-term liability.

_____ 14. (S.O. 5) If the market (effective) interest rate is higher than the contractual (stated) rate, the bonds will sell at less than face value, or at a discount.

_____ 15. (S.O. 5) The carrying value of bonds at maturity should be equal to the face value of the bonds.

_____ 16. (S.O. 5) Premium on Bonds Payable is a contra account to Bonds Payable.

_____ 17. (S.O. 5) The sale of bonds above face value causes the total cost at borrowing to be less than the bond interest cost.

_____ 18. (S.O. 6) When bonds are converted into common stock, the carrying value of the bonds is transferred to paid-in capital accounts.

_____ *19. (S.O. 9) The effective interest method results in a varying amount of interest expense but a constant rate of interest each interest period.

_____ *20. (S.O. 9) Generally accepted accounting principles require that the straight-line method be used when the annual amounts of bond interest expense for the straight-line method and the effective interest method are materially different.

The Navigator

MULTIPLE CHOICE

Circle the letter that best answers each of the following statements.

1. (S.O. 1) Which of the following statements concerning current liabilities is **incorrect?**
   a. Current liabilities include unearned revenues.
   b. A company that has more current liabilities than current assets is usually the subject of some concern.
   c. Current liabilities include prepaid expenses.
   d. A current liability is a debt that can reasonably be expected to be paid out of existing current assets or result in the creation of other current liabilities.

Items 2 and 3 pertain to the following information:

On October 1, 2006, Frederick Douglass Company issued a $28,000, 10%, nine-month interest-bearing note.

2. (S.O. 2) If the Frederick Douglass Company is preparing financial statements at December 31, 2006, the adjusting entry for accrued interest will include a:
   a. credit to Notes Payable of $700.
   b. debit to Interest Expense of $700.
   c. credit to Interest Payable of $1,400.
   d. debit to Interest Expense of $1,050.

3. (S.O. 2) Assuming interest was accrued on June 30, 2007, the entry to record the payment of the note on July 1, 2007, will include a:
   a. debit to Interest Expense of $700.
   b. credit to Cash of $28,000.
   c. debit to Interest Payable of $2,100.
   d. debit to Notes Payable of $30,100.

4. (S.O. 2) On August 1, 2006, a company borrowed cash and signed a one-year interest-bearing note on which both the face value and interest are payable on August 1, 2007. How will the note payable and the related interest be classified in the December 31, 2006, balance sheet?

	Note Payable	Interest Payable
a.	Current liability	Noncurrent liability
b.	Noncurrent liability	Current liability
c.	Current liability	Current liability
d.	Noncurrent liability	Not shown

5. (S.O. 3) The Pam Travis Company has total proceeds (before segregation of sales taxes) from sales of $2,100. If the sales tax is 5%, the amount to be credited to the account Sales is:
   a. $2,100.
   b. $1,995.
   c. $1,900.
   d. $2,000.

6. (S.O. 5) When bonds are sold at face value on the issue date, Bonds Payable is credited for:
   a. maturity value plus interest payable.
   b. face value.
   c. call price.
   d. conversion price.

7. (S.O. 5) On the maturity date, January 1, Mora Corporation pays the accrued interest recorded on December 31 and the face value of the bonds. The entry to record the payment will result in a credit to Cash and a debit to:
   a. Bonds Payable for the total payment.
   b. Bonds Payable for the face amount and as debit to Bond Interest Expense for the interest due.
   c. Bonds Payable for the face amount and a debit to Bond Interest Payable for the interest due.
   d. none of the above.

8. (S.O. 5) On the date of issue, ARCO Corporation sells $2 million 5-year bonds at 97. The entry to record the sale will include the following debits and credits.

	Bonds Payable	Discount on Bonds Payable
a.	$1,940,000 Cr.	$0 Dr.
b.	$2,000,000 Cr.	$60,000 Dr.
c.	$2,000,000 Cr.	$500,000 Dr.
d.	$2,000,000 Cr.	$6,000 Dr.

9. (S.O. 5) On the issue date, Rhoda Corporation sells $1,000,000 bonds at 103. The entry to record the sale will include a credit to Premium on Bonds Payable of:
   a. $0.
   b. $3,000.
   c. $30,000.
   d. $300,000

10. (S.O. 5) The market price of a bond is the:
    a. present value of its principal amount at maturity plus the present value of all future interest payments.
    b. principal amount plus the present value of all future interest payments.
    c. principal amount plus all future interest payments
    d. present value of its principal amount only.

11. (S.O. 5) The market rate of interest for a bond issue which sells for more than its par value is:
    a. independent of the interest rate stated on the bond.
    b. higher than the interest rate stated on the bond.
    c. equal to the interest rate stated on the bond.
    d. less than the interest rate stated on the bond.

12. (S.O. 6) Hoffman Corporation retires $100,000 of its bonds at 106 on January 1, following the payment of semiannuial interest. The carrying value of the bonds at the redemption date is $104,950. The entry to record the redemption will include a:
    a. credit of $4,950 to Loss on Bond Redemption.
    b. debit of $6,000 to Premium on Bonds Payable.
    c. credit of $1,050 to Gain on Bond Redemption.
    d. debit of $4,950 to Premium on Bonds Payable.

13. (S.O. 6) Ray Corporation's $100,000 convertible bonds are converted into 3,000 shares of $20 par value common stock when the market price of the stock is $40 per share. Using the book value method, the entry to record the conversion will include a:
    a. credit to Paid-in Capital in Excess of Par Value of $40,000.
    b. debit to Loss on Bond Conversion of $20,000.
    c. credit to Paid-in Capital in Excess of Par Value of $20,000.
    d. debit to Loss on Bond Conversion of $60,000.

14. (S.O. 7) Buffon Electronics Company issues a $300,000, 10%, 20-year mortgage note on January 1. The terms provide for semiannual installment payments, exclusive of real estate taxes and insurance of $17,483. After the first installment payment, the principal balance is:
    a. $300,000.
    b. $294,910.
    c. $297,517.
    d. $292,172.

15. (S.O. 7) Portly Cihla, Inc. issues a $1,000,000, 10%, 20-year mortgage note on January1, 2006. The note will be paid in annual installments of $140,000 each payable at the end of the year. What is the amount of interest expense that should be recognized by Portly Cihla, Inc. in the second year?
    a. $36,000.
    b. $86,000.
    c. $96,000.
    d. $100,000.

16. (S.O. 8) Using Table 1, the present value factor for 2 periods at a discount rate of 8% is:
    a. .89000.
    b. .92593.
    c. .91743.
    d. .85734.

17. (S.O. 8) A higher discount rate produces:
    a. a smaller present value.
    b. a higher present value.
    c. the same present value.
    d. a greater length of time.

18. (S.O. 8) The present value of $5,000 due in 10 years using a discount rate of 12% is:
    a. $1,609.85.
    b. $1,927.70.
    c. $2,837.15.
    d. $3,219.70.

19. (S.O. 8) Which of the following is not necessary to know when computing the present value of an annuity?
    a. The discount rate.
    b. The amount of the periodic receipts or payments.
    c. The number of discount periods.
    d. The probability of receiving the amount due.

*20. (S.O. 9) How does the amortization of discount on bonds payable affect each of the following?

	Carrying Value of Bond	Net Income
a.	Increase	Decrease
b.	Increase	Increase
c.	Decrease	Decrease
d.	Decrease	Increase

*21. (S.O. 9) How does the amortization of premium on bonds payable affect each of the following?

	Carrying Value of Bond	Net Income
a.	Increase	Decrease
b.	Increase	Increase
c.	Decrease	Decrease
d.	Decrease	Increase

*22. (S.O. 9) Under the effective interest method of amortization, interest expense is computed by multiplying:
a. the face value of the bonds by the contractual interest rate.
b. the carrying value of the bonds at the beginning of the period by the effective interest rate.
c. the carrying value of the bonds at the beginning of the period by the contractual interest rate.
d. the carrying value of the bonds at the end of the period by the effective interest rate.

*23. (S.O. 9) On January 1, Arawak, Inc. issued $2,000,000 of 9% bonds for $1,900,000. The bonds were issued to yield 10%. Interest is payable annually on December 31. Arawak uses the effective interest method of amortizing bond discount. At the end of the first year, Arawak should report unamortized bond discount of:
a. $90,000.
b. $71,000.
c. $51,610.
d. $51,000.

*24. (S.O. 9) On January 1, when the market interest rate was 14%, Santorio Corporation issued bonds in the face amount of $500,000, with interest at 12% payable semiannually. The bonds were issued at a discount of $53,180. How much of the discount should be amortized by the effective interest method for the first interest period?
a. $1,277.
b. $2,659.
c. $3,191.
d. $3,723.

*25. (S.O. 9) On January 1, Abbie Corporation issued $500,000 of 12%, six-year bonds with interest payable on July 1 and January 1. The bonds sold for $549,300 at an effective interest rate of 10%. On the first interest date, using the effective interest method, the debit entry to Bond Interest Expense is for:

a. $25,000.
b. $27,465.
c. $32,958.
d. $50,000.

*26. (S.O. 10) The effects of the straight-line method of amortization on the following in each interest period (assuming discount or premium amortization) are:

	Amount of Interest Expense	Carrying Value of Bonds
a.	Same	Increases or decreases
b.	Same	No effect
c.	Different	Increases or decreases
d.	Different	No effect

*27. (S.O. 10) On January 1, the Montesque Corporation sells $300,000 of 5-year, 10% bonds at 98 with interest payable on July 1 and January 1. The entry on July 1 to record payment of bond interest and the amortization of bond discount using the straight-line method will include a:

a. debit to Interest Expense, $15,000.
b. debit to Interest Expense, $30,000.
c. credit to Discount on Bonds Payable, $600.
d. credit to Discount on Bonds Payable, $1,200.

*28. (S.O. 10) For the bonds issued in question 27, above, what is the carrying value of the bonds at the end of the fourth interest period?

a. $297,600.
b. $296,400.
c. $294,000.
d. $291,600.

The Navigator

MATCHING

Match each term with its definition by writing the appropriate letter in the space provided.

Terms

_____ 1. Bond indenture.

_____ 2. Long-term liabilities.

_____ 3. Mortgage bond.

_____ 4. Current liability.

_____ 5. Callable bonds.

_____ 6. Convertible bonds.

_____ *7. Effective interest method of amortization.

_____ 8. Market (effective) interest rate.

_____ 9. Contractual (stated) interest rate.

_____ 10. Straight-line method of amortization.

Definitions

a. A method of writing off bond discount or bond premium that results in a periodic interest expense that is the same amount each interest period.

b. Obligations that are expected to be paid after one year.

c. Rate used to determine the amount of cash interest the borrower pays and the investor receives.

d. Bonds that permit bondholders to convert them into common stock at their option.

e. The rate investors demand for loaning funds to the corporation.

f. A legal document that sets forth the terms of the bond issue.

g. A bond secured by real estate.

h. A debt that can reasonably be expected to be paid from existing current assets or through the creation of other current liabilities within the next year or operating cycle, whichever is longer.

i. Bonds subject to call and retirement at a stated dollar amount prior to maturity at the option of the issuer.

j. A method of writing off bond discount or bond premium that results in a periodic interest expense equal to a constant percentage of the carrying value of the bonds.

The Navigator

EXERCISES

EX. 11-1 (S.O. 2 and 3) The following transactions took place during 2006 for Revel Pots and Pans Company:

Aug. 1 Borrowed $10,000 in cash from the Third National Bank by issuing a $10,000 eight-month, 12% interest-bearing note.

Dec. 1 Borrowed $20,000 in cash from the Second Federal Savings & Loan by issuing a six-month, 10% interest-bearing note.

Dec. 24 Determined from cash register readings that sales were $24,650 and sales taxes were $1,650.

Instructions

(a) Journalize the transactions above.
(b) Prepare the adjusting entries for the two notes at December 31, 2006.
(c) Record interest expense and payment of the two notes in 2007 at their maturity dates.

General Journal J1

Date	Account Title	Debit	Credit
2006 (a)	Dr. Cash	10,000	
	Dr. Notes payable		10,000
	Dr. Cash	20,000	
	Dr. Notes payable		20,000
	Dr. Cash	26,300	
	Cr. Sales		24,650
	Cr. Sales tax payable		1,650

General Journal J

Date	Account Title	Debit	Credit
(a) cont.			
2006 (b)	Dr. Interest Expense	500	
	Cr. Interest payable		500
	10,000 X .12 X 5/12		
	Dr. Interest Expense	167	
	Cr. Interest payable		167
	20,000 X .10 X 1/12		

General Journal

J

Date	Account Title	Debit	Credit
2007 (c)	Dr. Interest Expense	300	
	Cr. Interest Payable		300
	10,000 x 12% 3/12		
	Dr. Notes payable	10,000	
	Dr. Interest payable	800	
	Cr. Cash		10,800
	Dr. Interest Expense	833	
	Cr. Interest payable		833
	20000 x .10 x 5/12		
	Dr. Notes payable	20,000	
	Dr. Interest payable	1,000	
	Cr. Cash		21,000

EX. 11-2 (S.O. 5 and *9) On January 1, Gutenberg Printers Inc. issues $400,000, 10-year 12% bonds at 98 with interest payable on July 1 and January 1.

Instructions

(a) Journalize the issuance of the bonds and the entries on July 1 and December 31 for interest and the amortization of bond discount using the straight-line method. (Omit explanations.)

(b) Journalize the July 1 and December 31 entries assuming the effective interest rate on the bonds is 12.4% and the effective interest method is used. (Omit explanations.)

General Journal J1

Date	Account Title	Debit	Credit
(a)			
(b)			

EX. 11-3 (S.O. 6 and 7) Devers Computers Inc. has the following transactions concerning long-term liabilities during the current year.

April 1 Convertible bonds issued by Devers at face value are converted into common stock. The $100,000 bond issue has a conversion price of $25 per share of common stock with one $1,000 bond convertible into 40 shares of stock. The common stock has a par value of $10 and a fair market price of $30 at the time of conversion.

June 30 The first installment payment on a $100,000, 10%, 10-year mortgage note is made by Devers. The terms of the mortgage contract provided for semiannual installment payments, exclusive of real estate taxes and insurance of $8,024.

Dec. 31 The second installment payment is made on the mortgage note.

10%/2 10x2

Instructions

Journalize the transactions. (Omit explanations.)

General Journal J1

Date	Account Title	Debit	Credit
	Dr. Bonds payable	100,000	
	Cr. Common Stock		40,000
	Cr. APIC-common stk		60,000
	Dr. Interest exp	5,000	
	(100,000 x .10 x ½)		
	Dr. Mortgage Payable	3,024	
	Cr. Cash		8024
	Dr. Interest expense	4849	
	96976 x 10% x ½	3175	
	Dr. mortgage payable		8024
	Cr. Cash		

The Navigator

SOLUTIONS TO REVIEW QUESTIONS AND EXERCISES

TRUE-FALSE

1. (F) A current liability must meet **both** of the following criteria: (1) it is expected to be paid from existing current assets or through the creation of other current liabilities, and (2) it is expected to be paid within one year or the operating cycle, whichever is longer.
2. (F) Obligations in the form of written promissory notes are recorded as notes payable.
3. (F) Notes payable usually are issued to meet short-term financing needs.
4. (T)
5. (F) Unearned Revenues are classified as a current liability.
6. (T)
7. (F) Current liabilities are seldom listed in the order of maturity because of the varying maturity dates that may exist for a specific type of obligation such as notes payable. They are usually listed in order of magnitude.
8. (F) The fact that bondholders do not have voting rights is an advantage for common stockholders because their control is not affected.
9. (T)
10. (T)
11. (F) Bonds that permit bondholders to convert the bonds into common stock at their option are known as convertible bonds.
12. (T)
13. (F) Because interest on bonds is usually payable annually or semiannually, the interest is expected to be paid within the following year and thus is a current liability.
14. (T)
15. (T)
16. (F) The premium account is added to Bonds Payable on the balance sheet.
17. (T)
18. (T)

*19. (T)

*20. (F) Generally accepted accounting principles require that the effective interest method be used when the annual amounts of bond interest expense for the straight-line method and the effective interest method are materially different.

MULTIPLE CHOICE

1. (c) Prepaid expenses are current assets. Answers (a), (b), and (d) are all correct statements.

2. (b) The adjusting entry for the company is as follows:

Interest Expense	700	
Interest Payable ($28,000 X 10% X 3/12)		700

3. (c) The entry to record the payment of the note is as follows:

Notes Payable	28,000	
Interest Payable ($28,000 X 10% X 6/12 + $700)	2,100	
Cash		30,100

4. (c) Because the note and the accrued interest are payable within one year or the operating cycle whichever is longer from December 31, 2006, they both should be classified as current liabilities.

5. (d) The entry for Pam Travis Company to record sales and sales taxes is as follows:

Cash	2,100	
Sales ($2,100 ÷ 105%)		2,000
Sales Taxes Payable ($2,000 X 5%)		100

6. (b) When bonds are sold at face value on the issue date, Bonds Payable is credited for the face value of the bonds issued.

7. (c) The interest due was recorded on December 31 through an adjusting entry for accrued interest. Thus, the entry on January 1 will result in debits to Bonds Payable for the face amount and to Bond Interest Payable for the interest due.

8. (b) The proceeds from the sale are $1,940,000 ($2,000,000 X .97). Thus, Discount on Bonds Payable is debited for $60,000 and Bonds Payable is credited for the face amount, $2,000,000.

9. (c) The proceeds from the sale are $1,030,000 ($1,000,000 X 1.03). Thus, Premium on Bonds Payable is credited for $30,000 in the entry.

10. (a) The market price of a bond is equal to the present value of its principal amount at maturity plus the present value of all future interest payments.

11. (d) When bonds are sold at a premium, the market rate of interest is less than the contractual interest rate on the bonds.

12. (d) The entry to record the redemption is as follows:

Bonds Payable	100,000	
Premium on Bonds Payable	4,950	
Loss on Bond Redemption	1,050	
Cash		106,000

13. (a) The entry to record the conversion of the bonds into common stock is as follows:

Bonds Payable	100,000	
Common Stock (3,000 X $20)		60,000
Paid-in Capital in Excess of Par Value		40,000

No gain or loss is recognized when the book value method is used.

14. (c) The installment payment schedule for the first payment is:

Payment Date	Cash Payment	Interest Expense	Reduction of Principal	Principal Balance
7/1				$300,000
7/1	$17,483	$15,000*	$2,483	297,517

*Interest expense is the principal balance times the semiannual interest rate of 5%.

15. (c) The installment payment schedule for the first two payments is:

Payment Date	Cash Payment	Interest Expense	Reduction of Principal	Principal Balance
1/1/04				$1,000,000
12/31/04	$140,000	$100,000*	$40,000	960,000
12/31/05	$140,000	$ 96,000*		

*Interest expense is the principal balance times the annual interest rate of 10%.

16. (d) Using Table 1 going down the 8% column and across the 2 periods row, the number .85734 represents the present value of 1.

17. (a) A higher discount rate produces a smaller present value. A lower discount rate produces a higher present value.

18. (a) Using Table 1 going down the 12% column and across the 10 periods row, the number .32197 represents the present value of 1. Multiplying the amount from the table by $5,000 and the answer equals $1,609.85 ($5,000 X .32197).

19. (d) In computing the present value of an annuity, it is necessity to know (1) the discount rate, (2) the number of discount periods, and (3) the amount of the periodic receipts or payments.

*20. (a) The amortization of discount on bonds payable decreases Discount on Bonds Payable which is a contra account for Bonds Payable. Thus, the carrying value of the bonds **increases.** The amortized discount increases the amount of interest expense and therefore **decreases** net income.

*21. (d) The amortization of a premium on bonds payable decreases Premium on Bonds Payable which is reported as an addition to Bonds Payable. Thus, the carrying value of the bonds **decreases.** The amortized premium reduces the amount of interest expense and therefore **increases** net income.

*22. (b) The first step in the effective interest method is to determine the bond interest expense by multiplying the carrying value of the bonds at the beginning of the period by the effective interest rate.

*23. (a) The amount in Discount on Bonds Payable on January 1 is $100,000 ($2,000,000 - $1,900,000). At December 31, Bond Interest Expense is $190,000 ($1,900,000 X 10%) and the interest payable is $180,000 ($2,000,000 X 9%). The discount amortization is $10,000 and the balance in Discount on Bonds Payable is $90,000 ($100,000 - $10,000).

*24. (a) The entry on July 1 for the interest payment is:

Bond Interest Expense ($446,820 X 7%)	31,277	
Discount on Bonds Payable		1,277
Cash ($500,000 X 6%)		30,000

*25. (b) The debit to Bond Interest Expense is ($549,300 X 10% X 1/2) = $27,465.

*26. (a) Under the straight-line method, the amortization amount is the same each interest period. Thus, the amount of interest expense is the same each period but the carrying value of the bonds increases if a discount and decreases if a premium.

*27. (c) Bond discount of $6,000 ($300,000 - $294,000) should be amortized over 10 interest periods. The entry on July 1 is:

Bond Interest Expense	15,600	
Discount on Bonds Payable ($6,000 ÷ 10)		600
Cash ($300,000 X 10% X 1/2)		15,000

*28. (b) Under the straight-line method, the amortization amount is the same each interest period. After four periods, $2,400 will be amortized, and the balance in Discount on Bonds Payable will be $3,600 ($6,000 - $2,400). Thus, the carrying value of the bonds is $296,400 ($300,000 - $3,600).

MATCHING

1.	f	6.	d
2.	b	7.	j
3.	g	8.	e
4.	h	9.	c
5.	i	10.	a

EXERCISES

EX. 11-1

General Journal J1

Date	Account Title	Debit	Credit
(a) 2006			
Aug. 1	Cash	10,000	
	Notes Payable		10,000
	(To record receipt of cash and issuance		
	of $10,000, 12% eight-month note)		
Dec. 1	Cash	20,000	
	Notes Payable		20,000
	(To record receipt of cash and issuance		
	of six-month 10% interest-bearing note)		
Dec. 24	Cash	26,300	
	Sales		24,650
	Sales Taxes Payable		1,650
	(To record daily sales and sales taxes)		
(b)			
Dec. 31	Interest Expense ($10,000 X 12% X 5/12)	500	
	Interest Payable		500
	(To record interest expense for five months)		
31	Interest Expense ($20,000 x 10% X 1/12)	167	
	Interest Payable		167
	(To record interest expense for one month)		

General Journal			J2
Date	Account Title	Debit	Credit
(c)			
2007			
Mar. 31	Interest Expense	300	
	Interest Payable		300
	(To record interest expense for three		
	months on 12% interest-bearing note)		
Apr. 1	Notes Payable	10,000	
	Interest Payable	800	
	Cash		10,800
	(To record payment of Third National Bank		
	note)		
May 31	Interest Expense	833	
	Interest Payable		833
	(To record interest expense for five months		
	on 10% interest-bearing note)		
June 1	Notes Payable	20,000	
	Interest Payable	1,000	
	Cash		21,000
	(To record payment of the Second Federal		
	Savings & Loan note)		

EX. 11-2

General Journal

J1

Date	Account Title	Debit	Credit
(a)			
Jan. 1	Cash ($400,000 X 98%)	392,000	
	Discount on Bonds Payable	8,000	
	Bonds Payable		400,000
July 1	Bond Interest Expense	24,400	
	Discount on Bonds Payable ($8,000 ÷ 20)		400
	Cash ($400,000 X 6%)		24,000
Dec. 31	Bond Interest Expense	24,400	
	Discount on Bonds Payable		400
	Bond Interest Payable		24,000
(b)			
July 1	Bond Interest Expense ($392,000 X 6.2%)	24,304	
	Discount on Bonds Payable		304
	Cash ($400,000 X 6%)		24,000
Dec. 31	Bond Interest Expense [($392,000 + $304) X		
	6.2%]	24,323	
	Discount on Bonds Payable		323
	Bond Interest Payable		24,000

EX. 11-3

General Journal			J1
Date	Account Title	Debit	Credit
Apr. 1	Bonds Payable	100,000	
	Common Stock		40,000
	Paid-in Capital in Excess of Par Value		60,000
June 30	Interest Expense ($100,000 X 5%)	5,000	
	Mortgage Note Payable	3,024	
	Cash		8,024
Dec. 31	Interest Expense ($96,976 X 5%)	4,849	
	Mortgage Note Payable	3,175	
	Cash		8,024

CHAPTER 12

CORPORATIONS:
ORGANIZATION, STOCK TRANSACTIONS, DIVIDENDS, AND RETAINED EARNINGS

The Navigator ✓

- *Scan Study Objectives* ☐
- *Read Preview* ☐
- *Read Chapter Review* ☐
- *Work Demonstration Problem* ☐
- *Answer True-False Statements* ☐
- *Answer Multiple-Choice Questions* ☐
- *Match Terms and Definitions* ☐
- *Solve Exercises* ☐

CHAPTER STUDY OBJECTIVES

After studying this chapter, you should be able to:

1. Identify the major characteristics of a corporation.
2. Record the issuance of common stock.
3. Explain the accounting for treasury stock.
4. Differentiate preferred stock from common stock.
5. Prepare the entries for cash dividends and stock dividends.
6. Identify the items that are reported in a retained earnings statement.
7. Prepare and analyze a comprehensive stockholders' equity section.

*8. Describe the use and content of the stockholders' equity statement.

*9. Compute book value per share.

***Note:** All **asterisked** (*) items relate to material contained in the Appendix to the chapter.

PREVIEW OF CHAPTER 12

The corporation is the dominant form of business organization in the United States in terms of dollar volume of sales, earnings, and employees. All of the 500 largest companies in the United States are corporations. In this chapter we will explain the essential features of a corporation and the accounting for a corporation's capital stock transactions, dividends, and retained earnings. The content and organization of this chapter is as follows:

CORPORATIONS: ORGANIZATION, STOCK TRANSACTIONS, DIVIDENDS, AND RETAINED EARNINGS

Corporate Organization and Stock Transactions	Dividends	Retained Earnings	Stockholders' Equity Presentation and Analysis
▶ Corporate form of organization	▶ Cash dividends	▶ Retained earnings restrictions	▶ Presentation
▶ Common stock issues	▶ Stock dividends	▶ Prior period adjustments	▶ Analysis
▶ Treasury stock	▶ Stock splits	▶ Retained earnings statement	
▶ Preferred stock			

CHAPTER REVIEW

The Corporate Form of Organization

1. (S.O. 1) A **corporation** is an entity created by law that is separate and distinct from its owners and its continued existence is dependent upon the corporate statutes of the state in which it is incorporated.

2. The characteristics that distinguish a corporation from proprietorships and partnerships are:
   a. The corporation has separate legal existence from its owners.
   b. The stockholders have limited liability.
   c. Ownership is shown in shares of capital stock, which are transferable units.
   d. It is relatively easy for a corporation to obtain capital through the issuance of stock.
   e. The corporation can have a continuous life.
   f. The management in the corporation's organizational structure is at the discretion of the board of directors who are elected by the stockholders.
   g. The corporation is subject to numerous government regulations.
   h. The corporation must pay an income tax on its earnings, and the stockholders are required to pay taxes on the dividends they receive: the result is double taxation.

Forming a Corporation

3. The formation of a corporation involves (a) filing an application with the Secretary of State, (b) paying an incorporation fee, (c) receiving a charter (articles of incorporation), and (d) developing by-laws.
   a. Costs incurred in forming a corporation are called **organization costs.**
   b. These costs include fees to underwriters, legal fees, state incorporation fees, and promotional expenditures.
   c. Organization costs are expensed as incurred.

Ownership Rights of Stockholders

4. When chartered, the corporation may begin selling ownership rights in the form of shares of stock. Each share of common stock gives the stockholder the following **ownership rights:**
   a. To **vote** for the board of directors and in corporate actions that require stockholder approval.
   b. To **share in corporate earnings** through the receipt of dividends.
   c. To maintain the same percentage ownership when additional shares of common stock are issued **(preemptive right).**
   d. To share in assets upon liquidation **(residual claim).**

Stock Issue Considerations

5. **Authorized stock** is the amount of stock a corporation is allowed to sell as indicated by its charter.
   a. The authorization of capital stock does not result in a formal accounting entry.
   b. The difference between the shares of stock authorized and the shares issued is the number of unissued shares that can be issued without amending the charter.

6. A corporation has the choice of issuing common stock directly to investors or indirectly through an investment banking firm (brokerage house). Direct issue is typical in closely held companies, whereas indirect issue is customary for a publicly held corporation.

7. **Par value stock** is capital stock that has been assigned a value per share in the corporate charter. It represents the **legal capital** per share that must be retained in the business for the protection of corporate creditors.

8. **No-par stock** is capital stock that has not been assigned a value in the corporate charter. In many states the board of directors can assign a **stated value** to the shares which becomes the legal capital per share. When there is no assigned stated value, the entire proceeds are considered to be legal capital.

Common Stock Issues

9. (S.O. 2) When par value common stock is issued for cash, the par value of the shares is credited to Common Stock and the portion of the proceeds that is above or below par value is recorded in a separate paid-in capital account.

10. When no-par common stock has a stated value, the stated value is credited to Common Stock. When the selling price exceeds the stated value, the excess is credited to Paid-in Capital in Excess of Stated Value. When no-par stock does not have a stated value, the entire proceeds are credited to Common Stock.

Common Stock for Services or Non-Cash Assets

11. When common stock is issued for **services or non-cash assets,** cost is either the fair market value of the consideration given up or the consideration received, whichever is more clearly determinable.

Treasury Stock

12. (S.O. 3) **Treasury stock** is a corporation's own stock that has been issued, fully paid for, and reacquired but not retired.
    a. Under the cost method, Treasury Stock is debited at the price paid for the shares and the same amount is credited to Treasury Stock when the shares are reissued.
    b. When the Treasury Stock is resold and the selling price of the shares is greater than cost, the difference is credited to Paid-in Capital from Treasury Stock.
    c. When the selling price is less than cost, the excess of cost over selling price is usually debited to Paid-in Capital From Treasury Stock. When there is no remaining balance in Paid-in Capital From Treasury Stock, the remainder is debited to Retained Earnings.

Preferred Stock

13. (S.O. 4) **Preferred stock** has contractual claims that give it priority over common stock. Preferred stockholders usually have a preference to dividends and assets in the event of liquidation. However, they usually do not have voting rights.

14. Preferred stock should be identified separately from other stock (e.g., Preferred Stock, Paid-in Capital in Excess of Par Value—Preferred Stock). Preferred stock is shown first in the stockholders' equity section.

Cumulative Dividend

15. A **cumulative dividend** feature provides that preferred stockholders must be paid both current and prior year dividends before common stockholders receive any dividends.
    a. Preferred dividends not declared in a given period are called **dividends in arrears.**
    b. Dividends in arrears are not considered a liability, but the amount of the dividends in arrears should be disclosed in the notes to the financial statements.

Dividends

16. (S.O. 5) A dividend is a distribution by a corporation to its stockholders on a pro rata (proportional) basis. Dividends may be in the form of cash, property, scrip, or stock.

17. A **cash dividend** is a pro rata distribution of cash to stockholders. For a cash dividend to occur, a corporation must have (a) retained earnings, (b) adequate cash, and (c) declared dividends.

18. Three dates are important in connection with dividends:
    a. **Declaration date**—the date on which the board of directors formally authorizes a cash dividend and the liability is recorded.
    b. **Record date**—the date that marks the time when ownership of outstanding shares is determined from the stockholders' records maintained by the corporation.
    c. **Payment date**—the date dividend checks are mailed to the stockholders and the payment of the dividend is recorded.

19. **Preferred stockholders** must be paid any unpaid prior year dividends before common stockholders receive dividends.
    a. When preferred stock is **cumulative,** any dividends in arrears must be paid to preferred stockholders before allocating any dividends to common stockholders.
    b. When preferred stock is **not** cumulative, only the current year's dividend must be paid to preferred stockholders before paying any dividends to common stockholders.

Stock Dividend

20. A **stock dividend** is a pro rata distribution to stockholders of the corporation's stock. A stock dividend results in a decrease in retained earnings and an increase in paid-in capital. At a minimum, the par or stated value must be assigned to the dividend shares; in most cases, however, fair market value is used.

21. When the fair market value of the stock is used, the following entry is made at the declaration date:

Retained Earnings	XXX	
Common Stock Dividends Distributable		XXX
Paid-in Capital in Excess of Par Value		XXX

    a. Common Stock Dividends Distributable is reported in paid-in capital as an addition to common stock issued.
    b. Common Stock Dividends Distributable is debited and Common Stock is credited when the dividend shares are issued.

22. Stock dividends change the composition of stockholders' equity because a portion of retained earnings is transferred to paid-in capital. However, total stockholders' equity and the par or stated value per share remain the same.

Stock Split

23. A **stock split** involves the issuance of additional shares of stock to stockholders according to their percentage ownership.
    a. In a stock split, the number of shares is increased in the same proportion that par or stated value per share is decreased.
    b. A stock split has no effect on total paid-in capital, retained earnings, or total stockholders' equity.
    c. It is not necessary to formally journalize a stock split.

Retained Earnings

24. (S.O. 6) **Retained earnings** is net income that is retained in the business. The balance in retained earnings is part of the stockholders' claim on the total assets of the corporation.
    a. A **net loss** is recorded in Retained Earnings by a closing entry in which Retained Earnings is debited and Income Summary is credited.
    b. A debit balance in Retained Earnings is identified as a **deficit** and is reported as a deduction in the stockholders' equity section.

25. In some cases there may be **retained earnings restrictions** that make a portion of the balance currently unavailable for dividends. Restrictions result from one or more of the following causes: legal, contractual or voluntary. Retained earnings restrictions are generally disclosed in the notes to the financial statements.

26. A **prior period adjustment** is the correction of a material error in reporting net income in previously issued financial statements. The correction is:
    a. made directly to Retained Earnings.
    b. reported in the current year's retained earnings statement as an adjustment of the beginning balance of Retained Earnings.

27. Many corporations prepare a **retained earnings statement** to explain the changes in **retained earnings** during the year.

Stockholders' Equity Presentation

28. (S.O. 7) In the stockholders' equity section of the balance sheet, paid-in capital and retained earnings are reported and the specific sources of paid-in capital are identified. Within paid-in capital, two classifications are recognized.

a. **Capital stock,** which consists of preferred and common stock. Preferred stock is shown before common stock because of its preferential rights. Information as to the par value, shares authorized, shares issued, and shares outstanding is reported for each class of stock.

b. **Additional paid-in capital,** which includes the excess of amounts paid in over par or stated value and paid-in capital from treasury stock.

29. A widely used ratio that measures profitability from the common stockholder's viewpoint is **return on common stockholders' equity.** It is computed by dividing net income available to common stockholders (which is Net income - Preferred stock dividends) by average common stockholders' equity.

***Stockholders' Equity Statement**

*30. (S.O. 8) Instead of presenting a detailed stockholders' equity section in the balance sheet and a retained earnings statement, many companies prepare a **stockholders' equity statement.** The Appendix discusses this statement in more detail.

***Book Value Per Share**

*31. (S.O. 9) **Book value per share** represents the equity a common stockholder has in the net assets of the corporation from owning one share of stock.

a. The formula for computing book value per share when a company has only one class of stock outstanding is:

$$\text{Total Stockholders' Equity} \div \text{Number of Common Shares Outstanding} = \text{Book Value per Share}$$

b. Book value per share is not synonymous with the value of the stock in liquidation.

DEMONSTRATION PROBLEM (S.O. 3)

The Jefferson Corporation and the Franklin Company have the following stockholders' equity accounts on January 1, 2006.

Jefferson Corporation

Common stock, no par stated value $2	$ 600,000
Paid-in capital in excess of stated value	900,000
Retained earnings	300,000
Total	$1,800,000

Franklin Company

Common stock, $3 par	$ 900,000
Paid-in capital in excess of par value	450,000
Retained earnings	750,000
Total	$2,100,000

Both companies use the cost method of accounting for treasury stock. During 2006, the companies had the following treasury stock transactions.

Jefferson Corporation

Feb. 1	Purchased 10,000 shares at $9 per share.
May 2	Sold 2,000 shares at $10 per share.
Aug. 17	Sold 4,000 shares at $13 per share.
Dec. 15	Sold 3,000 shares at $8 per share.

Franklin Company

Mar. 6	Purchased 7,000 shares at $7 per share.
June 19	Sold 1,500 shares at $9 per share.
Sept. 2	Sold 3,000 shares at $6 per share.
Dec. 23	Sold 2,000 shares at $6 per share.

Instructions

(a) Journalize the treasury stock transactions for both companies (omit explanations).

(b) Prepare a stockholders' equity section for Franklin Company at December 31, 2006, assuming the company earned $75,000 of net income in 2006.

The Navigator

SOLUTION TO DEMONSTRATION PROBLEM

(a)

JEFFERSON CORPORATION--General Journal J1

Date	Account Title	Debit	Credit
2006			
Feb. 1	Treasury Stock	90,000	
	Cash		90,000
May 2	Cash	20,000	
	Treasury Stock		18,000
	Paid-in Capital from Treasury Stock		2,000
Aug. 17	Cash	52,000	
	Treasury Stock		36,000
	Paid-in Capital from Treasury Stock		16,000
Dec. 15	Cash	24,000	
	Paid-in Capital from Treasury Stock	3,000	
	Treasury Stock		27,000

FRANKLIN COMPANY--General Journal J1

Date	Account Title	Debit	Credit
2006			
Mar. 6	Treasury Stock	49,000	
	Cash		49,000
June 19	Cash	13,500	
	Treasury Stock (1,500 X $7)		10,500
	Paid-in Capital from Treasury Stock		3,000
Sept. 2	Cash (3,000 X 6)	18,000	
	Paid-in Capital from Treasury Stock	3,000	
	Treasury Stock (3,000 X $7)		21,000
Dec. 23	Cash (2,000 X $6)	12,000	
	Retained Earnings	2,000	
	Treasury Stock (2,000 X $7)		14,000

(b)

FRANKLIN COMPANY—Stockholders' Equity
December 31, 2006

Stockholders' equity	
Paid-in capital	
Common stock, $3 par value	$ 900,000
Paid-in capital in excess of par value	450,000
Total paid-in capital	1,350,000
Retained earnings	823,000
Total paid-in capital and retained earnings	2,173,000
Less: Treasury stock (500 shares)	3,500
Total stockholders' equity	$2,169,500

REVIEW QUESTIONS AND EXERCISES

TRUE—FALSE

Indicate whether each of the following is true (T) or false (F) in the space provided.

_____ 1. (S.O. 1) A corporation is a legal entity separate and distinct from its owners.

_____ 2. (S.O. 1) A successful corporation can have a continuous and perpetual life.

_____ 3. (S.O. 1) Stockholders have the right to directly formulate operating policies for the company.

_____ 4. (S.O. 1) An advantage of a corporation is that it is subject to very few government regulations.

_____ 5. (S.O. 1) The issuance of the charter, often referred to as the articles of incorporation, creates the corporation.

_____ 6. (S.O. 1) Organizational costs are capitalized by debiting an intangible asset entitled Organization Costs.

_____ 7. (S.O. 1) The amount of stock that a corporation is authorized to sell is indicated in its charter.

_____ 8. (S.O. 1) Upon the authorization of capital stock, a corporation will record a debit for the asset acquired and a credit to common stock.

_____ 9. (S.O. 1) Par value is indicative of the worth or market value of the stock.

_____ 10. (S.O. 2) The cash proceeds from issuing par value stock may be equal to or greater than, but not less than par value.

_____ 11. (S.O. 2) When no-par stock has a stated value, the entire proceeds from the issue are credited to Common Stock.

_____ 12. (S.O. 2) The cost of a noncash asset acquired in exchange for common stock should be either the fair market value of the consideration given up or the consideration received, whichever is more clearly determinable.

_____ 13. (S.O. 2) When stock is issued for noncash assets, the par value of the stock is never a factor in determining the cost of the assets received.

_____ 14. (S.O. 3) Under the cost method, Treasury Stock is debited at the price paid to reacquire the shares, and the same amount is credited to Treasury Stock when the shares are sold.

_____ 15. (S.O. 3) Treasury stock is a contra stockholders' equity account.

_____ 16. (S.O. 4) Preferred stockholders usually have the right to vote.

_____ 17. (S.O. 4) Preferred dividends in arrears should be recorded in a liability account.

_____ 18. (S.O. 5) A dividend is a distribution by a corporation to its stockholders on a pro rata basis.

_____ 19. (S.O. 5) A dividend based on paid-in capital is termed a liquidating dividend.

_____ 20. (S.O. 5) The date that the board of directors formally declares a cash dividend is the date of record.

_____ 21. (S.O. 5) A stock dividend results in a decrease in retained earnings and an increase in paid-in capital.

_____ 22. (S.O. 5) Common Stock Dividends Distributable is reported as a liability on the balance sheet.

_____ 23. (S.O. 5) A stock split must be formally journalized.

_____ 24. (S.O. 6) Retained earnings restrictions are generally disclosed in the notes to the financial statements.

_____ 25. (S.O. 6) A prior period adjustment is reported as an adjustment of the beginning balance of Retained Earnings.

_____ *26. (S.O. 9) Book value per share is the same thing as liquidation value per share.

_____ *27. (S.O. 9) When a company has both preferred and common stock, the computation of book value is more complex.

The Navigator

MULTIPLE CHOICE

Circle the letter that best answers each of the following statements.

1. (S.O. 1) Which of the following is an **incorrect** statement about a corporation?
   a. A corporation is an entity separate and distinct from its owners.
   b. Creditors ordinarily have recourse only to corporate assets in satisfaction of their claims.
   c. A corporation may be formed in writing, orally, or implied.
   d. A corporation is subject to numerous state and federal regulations.

2. (S.O. 1) Each share of common stock gives the stockholder the following ownership rights.

	Vote	Preemptive right	Residual claim
a.	yes	no	no
b.	yes	yes	no
c.	no	no	yes
d.	yes	yes	yes

3. (S.O. 1) Legal capital per share cannot be equal to the:
   a. par value per share of par value stock.
   b. total proceeds from the sale of par value stock above par value.
   c. stated value per share of no-par value stock.
   d. total proceeds from the sale of no-par value stock.

4. (S.O. 2) Mary Wells, Inc. issues 2,000 shares of $10 par value common stock at $22 per share. The entry for the issue will include a credit of $24,000 to:
   a. Gain from the Sale of Common Stock.
   b. Paid-in Capital from Treasury Stock.
   c. Paid-in Capital in Excess of Stated Value.
   d. Paid-in Capital in Excess of Par Value.

5. (S.O. 2) Aretha Franklin Inc. issues 10,000 shares of $1 stated value no-par value common stock at $8 per share. The entry for the issue will include a debit to Cash for $80,000 and credits to:
   a. Common Stock, $10,000 and Paid-in Capital in Excess of Stated Value, $70,000.
   b. Common Stock, $10,000 and Paid-in Capital in Excess of Par Value, $70,000.
   c. Common Stock, $80,000.
   d. Common Stock, $10,000 and Retained Earnings, $70,000.

6. (S.O. 2) When common stock is issued for services or non-cash assets, cost should be:
   a. only the fair market value of the consideration given up.
   b. only the fair market value of the consideration received.
   c. the book value of the common stock issued.
   d. either the fair market value of the consideration given up or the consideration received, whichever is more clearly evident.

7. (S.O. 3) Treasury stock was acquired for cash at more than its par value and then subsequently sold for cash at more than its acquisition price. What is the effect on additional paid-in capital from treasury stock transactions?

	Purchase of Treasury Stock	Sale of Treasury Stock
a.	No effect	No effect
b.	No effect	Increase
c.	Decrease	Increase
d.	Decrease	No effect

8. (S.O. 3) Elton John Corporation was organized on January 1, 2006, with authorized capital of 500,000 shares of $10 par value common stock. During 2006, Elton John issued 10,000 shares at $12 per share, purchased 1,000 shares of treasury stock at $13 per share, and sold 1,000 shares of treasury stock at $14 per share. What is the amount of additional paid-in capital at December 31, 2006?
   a. $0.
   b. $1,000.
   c. $20,000.
   d. $21,000.

9. (S.O. 3) Big Head Todd sells 2,000 shares of treasury stock purchased for $32,000 at $20 per share. The entry to record this sale should include a credit to:
   a. Gain from Sale of Treasury Stock $8,000.
   b. Paid-in Capital from Treasury Stock $8,000.
   c. Retained Earnings $8,000.
   d. Paid-in Capital from Treasury Stock $12,000.

10. (S.O. 3) The purchase of treasury stock:
   a. decreases common stock authorized.
   b. decreases common stock issued.
   c. decreases common stock outstanding.
   d. has no effect on common stock outstanding.

11. (S.O. 3) What is the effect of the purchase of treasury stock on the amount reported in the balance sheet for each of the following?

	Additional Paid-in Capital	Retained Earnings
a.	No effect	No effect
b.	No effect	Decrease
c.	Decrease	No effect
d.	Decrease	Decrease

12. (S.O. 3) Treasury stock is reported in the balance sheet as:
   a. an asset.
   b. a deduction in paid-in capital section.
   c. a deduction in the retained earnings section.
   d. a deduction from total paid-in capital and retained earnings.

13. (S.O. 3) Bob Marley Corporation was organized on January 2, 2006. During 2006, Bob Marley issued 20,000 shares at $12 per share, purchased 3,000 shares of treasury stock at $13 per share, and had net income of $150,000. What is the total amount of stockholders' equity at December 31, 2006?
   a. $320,000.
   b. $351,000.
   c. $354,000.
   d. $360,000.

14. (S.O. 4) On January 2, 2003, Fat Boy Slim Corporation issued 5,000 shares of 6% cumulative preferred stock at $100 par value. On December 31, 2006, Fat Boy Slim Corporation declared and paid its first dividend. What dividends are the preferred stockholders entitled to receive in the current year before any distribution is made to common stockholders?
   a. $0.
   b. $30,000.
   c. $90,000.
   d. $120,000.

15. (S.O. 4) Dividends in arrears should:
    a. be disclosed in the notes to the financial statements.
    b. be reported as a liability.
    c. be reported as a deduction from retained earnings.
    d. not be reported or disclosed.

16. (S.O. 5) Which of the following statements about a cash dividend is **incorrect?**
    a. The legality of a cash dividend depends on state corporation laws.
    b. The legality of a dividend does not indicate a company's ability to pay a dividend.
    c. Dividends are not a liability until declared.
    d. Shareholders usually vote to determine the amount of income to be distributed in the form of a dividend.

17. (S.O. 5) Remmers, Inc. declares a 10% common stock dividend when it has 20,000 shares of $10 par value common stock outstanding. If the market value of $24 per share is used, the amounts debited to Retained Earnings and credited to Paid-in Capital in Excess of Par Value are:

	Retained Earnings	Paid-in Capital in Excess of Par Value
a.	$20,000	$0
b.	$48,000	$28,000
c.	$48,000	$20,000
d.	$20,000	$28,000

18. (S.O. 5) Bussan Corporation splits its common stock 4 for 1, when the market value is $80 per share. Prior to the split, Bussan had 50,000 shares of $12 par value common stock issued and outstanding. After the split, the par value of the stock:
    a. remains the same.
    b. is reduced to $2 per share.
    c. is reduced to $3 per share.
    d. is reduced to $4 per share.

19. (S.O. 6) Which of the following statements about retained earnings restrictions is **incorrect?**
    a. Many states require a corporation to restrict retained earnings for the cost of treasury stock purchased.
    b. Long-term debt contracts may impose a restriction on retained earnings as a condition for the loan.
    c. The board of directors of a corporation may voluntarily create retained earnings restrictions for specific purposes.
    d. Retained earnings restrictions are generally disclosed through a journal entry on the books of a company.

20. (S.O. 6) A prior period adjustment should be reported in the:
    a. income statement after income from continuing operations and before extraordinary items.
    b. income statement after income from continuing operations and after extraordinary items.
    c. retained earnings statement after net income but before dividends.
    d. retained earnings statement as an adjustment of the beginning balance.

21. (S.O. 7) In the stockholders' equity section of the balance sheet, the classification of capital stock consists of:
    a. additional paid-in capital and common stock.
    b. common stock and treasury stock.
    c. common stock, preferred stock and treasury stock.
    d. common stock and preferred stock.

*22. (S.O. 9) At December 31, the stockholders' equity section shows:

Common stock, $5 par value, 1,100,000 shares issued and 1,000,000 shares outstanding	$5,500,000
Additional paid-in capital	1,400,000
Retained earnings	1,500,000
Treasury stock (100,000 shares)	(700,000)
Total stockholders' equity	$7,700,000

The book value per share of common stock is:
    a. $7.00.
    b. $7.70.
    c. $8.40.
    d. $7.20.

*23. (S.O. 6) Jim Lahey Corporation's stockholders' equity at June 30 consists of the following:

Preferred stock, 10% $50 par value; 20,000 shares issued and outstanding	$1,000,000
Common stock, $10 par value; 500,000 shares authorized; 150,000 shares issued and outstanding	1,500,000
Retained earnings	500,000

The book value per share of common stock is:
    a. $10.00.
    b. $12.67.
    c. $13.33.
    d. $17.65.

The Navigator

MATCHING

Match each term with its definition by writing the appropriate letter in the space provided.

Terms

______ 1. Authorized stock.

______ 2. Cash dividend.

______ 3. Par value stock.

______ 4. No-par value stock.

______ 5. Book value per share.

______ 6. Treasury stock.

______ 7. Declaration date.

______ 8. Cumulative dividend.

______ 9. Preferred stock.

______ 10. Legal capital.

______ 11. Record date.

______ 12. Payment date.

______ 13. Stock dividend.

______ 14. Retained earnings restrictions.

______ 15. Prior period adjustment.

Definitions

a. The amount per share of capital stock that must be retained in the business for the protection of corporate creditors.

b. The equity a common stockholder has in the net assets of the corporation from owning one share of stock.

c. Capital stock that has not been assigned a value in the corporate charter.

d. The date when ownership of outstanding shares is determined for dividend purposes.

e. A feature of preferred stock entitling the stockholder to receive current and unpaid prior-year dividends before common stock-holders receive any dividends.

f. Capital stock that has been assigned a value per share in the corporate charter.

g. A pro rata distribution of cash to stockholders.

h. The amount of stock a corporation is allowed to sell as indicated in its charter.

i. A pro rata distribution of the corporation's own stock to stockholders.

j. A corporation's own stock that has been issued, fully paid for, and reacquired but not retired.

k. Capital stock which has contractual preferences over common stock in certain areas.

l. The date dividend checks are mailed to stockholders.

m. The date the board of directors formally declares the dividend and announces it to stockholders.

n. The correction of an error in previously issued financial statements.

o. Circumstances that make a portion of retained earnings currently unavailable for dividends.

EXERCISES

EX. 12-1 (S.O. 2, 3) On January 2, The Soup Dragons receive a corporate charter authorizing the sale of 200,000 shares of $10 par value common stock. During the year, The Soup Dragons had the following transactions:

Jan.	5	Issued 20,000 shares of common stock for cash at $10 per share.
	10	Issued 30,000 shares of common stock for cash at $30 per share.
	23	Issued 10,000 shares of common stock for land that had a fair market price of $320,000.
Mar.	15	Issued 1,000 shares of common stock for attorney services used in organizing the corporation valued at $32,000.
Apr.	28	Acquired 5,000 shares of its common stock at $32 per share for the treasury.
June	18	Issued 15,000 shares of common stock for cash at $33 per share.
Sept.	23	Sold 2,000 shares of the treasury stock at $35 per share.

Instructions
Journalize the transactions. (Omit explanations)

General Journal

J1

Date	Account Title	Debit	Credit

EX. 12-2 (S.O. 5) Tycho Corporation started business operations on January 1, 2005. On January 1, 2006, Tycho has 400,000 shares of $10 par value common stock outstanding and $300,000 of retained earnings. During 2006, Tycho had the following transactions:

April 1	Declared a 10 cent per share cash dividend on common stock outstanding.
May 15	Paid the cash dividend declared on April 1.
July 1	Declared a 2% stock dividend when the fair market value of the stock was $15.
Aug. 1	Issued the shares for the stock dividend.
Nov. 1	Effected a 2 for 1 stock split.
Dec. 1	Declared a 10 cent per share cash dividend on common stock outstanding.

Instructions
Record the transactions above in the general journal. (Omit explanations).

General Journal J1

Date	Account Title	Debit	Credit
2006			

EX. 12-3 (S.O. 7) Charlatans Corporation had the following stockholders' equity accounts at December 31.

Common stock ($1 par value)	$ 150,000
Preferred stock ($50 par value, 6%)	500,000
Paid-in Capital in Excess of Par Value—Common	1,560,000
Paid-in Capital from Treasury Stock—Common	250,000
Retained Earnings	340,000
Treasury stock—common at cost	190,000

At December 31, the number of common and preferred shares were:

	Common	Preferred
Authorized	500,000	50,000
Issued	150,000	10,000
Outstanding	140,000	10,000

Instructions

Prepare the stockholders' equity section at December 31.

CHARLATANS CORPORATION

Stockholders' equity

The Navigator

SOLUTIONS TO REVIEW QUESTIONS AND EXERCISES

TRUE-FALSE

1. (T)
2. (T)
3. (F) The operating policies for the company are at the discretion of the board of directors, who are elected by the stockholders.
4. (F) A corporation is subject to numerous state and federal regulations that add considerably to the cost of doing business.
5. (T)
6. (F) Organizational costs are to be expensed as incurred.
7. (T)
8. (F) The authorization of capital stock does not result in a formal accounting entry, or the acquisition of an asset.
9. (F) Par value is not indicative of the worth or market value of the stock. The significance of par value is a legal matter.
10. (F) The sale of common stock may be below par value unless it is legally prohibited.
11. (F) When the selling price exceeds stated value, the excess is credited to Paid-in Capital in Excess of Stated Value and only the stated value is credited to Common Stock.
12. (T)
13. (T)
14. (T)
15. (T)
16. (F) Preferred stockholders usually do not have the right to vote.
17. (F) Dividends in arrears are not considered a liability because no obligation exists until the dividend is declared by the board of directors.
18. (T)
19. (T)
20. (F) The date that the board of directors formally declares a cash dividend is the date of declaration.
21. (T)
22. (F) Common Stock Dividends Distributable is reported in paid-in capital as an addition to common stock issued.
23. (F) Adequate disclosure of a stock split can be made through a memorandum notation in the capital stock account.
24. (T)
25. (T)

*26. (F) Book value per share is not synonymous with liquidation value per share because it is extremely unlikely that noncash assets would be converted into cash without gain or loss to the company.

*27. (T)

MULTIPLE CHOICE

1. (c) Answers (a), (b), and (d) are all correct statements. Answer (c) is incorrect because a corporation must file an application with the Secretary of State in the state in which incorporation is desired.

2. (d) Each share of common stock entitles the owner to vote in the election of the board of directors and other matters of concern. The stockholder has a preemptive right to maintain the same percentage ownership when additional shares of common stock are issued. And, upon liquidation, shareholders share in the distribution of assets according to their residual claim.

3. (b) Legal capital per share for par value stock is par value (a). Answers (c) and (d) are both equal to legal capital.

4. (d) The entry is:

Cash	44,000	
Common Stock		20,000
Paid-in Capital in Excess of Par value		24,000

5. (a) The entry is:

Cash	80,000	
Common Stock		10,000
Paid-in Capital in Excess of Stated Value		70,000

6. (d) When common stock is issued for services or non-cash assets, cost should be either the fair market value of the consideration given up or the consideration received, whichever is more clearly evident.

7. (b) The purchase of treasury stock affects only the treasury stock account and the cash account. The sale above cost affects these accounts and also increases paid-in capital from treasury stock.

8. (d) The additional paid-in capital will include both the excess of cash received over par value on the issuance of the stock, $20,000 (10,000 X $2) and Paid-in Capital from Treasury Stock when the treasury stock is sold, $1,000 ($14,000 - $13,000).

9. (b) Because the treasury stock was purchased at a cost of $32,000, the following entry should be made for the sale:

Cash	40,000	
Treasury Stock		32,000
Paid-in Capital from Treasury Stock		8,000

10. (c) Common stock outstanding includes any common stock issued less treasury stock. Treasury stock, however, is still issued stock.

11. (a) The purchase of the treasury stock decreases total stockholders' equity but has no effect on either additional paid-in capital or retained earnings.

12. (d) Treasury stock is not an asset (a). It is a contra stockholders' equity account that is deducted from total paid-in capital and retained earnings.

13. (b) The issuance of 20,000 shares at $12 per share results in $240,000 of stockholders' equity. The purchase of 3,000 shares of treasury stock decreases stockholders' equity by $39,000, and the net income causes stockholders equity to increase by $150,000.

14. (d) The preferred stockholders are entitled to four years of cumulative dividends of $30,000 per year (5,000 X $100 X .06) for each year between January 2, 2000 and December 31, 2006.

15. (a) Dividends in arrears are not considered to be a liability (b) because the dividends have not been declared. However, they should be disclosed in the notes to the financial statements.

16. (d) The board of directors has full authority to determine the amount of income to be distributed in the form of a dividend. The other answer choices are correct statements.

17. (b) The stock dividend results in the following entry:

Retained Earnings	48,000	
Common Stock Dividends Distributable		20,000
Paid-in Capital in Excess of Par Value		28,000

18. (c) The stock split results in an inversely proportional decrease in the par value of the stock ($3 = $12/4).

19. (d) Retained earnings restrictions are generally disclosed in the notes to the financial statements. The other answers are correct.

20. (d) A prior period adjustment is reported in the retained earnings statement as an adjustment of the beginning balance.

21. (d) In the stockholders' equity section of the balance sheet, the classification of capital stock consists of common stock and preferred stock.

*22. (b) The book value per share of common stock is: $\frac{\$7,700,000}{1,000,000} = \$7.70.$

*23. (c) The book value per share is: $\frac{\$3,000,000 - \$1,000,000}{150,000} = \$13.33.$

MATCHING

1.	h.	6.	j.	11.	d.
2.	g.	7.	m.	12.	l.
3.	f.	8.	e.	13.	i.
4.	c.	9.	k.	14.	o.
5.	b.	10.	a.	15.	n.

EXERCISES

EX. 12-1

General Journal J1

Date	Account Title	Debit	Credit
Jan. 5	Cash	200,000	
	Common Stock		200,000
10	Cash	900,000	
	Common Stock		300,000
	Paid-in Capital in Excess of Par Value		600,000
23	Land	320,000	
	Common Stock		100,000
	Paid-in Capital in Excess of Par Value		220,000
Mar. 15	Organization Expense	32,000	
	Common Stock		10,000
	Paid-in Capital in Excess of Par Value		22,000
Apr. 28	Treasury Stock	160,000	
	Cash		160,000
June 18	Cash	495,000	
	Common Stock		150,000
	Paid-in Capital in Excess of Par Value		345,000
Sept. 23	Cash	70,000	
	Treasury Stock (2,000 X $32)		64,000
	Paid-in Capital from Treasury Stock		6,000

EX. 12-2

General Journal J1

Date	Account Title	Debit	Credit
2006			
Apr. 1	Retained Earnings (400,000 x $.10)	40,000	
	Dividends Payable		40,000
May 15	Dividends Payable	40,000	
	Cash		40,000
July 1	Retained Earnings (400,000 X 2% X $15)	120,000	
	Common Stock Dividends Distributable		
	(400,000 X 2% X $10)		80,000
	Paid-in Capital in Excess of Par Value		40,000
Aug. 1	Common Stock Dividends Distributable	80,000	
	Common Stock		80,000
Nov. 1	No entry needed; total shares are 816,000		
	(408,000 X 2)		
Dec. 1	Retained Earnings (816,000 X $.10)	81,600	
	Dividends Payable		81,600

EX. 12-3

CHARLATANS CORPORATION

Stockholders' equity		
Paid-in capital		
Capital stock		
Preferred stock, $50 par value, 6%, 50,000 shares authorized, 10,000 shares issued and outstanding		$ 500,000
Common stock, $1 par value, 500,000 shares authorized, 150,000 shares issued and 140,000 shares outstanding		150,000
Total capital stock		650,000
Additional paid-in capital		
Excess over par value—common stock	$1,560,000	
From treasury stock—common	250,000	
Total additional paid-in capital		1,810,000
Total paid-in capital		2,460,000
Retained earnings		340,000
Total paid-in capital and retained earnings		2,800,000
Less: Treasury stock (10,000 common shares at cost)		(190,000)
Total stockholders' equity		$2,610,000

CHAPTER 13

The Navigator ✓

- Scan Study Objectives ☐
- Read Preview ☐
- Read Chapter Review ☐
- Work Demonstration Problem ☐
- Answer True-False Statements ☐
- Answer Multiple-Choice Questions ☐
- Match Terms and Definitions ☐
- Solve Exercises ☐

INVESTMENTS

CHAPTER STUDY OBJECTIVES

After studying this chapter, you should be able to:

1. Discuss why corporations invest in stocks and debt securities.
2. Explain the accounting for debt investments.
3. Explain the accounting for stock investments.
4. Describe the use of consolidated financial statements.
5. Indicate how debt and stock investments are valued and reported on the financial statements.
6. Distinguish between short-term and long-term investments.

*7. Describe the content of a work sheet for a consolidated balance sheet.

*8. Explain the form and content of consolidated financial statements.

***Note:** All **asterisked** (I) items relate to material contained in the Appendix to the chapter.

PREVIEW OF CHAPTER 13

Investment clubs represent one of a vast assortment of ways that investments can be purchased. Investments also can be made by individuals, mutual funds, banks, pension funds, and corporations. In addition, investments can be purchased for a short or a long period of time, as a passive investment, or with the intent to control the firm. As you will see in this chapter, the way in which a company accounts for its investments is determined by a number of factors. The content and organization of this chapter are as follows:

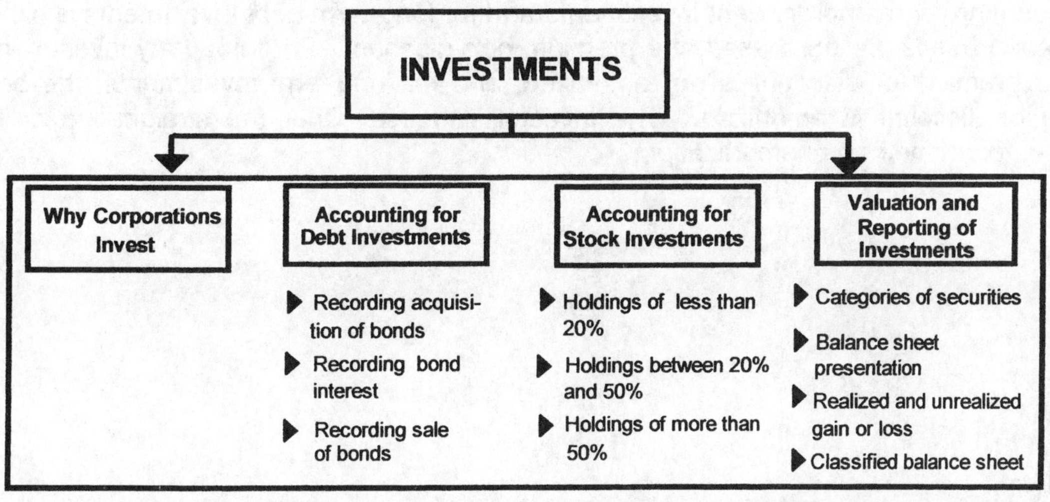

CHAPTER REVIEW

Temporary and Long-Term Investments

1. (S.O. 1) Corporations purchase investments because (1) they may have excess cash, (2) they generate earnings from investment income, and (3) for strategic reasons.

Accounting for Short-Term Debt Investments

2. (S.O. 2) **Debt investments** are investments in government and corporation bonds. At acquisition, the cost principle is applied and all expenditures necessary to acquire these investments are included in the cost (e.g., brokerage fees). At acquisition, Debt Investments is debited and Cash is credited for the cost of the investment.

3. Interest revenue must also be recorded on debt investments. Assume Bodhi Company (fiscal year ends December 31) receives $2,000 interest every six months on a debt investment purchased April 1, 2003. The following entries are required:

Date		Account	Debit	Credit
Oct.	1	Cash	2,000	
		Interest Revenue		2,000
Dec.	31	Interest Receivable	1,000	
		Interest Revenue		1,000
Apr.	1	Cash	2,000	
		Interest Receivable		1,000
		Interest Revenue		1,000

4. When bonds are sold, it is necessary to credit the investment account for the cost of the bonds, debit Cash, and any difference between the sale price and cost of bonds is recorded as a gain or loss. The gain or loss on the sale of debt investments is reported under Other Revenues and Gains or Other Expenses and Losses, respectively, in the income statement.

Accounting for Long-Term Debt Investments

5. The accounting for temporary debt investments and for long-term debt investments is similar except when bonds are purchased at a premium or a discount. For temporary investments, the bond premium or discount is **not** amortized, and for long-term investments, the bond premium or discount is amortized. The investor can use either the straight-line or the effective-interest method of amortization.

Accounting for Stock Investments

6. (S.O. 3) **Stock investments** are investments in the capital stock of corporations. The accounting for stock investments differs depending on the degree of influence the investor has over the issuing corporation. The presumed influences based on the investor's ownership interest and the accounting guidelines that are to be used are as follows:

Investor's Ownership Interest in Investee's Common Stock	Presumed Influence on Investee	Accounting Guidelines
Less than 20%	Insignificant	Cost Method
Between 20% and 50%	Significant	Equity Method
More than 50%	Controlling	Consolidated financial statements

Holdings Less than 20%

7. In accounting for stock investments of less than 20%, the **cost method** is used. Under the **cost method,** the investment is recorded at cost and revenue is recognized only when cash dividends are received.
   a. At acquisition, the cost principle applies and Stock Investments is debited and Cash is credited.
   b. When dividends are received, Cash is debited and Dividend Revenue is credited.
   c. When stock is sold, Cash is debited, Stock Investments is credited, and any difference between the two is debited or credited to Loss or Gain on Sale of Stock Investments, respectively. The loss or gain is reported under Other Expenses and Losses or Other Revenues and Gains on the income statement.

Holdings Between 20% and 50%

8. When an investor owns between 20% and 50% of the common stock of a corporation, it is generally presumed that the investor has a significant influence over the financial and operating activities of the investee; and therefore the **equity method** is used. Under the equity method, the investor does not record its share of the investee until the investee has earned income.
   a. At acquisition, the cost principle applies and Stock Investments is debited and Cash is credited.
   b. Each year, the investor records its share of the investee's income (investee's income X % of ownership in investee) with a debit to Stock Investments and a credit to Revenue from Investee Company (if the investee incurred a loss, then the opposite entry is made).
   c. Upon receiving dividends from the investee, the investor makes a debit to Cash and a credit to Stock Investments.

Holdings of More Than 50%

9. (S.O. 4) A company that owns more than 50% of the common stock of another entity is known as the **parent company.** The entity whose stock is owned by the parent company is called the **Subisidiary (affiliated) company.** Because of its stock ownership, the parent company has a **controlling interest** in the subsidiary company.

10. When a company owns more than 50% of the common stock of another company, **consolidated financial statements** are usually prepared. Consolidated financial statements present the assets and liabilities controlled by the parent company and the aggregate profitability of the subsidiary companies.

Valuation and Reporting of Investments

11. (S.O. 5) For purposes of valuation and reporting at a financial statement date, debt and stock investments are classified into the following three categories.
    a. **Trading securities** are securities bought and held primarily for sale in the near term to generate income on short-term price differences.
    b. **Available-for-sale securities** are securities that may be sold in the future.
    c. **Held-to-maturity securities** are debt securities that the investor has the intent and ability to hold to maturity.

12. The valuation guidelines for the above securities are as follows:

Trading	Available-for-sale	Held-to-maturity
At fair value with changes reported in net income	At fair value with changes reported in the stock-holders' equity section	At amortized cost

Trading Securities

13. When the trading securities are not sold as of the reporting date, the difference between the total cost of the securities and their total fair value are reported as unrealized gains or losses in the income statement. The adjusting entry to record an unrealized gain would include a debit to Market Adjustment—Trading and a credit to Unrealized Gain—Income. The adjusting entry to record an unrealized loss would include a debit to Unrealized Loss—Income and a credit to Market Adjustment—Trading. The unrealized gains or losses are reported in the income statement under Other Revenues and Gains or Other Expenses and Losses, respectively.

Available-for-Sale

14. If available-for-sale securities are held with the intent to sell them within the next year or operating cycle, the securities are classified as current assets in the balance sheet. Otherwise, they are classified as long-term assets in the investments section of the balance sheet.

15. The available-for-sale securities adjusting entry is made in the same way as the trading securities adjusting entry except that the unrealized gain or loss is reported in the stockholders' equity section of the balance sheet. This balance is then adjusted with the market adjustment account to show the difference between the cost and fair value at that time.

16. (S.O. 6) **Temporary investments** are securities held by a company that are (a) readily marketable and (b) intended to be converted into cash within the next year or operating cycle, whichever is longer. Investments that do not meet **both** criteria are classified as **long-term investments.**

17. An investment is **readily marketable** when it can be sold easily whenever the need for cash arises. **Intent to convert** means that management intends to sell the investment within the next year or the operating cycle, whichever is longer.

Balance Sheet Presentation

18. Temporary investments are listed immediately below cash in the current asset section of the balance sheet. Temporary investments are reported at fair value. Long-term investments are generally reported in a separate section of the balance sheet immediately below current assets; and available-for-sale securities are reported at fair value, and investments in common stock accounted for under the equity method are reported at equity.

19. In the income statement, the following items are reported in the nonoperating section:

Other Revenue and Gains	Other Expenses and Losses
Interest Revenue	Loss on Sale of Investments
Dividend Revenue	Unrealized Loss—Income
Gain on Sale of Investments	
Unrealized Gain—Income	

The unrealized gain or loss on available-for-sale securities is reported as a separate component of stockholders' equity.

***Preparing a Consolidated Balance Sheet**

*20. (S.O. 7) Consolidated balance sheets are prepared from the individual balance sheets of the affiliated companies. All items in the individual balance sheets are included in the consolidated balance sheet except amounts that pertain to transactions between the affiliated companies **(intercompany transactions).**

*21. The preparation of consolidated balance sheets is usually facilitated by the use of a work sheet. The intercompany eliminations are made solely on the work sheet to present correct consolidated data. They are not journalized or posted by either of the affiliated companies and therefore do not affect the ledger accounts.

***Cost Above Book Value**

*22. (S.O. 8) When the cost of acquiring the common stock of another company is above the book value, this amount is separately recognized in eliminating the parent company's investment account. Through the work sheet, the excess of cost over book value is first allocated to specific assets, such as inventory and plant equipment, if their fair market values on the acquisition date exceed their book values. Any remainder is considered to be goodwill.

***Consolidated Income Statement**

*23. The consolidated income statement shows the results of operations of affiliated companies as though they are one economic unit. Once again, all intercompany revenue and expense transactions must be eliminated.

The Navigator

DEMONSTRATION PROBLEM (S.O. 3)

During 2006, its first year of operation, the Zimmer Company had the following transactions in stock investments which are considered trading securities.

June 18 Purchased 1,000 shares of McClendon Corporation common stock for cash at $30 per share plus broker's fees of $300.

Aug. 3 Purchased 1,500 shares of Berryhill Corporation common stock for cash at $25 per share plus broker's fees of $400.

Dec. 31 Dividends are received from investments; McClendon Corporation $2 per share, and Berryhill Corporation $1.50 per share.

At December 31, the McClendon common stock had a market price of $29 per share and the Berryhill common stock had a $24 market price.

Instructions

(a) Journalize the transactions and the December 31 adjusting entry. (Omit explanations)

(b) Journalize the sale of 500 shares of McClendon common stock on March 1, 2007, assuming the shares were sold for $14,800 less broker's fees of $150. 14950

The Navigator

J/18 Dr. Stock Investments 30300
cr. cash 30300

aug/3 Dr. Stock Investments 37900
cr. cash 37900

Dec. 31st Dr. Cash 4250
cr. Dividend Revenue
[1000 × 2) + (1500 × 1.5) 4250

31st Dr. Unrealized Loss - Income 3200
cr. Market adjustment - Trading 3200
(1 × 1000) + 1 × 1500

	cost	Fair value	loss
MC	30300	29,000	1300
BH	37900	36,000	1900
			3200

SOLUTION TO DEMONSTRATION PROBLEM

(a)

General Journal J1

Date	Account Title	Debit	Credit
2006			
June 18	Stock Investments	30,300	
	Cash		30,300
Aug. 3	Stock Investments	37,900	
	Cash		37,900
Dec. 31	Cash	4,250	
	Dividend Revenue [(1,000 X $2.00) +		4,250
	(1,500 X $1.50)]		
31	Unrealized Loss--Income	3,200	
	Market Adjustment--Trading		3,200

	Cost	Fair Value	Unrealized Gain (Loss)
McClendon	$30,300	$29,000	$(1,300)
Berryhill	37,900	36,000	(1,900)
	$68,200	$65,000	$(3,200)

(b) 2007

Mar. 1	Cash ($14,800 - $150)............	14,650	
	Loss on Sale of Stock Investments............	500	
	Stock Investments ($30,300 X 1/2)		15,150

REVIEW QUESTIONS AND EXERCISES

TRUE—FALSE

Indicate whether each of the following is true (T) or false (F) in the space provided.

_____ 1. (S.O. 1) One of the reasons a corporation may purchase investments is that they have excess cash.

_____ 2. (S.O. 2) Debt investments are investments in government and corporation bonds.

_____ 3. (S.O. 2) When recording bond interest, Interest Receivable is reported as a fixed asset in the balance sheet.

_____ 4. (S.O. 2) The gain on sale of debt investments is reported as an extraordinary gain in the income statement.

_____ 5. (S.O. 2) For long-term debt investments, any bond premium or discount is amortized to interest revenue over the remaining term of the bonds.

_____ 6. (S.O. 3) If an investor's common stock ownership interest in an investee is less than 20%, the investment should be accounted for using the equity method.

_____ 7. (S.O. 3) Under the cost method, the investment is recorded at cost and revenue is recognized only when cash dividends are received.

_____ 8. (S.O. 3) Under the equity method, the investment in common stock is initially recorded at cost, and the investment account is adjusted annually to show the investor's equity in the investee.

_____ 9. (S.O. 3) Under the equity method, the investor debits revenue and credits the investment account for its share of the investee's net income.

_____ 10. (S.O. 4) If an investor has over a 50% ownership interest in the preferred stock of a company, it is generally assumed that the investor can exert significant influence over the affairs of the investee.

_____ 11. (S.O. 4) When a company owns more than 50% of the common stock of another company, consolidated financial statements are usually prepared.

_____ 12. (S.O. 4) Consolidated financial statements present a condensed version of the financial statements so investors will not experience information overload.

_____ 13. (S.O. 5) Trading securities are held with the intention of selling them in a short period of time (generally less than a month).

_____ 14. (S.O. 5) Available-for-sale securities are securities bought and held primarily for sale in the near term to generate income on short-term price differences.

_____ 15. (S.O. 5) The unrealized gain or loss on trading securities is reported in the income statement.

_____ 16. (S.O. 5) Available-for-sale securities can be classified as current assets or long-term assets.

_____ 17. (S.O. 5) The unrealized gain or loss on available-for-sale securities is reported in the income statement.

_____ 18. (S.O. 5) The adjusting entry to record an unrealized loss for available-for-sale securities would include a credit to Market Adjustment—Available-for-Sale Securities.

_____ 19. (S.O. 6) To be considered temporary, an investment must be readily marketable and management should intend to convert the investment into cash within the next year or operating cycle, whichever is longer.

_____ 20. (S.O. 6) "Intent to convert" does not include an investment used as a resource that will be used whenever the need for cash arises.

_____ *21. (S.O. 7) Consolidated statements are prepared from ledger accounts kept by the consolidated entity.

_____ *22. (S.O. 7) Intercompany eliminations are necessary in order to avoid understating the assets, liabilities, and ownership equity in the consolidated balance sheet.

_____ *23. (S.O. 7) Intercompany elimination entries are made solely on the work sheet and are not journalized or posted.

_____ *24. (S.O. 7) When acquisition cost exceeds book value, the work sheet elimination entry will include a debit to Excess of Cost Over Book Value of Subsidiary.

_____ *25. (S.O. 8) The goodwill portion of the excess of cost over book value should be amortized by the straight-line method over the period benefited but not in excess of 50 years.

_____ *26. (S.O. 8) The Excess of Cost Over Book Value of Subsidiary is specifically reported on a consolidated balance sheet.

_____ *27. (S.O. 8) A consolidated income statement shows the results of operations of affiliated companies as though they were one economic unit.

_____ *28. (S.O. 8) A work sheet does not facilitate the preparation of a consolidated income statement.

The Navigator

MULTIPLE CHOICE

Circle the letter that best answers each of the following statements.

1. (S.O. 1) Which of the following reasons best explains why a company that experiences seasonal fluctuations in sales may purchase investments in debt or equity securities?
   a. The company may have excess cash.
   b. The company may generate a significant portion of their earnings from investment income.
   c. The company may invest for the strategic reason of establishing a presence in a related industry.
   d. The company may invest for speculative reasons to increase the value in pension funds.

2. (S.O. 2) Debt investments are investments in:

	Government Bonds	Corporate Bonds
a.	Yes	Yes
b.	Yes	No
c.	No	Yes
d.	No	No

The following information is to be used for questions 3, 4, and 5.

Assume that Sutcliff Company acquires 100 Trout Inc. 10%, 20-year, $1,000 bonds on January 1, 2006, for $106,000, plus brokerage fees of $2,000 as a temporary investment.

3. (S.O. 2) The entry to record the investment includes a debit to Debt Investments of:
   a. $100,000.
   b. $106,000.
   c. $108,000.
   d. $110,000.

4. (S.O. 2) The entry for the receipt of semiannual interest on July 1 includes a credit to Interest Revenue of:
   a. $5,000.
   b. $5,600.
   c. $5,800.
   d. $10,000.

5. (S.O. 2) Assuming that Sutcliff Company receives net proceeds of $103,000 on the sale of Trout Inc. bonds on January 1, 2007, after receiving the interest due, the entry would include:
   a. a debit to Loss on Sale of Debt Investments of $3,000.
   b. a debit to Loss on Sale of Debt Investments of $5,000.
   c. a credit to Gain on Sale of Debt Investments of $3,000.
   d. a credit to Gain on Sale of Debt Investments of $5,000.

6. (S.O. 2) Which of the following is a major difference when accounting for long-term debt investments versus temporary debt investments?
   a. When selling long-term investments, no gain or loss is recognized.
   b. At the end of the year, any unrealized gain or loss on long-term debt investments must be recognized in the stockholders' equity section of the balance sheet.
   c. Interest revenue is not recognized for long-term investments.
   d. For temporary investments, bond premium or discount is not amortized to interest revenue.

7. (S.O. 3) A company that acquires less than 20% ownership interest in another company should account for the stock investment in that company using:
   a. the cost method.
   b. the equity method.
   c. the significant method.
   d. consolidated financial statements.

8. (S.O. 3) Under the cost method, cash dividends received by the investor from the investee should be recorded as:
   a. dividend revenue.
   b. an addition to the investor's share of the investee's profit.
   c. a deduction from the investor's share of the investee's profit.
   d. a deduction from the investment account.

9. (S.O. 3) On January 1, 2006, Moreland Company bought 15% of Lopes Corporation's common stock for $30,000. Lopes' net income for 2006 and 2007 were $10,000 and $50,000 respectively. During 2007, Lopes paid a cash dividend of $70,000. How much should Moreland show on its 2007 income statement as income from this investment under the cost method?
   a. $1,575.
   b. $7,500.
   c. $9,000.
   d. $10,500.

10. (S.O. 3) On January 1, 2007, Trillo Corporation paid $150,000 for 10,000 shares of Davis Corporation's common stock, representing a 15% investment in Davis. Davis declared and paid a cash dividend of $1 per share in 2007 when its net income was $130,000. At what amount should Trillo's investment in Davis be reported at December 31, 2007?
   a. $140,000.
   b. $150,000.
   c. $159,500.
   d. $169,500.

11. (S.O. 3) The equity method of accounting for an investment in the common stock of another company should be used by the investor when the investment:
   a. is composed of common stock and it is the investor's intent to vote the common stock.
   b. ensures a source of supply of raw materials for the investor.
   c. enables the investor to exercise significant influence over the investee.
   d. is obtained by an exchange of stock for stock.

12. (S.O. 3) Cash dividends declared out of current earnings are distributed to an investor. How will the investor's investment account be affected by those dividends under each of the following accounting methods?

	Cost Method	Equity Method
a.	Decrease	No effect
b.	Decrease	Decrease
c.	No effect	Decrease
d.	No effect	No effect

13. (S.O. 3) When an investor uses the equity method, the investment account will be increased when the investor recognizes a:
   a. proportionate equity in the net income of the investee.
   b. cash dividend received from the investee.
   c. stock dividend received from the investee.
   d. proportionate equity in the net loss of the investee.

14. (S.O. 3) When an investor uses the equity method to account for investments in common stock, cash dividends received by the investor from the investee should be recorded as:
   a. dividend revenue.
   b. a deduction from the investor's share of the investee's profits.
   c. a deduction from the investment account.
   d. a deduction from the stockholders' equity account, dividends to stockholders.

15. (S.O. 3) On January 2, Matthews Corporation acquired 20% of the outstanding common stock of Dernier Company for $700,000. For the year ended December 31, Dernier reported net income of $180,000 and paid cash dividends of $60,000 on its common stock. At December 31, the carrying value of Matthews' investment in Dernier under the equity method is:
   a. $688,000.
   b. $700,000.
   c. $712,000.
   d. $724,000.

16. (S.O. 4) Wilson Company purchases 54% of Pico Company's common stock. Wilson Company should present its interest in Pico Company using:
   a. the cost method.
   b. the equity method.
   c. the significant method.
   d. consolidated financial statements.

17. (S.O. 5) Securities bought and held primarily for sale in the near term to generate income on short-term price differences are:
   a. Trading securities.
   b. Available-for-sale securities.
   c. Never-sell securities.
   d. Held-to-maturity securities.

18. (S.O. 5) On December 31, 2006, Mumphrey Co. has the following costs and fair values for its investments classified as trading securities:

Investments	Cost	Fair Value
Cub Co.	$20,000	$25,000
Wrigley Co.	34,000	32,000

The adjusting entry for Mumphrey Co. will include a debit to:
a. Unrealized Loss—Income of $5,000.
b. Market Adjustment—Trading of $2,000.
c. Market Adjustment—Trading of $3,000.
d. Unrealized Gain—Income of $3,000.

19. (S.O. 5) On December 31, 2006, Dunston Co. has the following investments that are classified as available-for-sale securities:

Investments	Cost	Fair Value
Shawon Co.	$40,000	$35,000
Cihla Co.	38,000	39,000

The amount of the unrealized gain or loss would be reported on the income statement as a:
a. $5,000 unrealized loss.
b. $4,000 unrealized loss.
c. $1,000 unrealized gain.
d. No unrealized loss or gain is reported on the income statement.

20. (S.O. 7) Temporary investments are:
a. (1) readily marketable and (2) intended to be converted into cash after the current year or operating cycle, whichever is shorter.
b. (1) readily marketable and (2) intended to be converted into cash within the current year or operating cycle, whichever is longer.
c. (1) readily marketable and (2) intended to be converted into cash after the current year or operating cycle, whichever is longer.
d. (1) readily marketable and (2) intended to be converted into cash within the current year or operating cycle, whichever is shorter.

*21. (S.O. 8) Sutcliff Company acquires 100% of the net assets of Trout Company for $110,000. Trout Company's assets have a book value of $120,000 and its liabilities are $20,000. What is the amount of Excess of Cost Over Book Value of Subsidiary on the work sheet for the consolidated balance sheet?
a. $0.
b. $10,000.
c. $20,000.
d. $40,000.

*22. (S.O. 8) In a consolidated balance sheet, Excess of Cost Over Book Value of Subsidiary may be reported as:
   a. plant equipment.
   b. goodwill.
   c. both (a) and (b).
   d. neither (a) nor (b).

*23. (S.O. 8) One of the following statements about a consolidated income statement is **incorrect**. That statement is:
   a. In the work sheet, intercompany revenue and expense transactions should be eliminated.
   b. The statement shows the results of operations of affiliated companies as though they were one economic unit.
   c. The statement can be prepared directly from the work sheet.
   d. Intercompany sales between affiliates do not have to be eliminated.

The Navigator

MATCHING

Match each term with its definition by writing the appropriate letter in the space provided.

Terms

_____ 1. Equity method.

_____ 2. Parent company.

_____ 3. Available-for-sale securities.

_____ 4. Consolidated financial statements.

_____ 5. Trading securities.

_____ 6. Held-to-maturity securities.

_____ 7. Debt investments.

_____ 8. Affiliated companies.

_____ 9. Subsidiary company.

_____ 10. Fair value.

_____ 11. Temporary investments.

_____ 12. Cost method.

_____ 13. Stock investments.

Definitions

a. A company that owns more than 50% of the common stock of another entity.

b. Investments in government and corporate bonds.

c. Amount for which a security could be sold in a normal market.

d. Debt securities that the investor has the intent and ability to hold to maturity.

e. A method in which the investment in common stock is initially recorded at cost, and the investment account is adjusted annually to show the investors' equity in the investee.

f. Securities that may be sold in the future.

g. Financial statements that present the assets and liabilities controlled by a parent company and the aggregate profitability of the affiliated companies.

h. Securities bought and held primarily for sale in the near term to generate income on short-term price differences.

i. Companies under common control of a single company.

j. Investments in capital stock of corporations.

k. A method of accounting in which the investment in common stock is recorded at cost and revenue is recognized only when cash dividends are received.

l. A company in which more than 50% of its stock is owned by another company.

m. Investments that are readily marketable and intended to be converted into cash within the next year or operating cycle, whichever is longer.

The Navigator

EXERCISES

EX. 13-1 (S.O. 2 and 3) The Williams Corporation accumulated the following data for its investments made on January 1, 2006.

1. Purchased $100,000, 10%, 10-year Kilgus Corporation bonds for $105,000 in cash as a long-term investment. The bonds pay interest semi-annually on January 1 and July 1. Received the interest due on July 1.

2. Purchased for cash 10% of Walton Inc.'s 400,000 shares of common stock at a cost of $20 per share plus brokers' fees of $5,000. In 2006, Walton reports net income of $100,000, and it declares and pays a $30,000 cash dividend on December 31.

3. Acquired 40% of the common stock of Wilkerson Company for $500,000 cash. In 2006, Wilkerson Company reports net income of $70,000, and it declares and pays a $60,000 cash dividend on December 31.

Instructions

(a) Journalize the entries for the bonds on January 1 and July 1 assuming the straight-line method of amortization is used.
(b) Journalize the 2006 entries for the Walton stock, assuming the cost method is used.
(c) Journalize the 2006 entries for the Wilkerson stock, assuming the equity method is used.

General Journal

J1

Date	Account Title	Debit	Credit
2006	January		
(a)	Dr. Investment in Kilgus Corp	105,000	
	Cr. Cash		105,000
	July		
	Dr. Cash (100,000 x 10% 6/12)	5000	
(5000 ÷ 20)	Cr. Investment in Kilgus Corp	250	
	Cr. Interest Revenue		4750
(b)	Dr. Investment in Walton stock	805,000	
	Cr. Cash		805,000
	Dr. Cash	3000	
	Cr. Dividend Revenue		3000

General Journal J

Date	Account Title	Debit	Credit
(c)	Dr. Stock Investments	500,000	
	Cr. Cash		500,000
	Dr. Stock investmenst	28,000	
	Cr. Revenue from investment		28,000
	in Wilkerson's Company		
	Dr. Cash	24,000	
	Cr. Stock investments		24,000

EX. 13-2 (S.O. 5) Harry Caray Co. has the following data at December 31, 2006:

Securities	Cost	Fair value
Trading	$103,000	$99,000
Available-for-sale	70,000	75,000

The available-for-sale securities are held as a long-term investment.

Instructions

(a) Prepare the adjusting entries to report each class of securities at fair value.

(b) Indicate the statement presentation of each class of securities and the related unrealized gain (loss) accounts.

trading sec. + available for sale = market adjus. unrealized gain

(a)

General Journal J

Date	Account Title	Debit	Credit
	Dr. unrealized loss - income	4,000	
	Cr. market adjustment - trading		4,000
	Dr. market adj.	5,000	
	Cr. unrealized gain		5,000

(b)

***EX. 13-3** (S.O. 7) On January 2, 2006, Wilson Company acquires 100% of Pico Company's common stock for $160,000. The separate balance sheets of the two companies are presented in the work sheet.

Instructions

Complete the work sheet for the consolidated balance sheet for Wilson Company and its subsidiary, Pico Company.

WILSON COMPANY AND SUBSIDIARY
Work Sheet—Consolidated Balance Sheet
January 2, 2006

	Wilson Company	Pico Company	Eliminations Dr.	Eliminations Cr.	Consolidated Data
Assets					
Current assets	80,000	40,000			
Investments in Pico Company common stock	160,000				
Plant and equipment (net)	310,000	160,000			
Excess of cost over book value of subsidiary					
Totals	550,000	200,000			
Liabilities and Stockholders' Equity					
Current liabilities	110,000	50,000			
Common stock	350,000	90,000			
Retained earnings	90,000	60,000			
Totals	550,000	200,000			

The Navigator

SOLUTIONS TO REVIEW QUESTIONS AND EXERCISES

TRUE-FALSE

1. (T)
2. (T)
3. (F) When recording bond interest, Interest Receivable is reported as a current asset in the balance sheet.
4. (F) The gain on the sale of debt investments is reported under Other Revenues and Gains in the income statement.
5. (T)
6. (F) If an investor's common stock ownership interest in an investee is less than 20%, the investment should be accounted for using the cost method.
7. (T)
8. (T)
9. (F) Under the equity method, the investor debits the investment account and credits revenue for its share of the investee's net income.
10. (F) Regardless of the number of shares held, ownership of preferred stock does not give the investor an opportunity to exert significant influence over the affairs of the investee because preferred stock is usually nonvoting.
11. (T)
12. (F) Consolidated financial statements present the assets and liabilities controlled by the parent company and the aggregate profitability of the subsidiary companies.
13. (T)
14. (F) Trading securities are securities bought and held primarily for sale in the near term to generate income on short-term price differences.
15. (T)
16. (T)
17. (F) The unrealized gain or loss on available-for-sale securities is reported in the balance sheet as a separate component of stockholders' equity.
18. (T)
19. (T)
20. (F) "Intent to convert" is generally satisfied when the investment is considered a resource that will be used whenever the need for cash arises.

*21. (F) Consolidated statements are prepared from the individual financial statements of the affiliated companies.

*22. (F) Intercompany eliminations are necessary in order to avoid overstating the assets, liabilities, and ownership equity in the consolidated balance sheet.

*23. (T)

*24. (T)

*25. (F) The goodwill portion of the excess of cost over book value is not amortized.

*26. (F) In a consolidated balance sheet, the excess of cost over book value is first allocated to specific assets such as inventory and plant assets and the remainder is considered to be goodwill.

*27. (T)

*28. (F) A work sheet facilitates the preparation of a consolidated income statement in the same manner as it does for a balance sheet.

MULTIPLE CHOICE

1. (a) A company that experiences seasonal fluctuations in sales may have excess cash and therefore may be likely to purchase investments in debt or equity securities.

2. (a) Debt investments are investments in government and corporate bonds.

3. (c) At acquisition of debt investments, the cost principle applies. Cost includes all expenditures necessary to acquire these investments, such as the price paid plus brokerage fees (commissions), if any. Thus, the total cost of $108,000 is debited to Debt Investments.

4. (a) The bonds pay interest on July 1 of $5,000 ($100,000 X 10% X 1/2).

5. (b) Since the securities cost $108,000, a loss of $5,000 ($108,000 - $103,000) is realized.

6. (d) The accounting for temporary debt investments and for long-term debt investments is similar. The major exception is when bonds are purchased at a premium or discount. For temporary investments, the bond premium or discount is not amortized to interest revenue because the bonds are held for a short period of time and a misstatement of interest revenue for such a period is not considered material.

7. (a) A company that acquires less than 20% ownership interest in another company should account for the stock investment in that company using the cost method.

8. (a) Under the cost method, cash dividends received by the investor are recorded as dividend revenue.

9. (d) Under the cost method, the income statement of the investor is only affected by cash dividends received. During 2004 Lopes Company paid $70,000 of cash dividends of which Moreland received 15% or $10,500.

10. (b) Under the cost method, the investment in common stock is initially recorded at cost, and the investment account continues to be carried at cost until the shares are sold, with adjustments to fair value for financial statement presentation.

11. (c) The equity method of accounting for an investment in the common stock of another company should be used when the investment enables the investor to exercise significant influence over the investee.

12. (c) Under the cost method, cash dividends received by an investor are credited to Dividend Revenue. Under the equity method, the cash dividends received are credited to the Investment account.

13. (a) Each year, the investor debits the investment account and credits income for its share of the investee's net income.

14. (c) Each year, the investor credits cash dividends received to the investment account.

15. (d) Matthews should debit the investment account for $36,000 ($180,000 X 20%) and credit the investment account for $12,000 ($60,000 X 20%). Thus, the investment balance will increase to $724,000 ($700,000 + $36,000 - $12,000).

16. (d) Because Wilson Company has acquired over 50% of Pico Company's common stock, Wilson should present its interest in Pico Company using consolidated financial statements.

17. (a) Securities bought and held primarily for sale in the near term to generate income on short-term price differences are trading securities. Available-for-sale securities (b) are securities that may be sold in the future. Never-sell securities (c) is not a defined term. Held-to-maturity securities (d) are debt securities that the investor has the intent and ability to hold to maturity.

18. (c) Mumphrey Co. has an unrealized gain of $3,000 because total fair value ($57,000) is $3,000 greater than the total cost ($54,000). The adjusting entry would therefore be as follows:

Market Adjustment—Trading	3,000	
Unrealized Gain—Income		3,000

19. (d) An unrealized gain or loss on available-for-sale securities is not reported in the income statement. Instead, it is reported as a separate component of stockholders' equity. Therefore, Dunston would report a $4,000 ($5,000 - $1,000) unrealized loss as a separate component of stockholders' equity.

20. (b) Temporary investments are (1) readily marketable and (2) intended to be converted into cash within the current year or operating cycle, whichever is longer.

*21. (b) The net book value of Trout Company is $100,000 ($120,000 - $20,000). Since Sutcliff paid $110,000 for 100% of the net assets in Trout, the Excess of Cost over Book Value of Subsidiary is $10,000 ($110,000 - $100,000).

*22. (c) The excess may be reported as inventory or plant and equipment, and any remainder is reported as goodwill.

*23. (d) Intercompany sales between affiliates have to be eliminated in order to show the results of operations as though they were one economic unit.

MATCHING

1. e	6. d	11. m
2. a	7. b	12. k
3. f	8. i	13. j
4. g	9. l	
5. h	10. c	

EX. 13-1

General Journal J1

Date	Account Title	Debit	Credit
2006			
(a)			
Jan. 1	Investment in Kilgus Bonds	105,000	
	Cash		105,000
July 1	Cash ($100,000 X 10% X 6/12)	5,000	
	Investment in Kilgus Bonds ($5,000 ÷ 20)		250
	Interest Revenue		4,750
(b)			
Jan. 1	Investment in Walton Common Stock	805,000	
	Cash		805,000
Dec. 31	Cash ($30,000 X 10%)	3,000	
	Dividend Revenue		3,000
(c)			
Jan. 1	Investment in Wilkerson Common Stock	500,000	
	Cash		500,000
Dec. 31	Investment in Wilkerson Common Stock	28,000	
	Income from Investment in Wilkerson		
	Common Stock ($70,000 X 40%)		28,000
31	Cash ($60,000 X 40%)	24,000	
	Investment in Wilkerson Common Stock		24,000

EX. 13-2

General Journal			J1
Date	**Account Title**	**Debit**	**Credit**
(a)			
Dec. 31	Unrealized Loss--Income	4,000	
	Market Adjustment--Trading		4,000
	Market Adjustment--Available-for-sale	5,000	
	Unrealized Gain--Equity		5,000

(b) The trading securities are considered short-term and because of their high liquidity are listed immediately below cash in the current assets section of the balance sheet. They are reported at their fair value of $99,000. The available-for-sale securities are listed as long-term in this problem and therefore would generally be reported in a separate section of the balance sheet immediately below current assets at their fair value of $75,000.

The unrealized loss—income on the trading securities would be reported on the income statement in the Other Expenses and Losses section for $4,000. The unrealized gain—equity on the available-for-sale securities would be reported on the balance sheet as a separate component of stockholders' equity for $5,000.

***EX. 13-3**

WILSON COMPANY AND SUBSIDIARY
Work Sheet—Consolidated Balance Sheet
January 2, 2006

Assets	Wilson Company	Pico Company	Eliminations Dr.	Eliminations Cr.	Consolidated Data
Current assets	80,000	40,000			120,000
Investments in Pico Company common stock	160,000			160,000	
Plant and equipment (net)	310,000	160,000			470,000
Excess of cost over book value of subsidiary			10,000		10,000
Totals	550,000	200,000			600,000
Liabilities and Stockholders' Equity					
Current liabilities	110,000	50,000			160,000
Common stock	350,000	90,000	90,000		350,000
Retained earnings	90,000	60,000	60,000		90,000
Totals	550,000	200,000	160,000	160,000	600,000

The Navigator ✓

- Scan Study Objectives ☐
- Read Preview ☐
- Read Chapter Review ☐
- Work Demonstration Problem ☐
- Answer True-False Statements ☐
- Answer Multiple-Choice Questions ☐
- Match Terms and Definitions ☐
- Solve Exercises ☐

Chapter **14**

THE STATEMENT OF CASH FLOWS

CHAPTER STUDY OBJECTIVES

After studying this chapter, you should be able to:

1. Indicate the usefulness of the statement of cash flows.
2. Distinguish among operating, investing, and financing activities.
3. Prepare a statement of cash flows using the indirect method.
4. Prepare a statement of cash flows using the direct method.
5. Analyze the statement of cash flows.

*6. Explain the guidelines and procedural steps in using a work sheet to prepare the statement of cash flows using the indirect method.

***Note:** All **asterisked** (*) items relate to material contained in the Appendix to the chapter.

The Navigator

PREVIEW OF CHAPTER 14

The balance sheet, income statement, and retained earnings statement do not always show the whole picture of the financial condition of a company or institution. For example, how did Eastman Kodak finance cash dividends of $649 million in a year in which it earned only $17 million? The answer to this and similar questions can be found in this chapter, which presents the **statement of cash flows.** The content and organization of this chapter are as follows:

THE STATEMENT OF CASH FLOWS

The Statement of Cash Flows: Purpose and Format
- Usefulness
- Classifications
- Significant noncash activities
- Format
- Preparation
- Indirect and direct methods

Section 1: Indirect Method (OR)
- Step 1: Operating activities
- Step 2: Investing and financing activities
- Step 3: Net change in cash

Section 2: Direct Method
- Step 1: Operating activities
- Step 2: Investing and financing activities
- Step 3: Net change in cash

Using Cash Flows to Evaluate a Company
- Free cash flow

The Navigator

CHAPTER REVIEW

Purpose and Usefulness of the Statement of Cash Flows

1. (S.O. 1) The fourth basic financial statement is the **statement of cash flows.** The primary purpose of the statement is to provide information about an entity's cash receipts and cash payments during a period.

2. The information in the statement of cash flows should help investors to assess the:
   a. entity's ability to generate future cash flows.
   b. entity's ability to pay dividends and meet obligations.
   c. reasons for the difference between net income and net cash flow from operating activities.
   d. cash investing and financing transactions during the period.

Classification of Cash Flows

3. (S.O. 2) The statement of cash flows classifies cash receipts and cash payments by:
   a. **Operating activities** which include cash effects of transactions that create revenues and expenses and thus enter into the determination of net income.
   b. **Investing activities** which include (1) acquiring and disposing of investments and productive long-lived assets, and (2) lending money and collecting the loans.
   c. **Financing activities** which involve liability and stockholders' equity items and include (1) obtaining cash from issuing debt and repaying the amounts borrowed, and (2) obtaining cash from stockholders and providing them with a return on their investment.

4. **Significant noncash transactions** will include the conversion of bonds into common stock and the acquisition of assets through the issuance of bonds or capital stock. These transactions are individually reported at the bottom of the statement of cash flows or they may appear in a separate note or supplementary schedule to the financial statements.

General Format

5. The three classes of activities constitute the general **format** of the statement with the operating activities section appearing first, followed by the investing activities and financing activities sections.
   a. The **net cash** provided or used by each activity is totaled to show the **net increase (decrease) in cash** for the period.
   b. The net change in cash for the period is then added to or subtracted from the beginning-of-the-period cash balance.
   c. Finally, any significant noncash investing and financing activities are reported in a **separate schedule** at the bottom of the statement.

Preparing the Statement of Cash Flows

6. The statement of cash flows is not prepared from the adjusted trial balance. The information to prepare this statement usually comes from three sources: (a) a comparative balance sheet, (b) the current income statement, and (c) additional information.

7. The **major steps** in preparing the statement are:
   Step 1: Determine the net cash provided/used by operating activities by converting net income from an accrual basis to a cash basis.
   Step 2: Analyze changes in noncurent asset and liablility accounts and record as investing and financing activities, or as significant noncash transactions.
   Step 3: Compare the net change in cash on the statement of cash flows with the change in the cash account reported on the balance sheet to make sure the amounts agree.

8. In performing step 1, the operating activities section must be **converted** from an accrual basis to a cash basis. This may be done by either the **indirect method** or the **direct method.**
   a. Both methods arrive at the same total amount for "net cash provided by operations" but they differ in disclosing the items that comprise the total amount.
   b. The indirect method is used extensively in practice.
   c. The FASB has expressed a preference for the direct method.

The Indirect Method

9. (S.O. 3) The following points 10 through 15 explain and illustrate the indirect method.

The First Step--Indirect

10. The first step is to determine **net cash provided/used** by operating activities.
    a. Under **generally accepted accounting principles** the accrual basis of accounting is used and results in recognizing revenues when earned and expenses when incurred.
    b. In order to determine cash provided from operations it is necessary to report revenues and expenses on a **cash basis.** This is determined by adjusting net income for items that did not affect cash.

11. The operating section of the statement of cash flows should (a) begin with net income, (b) add (or deduct) items not affecting cash, and (c) show net cash provided by operating activities.

12. The noncash items that require adjustments to net income are:
    (a) Add back noncash expenses, such as depreciation expense, amortization, or depletion.
    (b) Deduct gains and add losses that resulted from investing and financing activities.
    (c) Analyze changes to noncash current asset and current liability accounts.

The Second Step--Indirect

13. The second step, **net cash provided/used by investing and financing activities** is generally determined from changes in noncurrent accounts reported in the comparative balance sheet and selected additional data.
    a. If the account, Land, increases $50,000 and the transaction data indicates that land was purchased for cash, a cash outflow from an investment activity has occurred.
    b. If the account, Common Stock, increases $100,000 and the transaction data indicates that additional capital stock was issued for cash, a cash inflow from a financing activity has resulted.

14. The redemption of debt and the retirement or reacquisition of capital stock is a cash outflow from a financing activity.

The Third Step--Indirect

15. To prepare a statement of cash flows, the third step is determining the net increase or decrease in cash. This is simply the difference between cash at the beginning of the year and cash at the end of the year.

The Direct Method

16. (S.O. 4) The following points 17 through 24 explain and illustrate the direct method.

The First Step--Direct

17. The first step is to determine net cash provided/used by operating activities by adjusting each item in the income statement from the accrual basis to the cash basis.
    a. If the income statement shows revenue of $120,000 and accounts receivable (net) increased $20,000 during the year, cash revenue is $100,000 ($120,000 - $20,000).
    b. If the income statement reports operating expenses of $60,000 but accounts payable have increased $12,000 during the year, cash operating expenses are $48,000 ($60,000 - $12,000).

18. In the operating activities section, only **major classes** of cash receipts and cash payments are reported as follows:
    a. **Cash receipts** from (1) sales of goods and services to customers and (2) interest and dividends on loans and investments.
    b. **Cash payments** (1) to suppliers, (2) to employees, (3) for operating expenses, (4) for interest, and (5) for taxes.

19. The formula for computing **cash receipts from customers** is:

Revenue from sales [+ Decrease in accounts receivable or - Increase in accounts receivable]

20. The formula for computing **cash payments to suppliers** is:

Cost of goods sold [+ Increase in inventory or - Decrease in inventory] [+ Decrease in accounts payable or - Increase in accounts payable]

21. The formula for computing **cash payments for operating expenses** is:

Operating expenses (exclusive of depreciation expense) [+ Increase in prepaid expenses or - Decrease in prepaid expenses] [+ Decrease in accrued expenses payable or - Increase in accued expenses payable]

22. The formula for computing **cash payments for income taxes** is:

Income tax expense	+ Decrease in income taxes payable or - Increase in income taxes payable

The Second Step--Direct

23. The second step, **net cash provided/used by investing and financing activities** is generally determined from changes in noncurrent accounts reported in the comparative balance sheet and selected additional data.

The Third Step--Direct

24. The third step is to determine the net increase or decrease in cash by determining the difference between cash at the beginning of the year and cash at the end of the year as reported on comparative balance sheets.

Analysis of the Statement of Cash Flows

25. (S.O. 5) A measurement that provides additional insight into a company's cash generating ability is **free cash flow**. Free cash flow is calculated with the following formula:

Free Cash Flow = Cash Provided by Operations - Capital Expenditures - Cash Dividends

Use of a Work Sheet

*26. (S.O. 6) A **work sheet** may be used to assemble and classify the data that will appear on the statement of cash flows. The work sheet is divided into two parts:
   a. Balance sheet accounts with columns for (1) end of last year balances, (2) reconciling items (debit and credit), and (3) end of current year balances.
   b. Statement of cash flows effects with debit and credit columns. This part of the work sheet consists of the operating, investing, and financing sections.

*27. The following **guidelines** are important in **using** a work sheet.
   a. In the **balance sheet section,** accounts with debit balances are listed separately from those with credit balances.
   b. In the **cash flow effects section,** inflows of cash are entered as debits in the reconciling columns and outflows of cash are entered as credits in the reconciling columns.
   c. The reconciling items shown in the work sheet are not entered in any journal or posted to any account.

*28. The steps in preparing a work sheet are:
   a. Enter the balance sheet accounts and their beginning and ending balances in the balance sheet accounts section.
   b. Enter the data that explains the changes in the balance sheet accounts (other than cash) and their effects on the statement of cash flows in the reconciling columns of the work sheet.

c. Enter the increase or decrease in cash on the Cash line and at the bottom of the work sheet. This entry should enable the totals of the reconciling columns to be in agreement.

*29. The statement of cash flows is prepared entirely from the data that appears in the work sheet under Statement of Cash Flows Effects.

The Navigator

DEMONSTRATION PROBLEM (S.O. 3 and 4)

Presented below is the comparative balance sheet for Kinports Company as of December 31, 2006 and 2005, and the income statement for 2006:

KINPORTS COMPANY
Comparative Balance Sheet
December 31

Assets	2006	2005
Cash	$ 52,000	$ 63,000
Accounts receivable (net)	64,000	75,000
Inventory	193,000	179,000
Prepaid expenses	21,000	27,000
Land	95,000	120,000
Equipment	277,000	221,000
Accumulated depreciation—equipment	(51,000)	(42,000)
Building	300,000	300,000
Accumulated depreciation—building	(100,000)	(75,000)
	$851,000	$868,000
Liabilities and Stockholders' Equity		
Accounts payable	$ 34,000	$ 77,000
Bonds payable	245,000	290,000
Common stock, $1 par	275,000	230,000
Retained earnings	297,000	271,000
	$851,000	$868,000

KINPORTS COMPANY
Income Statement
For the Year Ended December 31, 2006

Sales		$600,000
Less:		
Cost of goods sold	$380,000	
Operating expenses	90,000	
Loss on sale of equipment	2,000	
Income tax expense	27,000	499,000
Net income		$101,000

Additional information:

1. Operating expenses include depreciation expense of $54,000.
2. Land was sold at book value.
3. Cash dividends of $75,000 were declared and paid.
4. Equipment was purchased for $82,000. In addition, equipment costing $26,000 with a book value of $6,000 was sold for $4,000.
5. Bonds with a face value of $45,000 were converted into 45,000 shares of $1 par value common stock.
6. Accounts payable pertain to merchandise suppliers.

Instructions

(a) Prepare a statement of cash flows for the year ended December 31, 2006 using the indirect method.

(b) Prepare a statement of cash flows for the year ended December 31, 2006 using the direct method.

SOLUTION TO DEMONSTRATION PROBLEM

(a)

KINPORTS COMPANY
Statement of Cash Flows
For the Year Ended December 31, 2006

Cash flows from operating activities		
Net income		$101,000
Adjustments to reconcile net income to net cash provided by operating activities		
Depreciation expense	$ 54,000	
Loss on sale of equipment	2,000	
Decrease in accounts receivable	11,000	
Increase in inventory	(14,000)	
Decrease in prepaid expenses	6,000	
Decrease in accounts payable	(43,000)	16,000
Net cash provided by operating activities		117,000
Cash flows from investing activities		
Sale of equipment	4,000	
Sale of land	25,000	
Purchase of equipment	(82,000)	
Net cash used by investing activities		(53,000)
Cash flows from financing activities		
Cash dividend to stockholders		(75,000)
Net decrease in cash		(11,000)
Cash at beginning of period		63,000
Cash at end of period		$ 52,000
Noncash investing and financing activities		
Conversion of bonds into common stock		$ 45,000

(b)

KINPORTS COMPANY
Statement of Cash Flows
For the Year Ended December 31, 2006

Cash flows from operating activities		
Cash receipts from customers (1)		$611,000
Cash payments		
To suppliers (2)	$437,000	
For operating expenses (3)	30,000	
For income taxes	27,000	494,000
Net cash provided by operating activities		117,000
Cash flows from investing activities		
Sale of equipment	4,000	
Sale of land	25,000	
Purchase of equipment	(82,000)	
Net cash used by investing activities		(53,000)
Cash flows from financing activities		
Cash dividend to stockholders		(75,000)
Net decrease in cash		(11,000)
Cash at beginning of period		63,000
Cash at end of period		$ 52,000
Noncash investing and financing activities		
Conversion of bonds into common stock		$ 45,000

(1) Cash receipts from customers:

Sales per income statement	$600,000
Add: Decrease in accounts receivable	11,000
Cash receipts from customers	$611,000

(2) Cash payments to suppliers:

Cost of goods sold per income statement	$380,000
Add: Increase in inventory	14,000
Purchases	394,000
Add: Decrease in accounts payable	43,000
Cash payments to suppliers	$437,000

(3) Cash payments for operating expenses:

Operating expenses per income statement		$90,000
Deduct: Depreciation expense	$54,000	
Decrease in prepaid expenses	6,000	60,000
Cash payments for operating expenses		$30,000

REVIEW QUESTIONS AND EXERCISES

TRUE—FALSE

Indicate whether each of the following is true (T) or false (F) in the space provided.

_____ 1. (S.O. 1) The statement of cash flows is an optional financial statement.

_____ 2. (S.O. 1) The statement of cash flows provides information about the cash receipts and cash payments of an entity during a period.

_____ 3. (S.O. 2) The statement of cash flows classifies cash receipts and cash payments into two categories: operating activities and nonoperating activities.

_____ 4. (S.O. 2) Investing activities pertain only to cash flows from acquiring and disposing of investments and productive long-lived assets.

_____ 5. (S.O. 2) Financing activities include the obtaining of cash from issuing debt and repaying the amounts borrowed.

_____ 6. (S.O. 2) A cash inflow from the sale of equity securities of another entity is an investing activity.

_____ 7. (S.O. 2) Cash outflows to pay employees for services rendered are an operating activity.

_____ 8. (S.O. 2) A significant noncash transaction occurs when plant assets are acquired by issuing bonds.

_____ 9. (S.O. 2) Significant noncash transactions are reported in the statement of cash flows in a separate section entitled Significant Noncash Transactions.

_____ 10. (S.O. 2) In the statement of cash flows, the operating activities section is usually presented last.

_____ 11. (S.O. 2) The statement of cash flows helps investors assess the company's ability to pay cash dividends.

_____ 12. (S.O. 2) The adjusted trial balance is the only item needed to prepare the Statement of Cash Flows.

_____ 13. (S.O. 2) The indirect method is used more often in practice than the direct method.

_____ 14. (S.O. 2) In determining net cash provided by operating activities, accrual basis net income is converted to cash basis net income.

_____ 15. (S.O. 3) Under the indirect method, retained earnings is adjusted for items that affected reported net income but did not affect cash.

_____ 16. (S.O. 3) Under the indirect method, noncash charges in the income statement are added back to net income.

_____ 17. (S.O. 3) Under the indirect method, in determining net cash provided by operating activities, an increase in accounts receivable and an increase in accounts payable are added to net income.

_____ 18. (S.O. 4) Under the direct method of determining net cash provided by operating activities, cash revenues and cash expenses are computed.

_____ 19. (S.O. 4) Under the direct method, the formula for computing cash collections from customers is sales revenues plus the increase in accounts receivable or minus the decrease in accounts receivable.

_____ 20. (S.O. 4) Under the direct method, cash payments for operating expenses is computed by adding increases in prepaid expenses and decreases in accrued expenses payable to operating expenses.

_____ *21. (S.O. 6) The work sheet for the statement of cash flows contains a balance sheet accounts section and a statement of cash flows effects section.

_____ *22. (S.O. 6) The reconciling items shown on the work sheet are journalized and posted to the accounts.

_____ *23. (S.O. 6) The reconciling entry for depreciation expense in a work sheet is a credit to Accumulated Depreciation and a debit to Operating-Depreciation Expense.

MULTIPLE CHOICE

Circle the letter that best answers each of the following statements.

1. (S.O. 1) The primary purpose of the statement of cash flows is to:
   a. distinguish between debits and credits to the cash account.
   b. provide information about the cash receipts and cash payments of an entity during a period.
   c. provide an analysis of the different cash accounts.
   d. provide information about the cash available at a particular time.

2. (S.O. 2) Financing activities involve:
   a. lending money to other entities and collecting on those loans.
   b. cash receipts from sales of goods and services.
   c. acquiring and disposing of productive long-lived assets.
   d. long-term liability and owners' equity items.

3. (S.O. 2) Investing activities include all of the following except cash:
   a. inflows from the sale of debt securities of other entities.
   b. outflows to redeem the entity's long-term debt.
   c. outflows to purchase property, plant, and equipment.
   d. outflows to make loans to other entities.

4. (S.O. 2) Which of the following statements about significant noncash transactions is **incorrect?**
   a. The reporting of these transactions in the financial statements or notes is optional.
   b. The conversion of bonds into common stock is an example of a significant noncash transaction.
   c. These transactions can be individually reported in a separate note.
   d. These transactions can be reported in a separate section at the bottom of the statement of cash flows.

5. (S.O. 2) The statement of cash flows is prepared from all of the following except:
   a. the adjusted trial balance.
   b. comparative balance sheets.
   c. selected transaction data.
   d. current income statement.

6. (S.O. 2) Which of the following steps is **not** required in preparing the statement of cash flows?
   a. Determine the change in cash.
   b. Determine net cash provided by operating activities.
   c. Determine cash from investing and financing activities.
   d. Determine the change in current assets.

7. (S.O. 2) In determining net cash provided by operating activities it is **incorrect** to:
   a. eliminate noncash revenues from net income.
   b. eliminate noncash expenses from net income.
   c. include the issuance of the company's bonds for cash.
   d. convert accrual based net income to a cash basis.

8. (S.O. 2) The information in a statement of cash flows will not help investors to assess the entity's ability to:
   a. generate future cash flows.
   b. obtain favorable borrowing terms at a bank.
   c. pay dividends.
   d. pay its obligations when they become due.

9. (S.O. 3) In the Ulen Company, net income is $65,000. If accounts receivable increased $35,000 and accounts payable decreased $10,000, net cash provided by operating activities using the indirect method is:
   a. $20,000.
   b. $40,000.
   c. $90,000.
   d. $110,000.

10. (S.O. 3) Under the indirect method, when accounts receivable decrease during the period,
    a. to convert net income to net cash provided by operating activities, the decrease in accounts receivable must be added to net income.
    b. revenues on a cash basis are less than revenues on an accrual basis.
    c. to convert net income to net cash provided by operating activities, the decrease in accounts receivable must be subtracted from net income.
    d. revenues on an accrual basis are greater than revenues on a cash basis.

11. (S.O. 3) Which of the following is the correct treatment for changes in current liabilities in the cash flow statement using the indirect method?

	Add to Net Income	Deduct from Net Income
a.	Decreases	Increases
b.	Decreases	Decreases
c.	Increases	Decreases
d.	Increases	Increases

12. (S.O. 3 and 4) In the Freyfogle Company, land decreased $75,000 because of a cash sale for $75,000, the equipment account increased $30,000 as a result of a cash purchase, and Bonds Payable increased $100,000 from an issuance for cash at face value. The net cash provided by investing activities is:
    a. $75,000.
    b. $145,000.
    c. $45,000.
    d. $70,000.

13. (S.O. 3 and 4) In the Tabb Company, Treasury Stock increased $15,000 from a cash purchase, and Retained Earnings increased $40,000 as a result of net income of $62,000 and cash dividends paid of $22,000. Net cash used by financing activities is:
    a. $15,000.
    b. $22,000.
    c. $55,000.
    d. $37,000.

14. (S.O. 3) In converting net income to net cash provided by operating activities, under the indirect method:
    a. decreases in accounts receivable and increases in prepaid expenses are added.
    b. decreases in inventory and increases in accrued liabilities are added.
    c. decreases in accounts payable and decreases in inventory are deducted.
    d. increases in accounts receivable and increases in accrued liabilities are deducted.

15. (S.O. 3 and 4) In the Hayes Company, there was an increase in the land account during the year of $24,000. Analysis reveals that the change resulted from a cash sale of land at cost $55,000, and a cash purchase of land for $79,000. In the statement of cash flows, the change in the land account should be reported in the investment section:
    a. as a net purchase of land, $24,000.
    b. only as a purchase of land $79,000.
    c. as a purchase of land $79,000 and a sale of land $55,000.
    d. only as a sale of land $55,000.

16. (S.O. 3) In the Merrit Company, machinery with a book value of $8,000 is sold for $5,000 cash. In the statement of cash flows, the cash proceeds are reported in the:
    a. investing section and the loss is added to net income in the operating section.
    b. financing section and the loss is added to net income in the operating section.
    c. investing section and no adjustment is made to net income.
    d. financing section and no adjustment is made to net income.

17. (S.O. 4) In the Phander Corporation, cash receipts from customers were $92,000, cash payments for operating expenses were $68,000, and one-third of the company's $4,200 of income taxes were paid during the year. Net cash provided by operating activities is:
    a. $24,000.
    b. $19,800.
    c. $22,600.
    d. $21,200.

18. (S.O. 4) The Rotunda Company uses the direct method in determining net cash provided by operating activities. If reported cost of goods sold is $140,000, inventory increased $20,000, and accounts payable increased $15,000, cash payments to suppliers are:
    a. $135,000.
    b. $145,000.
    c. $175,000.
    d. $105,000.

19. (S.O. 4) The Cribbets Company uses the direct method in determining net cash provided by operating activities. During the year operating expenses were $260,000, prepaid expenses increased $20,000, and accrued expenses payable increased $30,000. Cash payments for operating expenses were:
    a. $210,000.
    b. $310,000.
    c. $270,000.
    d. $250,000.

20. (S.O. 4) The Bainbridge Company uses the direct method in determining net cash provided by operating activities. The income statement shows income tax expense $70,000. Income taxes payable were $25,000 at the beginning of the year and $18,000 at the end of the year. Cash payments for income taxes are:
    a. $63,000.
    b. $70,000.
    c. $77,000.
    d. none of the above.

*21. (S.O. 6) When a work sheet is used, all but one of the following statements is correct. The **incorrect** statement is:
    a. Reconciling items on the work sheet are not journalized or posted.
    b. The bottom portion of the work sheet shows the statement of cash flows effects.
    c. The balance sheet accounts portion of the work sheet is divided into two parts: assets, and liabilities and stockholders' equity.
    d. Each line pertaining to a balance sheet account should foot across.

*22. (S.O. 6) In the Nowak Company, the beginning and ending balances in Land were $132,000 and $160,000 respectively. During the year, land costing $30,000 was sold for $30,000 cash, and land costing $58,000 was purchased for cash. The entries in the reconciling columns of the work sheet will include a:

a. credit to Land $30,000 and a debit to Sale of Land $30,000 under investing activities.
b. debit to Land $58,000 and a credit to Purchase of Land $58,000 under financing activities.
c. net debit to Land $28,000 and a credit to Purchase of Land $28,000 under investing activities.
d. credit to Land $30,000 and a debit to Sale of Land $30,000 under financing activities.

The Navigator

MATCHING

The Ross Company had the following transactions. In the space provided, classify each transaction by using the following code letters: (A) operating activity (indirect method), (B) investing activity, (C) financing activity, and (D) significant noncash investing and financing activity. (Note: a transaction may be reported in more than one section.)

_____ 1. Payment of cash dividends to stockholders.

_____ 2. Sale of land for cash at cost.

_____ 3. Purchase of treasury stock for cash.

_____ 4. Issuance of long-term bonds for cash.

_____ 5. Exchange of equipment for a patent.

_____ 6. Payment of cash to lenders for interest.

_____ 7. Loan of money to a supplier.

_____ 8. Purchase of equity securities of another entity for cash.

_____ 9. Cash payments to the IRS for income taxes.

_____ 10. Redemption of bonds at book value.

_____ 11. Receipt of cash dividends from another entity.

_____ 12. Sale of treasury stock above its cost.

_____ 13. Sale of equity securities of another entity at book value for cash.

_____ 14. Collection of loan made to a supplier.

_____ 15. Collection from customers for sales of goods.

_____ 16. Conversion of bonds into common stock.

_____ 17. Cash payments to employees for services.

_____ 18. Purchase of land for cash.

_____ 19. Cash payments to suppliers for inventory.

_____ 20. Receipt of interest on loans to another entity.

The Navigator

EXERCISES

EX. 14-1 (S.O. 3 and 4) Lafave Inc., a service company, has the following selected information at December 31, 2006.

Balance Sheets	2006	2005
Cash	$ 83,000	$ 61,000
Accounts receivable	78,000	86,000
Prepaid expenses	12,000	6,000
Accounts payable	92,000	87,000
Income taxes payable	17,000	13,000

Income statement for 2006	
Sales revenues	$173,000
Operating expenses	160,000
Income before income taxes	13,000
Income tax expense	6,000
Net income	$ 7,000

Operating expenses include $4,000 of depreciation expense.

Instructions

(a) Using the direct method, prepare the operating activities section of the statement of cash flows for 2006.

(b) Using the indirect method, prepare the operating activities section of the statement of cash flows for 2006.

(a) Cash flows from operating activities using the direct method.

(b) Cash flows from operating activities using the indirect method.

EX. 14-2 (S.O. 4) Illini Law Company reports the following condensed balance sheets at December 31:

Assets	2006	2005
Cash	$ 53,000	$ 38,000
Accounts receivable	72,000	76,000
Inventory	65,000	58,000
Property, plant and equipment (net)	196,000	172,000
Total	$386,000	$344,000
Liabilities and Stockholders' Equity		
Accounts payable	$ 48,000	$ 52,000
Notes payable, long-term	83,000	71,000
Common stock	212,000	180,000
Retained earnings	43,000	41,000
Total	$386,000	$344,000

Other information:

1. Net income was $10,000 in 2006 and $25,000 in 2005.
2. Depreciation expense was $8,000 in 2006 and $10,000 in 2005.
3. Machinery costing $62,000 was purchased for cash in 2006.
4. Dividends of $8,000 were paid during 2006.
5. Equipment was sold for cash during 2006 at $2,000 below its book value of $30,000.
6. A $12,000, long-term note payable was issued for cash in 2006.
7. Common stock of $32,000 was issued for cash in 2006.
8. Sales revenue per the income statement was $150,000 in 2006.
9. Cost of goods sold per the 2006 income statement was $110,000.
10. Operating expenses (all paid in cash) per the 2006 income statement were $20,000, excluding depreciation expense.
11. Accounts payable pertain to suppliers.

Instructions

(a) Prepare a statement of cash flows for 2006 using the indirect method.
(b) Prepare a statement of cash flows for 2006 using the direct method.

(a)

ILLINI LAW COMPANY
Statement of Cash Flows
For the Year Ended December 31, 2006

(b)

ILLINI LAW COMPANY
Statement of Cash Flows
For the Year Ended December 31, 2006

The Navigator

SOLUTIONS TO REVIEW QUESTIONS AND EXERCISES

TRUE-FALSE

1. (F) The statement of cash flows is the fourth basic financial statement that companies are required to prepare.
2. (T)
3. (F) The statement classifies cash receipts and cash payments into three categories of activity: investing, financing, and operating.
4. (F) Investing activities also include lending money and collecting on these loans.
5. (T)
6. (T)
7. (T)
8. (T)
9. (F) The section is entitled noncash investing and financing activities.
10. (F) The operating section is always listed first.
11. (T)
12. (F) The statement of cash flows requires detailed information concerning the changes in account balances.
13. (T)
14. (T)
15. (F) It is net income and not retained earnings that is adjusted under the indirect method.
16. (T)
17. (F) An increase in accounts receivable is deducted from net income.
18. (T)
19. (F) Increases in accounts receivable are deducted and decreases in accounts receivable are added.
20. (T)

*21. (T)
*22. (F) Reconciling items are not journalized or posted to any account.
*23. (T)

MULTIPLE CHOICE

1. (b) The primary purpose of the statement of cash flows is to provide information about the cash receipts and cash payments of an entity during a period.

2. (d) Financing activities involve long-term liability and owners' equity items and include (1) obtaining cash from issuing debt and repaying the amounts borrowed, and (2) obtaining cash from stockholders and providing them with a return on their investment. Answers (a) and (c) are investing activities and answer (b) is an operating activity.

3. (b) Cash outflows to redeem the entity's long-term debt are a financing activity.

4. (a) The reporting of significant noncash transactions in the financial statements or notes is required because they represent significant financing and investing activities that merit disclosure.

5. (a) The statement is not prepared from an adjusted trial balance.

6. (d) It is not necessary to determine the change in current assets because the statement pertains to cash flows.

7. (c) The issuance of a company's bonds is a financing transaction that is not included in determining cash provided by operations.

8. (b) Information in the statement does not permit an assessment of an entity's credit rating or the borrowing terms at a bank.

9. (a) The computation is:

Net income		$65,000
Deduct: Increase in accounts receivable	$35,000	
Decrease in accounts payable	10,000	45,000
Net cash provided by operations		$20,000

10. (a) To convert net income to net cash provided by operating activities, a decrease in accounts receivable must be added to net income. Also, a decrease in accounts receivable results in revenues on a cash basis being higher than revenues on an accrual basis.

11. (c) In determining net cash from operating activities under the indirect method, when there is an increase in current liabilities the amount is added to net income; and when there is a decrease, the amount is subtracted from net income.

12. (c) The issuance of bonds is a financing activity. The sale of land and the purchase of equipment are investing activities. Therefore, net cash provided by investing activities is $45,000 ($75,000 - $30,000).

13. (d) Net income is an operating activity. The other transactions are financing activities. Thus, net cash used by financing activities is $37,000 ($15,000 + $22,000).

14. (b) Increases in prepaid expenses are deducted (a). Decreases in inventory are added (c). Increases in accrued liabilities are added (d).

15. (c) Both the gross cash inflow, $55,000 and the gross cash outflow $79,000 should be reported.

16. (a) The sale of machinery is an investing activity and the cash proceeds of $5,000 should be reported in this section. The $3,000 loss is a noncash charge that must be added back to net income in the operating section.

17. (c) Cash receipts were $92,000 and cash payments for operating expenses and income taxes were $69,400 ($68,000 + $1,400) or a difference of $22,600.

18. (b) An increase in inventory is added and an increase in accounts payable is deducted. Thus $140,000 + $20,000 - $15,000 = $145,000.

19. (d) An increase in prepaid expenses is added and an increase in accrued expenses payable is deducted. Thus, $260,000 + $20,000 - $30,000 = $250,000.

20. (c) A decrease in income taxes payable is added to income tax expense. Thus $70,000 + $7,000 = $77,000.

*21. (c) The balance sheet accounts are divided into two parts. However, the parts are debit balance accounts and credit balance accounts.

*22. (a) The entries in the reconciling columns are: (1) Cr. Land $30,000 and Dr. Sale of Land $30,000 under investing activities, and (2) Dr. Land $58,000 and Cr. Purchase of Land $58,000 under investing activities.

MATCHING

1. C	6. A	11. A	16. D
2. B	7. B	12. C	17. A
3. C	8. B	13. B	18. B
4. C	9. A	14. B	19. A
5. D	10. C	15. A	20. A

EXERCISES

EX. 14-1

(a) Cash flows from operating activities

Cash receipts from customers (1)	$181,000
Cash payments for operating expenses (2)	157,000
Income before income taxes	24,000
Cash payments for income taxes (3)	2,000
Net cash provided by operations	$ 22,000

(1) Computation of cash receipts from customers:

Sales revenues per income statement	$173,000
Add: Decrease in receivables (net)	8,000
Cash receipts from revenues	$181,000

(2) Computation of cash payments for operating expenses:

Operating expense per income statement	$160,000
Deduct: Depreciation expense	(4,000)
Deduct: Increase in accounts payable	(5,000)
Add: Increase in prepaid expenses	6,000
Cash payments for operating expenses	$157,000

(3) Computation of cash payments for income taxes:

Income taxes per income statement	$ 6,000
Deduct: Increase in income taxes payable	(4,000)
Cash payments for income taxes	$ 2,000

(b)

Cash flows from operating activities		
Net income		$ 7,000
Add (deduct) items not affecting cash		
Depreciation expense	$ 4,000	
Decrease in accounts receivable	8,000	
Increase in prepaid expense	(6,000)	
Increase in accounts payable	5,000	
Increase in taxes payable	4,000	15,000
Cash provided by operations		$22,000

EX. 14-2

(a)

ILLINI LAW COMPANY
Statement of Cash Flows
For the Year Ended December 31, 2006

Cash flows from operating activities		
Net income		$10,000
Adjustments to reconcile net income to net cash provided by operating activities		
Depreciation expense	$ 8,000	
Decrease in accounts receivable	4,000	
Increase in inventory	(7,000)	
Decrease in accounts payable	(4,000)	
Loss on sale of equipment	2,000	3,000
Net cash provided by operating activities		13,000
Cash flows from investing activities		
Sale of equipment	$ 28,000	
Purchase of machinery	(62,000)	
Cash used by investing activities		(34,000)
Cash flows from financing activities		
Issuance of long-term note payable	12,000	
Issuance of common stock	32,000	
Payment of cash dividends	(8,000)	
Cash provided by financing activities		36,000
Net increase in cash		15,000
Cash balance at beginning of period		38,000
Cash balance at end of period		$53,000

(b)

ILLINI LAW COMPANY
Statement of Cash Flows
For the Year Ended December 31, 2006

Cash flows from operating activities		
Cash receipts from customers (1)		$154,000
Cash payments		
To suppliers (2)	$121,000	
For operating expenses	20,000	141,000
Net cash provided by operating activities		13,000
Cash flows from investing activities		
Sale of equipment	$ 28,000	
Purchase of machinery	(62,000)	
Net cash used by investing activities		(34,000)
Cash flows from financing activities		
Issuance of long-term note payable	12,000	
Issuance of common stock	32,000	
Payment of cash dividends	(8,000)	
Net cash provided by financing activities		36,000
Net increase in cash		15,000
Cash balance at beginning of period		38,000
Cash balance at end of period		$53,000

(1) Computation of cash receipts from customers:

Sales revenue per income statement	$150,000
Add: Decrease in receivables	4,000
Cash receipts from receivables	$154,000

(2) Computation of cash payments to suppliers:

Cost of goods sold per income statement	$110,000
Add: Increase in inventory	7,000
Add: Decrease in accounts payable	4,000
Cash payments to suppliers	$121,000

Chapter **15**

FINANCIAL STATEMENT ANALYSIS

The Navigator ✓

- Scan Study Objectives ☐
- Read Preview ☐
- Read Chapter Review ☐
- Work Demonstration Problem ☐
- Answer True-False Statements ☐
- Answer Multiple-Choice Questions ☐
- Match Terms and Definitions ☐
- Solve Exercises ☐

CHAPTER STUDY OBJECTIVES

After studying this chapter, you should be able to:

1. Discuss the need for comparative analysis.
2. Identify the tools of financial statement analysis.
3. Explain and apply horizontal analysis.
4. Describe and apply vertical analysis.
5. Identify and compute ratios and describe their purpose and use in analyzing a firm's liquidity, profitability and solvency.
6. Understand the concept of earning power, and indicate how material items not typical of regular operations are presented.
7. Recognize the limitations of financial statement analysis.

The Navigator

PREVIEW OF CHAPTER 15

Financial statement analysis, the topic of this chapter, enhances the usefulness of published financial statements in making decisions about a company. The content and organization of this chapter are shown below.

FINANCIAL STATEMENT ANALYSIS

Basics of Financial Statement Analysis	Horizontal Analysis and Vertical Analysis	Ratio Analysis	Earning Power and Irregular Items	Limitations of Financial Statement Analysis
▶ Need for comparative analysis	▶ Balance sheet	▶ Liquidity	▶ Discontinued operations	▶ Estimates
▶ Tools of analysis	▶ Income statement	▶ Profitability	▶ Extraordinary items	▶ Cost
	▶ Retained earnings statement	▶ Solvency	▶ Change in accounting principle	▶ Accounting methods
		▶ Summary	▶ Comprehensive income	▶ Atypical Data
				▶ Diversification

The Navigator

CHAPTER REVIEW

Characteristics

1. **Financial statement analysis** enables the financial statement user to make informed decisions about a company.

2. When analyzing financial statements, three major characteristics of a company are generally evaluated: (a) liquidity, (b) profitability, and (c) solvency.

3. (S.O. 1) Comparative analysis may be made on a number of different bases.
   a. **Intracompany basis**—Compares an item or financial relationship within a company in the current year with the same item or relationship in one or more prior years.
   b. **Industry averages**—Compares an item or financial relationship of a company with industry averages.
   c. **Intercompany basis**—Compares an item or financial relationship of one company with the same item or relationship in one or more competing companies.

Tools of Financial Analysis

4. (S.O. 2) There are three **basic tools** of analysis: (a) horizontal, (b) vertical, and (c) ratio.

Horizontal Analysis

5. (S.O. 3) **Horizontal analysis,** also called **trend analysis,** is a technique for evaluating a series of financial statement data over a period of time to determine the increase or decrease that has taken place, expressed as either an amount or a percentage. In horizontal analysis, a base year is selected and changes are expressed as percentages of the base year amount.

Vertical Analysis

6. (S.O. 4) **Vertical analysis,** also called **common size analysis,** expresses each item within a financial statement as a percent of a base amount. Generally, the base amount is total assets for the balance sheet, and net sales for the income statement. For example, it may be determined that current assets are 22% of total assets, and selling expenses are 15% of net sales.

Ratio Analysis

7. (S.O. 5) A **ratio** expresses the mathematical relationship between one quantity and another as either a percentage, rate, or proportion. Ratios can be classified as:
   a. **Liquidity ratios**—measures of the short-term ability of the enterprise to pay its maturing obligations and to meet unexpected needs for cash.
   b. **Solvency ratios**—measures of the ability of the enterprise to survive over a long period of time.
   c. **Profitability ratios**—measures of the income or operating success of an enterprise for a given period of time.

8. There are four **liquidity ratios:** the current ratio, the acid test ratio, receivables turnover, and inventory turnover.

9. The **current ratio** expresses the relationship of current assets to current liabilities. It is a widely used measure for evaluating a company's liquidity and short-term debt paying ability. The formula for this ratio is:

$$\text{Current ratio} = \frac{\text{Current assets}}{\text{Current liabilities}}$$

10. The **acid-test** or **quick ratio** relates cash, short-term investments, and net receivables to current liabilities. This ratio indicates a company's immediate liquidity. It is an important complement to the current ratio. The formula for the acid-test ratio is:

$$\text{A}\ \frac{\text{Cash + short-term investments + receivables (net)}}{\text{Current liabilities}}$$

11. The **receivables turnover ratio** is used to assess the liquidity of the receivables. This ratio measures the number of times, on average, receivables are collected during the period. The formula for the ratio is:

$$\text{Receivables turnover} = \frac{\text{Net credit sales}}{\text{Average net receivables}}$$

Average net receivables can be computed from the beginning and ending balances of the net receivables. A popular variant of the receivables turnover ratio is to convert it into an average collection period in terms of days. This is done by dividing the turnover ratio into 365 days.

12. **Inventory turnover** measures the number of times, on average, the inventory is sold during the period. It indicates the liquidity of the inventory. The formula for the ratio is:

$$\text{Inventory turnover} = \frac{\text{Cost of goods sold}}{\text{Average inventory}}$$

Average inventory can be computed from the beginning and ending inventory balances. A variant of the inventory turnover ratio is to compute the **average days to sell the inventory.** This is done by dividing the inventory turnover ratio into 365 days.

13. The profitability ratios are explained in review points 14 to 23.

14. The **profit margin ratio** is a measure of the percentage of each sales dollar that results in net income. The formula is:

$$\text{Profit margin on sales} = \frac{\text{Net income}}{\text{Net sales}}$$

15. **Asset turnover** measures how efficiently a company uses its assets to generate sales. The formula for this ratio is:

$$\text{Asset turnover} = \frac{\text{Net sales}}{\text{Average assets}}$$

16. **Return on assets** is an overall measure of profitability. It measures the rate of return on each dollar invested in assets. The formula is:

$$\text{Return on assets} = \frac{\text{Net income}}{\text{Average assets}}$$

17. **Return on common stockholders' equity** measures profitability from the common stockholders' viewpoint. The ratio shows the dollars of income earned for each dollar invested by the owners. The formula is:

$$\text{Return on common stockholders' equity} = \frac{\text{Net income}}{\text{Average common stockholders' equity}}$$

    a. When preferred stock is present, preferred dividend requirements are deducted from net income to compute income available to common stockholders. Similarly, the par value of preferred stock (or call price, if applicable) must be deducted from total stockholders' equity to arrive at the amount of common stock equity used in this ratio.

    b. Leveraging or trading on the equity at a gain means that the company has borrowed money through the issuance of bonds or notes at a lower rate of interest than it is able to earn by using the borrowed money. A comparison of the rate of return on total assets with the rate of interest paid for borrowed money indicates the profitability of trading on the equity.

18. **Earnings per share** measures the amount of net income earned on each share of common stock. The formula is:

$$\text{Earnings per share} = \frac{\text{Net income}}{\text{Weighted average common shares outstanding}}$$

    Any preferred dividends declared for the period must be subtracted from net income.

19. The **price-earnings ratio** measures the ratio of market price per share of common stock to earnings per share. It is an oft-quoted statistic that reflects investors' assessments of a company's future earnings. The formula for the ratio is:

$$\text{Price-earnings ratio} = \frac{\text{Market price per share of stock}}{\text{Earnings per share}}$$

20. The **payout ratio** measures the percentage of earnings distributed in the form of cash dividends. The formula is:

$$\text{Payout ratio} = \frac{\text{Cash dividends}}{\text{Net income}}$$

Companies with high growth rates generally have low payout ratios because they reinvest most of their income into the business.

21. There are two **solvency** ratios: debt to total assets and times interest earned.

22. The **debt to total assets ratio** measures the percentage of total assets provided by creditors. The formula for this ratio is:

$$\text{Debt to total assets} = \frac{\text{Total debt}}{\text{Total assets}}$$

The adequacy of this ratio is often judged in the light of the company's earnings. Companies with relatively stable earnings, such as public utilities, have higher debt to total assets ratios than cyclical companies with widely fluctuating earnings, such as many high-tech companies.

23. The **times interest earned ratio** measures a company's ability to meet interest payments as they become due. The formula is:

$$\text{Times interest earned} = \frac{\text{Income before income taxes and interest expense}}{\text{Interest expense}}$$

Discontinued Operations

24. (S.O. 6) **Discontinued operations** refers to the disposal of a significant segment of a business, such as the cessation of an entire activity or the elimination of a major class of customers.
    a. When the disposal occurs, the income statement should report both income from continuing operations and income (loss) from discontinued operations.
    b. The income (loss) from discontinued operations consists of (1) income (loss) from operations and (2) gain (loss) on disposal of the segment.
    c. Both components are reported net of applicable taxes in a section entitled Discontinued Operations, which follows income from continuing operations.

Extraordinary Items

25. **Extraordinary items** are events and transactions that meet two conditions: (a) unusual in nature and (b) infrequent in occurrence.
    a. To be **"unusual,"** the item should be abnormal and only incidentally related to customary activities of the entity.
    b. To be **"infrequent,"** the item should not be reasonably expected to recur in the foreseeable future.
    c. Extraordinary items are reported net of taxes in a separate section of the income statement immediately below discontinued operations.

Change in Accounting Principle

26. A **change in an accounting principle** occurs when the principle used in the current year is different from the one used in the preceding year. When a change has occurred:
    a. The new principle should be used in reporting the results of operations of the current year.
    b. The cumulative effect of the change on all prior year income statements should be disclosed net of applicable taxes in a special section immediately preceding net income.

Income Statement with Nontypical Items

27. A partial income statement showing the additional sections and the material items not typical of regular operations is as follows:

Income Statement (partial)

Income before income taxes		$XXX
Income tax expense		XXX
Income from continuing operations		XXX
Discontinued operations:		
Loss from operations of discontinued segment, net of $XXX income tax savings	$XXX	
Gain on disposal of segment, net of $XXX income taxes	XXX	XXX
Income before extraordinary item and cumulative effect of change in accounting principle		XXX
Extraordinary item:		
Gain or loss, net of $XXX income taxes		XXX
Cumulative effect of change in accounting principle:		
Effect on prior years of change, net of $XXX income taxes		XXX
Net Income		$XXX

28. **Comprehensive income** includes all changes in stockholders' equity during a period except those resulting from investments by stockholders and distributions to stockholders.

29. (S.O. 7) The limitations of financial statement analysis are:
    a. **Estimates.** The financial statements contain numerous estimates. To the extent that these estimates are inaccurate, the financial ratios and percentages are inaccurate.
    b. **Cost.** Traditional financial statements are based on cost and are not adjusted for price-level changes.
    c. **Alternative accounting methods.** Variations among companies in the application of generally accepted accounting principles may hamper comparability.
    d. **Atypical data.** Companies frequently establish a fiscal year-end that coincides with the low point in operating activity or in inventory levels. Therefore, year-end data may not be typical of the financial condition during the year.
    e. **Diversification of firms.** Many firms are so diversified that they cannot be classified by industry.

DEMONSTRATION PROBLEM No. 1 (S.O. 5)

The condensed financial statements of Carpenter Company for the years 2006 and 2005 are presented below:

CARPENTER COMPANY
Balance Sheet
December 31

Assets

	(In thousands) 2006	2005
Current assets		
Cash and short-term investments	$ 276	$ 232
Accounts receivable (net)	523	379
Inventories	438	382
Prepaid expenses	97	81
Total current assets	1,334	1,074
Property, plant and equipment (net)	3,251	2,799
Intangibles and other assets	177	251
Total assets	$4,762	$4,124

Liabilities and Stockholders' Equity

	2006	2005
Current liabilities	$1,994	$1,621
Long-term liabilities	793	752
Stockholders' equity	1,975	1,751
Total liabilities and stockholders' equity	$4,762	$4,124

CARPENTER COMPANY
Income Statement
For the Year Ended December 31

	(In thousands) 2006	2005
Revenues	$5,194	$4,873
Expenses		
Cost of goods sold	2,596	2,364
Selling and administrative expenses	1,963	1,732
Interest expense	52	46
Total expenses	4,611	4,142
Income before income taxes	583	731
Income tax expense	175	219
Net income	$ 408	$ 512

Instructions

Compute the following ratios for Carpenter for 2006 and 2005.

(a) Current ratio.
(b) Receivables turnover (Receivables 12/31/04, $373).
(c) Profit margin ratio.
(d) Rate of return on assets (Assets 12/31/04, $3,926).
(e) Return on common stockholders' equity (Equity 12/31/04, $1,492).
(f) Debt to total assets
(g) Times interest earned.
(h) Acid-test ratio.
(i) Asset turnover.

The Navigator

SOLUTION TO DEMONSTRATION PROBLEM

		2006	2005
(a)	Current ratio:		
	$1,334 ÷ $1,994 =	.67 : 1	
	$1,074 ÷ $1,621 =		.66 : 1
(b)	Receivables turnover:		
	$5,194 ÷ [($523 + $379) ÷ 2] =	11.52 times	
	$4,873 ÷ [($379 + $373) ÷ 2] =		12.96 times
(c)	Profit margin ratio:		
	$408 ÷ $5,194 =	7.9%	
	$512 ÷ $4,873 =		10.5%
(d)	Rate of return on assets:		
	$408 ÷ [$4,762 + $4,124) ÷ 2] =	9.2%	
	$512 ÷ [$4,124 + $3,926) ÷ 2] =		12.7%
(e)	Return on common stockholders' equity:		
	$408 ÷ [($1,975 + $1,751) ÷ 2] =	21.9%	
	$512 ÷ [($1,751 + $1,492) ÷ 2] =		31.6%
(f)	Debt to total assets:		
	$2,787 ÷ $4,762 =	58.5%	
	$2,373 ÷ $4,124 =		57.5%
(g)	Times interest earned:		
	($583 + $52) ÷ $52 =	12.21 times	
	($731 + $46) ÷ $46 =		16.89 times
(h)	Acid-test ratio:		
	($276 + $523) ÷ $1,994 =	.40 : 1	
	($232 + $379) ÷ $1,621 =		.38 : 1
(i)	Asset turnover:		
	$5,194 ÷ [($4,762 + $4,124) ÷ 2] =	1.17 times	
	$4,873 ÷ [($4,124 + $3,926) ÷ 2] =		1.21 times

DEMONSTRATION PROBLEM No. 2 (S.O. 6)

The Julitta Company has income from continuing operations of $180,000 for the year ended December 31, 2006. It also has the following items (before considering income taxes): (1) an extraordinary flood loss of $37,000, (2) a gain of $45,000 on the discontinuance of a division, and (3) a cumulative change in an accounting principle that resulted in an increase in prior year's depreciation of $30,000. Assume all items are subject to income taxes at a 30% tax rate.

Instructions

Prepare an income statement, beginning with income from continuing operations.

SOLUTION TO DEMONSTRATION PROBLEM

JULITTA COMPANY
Income Statement (partial)
For the Year Ended December 31, 2006

Income from continuing operations	$180,000
Discontinued operations:	
Gain on disposal of division, net of $13,500 income taxes	31,500
Income before extraordinary item and cumulative effect of change in accounting principle	211,500
Extraordinary item:	
Loss from flood, net of $11,100 taxes	(25,900)
Cumulative effect of change in accounting principle:	
Effect on prior years of change, net of $9,000 taxes	(21,000)
Net income	$164,600

REVIEW QUESTIONS AND EXERCISES

TRUE—FALSE

Indicate whether each of the following is true (T) or false (F) in the space provided.

_____ 1. (S.O. 2) Comparative analysis may be made on an intracompany basis, an intercompany basis, and on the basis of industry averages.

_____ 2. (S.O. 2) The three basic tools of analysis are horizontal analysis, vertical analysis, and ratio analysis.

_____ 3. (S.O. 3) Trend analysis and vertical analysis mean the same thing.

_____ 4. (S.O. 3) Horizontal analysis involves determining percentage increases or decreases in financial statement data over a period of time.

_____ 5. (S.O. 3) A percentage change can be computed only if the base amount is zero or positive.

_____ 6. (S.O. 4) In vertical analysis, the base amount in an income statement is usually net sales.

_____ 7. (S.O. 5) A short-term creditor is primarily interested in the solvency of a company.

_____ 8. (S.O. 5) A long-term creditor is interested in the profitability and solvency of a company.

_____ 9. (S.O. 5) Profitability ratios measure the ability of the enterprise to survive over a long period of time.

_____ 10. (S.O. 5) Liquidity ratios include the current ratio, the acid-test ratio, receivables turnover, and inventory turnover.

_____ 11. (S.O. 5) Solvency ratios include debt to total assets, the price-earnings ratio, and times interest earned.

_____ 12. (S.O. 5) The formula for the current ratio is current liabilities divided by current assets.

_____ 13. (S.O. 5) The formula for the acid-test ratio is the sum of cash, short-term investments, and receivables (net) divided by current liabilities.

_____ 14. (S.O. 5) The receivables turnover ratio indicates how quickly receivables can be converted to cash.

_____ 15. (S.O. 5) The average days to sell inventory is computed by multiplying the inventory turnover ratio by 365.

_____ 16. (S.O. 5) The formula for the profit margin ratio is net income divided by average assets.

_____ 17. (S.O. 5) The asset turnover ratio is an overall measure of profitability.

_____ 18. (S.O. 5) Preferred dividend requirements must be subtracted from net income when computing the rate of return on common stockholders' equity.

_____ 19. (S.O. 5) Trading on the equity at a gain means that the company's rate of return on total assets is less than the rate of interest paid for borrowed money.

_____ 20. (S.O. 5) The payout ratio measures the percentage of earnings distributed in the form of cash dividends.

_____ 21. (S.O. 6) The phasing out of a product line because of a changing market or technological improvements is considered a disposal of a segment.

_____ 22. (S.O. 6) When the disposal of a significant segment occurs, the income statement should report both income from continuing operations and income (loss) from discontinued operations.

_____ 23. (S.O. 6) Extraordinary items are changes in accounting principles that are infrequent in occurrence.

_____ 24. (S.O. 6) An employee labor strike would be considered an extraordinary item.

_____ 25. (S.O. 6) Extraordinary items are reported net of applicable taxes in a separate section of the income statement.

_____ 26. (S.O. 6) A change from the declining-balance method of depreciation to the straight-line method would be considered a change in accounting principle.

_____ 27. (S.O. 6) The cumulative effect of a change in an accounting principle is shown in the retained earnings statement as a prior period adjustment.

The Navigator

MULTIPLE CHOICE

Circle the letter that best answers each of the following statements.

1. (S.O. 1) Comparisons of data within a company are an example of the following comparative basis:
   a. Industry averages.
   b. Intercompany.
   c. Intracompany.
   d. None of the above.

2. (S.O. 3) Horizontal analysis is also known as:
   a. trend analysis.
   b. vertical analysis.
   c. ratio analysis.
   d. common-size analysis.

3. (S.O. 3) Silva Corporation reported net sales of $200,000, $350,000, and $450,000 in the years 2004, 2005, and 2006 respectively. If 2004 is the base year, what is the trend percentage for 2006?
   a. 129%.
   b. 135%.
   c. 164%.
   d. 225%.

4. (S.O. 3) Evans Enterprises reported current assets of $50,000 at December 31, 2005 and $40,000 at December 31, 2006. If 2005 is the base year, this is a percentage increase (decrease) of:
   a. (25%).
   b. (20%).
   c. 25%.
   d. 80%.

5. (S.O. 4) When performing vertical analysis, the base amount for administrative expense is generally:
   a. administrative expense in a previous year.
   b. net sales.
   c. gross profit.
   d. fixed assets.

6. (S.O. 4) When performing vertical analysis, the base amount for cash is:
   a. Cash in a previous-year balance sheet.
   b. Total current assets.
   c. Total liabilities.
   d. Total assets.

7. (S.O. 4) Vertical analysis facilitates comparison of:
   a. companies of different size in the same industry.
   b. the income statement to the balance sheet.
   c. different years for the same company.
   d. more than one of the above.

8. (S.O. 5) A ratio can be expressed as a:
   a. percentage.
   b. rate.
   c. proportion.
   d. all of the above.

9. (S.O. 5) What type of ratios best measure the short-term ability of the enterprise to pay its maturing obligations and to meet unexpected needs for cash?
   a. Leverage.
   b. Solvency.
   c. Profitability.
   d. Liquidity.

10. (S.O. 5) Profitability ratios measure an enterprise's:
    a. ability to survive over a long period of time.
    b. short-term ability to meet its obligations.
    c. income or operating success for a given period of time.
    d. short-term ability to meet unexpected needs for cash.

11. (S.O. 5) Which of the following is **not** a liquidity ratio?
    a. Acid-test ratio.
    b. Inventory turnover.
    c. Payout ratio.
    d. Receivables turnover.

12. (S.O. 5) The acid-test ratio is also known as the:
    a. current ratio.
    b. quick ratio.
    c. fast ratio.
    d. times interest earned ratio.

13. (S.O. 5) Cash, marketable securities, and receivables (net) are included in the acid-test ratio because they are:
    a. highly liquid.
    b. not readily saleable.
    c. not transferable to others.
    d. included in the current asset section.

14. (S.O. 5) Avanti Corporation had beginning inventory $50,000, cost of goods purchased $350,000, and ending inventory $100,000. What was Avanti's inventory turnover?
    a. 3 times.
    b. 4 times.
    c. 5.33 times.
    d. 6 times.

15. (S.O. 5) The average net receivables for Merchant Company was $40,000, and net credit sales were $400,000. What was the average collection period?
    a. 10 days.
    b. 36.5 days.
    c. 70 days.
    d. Cannot be computed from the information given.

16. (S.O. 5) Reams Corporation reported net income $36,000, net sales $300,000, and average assets $600,000 for 2006. The 2006 profit margin was:
    a. 6%.
    b. 12%.
    c. 50%.
    d. 200%.

17. (S.O. 5) Perez Company reports the following amounts for 2006:

Net income	$ 100,000
Average stockholders' equity	1,000,000
Preferred dividends	28,000
Par value preferred stock	200,000

    The 2006 rate of return on common stockholders' equity is:
    a. 7.2%.
    b. 9.0%.
    c. 10.0%.
    d. 12.5%.

18. (S.O. 5) The debt to total assets ratio:
    a. is a solvency ratio.
    b. is computed by dividing total assets by total debt.
    c. measures the total assets provided by stockholders.
    d. is a profitability ratio.

19. (S.O. 5) In 2006 Johnson Corporation reported income from operations $225,000, interest expense $75,000, and income tax expense $120,000. Johnson's times interest earned ratio was:
    a. 1.4 times.
    b. 2.5 times.
    c. 3 times.
    d. 4 times.

20. (S.O. 6) The Heather Corporation has income before income taxes of $300,000 and an extraordinary loss from a hurricane of $100,000. Both the extraordinary loss and taxable income are subject to a 30% tax rate. The extraordinary loss should be reported as follows:
    a. Extraordinary loss from hurricane—$100,000.
    b. Extraordinary loss from hurricane, net of $30,000 income tax loss—$130,000.
    c. Extraordinary loss from hurricane, net of $60,000 income tax loss—$160,000.
    d. Extraordinary loss from hurricane, net of $30,000 income tax savings—$70,000.

21. (S.O. 6) A loss from the disposal of a segment of a business enterprise should be reported separately in the income statement:
    a. after cumulative effect of changes in accounting principle and before extraordinary items.
    b. before cumulative effect of changes in accounting principle and after extraordinary items.
    c. after extraordinary items and cumulative effect of changes in accounting principle.
    d. before extraordinary items and cumulative effect of changes in accounting principle.

22. (S.O. 6) Galileo, Inc. decides on January 1 to discontinue its telescope manufacturing division. On July 1, the division's assets with a book value of $420,000 are sold for $300,000. Operating income from January 1 to June 30 for the division amounted to $50,000. Ignoring income taxes, what total amount should be reported on Galileo's income statement for the current year under the caption, Discontinued Operations?
    a. $50,000.
    b. $70,000 loss.
    c. $120,000 loss.
    d. $170,000.

23. (S.O. 6) An extraordinary item is one that:
    a. occurs infrequently and is uncontrollable in nature.
    b. occurs infrequently and is unusual in nature.
    c. is material and is unusual in nature.
    d. is material and is uncontrollable in nature.

24. (S.O. 6) An extraordinary item should be reported separately in the income statement:
    a. before cumulative effect of changes in accounting principles and after discontinued operations.
    b. before cumulative effect of changes in accounting principles and before discontinued operations.
    c. after cumulative effect of changes in accounting principles and after discontinued operations.
    d. after cumulative effect of changes in accounting principles and before discontinued operations.

25. (S.O. 6) An earthquake destroyed Hooke Company's operating plant, resulting in a loss of $2,200,000. Hooke's income tax rate is 30%. In Hooke's income statement, the net effect of the extraordinary loss should be reported at:
    a. $0.
    b. $660,000.
    c. $1,540,000.
    d. $2,200,000.

26. (S.O. 6) The Ricci Company changed from the double-declining-balance method of depreciation to the straight-line method. The cumulative effect of the change on prior year income statements should be reported separately as a (an)
    a. extraordinary item.
    b. component of income after extraordinary items.
    c. component of income from continuing operations.
    d. prior period adjustment.

27. (S.O. 6) When there has been a change in an accounting principle,
    a. the old principle should be used in reporting the results of operations for the current year.
    b. the cumulative effect of the change should be reported in the current year's retained earnings statement.
    c. the cumulative effect of the change does not have to be reported.
    d. the new principle should be used in reporting the results of operations of the current year.

28. (S.O. 6) Henlein Company changed from an accelerated method of depreciation to the straight-line method in 2006. Information concerning depreciation under each method is as follows:

Year	Accelerated method	Straight-line method
2004	$200,000	$150,000
2005	340,000	200,000
2006	420,000	260,000
	$960,000	$610,000

What should be reported in Henlein's 2006 income statement as the cumulative effect on prior years of changing to a different depreciation method assuming a 30% income tax rate?

a. $57,000.
b. $133,000.
c. $105,000.
d. $245,000.

29. (S.O. 7) Which of the following is **not** generally considered to be a limitation of financial analysis?

a. Use of estimates.
b. Use of historical cost.
c. Use of ratio analysis.
d. Use of alternative accounting methods.

The Navigator

MATCHING—TERMS

Match each term with its definition by writing the appropriate letter in the space provided.

Terms

______ 1. Liquidity ratios.

______ 2. Trend analysis.

______ 3. Profitability ratios.

______ 4. Common size analysis.

______ 5. Solvency ratios.

______ 6. Horizontal analysis.

______ 7. Trading on the equity.

______ 8. Vertical analysis.

______ 9. Ratio.

______ 10. Leveraging.

______ 11. Change in accounting principle.

______ 12. Discontinued operations.

______ 13. Extraordinary item.

Definitions

a. Borrowing money at a rate of interest lower than the rate of return earned by investing the borrowed money.

b. The disposal of a significant segment of the business such as the cessation of an entire activity or the elimination of a major class of customers.

c. Measures of the short-term ability of the enterprise to pay its maturing obligations and to meet unexpected needs for cash.

d. An expression of the mathematical relationship between one quantity and another that may be expressed as a percentage, a rate, or a simple proportion.

e. Events and transactions that are unusual in nature and infrequent in occurrence.

f. Measures of the income or operating success of an enterprise for a given period of time.

g. The use of a principle in the current year that is different from the one used in the preceding year.

h. A technique for evaluating financial statement data that expresses each item within a financial statement as a percent of a base amount within the statement.

i A technique for evaluating a series of financial statement data over a period of time to determine the amount and/or percentage increase (decrease) that has taken place, expressed as either an amount or a percentage.

j. Measures of the ability of the enterprise to survive over a long period of time.

MATCHING—RATIOS

Match each ratio with its formula by writing the appropriate letter in the space provided.

Ratios

_____ 1. Current ratio.

_____ 2. Inventory turnover.

_____ 3. Return on assets.

_____ 4. Price-earnings ratio.

_____ 5. Times interest earned.

_____ 6. Acid-test ratio.

_____ 7. Profit margin.

_____ 8. Return on common stockholders' equity.

_____ 9. Payout ratio.

_____ 10. Receivables turnover.

_____ 11. Asset turnover.

_____ 12. Earnings per share.

_____ 13. Debt to total assets.

Formulas

a. $\dfrac{\text{Net income}}{\text{Net sales}}$

b. $\dfrac{\text{Income before income taxes and interest expense}}{\text{Interest expense}}$

c. $\dfrac{\text{Net sales}}{\text{Average assets}}$

d. $\dfrac{\text{Cash + short-term investments + receivables (net)}}{\text{Current liabilities}}$

e. $\dfrac{\text{Cash dividends}}{\text{Net income}}$

f. $\dfrac{\text{Net income}}{\text{Average common stockholders' equity}}$

g. $\dfrac{\text{Market price of stock}}{\text{Earnings per share}}$

h. $\dfrac{\text{Cost of goods sold}}{\text{Average inventory}}$

i. $\dfrac{\text{Net income}}{\text{Weighted average common shares outstanding}}$

j. $\dfrac{\text{Net credit sales}}{\text{Average net receivables}}$

k. $\dfrac{\text{Current assets}}{\text{Current liabilities}}$

l. $\dfrac{\text{Total debt}}{\text{Total assets}}$

m. $\dfrac{\text{Net income}}{\text{Average assets}}$

EXERCISES

EX. 15-1 (S.O. 3) Using horizontal analysis, compute the percentage increase or decrease for Stevens Co. for each current asset and for current assets in total.

Current Assets	2006	2005	Increase or (Decrease) Amount	Percentage
Cash	$ 50,000	$ 40,000		
Receivables (net)	54,000	72,000		
Inventories	90,000	100,000		
Prepaid expenses	42,000	35,000		
Total	$236,000	$247,000		

EX. 15-2 (S.O. 4) Using vertical analysis, prepare a common-size income statement for Larry Budd, using net sales as the base.

LARRY BUDD CORPORATION
Condensed Income Statement
For the Year Ended December 2006

	Amount	Percent
Net sales	$780,000	
Cost of goods sold	470,000	
Gross profit	310,000	
Operating expenses	140,000	
Income from operations	170,000	
Interest expense	16,000	
Income before income taxes	154,000	
Income tax expense	62,000	
Net income	$ 92,000	

EX. 15-3 (S.O. 5) Letterman Corporation decides to expand its operations by issuing $500,000 of 10% bonds. As a result of the additional financing, income from operations is expected to increase $70,000. Financial data prior to and after the expansion are as follows:

	Before Expansion	After Expansion
Total assets	$2,000,000	$2,514,000
Total liabilities	700,000	1,200,000
Total common stock equity	1,300,000	1,314,000
	$2,000,000	$2,514,000
Income from operations	$ 550,000	$ 620,000
Interest expense	50,000	100,000
Income before income taxes	500,000	520,000
Income tax expense (30%)	150,000	156,000
Net income	$ 350,000	$ 364,000

Instructions

Compute the following ratios before and after expansion. Assume year-end balance sheet amounts are representative of average balances.

1. Return on assets.
2. Return on common stockholders' equity.
3. Debt to total assets.
4. Times interest earned.

Ratio	Before Expansion	After Expansion
1. Return on assets.		
2. Return on common stockholders' equity.		
3. Debt to total assets.		
4. Times interest earned.		

EX. 15-4 (S.O. 6) On December 31, 2006, Fortcamp Company's controller accumulated the following data before considering income taxes of 30%.

Extraordinary gains resulting from a condemnation award by a state government $50,000.
Cumulative effect of change from a straight-line depreciation to declining-balance depreciation $40,000.
Loss on disposal of Division B, $60,000.
Income before income taxes $500,000.

Instructions
Prepare a partial income statement beginning with income before income taxes.

FORTCAMP COMPANY
Income Statement (partial)
For the Year Ended December 31, 2006

The Navigator

SOLUTIONS TO REVIEW QUESTIONS AND EXERCISES

TRUE-FALSE

1. (T)
2. (T)
3. (F) Trend analysis and horizontal analysis mean the same thing.
4. (T)
5. (F) A percentage change can be computed only if the base year amount is positive.
6. (T)
7. (F) A short-term creditor is primarily interested in the liquidity of a company.
8. (T)
9. (F) Profitability ratios measure the income or operating success of the enterprise for a given period of time.
10. (T)
11. (F) The price-earnings ratio is a profitability ratio.
12. (F) The current ratio is current assets divided by current liabilities.
13. (T)
14. (T)
15. (F) The average days to sell inventory is computed by dividing 365 by the inventory turnover ratio.
16. (F) The formula for the profit margin ratio is net income ÷ net sales.
17. (F) The asset turnover ratio measures how efficiently a company uses its assets to generate sales. It is the return on assets ratio that is an overall measure of profitability.
18. (T)
19. (F) Trading on the equity at a gain means that the company's rate of return on total assets exceeds the rate of interest paid for borrowed money.
20. (T)
21. (F) A disposal of a segment refers to the disposal of a significant segment of the business such as the cessation of an entire activity or the elimination of a major class of customers.
22. (T)
23. (F) Extraordinary items are events and transactions that are: (a) unusual in nature, and (b) infrequent in occurrence.
24. (F) Losses attributable to labor strikes are not considered extraordinary.
25. (T)
26. (T)
27. (F) The cumulative effect of the change on all prior year income statements should be disclosed net of applicable taxes in a special section of the income statement immediately preceding net income.

MULTIPLE CHOICE

1. (c) Comparisons of data within a company are an example of the intracompany basis of comparison.

2. (a) Vertical analysis (b) is also known as common-size analysis (d). Ratio analysis (c) is different from both horizontal analysis and vertical analysis.

3. (d) In trend analysis, the base year is assigned a value of 100%. The amounts for the other years are divided by the amount in the base year and expressed as a percentage. The percentage for 2006 is 225% ($450,000 ÷ $200,000).

4. (b) Current assets decreased by $10,000 from $50,000 to $40,000. This is a percentage decrease of 20% ($10,000 ÷ $50,000).

5. (b) When performing vertical analysis, the base amount for income statement items is that year's net sales. Answer (a), administrative expense in a previous year, would be the correct answer for horizontal analysis.

6. (d) When performing vertical analysis, the base amount for balance sheet items is that year's total assets. Answer (a), cash in a previous-year balance sheet, would be the correct answer for horizontal analysis.

7. (a) Vertical analysis would facilitate comparison of two companies in the same industry by making companies of different sizes comparable. Horizontal analysis would be best for comparing different years for the same company (c).

8. (d) A ratio expresses the mathematical relationship between one quantity and another, and can be expressed as either a percentage, a rate, or a proportion.

9. (d) Solvency ratios (b) measure the ability of the enterprise to survive over a long period of time. Profitability ratios (c) measure the operating success (ability to earn income) of the enterprise for a given period of time. Leverage ratios (a) are not a type of ratio.

10. (c) Choice (a) refers to solvency ratios. Choices (b) and (d) pertain to liquidity ratios.

11. (c) The payout ratio is a profitability ratio.

12. (b) The acid-test ratio is also known as the quick ratio.

13. (a) The acid-test ratio measures a company's immediate ability to pay its short-term debt. The assets in the numerator are highly liquid (quickly convertible into cash) and therefore are immediately available to pay short-term debt.

14. (b) Cost of goods sold is $300,000 ($50,000 + $350,000 - $100,000). Average inventory is $75,000 [($50,000 + $100,000) ÷ 2]. Thus, the ratio is 4 times ($300,000 ÷ $75,000).

15. (b) Receivables turnover is 10 times ($400,000 ÷ $40,000). The average collection period is 36.5 days (365 ÷ 10).

16. (b) The profit margin is net income ($36,000) divided by net sales ($300,000) or 12%.

17. (b) The basic computation for the rate of return on common stockholders' equity is net income divided by average common stockholders' equity. When preferred stock is present, preferred dividends must be subtracted from the numerator and the par value of preferred stock must be subtracted from the denominator.

The result is: $\frac{\$100,000\ -\ \$28,000}{\$1,000,000\ -\ \$200,000} = 9\%$.

18. (a) The debt to total assets ratio is computed by dividing total debt by total assets (b). It measures the total assets provided by creditors (c), and it is not a profitability ratio (d).

19. (d) The formula for times interest earned is income before income taxes and interest expense divided by interest expense. The numerator is $300,000 ($225,000 + $75,000). Thus, the times interest earned is 4 ($300,000 ÷ $75,000).

20. (d) The tax rate of 30% is applied to income before income taxes of $300,000 to show income taxes of $90,000, and the extraordinary item of $100,000 is reported net of the $30,000 tax savings.

21. (d) A loss from the disposal of a segment of a business enterprise should be reported separately immediately following income from continuing operations and before the other additional sections.

22. (b) Within the "Discontinued Operations" section both the operating income and the loss on the disposal are reported ($120,000 loss - $50,000 income from operations = $70,000 loss).

23. (b) An extraordinary item is one that occurs infrequently and is unusual in nature.

24. (a) An extraordinary item should be reported separately as a component of income before cumulative effect of changes in accounting principles and after discontinued operations of a segment of a business.

25. (c) Extraordinary items should be reported net of income taxes [$2,200,000 X 1 - .30)].

26. (b) A change in accounting principle should be reported separately as a component of income after extraordinary items.

27. (d) In the income statement, the new principle should be used in reporting the results of operations for the current year. In addition, the cumulative effect of the change on all prior years should be reported in a special section of the income statement.

28. (b) The cumulative effect on prior years of the change in accounting principle reflects the difference in depreciation for 2004 and 2005. The amount net of tax is $133,000 [($50,000 + $140,000) X (1 - .30)].

29. (c) Choices (a), (b), and (d) all limit comparability. The use of ratios is one of the accepted tools of analysis; it is not a limitation.

MATCHING—TERMS

1. c
2. i
3. f
4. h
5. j
6. i
7. a
8. h
9. d
10. a
11. g
12. b
13. e

MATCHING—RATIOS

1. k
2. h
3. m
4. g
5. b
6. d
7. a
8. f
9. e
10. j
11. c
12. i
13. l

EXERCISES

EX. 15-1

Current Assets	2006	2005	Increase or (Decrease) Amount	Percentage
Cash	$ 50,000	$ 40,000	$ 10,000	25.0%
Receivables (net)	54,000	72,000	(18,000)	(25.0%)
Inventories	90,000	100,000	(10,000)	(10.0%)
Prepaid expenses	42,000	35,000	7,000	20.0%
Total	$236,000	$247,000	$(11,000)	(4.5%)

EX. 15-2

LARRY BUDD CORPORATION
Condensed Income Statement
For the Year Ended December 31, 2006

	Amount	Percent
Net sales	$780,000	100.0%
Cost of goods sold	470,000	(60.3%)
Gross profit	310,000	39.7%
Operating expenses	140,000	(17.9%)
Income from operations	170,000	21.8%
Interest expense	16,000	(2.1%)
Income before income taxes	154,000	19.7%
Income tax expense	62,000	(7.9%)
Net income	$ 92,000	11.8%

EX. 15-3

Ratio	Before Expansion	After Expansion
1. Return on assets.	$\frac{\$350,000}{\$2,000,000} = 17.5\%$	$\frac{\$364,000}{\$2,514,000} = 14.5\%$
2. Return on common stockholders' equity.	$\frac{\$350,000}{\$1,300,000} = 26.9\%$	$\frac{\$364,000}{\$1,314,000} = 27.7\%$
3. Debt to total assets.	$\frac{\$700,000}{\$2,000,000} = 35\%$	$\frac{\$1,200,000}{\$2,514,000} = 47.7\%$
4. Times interest earned.	$\frac{\$500,000 + \$50,000}{\$50,000} = 11 \text{ times}$	$\frac{\$520,000 + \$100,000}{\$100,000} = 6.2 \text{ times}$

EX. 15-4

FORTCAMP COMPANY
Income Statement (partial)
For the Year Ended December 31, 2006

Income before income taxes	$500,000
Income tax expense (30%)	150,000
Income from continuing operations	350,000
Discontinued operations	
Loss on disposal of Division B, net of $18,000 income tax saving	(42,000)
Income before extraordinary item and cumulative effect of change in accounting principle	308,000
Extraordinary item	
Condemnation award, net of $15,000 income tax expense	35,000
Cumulative effect of change in accounting principle	
Effect on prior years of change in depreciation method, net of $12,000 income tax saving	(28,000)
Net income	$315,000

APPENDIX C

TIME VALUE OF MONEY

The Navigator	✓
■ *Scan Study Objectives*	☐
■ *Read Preview*	☐
■ *Read Chapter Review*	☐
■ *Work Demonstration Problem*	☐
■ *Answer True-False Statements*	☐
■ *Answer Multiple-Choice Questions*	☐
■ *Match Terms and Definitions*	☐
■ *Solve Exercises*	☐

STUDY OBJECTIVES

After studying this appendix, you should be able to:

1. Distinguish between simple and compound interest.
2. Solve for future value of a single amount.
3. Solve for future value of an annuity.
4. Identify the variables fundamental to solving present value problems.
5. Solve for present value of a single amount.
6. Solve for present value of an annuity.
7. Compute the present value of notes and bonds.

The Navigator

APPENDIX C REVIEW

Value of Interest

1. (S.O. 1) **Interest** is payment for the use of another person's money. The amount of interest involved in any financing transaction is based on three elements:
   a. **Principal:** The original amount borrowed or invested.
   b. **Interest Rate:** An annual percentage of the principal.
   c. **Time:** The number of years that the principal is borrowed or invested.

2. **Simple interest** is computed on the principal amount only. Simple interest is usually expressed as:

   Interest = Principal X Rate X Time

3. **Compound interest** is computed on principal and on any interest earned that has not been paid or withdrawn. It is the return on (or growth of) the principal for two or more time periods.

Future Value of a Single Amount

4. (S.O. 2) The **future value of a single amount** is the value at a future date of a given amount invested assuming compound interest. Future value is usually expressed as:

   $$FV = P \times (1 + i)^n$$

   FV = future value of a single amount
   P = principal
   i = interest rate for one period
   n = number of periods

5. The Future Value of 1 table is used for obtaining a 5-digit decimal number which is multiplied by the principal to calculate the future value.

Future Value of an Annuity

6. (S.O. 3) The **future value of an annuity** is the sum of all the payments (receipts) plus the accumulated compound interest on them. In computing the future value of an annuity, it is necessary to know the (1) interest rate, (2) the number of compounding periods, and (3) the amount of the periodic payments or receipts. When the periodic payments or receipts are the same in each period, the future value can be computed by using a future value of an annuity of 1 table.

Present Value Variables

7. (S.O. 4 and 5) The **present value** is based on three variables: (1) the dollar amount to be received (future amount), (2) the length of time until the amount is received (number of periods), and (3) the interest rate (the discount rate).

   $PV = FV/(1 + i)$

   PV = present value
   FV = future value
   i = interest rate

8. The present value of 1 may also be determined through tables that show the present value of 1 for n periods.

Present Value of an Annuity

9. (S.O. 6) In computing the present value of an annuity, it is necessary to know (1) the discount rate, (2) the number of discount periods, and (3) the amount of the periodic receipts or payments. When the future receipts are the same in each period, there are two other ways to compute the present value. First, the annual cash flow can be multiplied by the sum of the three present value factors. Second, annuity tables may be used.

Time Periods and Discounting

10. Discounting may also be done over shorter periods of time such as monthly, quarterly, or semiannually. When the time frame is less than one year, it is necessary, to convert the annual interest rate to the applicable time frame.

Computing the Present Value of a Long-Term Note or Bond

11. (S.O. 7) The present value (or market price) of a long-term note or bond is a function of three variables: (1) the payment amounts, (2) the length of time until the amounts are paid, and (3) the discount rate. When the investor's discount rate is equal to the bond's contractual interest rate, the present value of the bonds will equal the face value of the bonds.

The Navigator

DEMONSTRATION PROBLEM (S.O. 3)

Gardner Co. is about to issue $1,000,000 of 10-year bonds paying a 10% interest rate, with interest payable semiannually. The discount rate for such securities is 8%. How much can Gardner expect to receive for the sale of these bonds?

The Navigator

SOLUTION TO DEMONSTRATION PROBLEM

Present value of principal to be received at maturity	
$1,000,000 X PV of 1 due in 20 periods at 4%	
$1,000,000 X .45639 (Table 1)	$ 456,390
Present value of interest to be received periodically over the terms of the bonds	
$50,000 X PV of 1 due periodically for 20 periods at 4%	
$50,000 X 13.5903 (Table 2)	679,515
Present value of bonds	$1,135,905

REVIEW QUESTIONS AND EXERCISES

TRUE—FALSE

Indicate whether each of the following is true (T) or false (F) in the space provided.

_____ 1. Present value is based on three variables: (1) the dollar amount to be received (future amount), (2) the probability of receiving that amount in the future, and (3) the interest rate (the discount rate).

_____ 2. The process of determining the present value is referred to as discounting the future amount.

_____ 3. In computing the present value of an annuity, it is necessary to know the (1) discount rate, (2) the number of discount periods, and (3) the present value.

_____ 4. Discounting may also be done over shorter periods of time such as monthly, quarterly, or semiannually.

_____ 5. The present value (or market price) of a bond is a function of three variables: (1) the payment amounts, (2) the length of time until the amounts are paid, and (3) the discount rate.

The Navigator

MULTIPLE CHOICE

Circle the letter that best answers each of the following statements.

1. Using Table 1, the present value factor for 2 periods at a discount rate of 8% is:
   a. .89000.
   b. .92593.
   c. .91743.
   d. .85734.

2. A higher discount rate produces:
   a. a smaller present value.
   b. a higher present value.
   c. the same present value.
   d. a greater length of time.

3. The present value of $5,000 due in 10 years using a discount rate of 12% is:
   a. $1,609.85.
   b. $1,927.70.
   c. $2,837.15.
   d. $3,219.70.

4. Which of the following is not necessary to know when computing the present value of an annuity?
   a. The discount rate.
   b. The amount of the periodic receipts or payments.
   c. The number of discount periods.
   d. The probability of receiving the amount due.

5. Alan Hirsch earns 15% on an investment that pays back $12,000 at the end of each of the next five years. Using Table 2, what is the amount Hirsch invested to earn the 15% rate of return?
   a. $201,129.60.
   b. $60,000.00.
   c. $40,225.92.
   d. $34,259.76.

The Navigator

EXERCISES

EX. C-1

a. If Tim Foran invests $20,900 now and wants to receive $100,000 at the end of 15 years, what annual rate of interest will Tim Foran earn on his investment?

b. Bova Corporation receives a $20,000, 8-year note bearing interest of 10% (paid annually) from a customer at a time when the discount rate is 8%. What is the present value of the note received by Bova?

SOLUTIONS TO REVIEW QUESTIONS AND EXERCISES

TRUE-FALSE

1. (F) Present value is based on three variables: (1) the dollar amount to be received (future amount), (2) the length of time until the amount is received (number of periods), and (3) the interest rate (the discount rate).
2. (T)
3. (F) In computing the present value of an annuity, it is necessary to know (1) the discount rate, (2) the number of discount periods, and (3) the amount of the periodic receipts or payments.
4. (T)
5. (T)

MULTIPLE CHOICE

1. (d) Using Table 1 going down the 8% column and across the 2 periods row, the number .85734 represents the present value of 1.

2. (a) A higher discount rate produces a smaller present value. A lower discount rate produces a higher present value.

3. (a) Using Table 1 going down the 12% column and across the 10 periods row, the number .32197 represents the present value of 1. Multiplying the amount from the table by $5,000 and the answer equals $1,609.85 ($5,000 X .32197).

4. (d) In computing the present value of an annuity, it is necessary to know (1) the discount rate, (2) the number of discount periods, and (3) the amount of the periodic receipts or payments.

5. (c) The present value of interest to be received periodically over the term of the note is equal to $12,000 multiplied by the present value of 1 due in five periods at 15% ($12,000 X 3.35216 = $40,225.92).

EXERCISES

EX. C-1

a. $20,900 ÷ $100,000 = .20900.
Using Table 1 and going across period row 15, .20900 is under the 11% column indicating an annual rate of interest of 11% must be earned.

b. Present value of principal to be received at maturity:

$20,000 X PV of 1 due in 8 periods at 8%	
$20,000 X .54027 (Table 1)	$10,805
Present value of interest to be received periodically over the term of the note:	
$2,000 X PV of 1 due periodically for 8 periods at 8%	
$2,000 X 5.74664 (Table 2)	11,493
Present value of note	$22,298

APPENDIX D

PAYROLL ACCOUNTING

The Navigator	✓
■ *Scan Study Objectives*	☐
■ *Read Preview*	☐
■ *Read Chapter Review*	☐
■ *Work Demonstration Problem*	☐
■ *Answer True-False Statements*	☐
■ *Answer Multiple-Choice Questions*	☐
■ *Match Terms and Definitions*	☐
■ *Solve Exercises*	☐

STUDY OBJECTIVES

After studying this appendix, you should be able to:

1. Discuss the objectives of internal control for payroll.
2. Compute and record the payroll for a pay period.
3. Describe and record employer payroll taxes.

The Navigator

APPENDIX D REVIEW

Payroll Accounting

1. (S.O. 1) The term **payroll** pertains to all salaries and wages paid to employees. Payments made to professional individuals who are independent contractors are called fees. Payroll regulations relating to such areas as taxes and reporting, only apply to employees.

Internal Controls for Payroll

2. The objectives of **internal accounting control** concerning payroll are (a) to safeguard company assets from unauthorized payments of payrolls, and (b) to ensure the accuracy and reliability of the accounting records pertaining to payrolls.

3. The payroll activities consist of four functions: (a) hiring employees, (b) timekeeping, (c) preparing the payroll, and (d) paying the payroll. These four functions should be assigned to different departments or individuals.

4. The **human resources (personnel) department** is responsible for the posting of job openings, the screening and interviewing of applicants, and hiring employees. The human resources department is also responsible for authorizing changes in pay rates during employment and terminations of employment.

5. In **timekeeping,** employees usually are required to record time worked on a time card by punching a time clock. A supervisor often monitors the time clock procedures.

6. The **payroll department** prepares the payroll based on (a) personnel department authorizations and (b) approved time cards from timekeeping. The payroll department is also responsible for preparing payroll checks, maintaining payroll records, and preparing payroll tax returns.

7. The **treasurer's department** is responsible for the payment of the payroll.
   a. Payment by check minimizes the risk of loss from theft, and the endorsed check provides proof of payment.
   b. All checks must be signed by the treasurer and their distribution should be controlled by the treasurer's department.

Gross Earnings

8. (S.O. 2) **Gross earnings** is the total compensation earned by an employee. There are three types of gross earnings: wages, salaries, and bonuses.
   a. Total wages are determined by applying the hourly rate of pay to the hours worked.
   b. Most companies are required to pay a minimum of one and one-half times the regular hourly rate for overtime work.

Payroll Deductions

9. Mandatory payroll deductions consist of FICA taxes and income taxes.
   a. These deductions do not result in payroll tax expense to the employer.
   b. **FICA taxes** are designed to provide workers with supplemental retirement, employment disability, and medical benefits.
   c. FICA taxes are also known as Social Security Taxes.

10. **Income taxes** are required to be withheld from employees each pay period and the amount is determined by three variables: (a) the employee's gross earnings; (b) the number of allowances claimed by the employee for herself or himself, his or her spouse, and other dependents; and (c) the length of the pay period.

11. **Voluntary deductions** pertain to withholdings for charitable, retirement, and other purposes and are authorized by the employee.

12. **Net pay** is determined by subtracting payroll deductions from gross earnings.

Recording the Payroll

13. The **employee earnings record** provides a cumulative record of each employee's gross earnings, deductions, and net pay during the year. This record is used by the employer in:
    a. Determining when an employee has earned the maximum earnings subject to FICA taxes.
    b. Filing state and federal payroll tax returns.
    c. Providing each employee with a statement of gross earnings and tax withholdings for the year.

14. Many companies use a **payroll register** to accumulate gross earnings, deductions, and net pay by employee for each period. In some cases, this record is a journal or book of original entry.

15. The typical journal entry to record a payroll is as follows:

Account	Debit	Credit
Office Salaries Expense	XXX	
Wages Expense	XXX	
FICA Taxes Payable		XXX
Federal Income Taxes Payable		XXX
State Income Taxes Payable		XXX
United Fund Payable		XXX
Union Dues Payable		XXX
Salaries and Wages Payable		XXX

16. When the payroll is paid, Salaries and Wages Payable is debited and Cash is credited.

Employer Payroll Taxes

17. (S.O. 3) There are three taxes imposed on employers by governmental agencies that result in payroll tax expense:
    a. **FICA Taxes.** The employer must match each employee's FICA contribution.
    b. **Federal Unemployment Taxes.** The employer is required to pay a tax on the first $9,000 of gross wages paid to each employee during a calendar year.
    c. **State Unemployment Taxes.** All states have unemployment compensation programs that require the employer to pay a tax on the first $9,000 of gross wages paid to each employee during a calendar year.

18. The typical entry for recording payroll tax expense is as follows:

Account	Debit	Credit
Payroll Tax Expense	XXX	
FICA Taxes Payable		XXX
Federal Unemployment Taxes Payable		XXX
State Unemployment Taxes Payable		XXX

19. Preparation of payroll tax returns is the responsibility of the payroll department; payment of the taxes is made by the treasurer's department.

20. The employer is required to provide each employee with a **Wage and Tax Statement (Form W-2)** by January 31 following the end of a calendar year. This statement shows gross earnings, FICA taxes withheld, and income taxes withheld for the year.

The Navigator

REVIEW QUESTIONS AND EXERCISES

TRUE—FALSE

Indicate whether each of the following is true (T) or false (F) in the space provided.

_____ 1. (S.O. 1) Payments made for personal service to the company by professionals, such as an attorney, should be included as a part of salaries and wages.

_____ 2. (S.O. 1) The objectives of internal accounting control for payrolls are (a) to safeguard company assets from unauthorized payments of payrolls, and (b) to assure the accuracy and reliability of the accounting records pertaining to payrolls.

_____ 3. (S.O. 1) The posting of job openings, the screening and interviewing of applicants, and the hiring of employees is the responsibility of the payroll department.

_____ 4. (S.O. 1) For good internal control, payroll checks should be prenumbered and signed by the treasurer.

_____ 5. (S.O. 2) FICA taxes are a voluntary deduction from employee earnings.

_____ 6. (S.O. 2) Income taxes to be withheld are determined by (a) the employee's gross earnings; (b) the number of allowances claimed by the employee for herself or himself, his or her spouse, and other dependents; and (c) the length of the pay period.

_____ 7. (S.O. 2) The statement of earnings document is a cumulative record of each employee's earnings during the year and provides other essential data, such as total taxes withheld for each employee.

_____ 8. (S.O. 3) FICA taxes are a deduction from employee earnings and are also imposed upon employers as an expense.

_____ 9. (S.O. 3) An employer is required to provide each employee with a Wage and Tax Statement (Form W-2).

The Navigator

MULTIPLE CHOICE

Circle the letter that best answers each of the following statements.

1. (S.O. 1) Which of the following is not considered a function of payroll activities?
   a. Preparing payroll tax returns.
   b. Timekeeping.
   c. Preparing the payroll.
   d. Paying independent contractors for personal service.

2. (S.O. 1) The department responsible for paying payroll is the:
   a. treasurer's department.
   b. personnel department.
   c. timekeeping department.
   d. payroll department.

3. (S.O. 2) Jan Turner earns $16 per hour for a 40 hour work week and $24 per hour for overtime work. If Turner works 44 hours, her gross earnings are:
   a. $704.
   b. $736.
   c. $836.
   d. $1,056.

4. (S.O. 2) Lewis Latimer, an employee of Spottswood Company, has gross earnings for the month of October of $4,000. FICA taxes are 8% of gross earnings, federal income taxes amount to $635 for the month, state income taxes are 2% of gross earnings, and Lewis authorizes voluntary deductions of $10 per month to the United Fund. What is the net pay for Lewis Latimer?
   a. $2,961.40.
   b. $2,955.00.
   c. $2,965.00.
   d. $2,967.70.

5. (S.O. 2) The journal entry to record the payroll for Marcus Garvey Company for the week ending January 8 would probably include a:
   a. credit to Office Salaries Expense.
   b. credit to Wages Expense.
   c. debit to Federal Income Taxes Payable.
   d. credit to FICA Taxes Payable.

6. (S.O. 2) A tax that is also known as social security taxes is:
   a. state income taxes.
   b. federal income taxes.
   c. Federal Insurance Contribution Act (FICA) taxes.
   d. federal unemployment taxes.

7. (S.O. 3) The journal entry for Hansberry Corporation to record employer payroll taxes will include a:
   a. debit to Wages Expense.
   b. debit to State Unemployment Expense.
   c. debit to FICA Taxes Payable.
   d. debit to Payroll Tax Expense.

8. (S.O. 3) The record that provides a cumulative summary of each employee's gross earnings, payroll deductions, and net pay during the year is required to be maintained to comply with state and federal laws is the:
   a. payroll register.
   b. employee earnings record.
   c. statement of earnings.
   d. Wage and Tax Statement.

The Navigator

MATCHING

Match each term with its definition by writing the appropriate letter in the space provided.

Terms

_____ 1. FICA taxes.

_____ 2. Payroll register.

_____ 3. Statement of earnings.

_____ 4. State unemployment taxes.

_____ 5. Employee earnings record.

_____ 6. Federal unemployment taxes.

_____ 7. Wage and Tax Statement (Form W-2).

_____ 8. Employee's Withholding Allowance Certificate (Form W-4).

_____ 9. Gross earnings.

Definitions

a. A record showing the gross earnings, payroll deductions, and net pay of each employee for a pay period.

b. A document that accompanies each payroll check and indicates the employee's gross earnings, payroll deductions, and net pay.

c. A statement showing an employee's gross earnings, FICA taxes withheld, and income taxes withheld for the year.

d. A cumulative record that provides information concerning each employee's gross earnings, deductions, and net pay during the year.

e. An Internal Revenue Service form showing the number of allowances claimed by an employee for the purpose of withholding income taxes from the employee's gross earnings.

f. Taxes imposed on an employer by state governments that provide benefits to employees who lose their jobs.

g. Total compensation earned by an employee.

h. Taxes imposed on an employer by the federal government that provide benefits to employees who lose their jobs.

i. Taxes designed to provide workers with supplemental retirement, employment disability, and medical benefits.

EXERCISES

EX. D-1 (S.O. 1)

The following information pertains to the payroll of B.T. Washington Company for the week ended January 24, 2006. All hours over 40 are paid at one and one-half times the regular hourly rate.

Employee	Total Hours Worked	Hourly Rate	Federal Income Taxes	United Fund	Union Dues
E. Bouchet	45	$13.00	$110	$10	$5
C. Cullen	44	15.00	138	12	5
M. Henson	38	10.00	64	10	5
B. Mays	48	12.00	100	14	5

Instructions

(a) Complete the schedule below. The state income tax rate is 4% of earnings and the FICA tax rate is 8% of gross earnings.
(b) Prepare the entry to record the payroll on January 24.
(c) Prepare the journal entry to record payment of the payroll on January 26.
(d) Record the employer's payroll taxes assuming state unemployment taxes are 5.4% and federal unemployment taxes are 0.8%.

(a)

Employee	Gross Earnings	FICA Taxes	Federal Income Taxes	State Income Taxes	United Fund	Union Dues	Net Pay
E. Bouchet							
C. Cullen							
M. Henson							
B. Mays							

General Journal J1

Date	Account Title	Debit	Credit
2006			
(b)			
(c)			
(d)			

The Navigator

SOLUTIONS TO REVIEW QUESTIONS AND EXERCISES

TRUE-FALSE

1. (F) The term payroll does not extend to payments made for personal service to the company by professionals, such as attorneys. These and other professional individuals are independent contractors, and payments to them are called fees rather than salaries and wages.
2. (T)
3. (F) The posting of job openings, the screening and interviewing of applicants, and the hiring of employees is the responsibility of the personnel department.
4. (T)
5. (F) FICA taxes are considered a mandatory deduction from employee earnings.
6. (T)
7. (F) The statement of earnings accompanies each payroll check and indicates the employee's gross earnings, payroll deductions, and net pay. The document that shows the data given in the true-false statement is the employee earnings record which is an internal document maintained by an employer to comply with state and federal laws.
8. (T)
9. (T)

MULTIPLE CHOICE

1. (d) Preparing payroll tax returns (a), timekeeping (b), and preparing the payroll (c) are all considered functions of payroll activities. Payments to professionals are called fees; such payments extend beyond the term "payroll."

2. (a) The treasurer's department should be responsible for the payment of the payroll. The other departments perform other important payroll functions but not paying the payroll.

3. (b) Gross earnings are $736. (Regular 40 X $16 = $640 + overtime 4 X $24 = $96).

4. (b) The net pay is computed as follows:

Gross earnings		$4,000.00
Payroll deductions:		
FICA taxes ($4,000 X 8%)	$320.00	
Federal income taxes	635.00	
State income taxes ($4,000 X 2%)	80.00	
United Fund	10.00	1,045.00
Net pay		$2,955.00

5. (d) An example of a typical payroll entry is as follows:

Office Salaries Expense	XXXX	
Wages Expense	XXXX	
FICA Taxes Payable		XXXX
Federal Income Taxes Payable		XXXX
State Income Taxes Payable		XXXX
United Fund Payable		XXXX
Wages Payable		XXXX

6. (c) FICA taxes are also known as social security taxes. This tax is both withheld from employees and is matched by the employer as a payroll tax expense.

7. (d) An example of a typical employer payroll taxes entry is as follows:

Payroll Tax Expense	XXXX	
FICA Taxes Payable		XXXX
Federal Unemployment Taxes Payable		XXXX
State Unemployment Taxes Payable		XXXX

8. (b) Both the payroll register (a) and the statement of earnings (c) relate to a given pay period. The Wage and Tax Statement (d) does contain cumulative data on each employee but it does not show all payroll deductions or net pay.

MATCHING

1.	i	6.	h
2.	a	7.	c
3.	b	8.	e
4.	f	9.	g
5.	d		

EXERCISES

EX. D-1

(a)

Employee	Gross Earnings	FICA Taxes	Federal Income Taxes	State Income Taxes	United Fund	Union Dues	Net Pay
E. Bouchet	$ 617.50	$ 49.40	$110.00	$24.70	$10.00	$ 5.00	$ 418.40
C. Cullen	690.00	55.20	138.00	27.60	12.00	5.00	452.20
M. Henson	380.00	30.40	64.00	15.20	10.00	5.00	255.40
B. Mays	624.00	49.92	100.00	24.96	14.00	5.00	430.12
	$2,311.50	$184.92	$412.00	$92.46	$46.00	$20.00	$1,556.12

General Journal			
			J1
Date	**Account Title**	**Debit**	**Credit**
2006			
(b)			
Jan. 24	Wages Expense	2,311.50	
	FICA Taxes Payable (Employee Contribution)		184.92
	Federal Income Taxes Payable		412.00
	State Income Taxes Payable		92.46
	United Fund Payable		46.00
	Union Dues Payable		20.00
	Wages Payable		1,556.12
	(To record January 24 payroll)		
(c)			
Jan. 26	Wages Payable	1,556.12	
	Cash		1,556.12
	(To record payment of Jan. 24 payroll)		
(d)			
Jan. 26	Payroll Tax Expense	328.23	
	FICA Taxes Payable (Employer's Contribution)		184.92
	Federal Unemployment Taxes Payable		
	[($2,311.50 X (0.062 - 0.054)]		18.49
	State Unemployment Taxes Payable		
	($2,311.50 X 0.054)		124.82

APPENDIX E

SUBSIDIARY LEDGERS AND SPECIAL JOURNALS

The Navigator	✓
■ *Scan Study Objectives*	☐
■ *Read Preview*	☐
■ *Read Chapter Review*	☐
■ *Work Demonstration Problem*	☐
■ *Answer True-False Statements*	☐
■ *Answer Multiple-Choice Questions*	☐
■ *Match Terms and Definitions*	☐
■ *Solve Exercises*	☐

STUDY OBJECTIVES

After studying this chapter, you should be able to:

1. Describe the nature and purpose of a subsidiary ledger.
2. Explain how special journals are used in journalizing.
3. Indicate how a multi-column journal is posted.

The Navigator

APPENDIX E REVIEW

Subsidiary Ledgers

1. (S.O. 1) A **subsidiary ledger** is a group of accounts with a common characteristic, assembled together to facilitate the recording process by freeing the general ledger from details concerning individual balances.

2. Two common subsidiary ledgers are:
   a. The accounts receivable (or customers') ledger which collects transaction data with individual customers.
   b. The accounts payable (or creditors') ledger which collects transaction data with individual creditors.

3. The summary account in the general ledger is called a **control account** and the balance in the control account must equal the composite balance of the individual accounts in the subsidiary ledger at the end of the period.

4. The advantages of using subsidiary ledgers are that they:
   a. Show transactions affecting one customer or one creditor in a single account, thus providing up-to-date information on specific account balances.
   b. Free the general ledger of excessive details. As a result, a trial balance of the general ledger does not contain vast numbers of individual account balances.
   c. Help locate errors in individual accounts by reducing the number of accounts in one ledger and by using control accounts.
   d. Make possible a division of labor in posting by having one employee post to the general ledger while a different employee(s) post to the subsidiary ledgers.

Special Journals

5. (S.O. 2) To expedite journalizing and posting transactions, most companies use **special journals** in addition to the general journal. A special journal is used to group similar types of transactions, such as all sales of merchandise on account or all cash receipts.

6. The following are types of special journals:
   a. Sales journal—all sales of merchandise on account.
   b. Cash receipts journal—all cash received (including cash sales).
   c. Purchases journal—all purchases of merchandise on account.
   d. Cash payments journal—all cash paid (including cash purchases).

7. If a transaction cannot be recorded in a special journal, it is recorded in the general journal. Special journals permit greater division of labor and reduce the time necessary to complete the posting process.

Sales Journal

8. For the **sales journal,**
   a. Each entry results in a debit to Accounts Receivable and a credit to Sales at selling price; and a debit to Cost of Goods Sold and a credit to Merchandise Inventory at cost.
   b. Only one line is needed to record each transaction.
   c. All entries are made from sales invoices.
   d. Postings are made daily to the individual accounts receivable in the subsidiary ledger and monthly, in total, to Accounts Receivable, Sales, Cost of Goods Sold and Merchandise Inventory in the general ledger.

Cash Receipts Journal

9. The **cash receipts journal** is a columnar journal with debit columns for cash and sales discounts, and credit columns for accounts receivable, sales, and "other" accounts. In addition there is a separate column for a debit to Cost of Goods Sold and a credit to Merchandise Inventory. In journalizing cash receipts transactions:
   a. Only one line is needed for each entry.
   b. Each sale entry is accompanied by another entry that debits Cost of Goods Sold and credits Merchandise Inventory for cost.

10. (S.O. 3) The **posting of a columnar journal** such as the cash receipts journal involves the following procedures:
    a. All column totals except the total for the Other Accounts column are posted once at the end of the month to the account title or titles specified in the column heading.
    b. The total of the Other Accounts column is not posted. Instead, the individual amounts comprising the total are posted separately to the general ledger accounts specified in the Accounts Credited column.
    c. The individual amounts in a column, posted in total to a control account, are posted daily to the subsidiary ledger account specified in the Accounts Credited column.

Purchases Journal

11. For the **purchases journal,**
    a. Each entry results in a debit to Merchandise Inventory and a credit to Accounts Payable.
    b. Only one line is needed to record each transaction.
    c. All entries are made from purchase invoices.
    d. Postings are made daily to the individual creditor accounts in the accounts payable subsidiary ledger and monthly, in total, to Merchandise Inventory and Accounts Payable in the general ledger.

12. The purchases journal can be expanded into a columnar journal by adding columns for office supplies, store supplies, and other accounts.

Cash Payments Journal

13. The **cash payments journal** has multiple columns because cash payments may be made for a variety of purposes.
    a. The journalizing procedures are similar to those described earlier for the cash receipts journal.
    b. All entries are made from prenumbered checks.
    c. The posting procedures are similar to those described earlier for the cash receipts journal.

Effects of Special Journals on General Journal

14. Only transactions that cannot be entered in a special journal are recorded in the **general journal.** When the entry involves both control and subsidiary accounts the following modifications are required:
    a. In journalizing, both the control and subsidiary accounts must be identified.
    b. In posting, there must be a dual posting: once to the control account and once to the subsidiary account.

The Navigator

DEMONSTRATION PROBLEM (S.O. 2 and 3)

The Gauguin Company uses a five column cash payments journal with columns for Cash (Cr.), Merchandise Inventory (Cr.), Store Supplies (Dr.), Accounts Payable (Dr.), and Other Accounts (Dr.). Cash payments for the month of October are as follows:

October	2	Check No. 101 for $1,100 is issued to Toulouse-Lautrec Realty for October rent.
	5	Check No. 102 for $600 is issued for the purchase of merchandise.
	9	Check No. 103 for $8,820 is sent to Cassatt Inc. in payment of October 4 invoice for $9,000 less a 2% discount.
	13	Check No. 104 for $550 is issued for store supplies.
	17	Check No. 105 for $8,000 is sent to Picasso Company in payment of October 3 invoice for $8,000.
	21	Check No. 106 for $400 is issued to Paul Gauguin as a cash withdrawal for personal use.
	28	Check No. 107 for $300 is issued for store supplies.

Instructions

Journalize the transactions in the cash payments journal.

The Navigator

SOLUTION TO DEMONSTRATION PROBLEM

Cash Payments Journal

Date	Ck. No.	Explanation	Accounts Debited	Ref.	Other Accounts Dr.	Accounts Payable Dr.	Store Supplies Dr.	Merchandise Inventory Cr.	Cash Cr.
Oct. 2	101	Toulouse-Lautrec, Realty	Rent Expense		1,100				1,100
5	102	Buy merchandise.	Merchandise Inventory		600				600
9	103	Pay in full.	Cassatt, Inc.			9,000		180	8,820
13	104	Purchase supplies.					550		550
17	105	Pay in full.	Picasso Company			8,000			8,000
21	106	Withdraw cash.	Paul Gauguin, Drawing		400				400
28	107	Purchase supplies.					300		300
					2,100	17,000	850	180	19,770

REVIEW QUESTIONS AND EXERCISES

TRUE—FALSE

Indicate whether each of the following is true (T) or false (F) in the space provided.

_____ 1. (S.O. 1) A subsidiary ledger is a group of accounts with a common characteristic.

_____ 2. (S.O. 1) The summary account in the general ledger that controls the subsidiary ledger is called a special account.

_____ 3. (S.O. 1) Each general ledger control account balance must equal the composite balance of the individual accounts in the related subsidiary ledger at the end of an accounting period.

_____ 4. (S.O. 1) An advantage of using a subsidiary ledger control account is that it assists in locating errors in individual accounts by reducing the number of accounts combined in one ledger.

_____ 5. (S.O. 2) A special journal is used to group unusual types of transactions.

_____ 6. (S.O. 2) If a transaction cannot be recorded in a special journal, it should not be recorded.

_____ 7. (S.O. 2) When special journals are employed, all postings must be monthly or daily but cannot be both.

_____ 8. (S.O. 2) A disadvantage of the sales journal is that recording transactions takes longer.

_____ 9. (S.O. 2) At the end of the month, the column totals in the sales journal need only to be posted to the Sales account.

_____ 10. (S.O. 2) A cash sale of merchandise will result in the use of one line in the cash receipts journal.

_____ 11. (S.O. 2) Totaling the columns of a journal and proving the equality of the totals is called footing and cross-footing a journal.

_____ 12. (S.O. 2) The cash receipts journal will usually include a Sales Discounts column.

_____ 13. (S.O. 3) All purchases of merchandise on account are recorded in the purchases journal.

_____ 14. (S.O. 3) Entries in the purchases journal are made from sales invoices.

_____ 15. (S.O. 3) Postings from the one-column purchases journal are made daily to the accounts payable subsidiary ledger and monthly to the general ledger.

_____ 16. (S.O. 3) The total of the Other Accounts column of the cash payments journal is posted to the general ledger at the end of the month.

_____ 17. (S.O. 3) Only transactions that cannot be entered in a special journal are recorded in the general journal.

The Navigator

MULTIPLE CHOICE

Circle the letter that best answers each of the following statements.

1. (S.O. 1) Which of the following accounts may a business not use as a controlling account and subsidiary ledger?
   a. Inventory.
   b. Accounts Payable.
   c. Selling and Administrative Expenses.
   d. A business may use all of the above as controlling accounts and subsidiary ledgers.

2. (S.O. 1) Which of the following is **not** an advantage of a subsidiary ledger?
   a. Shows transactions affecting one customer or one creditor in a single account.
   b. Help locate errors in individual accounts.
   c. Puts greater detail in the general ledger.
   d. Makes possible a division of labor.

3. (S.O. 2) Which of the following is a journal that most merchandising enterprises will not use?
   a. Cash payments journal.
   b. Purchases journal.
   c. Sales journal.
   d. Equipment journal.

4. (S.O. 2) When the totals of the sales journal are posted at the end of the month there will be credits to:
   a. Sales and Merchandise Inventory and debits to Accounts Receivable and Cost of Goods Sold.
   b. Accounts Receivable and Cost of Goods Sold and debits to Sales and Merchandise Inventory.
   c. Sales and debits to each individual customer account.
   d. the Sales account only, and no debits.

5. (S.O. 2) The entries in the sales journal must be posted daily to the:
   a. Sales Account.
   b. Accounts Receivable subsidiary ledger.
   c. the Accounts Payable subsidiary ledger.
   d. none of the above.

6. (S.O. 2) A cash receipts journal will be used for:

	Cash sales	Sales discounts	Cost of Goods Sold
a.	yes	yes	yes
b.	yes	no	yes
c.	no	yes	yes
d.	yes	yes	no

7. (S.O. 2) Which of the following transactions will not involve the cash receipts journal?
   a. Cash sales of merchandise totaling $2,000.
   b. Cash is received by signing a note for $3,000.
   c. The owner makes a cash investment in the business.
   d. A company gives a purchase refund to a purchaser following a cash purchase.

8. (S.O. 2) The Other Accounts column of a columnar journal is often referred to as the:
   a. Sundry Accounts column.
   b. Controlling Account column.
   c. Credit Account column.
   d. Debit Account column.

9. (S.O. 2) In the cash receipts journal, debits are made in which columns?
   a. Cash, Sales Discounts, and Cost of Goods Sold.
   b. Accounts Receivable, Cash, and Cost of Goods Sold.
   c. Sales Discounts, Sales, and Merchandise Inventory.
   d. Accounts Receivable, Sales, and Merchandise Inventory.

10. (S.O. 3) The purchases journal will include:

	Cash purchases	Credit purchases	Merchandise Inventory
a.	yes	yes	yes
b.	yes	no	yes
c.	no	yes	no
d.	no	yes	yes

11. (S.O. 3) In the expanded purchases journal, debits are made in which columns?
    a. Accounts Payable, Merchandise Inventory, and Office Supplies.
    b. Merchandise Inventory, Office Supplies, and Store Supplies.
    c. Cash, Office Supplies, and Store Supplies.
    d. Accounts Payable, Cash, and Merchandise Inventory.

12. (S.O. 3) The cash payments journal may include a column for:
    a. store supplies.
    b. accounts receivable.
    c. sales.
    d. sales discounts.

13. (S.O. 3) If a customer returns goods for credit, an entry is normally made in the:
    a. cash receipts journal.
    b. sales journal.
    c. cash payments journal.
    d. general journal.

14. (S.O. 3) If a customer takes a sales discount, an entry is made in the:
    a. cash receipts journal.
    b. sales journal.
    c. cash payments journal.
    d. general journal.

15. (S.O. 3) Totaling the columns of a multi-column journal and proving the equality of the totals is called:
    a. totaling and balancing.
    b. footing and cross-footing.
    c. totaling and cross-footing.
    d. footing and balancing.

The Navigator

MATCHING

Match each term with its definition by writing the appropriate letter in the space provided.

Terms

_____ 1. Subsidiary ledger.

_____ 2. Control account.

_____ 3. Special journal.

_____ 4. Sales journal.

_____ 5. Cash receipts journal.

_____ 6. Purchases journal.

_____ 7. Cash payments journal.

_____ 8. Multi-column journal.

Definitions

a. An account in the general ledger that controls a subsidiary ledger.
b. A special journal used to record all sales of merchandise on account.
c. A group of accounts with a common characteristic that is controlled by an account in the general ledger.
d. A special journal used to record all cash paid.
e. A journal that is used to group similar types of transactions such as all credit sales or all cash receipts.
f. A special journal used to record all purchases of merchandise on account.
g. A special journal used to record all cash received.
h. A special journal with more than one column.

The Navigator

EXERCISES

EX. E-1 (S.O. 2 and 3) Cartoonist Inc., had the following transactions during the month.

1. Merchandise is sold on credit to Gary Trudeau for $2,500.
2. Merchandise is sold to Charles Schulz for $1,000 cash.
3. Merchandise purchased by Charlie Brown on account is returned for credit.
4. A check for $2,940 is received from Al Capp in payment of invoice no. 101 for $3,000 less 2% discount.
5. Merchandise is purchased on credit from Disney Company for $2,000, terms 1/20, n/30.
6. Check no. 101 for $3,100 is issued for store supplies bought from Jim Davis.
7. Check no. 102 for $1,980, $2,000 less the 1% discount is mailed to Disney Company to pay for merchandise purchased on credit.
8. Merchandise is purchased for $1,000 (check no. 103) cash from Mary Worth.
9. Equipment is purchased from Mort Walker for $4,000 on credit.
10. Cash is received from R. Dagwood in payment of a $5,000 note receivable, plus $75 of accrued interest.

Instructions

(a) Indicate the journal in which each transaction should be entered using the following letters:

G = General journal
S = Sales journal
P = Purchases journal (one-column)
CR = Cash receipts journal
CP = Cash payments journal

(b) For each journal selected in (a) above, indicate by inserting a check mark in the appropriate column whether the journalized data should be posted (1) only at the end of the month, (2) daily and at the end of the month, or (3) only daily. (Note: Assume that the columnar journals have the same columns as those in the chapter and subsidiary and control accounts are used.)

		(b) Posting		
Transaction	(a) Journal	Monthly Only	Daily and Monthly	Daily Only
1.				
2.				
3.				
4.				
5.				
6.				
7.				
8.				
9.				
10.				

EX. E-2 (S.O. 3) The following transactions were made by George Baker Company during the month of October 2006.

Oct. 3 Received a $3,000 payment from Chic Young in full for invoice no. 101 when terms were n/30.

6 Bought store supplies from Chester Gould Co. for $500—used check no. 101.

9 Purchased merchandise from Harold Gray Company for $3,500—used check no. 102.

13 Received $2,000 cash from Harold Gray Company as an allowance for defective goods purchased on Oct. 9.

16 Purchased merchandise from Hank Ketcham Company for $1,500 on credit.

20 Sold merchandise to Jack Kirby for $2,250 on credit—used sales invoice no. 10. The cost of goods sold was $1,600.

23 Purchased merchandise from Bob Montana, Inc. for $6,000 on credit.

25 Received $2,205 from Jack Kirby for the sale made on Oct. 20 less a 2% discount.

27 Paid Hank Ketcham Company $1,485 cash for the purchase on Oct. 16 less a 1% discount–used check no. 103.

Instructions
In the journals provided, enter the transactions for the George Baker Company for the month ended October 31, 2006.

Sales Journal

S1

Date	Account Debited	Invoice No.	Ref.	Accts. Receivable Dr. Sales Cr.	Cost of Goods Sold Dr. Merchandise Inventory Cr.
2006					

Purchases Journal

P1

Date	Account Credited	Terms	Ref.	Merchandise Inventory Dr. Accounts Payable Cr.
2006				

Cash Receipts Journal

CR1

Date	Account Credited	Ref.	Cash Dr.	Sales Discounts Dr.	Accounts Receivable Cr.	Sales Cr.	Other Accounts Cr.	Cost of Goods Sold Dr. Merchandise Inventory Cr.
2006								

Cash Payments Journal

CP1

Date	Ck No.	Accounts Debited	Ref.	Other Accounts Dr.	Accounts Payable Dr.	Store Supplies Dr.	Merchandise Inventory Cr.	Cash Cr.
2006								

The Navigator

SOLUTIONS TO REVIEW QUESTIONS AND EXERCISES

TRUE-FALSE

1. (T)
2. (F) The summary account in the general ledger is called a control account.
3. (T)
4. (T)
5. (F) A special journal is used to group similar types of transactions.
6. (F) If a transaction cannot be recorded in a special journal, it is recorded in the general journal.
7. (F) When special journals are employed, daily postings are usually made to the subsidiary ledgers and monthly postings to the general ledger.
8. (F) An advantage of the sales journal is that one-line entry for each sales transaction saves time.
9. (F) The column totals of the Sales journal are posted to the Sales account and the Accounts Receivable account, and the Cost of Goods Sold account and the Merchandise Inventory account.
10. (T)
11. (T)
12. (T)
13. (T)
14. (F) Entries in the purchases journal are made from purchase invoices. Sales invoices are used to make entries in the sales journal.
15. (T)
16. (F) The total of the Other Accounts column is not posted because each individual transaction is posted to the appropriate account affected.
17. (T)

MULTIPLE CHOICE

1. (d) Two common subsidiary ledgers are the accounts receivable ledger and the accounts payable ledger. Businesses may also use controlling accounts and subsidiary ledgers for other accounts such as inventory, equipment, and selling and administrative expenses.

2. (c) Advantages of the subsidiary ledger are: (a) shows transactions affecting one customer or one creditor in a single account, (b) helps locate errors in individual accounts, and (d) makes possible a division of labor. Another advantage is that subsidiary ledgers free the general ledger of excessive details.

3. (d) Most merchandising enterprises use a (c) sales journal, (b) purchases journal, and (a) cash payments journal as well as a cash receipts journal. An equipment journal is generally not used as a special journal because there are not that many equipment purchases during an accounting period.

4. (a) At the end of the month, the totals are posted to the general ledger as debits to Accounts Receivable and Cost of Goods Sold, and as credits to Sales and Merchandise Inventory.

5. (b) Postings from the sales journal are made daily to the individual accounts receivable in the subsidiary ledger and monthly to the general ledger.

6. (a) The cash receipts journal will be used for cash sales, collections of accounts, and other receipts of cash. Since the sales discount is not determined until the receipt of cash, it also is recorded in the cash receipts journal. Cost of Goods Sold is also debited when goods are sold.

7. (d) The cash receipts journal is used for all receipts of cash. When a refund is given on a cash purchase, cash is paid. Thus, the entry should be made in the cash payments journal.

8. (a) The Other Accounts column is often referred to as the sundry accounts column because a variety of general ledger account titles may be used. The other choices are not used referring to a miscellaneous accounts column.

9. (a) In the cash receipts journal, debits are made in the cash and sales discounts columns. In the same journal, credits are made in the accounts receivable, sales, and other accounts columns. In addition debits and credits are made in the Cost of Goods Sold and Merchandise Inventory column.

10. (d) The purchases journal is a special journal that is used to record all purchases of merchandise on account. Cash purchases are recorded in the cash payments journal.

11. (b) In the Purchases Journal, credits are made to the Accounts Payable column and debits to the Merchandise Inventory, Office Supplies, Store Supplies and Other Accounts columns.

12. (a) The cash payments journal may have a column for Store Supplies because supplies may be purchased for cash. It would not have columns for the other choices because they pertain to sales and cash receipts.

13. (d) The return of goods for credit cannot be made in any of the special journals. Therefore, the entry must be made in the general journal.

14. (a) The sales discount is not taken until the cash is received. Therefore, the entry is made in the cash receipts journal.

15. (b) The correct terminology is footing and cross-footing.

MATCHING

1. c	4. b	7. d
2. a	5. g	8. h
3. e	6. f	

EXERCISES

EX. E-1

Transaction	(a) Journal	(b) Posting: Monthly Only	(b) Posting: Daily and Monthly	(b) Posting: Daily Only
1.	S		✓	
2.	CR	✓		
3.	G			✓
4.	CR		✓	
5.	P		✓	
6.	CP	✓		
7.	CP		✓	
8.	CP	✓		
9.	G			✓
10.	CR		✓	

EX. E-2

Sales Journal

S1

Date	Account Debited	Invoice No.	Ref.	Accts. Receivable Dr. Sales Cr.	Cost of Goods Sold Dr. Merchandise Inventory Cr.
2006					
Oct. 20	Jack Kirby	10		2,250	1,600

Purchases Journal

P1

Date	Account Credited	Terms	Ref.	Merchandise Inventory Dr. Accounts Payable Cr.
2006				
Oct. 16	Hank Ketcham Company			1,500
23	Bob Montana, Inc.			6,000

Cash Receipts Journal

CR1

Date	Account Credited	Ref.	Cash Dr.	Sales Discounts Dr.	Accounts Receivable Cr.	Sales Cr.	Other Accounts Cr.	Cost of Goods Sold Dr. Merchandise Inventory Cr.
2006								
Oct. 3	Chic Young		3,000		3,000			
13	Merchandise Inventory		2,000				2,000	
25	Jack Kirby		2,205	45	2,250			

Cash Payments Journal

CP1

Date	Ck No.	Accounts Debited	Ref.	Other Accounts Dr.	Accounts Payable Dr.	Store Supplies Dr.	Merchandise Inventory Cr.	Cash Cr.
2006								
Oct. 6	101					500		500
9	102	Merchandise Inventory		3,500				3,500
27	103	Hank Ketcham Company			1,500		15	1,485

APPENDIX F

The Navigator	✓
■ *Scan Study Objectives*	☐
■ *Read Preview*	☐
■ *Read Chapter Review*	☐
■ *Work Demonstration Problem*	☐
■ *Answer True-False Statements*	☐
■ *Answer Multiple-Choice Questions*	☐
■ *Match Terms and Definitions*	☐
■ *Solve Exercises*	☐

OTHER SIGNIFICANT LIABILITIES

STUDY OBJECTIVES

After studying this appendix, you should be able to:

1. Describe the accounting and disclosure requirements for contingent liabilities.
2. Contrast the accounting for operating and capital leases.
3. Identify additional liabilities for fringe benefits associated with employee compensation.

The Navigator

APPENDIX F REVIEW

Contingent Liabilities

1. (S.O. 1) A **contingent liability** is a potential liability that may become an actual liability in the future. The accounting guidelines require that:
   a. If it is **probable** that the contingency will happen and the amount can be reasonably estimated, the liability should be recorded in the accounts.
   b. If it is only **reasonably possible**, then it need be disclosed only in the notes accompanying the financial statements.
   c. If the possibility of occurrence is **remote**, the contingency need not be recorded or disclosed.

Product Warranties

2. **Product warranties** are a good example of a contingent liability. They are recorded by estimating the cost of honoring product warranty contracts and expensing the amount in the period in which the sale occurs. Warranty expense is reported under selling expenses in the income statement, and estimated warranty liability is classified as a current liability on the balance sheet.

Leases

3. (S.O. 2) **A lease** is a contractual agreement between a lessor (owner) and a lessee (renter) that grants the right to use specific property for a specified period in return for cash payments.

Operating Leases

4. In an **operating lease,** the intent is temporary use of the property by the lessee with continued ownership of the property by the lessor. The lease (or rental) payments are recorded as an expense by the lessee and as revenue by the lessor.

Capital Leases

5. A **capital lease** transfers substantially all the benefits and risks of ownership from the lessor to the lessee:
   a. The lessee is required to record an asset and the related obligation at the present value of the future lease payments.
   b. The leased asset is reported on the balance sheet under plant assets.
   c. The portion of the lease liability to be paid in the next year is a current liability, and the remainder is classified as a long-term liability.

Employee Compensation

6. (S.O. 3) When the compensation for **paid absences** (paid vacations, sick pay benefits, and paid holidays) is probable and the amount can be reasonably estimated, a liability should be accrued. When the amount cannot be reasonably estimated, the potential liability should be disclosed.

7. A **pension plan** is an agreement whereby an employer provides benefits to employees after they retire. Three parties are generally involved in a pension plan:
   a. The employer sponsors the plan.
   b. The plan administrator receives the contributions, invests the pension assets, and makes the benefit payments.
   c. The retired employees receive the pension payments.

8. There are two common types of pension arrangements:
   a. In a **defined contribution plan,** the employer's contribution to the plan is defined by the terms of the plan, and this contribution is recognized as pension expense.
   b. In a **defined benefit plan,** the benefits the employee will receive are defined, and pension expense is based on actuarial methods and accounting standards that may not equal the employer's cash contribution.

The Navigator

REVIEW QUESTIONS AND EXERCISES

TRUE—FALSE

Indicate whether each of the following is true (T) or false (F) in the space provided.

_____ 1. (S.O. 1) If it is remote that a contingency will happen and it is reasonably estimable, the liability should be recorded in the accounts.

_____ 2. (S.O. 1) For the current year, total warranty expense is equal to the estimated cost of servicing the units sold in the current year.

_____ 3. (S.O. 2) Operating leases are leases that the lessee must capitalize on its balance sheet as an asset.

_____ 4. (S.O. 2) A capital lease occurs when the lease transfers substantially all the benefits and risks of ownership from the lessor to the lessee.

_____ 5. (S.O. 2) Under a capital lease the leased asset is reported on the balance sheet under plant assets.

_____ 6. (S.O. 3) When the payment of a future paid absence is probable and can be reasonably estimated, a liability should be accrued.

MULTIPLE CHOICE

Circle the letter that best answers each of the following statements.

1. (S.O. 1) How should a contingency that is reasonably possible and for which the amount can be reasonably estimated be handled?

	Accrued	**Disclosed**
a.	Yes	No
b.	No	Yes
c.	Yes	Yes
d.	No	No

2. (S.O. 1) A contingency need not be recorded nor disclosed when:
   a. it is probable the contingency will happen and the amount can be reasonably estimated.
   b. it is probable the contingency will happen but the amount cannot be reasonably estimated.
   c. it is reasonably possible the contingency will happen and the amount can be reasonably estimated.
   d. the possibility of the contingency happening is remote.

3. (S.O. 1) A contingency for which the amount can be reasonably estimated should be disclosed when the outcome of the contingency is:

	Reasonably Possible	Remote
a.	Yes	No
b.	Yes	Yes
c.	No	No
d.	No	Yes

4. (S.O. 2) Which of the following is **not** a condition under which the lessee must record the lease as an asset?
   a. The lease contains a bargain purchase option.
   b. The lease transfers ownership of the property to the lessee.
   c. The lease term is equal to 60% or more of the economic life of the leased property.
   d. The present value of the lease payments exceeds 90% of the fair market value of the leased property.

5. (S.O. 3) Du Bois Company employees are entitled to one day's vacation for each month worked. If an employee earns an average of $150 per day in a given month, the entry to accrue vacation benefits expense for the year for one employee will be as follows:

		Debit	Credit
a.	Vacation Benefits Expense	150	
	Liability for Vacation Benefits		150
b.	Pension Expense	1,800	
	Pension Liability		1,800
c.	No entry.		
d.	Vacation Benefits Expense	1,800	
	Liability for Vacation Benefits		1,800

6. (S.O. 3) Which of the following statements about a pension plan is correct?
   a. A pension plan involves two parties: the employer and the retired employees.
   b. In a defined contribution plan, the benefits the employee will receive at retirement are defined.
   c. In a defined contribution plan, the employer's contribution to the plan is reported as pension expense.
   d. In a defined benefit plan, the employer's pension expense must equal the pension contribution.

The Navigator

MATCHING

Match each term with its definition by writing the appropriate letter in the space provided.

Terms

_____ 1. Contingent liability.

_____ 2. Pension plan.

_____ 3. Defined benefit plan.

_____ 4. Defined contribution plan.

_____ 5. Capital lease.

_____ 6. Operating lease.

Definitions

a. An arrangement whereby an employer provides benefits to employees after they retire.

b. A contractual arrangement that transfers substantially all the benefits and risks of ownership to the lessee.

c. A type of pension arrangement in which the employer's contribution to the plan is defined by the terms of the plan.

d. A contractual arrangement giving the lessee temporary use of the property.

e. A type of pension plan in which the benefits that the employee will receive at the time of retirement are defined.

f. A potential liability that may become an actual liability in the future.

EXERCISES

EX. F-1 (S.O. 1 and 2)

The following transactions took place during 2006 for Revel Pots and Pans Company.

Aug. 1 Made a lease payment of $75,000 to Zullo, Inc. in an operating lease transaction for fire trucks.

Dec. 1 Leased a new building from Gardner, Inc. The present value of the lease payments is $600,000. The lease qualifies as a capital lease.

Dec. 31 Determined that it is probable and reasonably estimated that 400 units sold under warranty will be defective and that warranty repair costs will average $20 per unit. No warranty entries have been reported during the year.

Instructions

Journalize the above transactions.

General Journal J1

Date	Account Title	Debit	Credit
2006			

The Navigator

SOLUTIONS TO REVIEW QUESTIONS AND EXERCISES

TRUE-FALSE

1. (F) If it is probable that a contingency will happen and it is reasonably estimable, the liability should be recorded in the accounts; a contingency that is remote need not be recorded or disclosed.
2. (T)
3. (F) The lessee simply records the lease payments as an expense in the income statement. No asset or liability is recorded.
4. (T)
5. (T)
6. (T)

MULTIPLE CHOICE

1. (b) When a contingency is probable and reasonably estimable, the liability should be recorded in the accounts. When a contingency does not meet the two conditions for accrual described above, only disclosure of the contingency is required, unless it is remote in which case no disclosure is made.

2. (d) If the possibility of the contingency happening is remote, it need not be recorded nor disclosed.

3. (a) A contingency for which the amount of loss can be reasonably estimated should be disclosed when the outcome of the contingency is reasonably possible.

4. (c) The lease term must be equal to 75% or more of the economic life of the lease.

5. (d) Since the employee is entitled to one day's vacation for each month worked, at the end of the year he would be entitled to 12 days. Therefore, the vacation benefits expense would amount to $1,800 and the entry in (d) would be made.

6. (c) Answer (a) is incorrect because a fund administrator is also involved. In a defined contribution plan, the employer's contribution is defined but not the retiree's benefits (b). Answer (d) is incorrect because in a defined benefit plan pension expense is not necessarily equal to the cash contribution.

MATCHING

1. f	4. c
2. a	5. b
3. e	6. d

EXERCISES

EX. F-1

General Journal			
			J1
Date	**Account Title**	**Debit**	**Credit**
2006			
Aug. 1	Truck Rental Expense	75,000	
	Cash		75,000
	(To record payment of lease rental charge)		
Dec. 1	Leased Asset--Building	600,000	
	Lease Liability		600,000
	(To record leased asset and lease liability)		
Dec. 31	Warranty Expense (400 X $20)	8,000	
	Estimated Warranty Liability		8,000
	(To accrue estimated warranty costs)		